Local and Urban Governance

Series Editor
Carlos Nunes Silva ⓘ, Institute of Geography and Spatial Planning,
University of Lisbon, Lisbon, Portugal

This series contains research studies with policy relevance in the field of sub-national territorial governance, at the micro, local and regional levels, as well as on its connections with national and supranational tiers. The series is multidisciplinary and brings together innovative research from different areas within the Social Sciences and Humanities. The series is open for theoretical, methodological and empirical ground breaking contributions. Books included in this series explore the new modes of territorial governance, new perspectives and new research methodologies. The aim is to present advances in Governance Studies to scholars and researchers in universities and research organizations, and to policy makers worldwide. The series includes monographs, edited volumes and textbooks. Book proposals and final manuscripts are peer-reviewed.

The areas covered in the series include but are not limited to the following subjects:

- Local and regional government
- Urban and metropolitan governance
- Multi-level territorial governance
- Post-colonial local governance
- Municipal merger reforms
- Inter-municipal cooperation
- Decentralized cooperation
- Governance of spatial planning
- Strategic spatial planning
- Citizen participation in local policies
- Local governance, spatial justice and the right to the city
- Local public services
- Local economic development policies
- Entrepreneurialism and municipal public enterprises
- Local government finance
- Local government and sustainable development
- Anthropocene and green local governance
- Climate change and local governance
- Smart local governance

The series is intended for geographers, planners, political scientists, sociologists, lawyers, historians, urban anthropologists and economists. **Local and Urban Governance—now indexed in Scopus**.

Yu Noda

Editor

Local Governance in Japan

 Springer

Editor
Yu Noda (iD)
Faculty of Policy Studies
Doshisha University
Kyoto, Japan

ISSN 2524-5449   ISSN 2524-5457   (electronic)
Local and Urban Governance
ISBN 978-3-031-77321-1   ISBN 978-3-031-77322-8   (eBook)
https://doi.org/10.1007/978-3-031-77322-8

To our families

Preface

The book *Local Governance in Japan* identifies strategies to facilitate effective local governance from the perspectives of scientists from diverse disciplines. Japanese local governments provide a vast array of governmental services based on a detailed and complicated system of laws and procedures. Japanese culture, which emphasizes the comprehensiveness and granularity of such a vast and extensive range of services, is not limited to government services. This is similar to the characteristics of Japanese industries, such as the traditional textile, automobile, electrical machinery, and metalworking industries, as well as the accumulated technology in the agricultural and service sectors. Japan, which was a depleted country immediately after World War II, achieved high economic growth from the 1950s onward because of its meticulousness and diligence to steadily underpin economic growth. In addition, Japan has maintained a wide range of defensible administrative services to date, although it has experienced a prolonged recession since the 1990s. However, as Japan has already become a society with a declining population, maintaining these services will become more difficult in the near future.

The Japanese governance system under which local governments promote their administrative activities is uniform throughout the country, and the scope of services provided by local governments is versatile. Therefore, local governments are faced with the challenge of improving their governance with limited policy resources. In addition, the fundamental management strategy of Japanese local governments has been to maintain services by increasing the size of the government through repeated mergers. However, the geographical conditions of municipalities and differences in living areas make it difficult to increase the size of the government indefinitely. This book attempts to explain, from a systematic, comprehensible, and informative perspective, how Japan's local governments are trying to overcome this extremely serious challenge. The Japanese experience that this book presents, which explores clues to help local governments solve this difficult puzzle, could be beneficial to other countries with diverse local government systems. One of the major issues that this book focuses on is how to establish relationships with other actors who can serve as policy actors, which is a central theme of local governance.

Local governance appears to be an ambiguous concept that is difficult to address systematically because scholars can view it in multiple ways. However, as approaching local governance from only one particular academic discipline fails to provide a clear-cut solution, it is essential to approach it from the perspectives of scholars from diverse disciplines. In this book, various experts discuss local governance and focus on the relationships among actors, especially local governments, to clarify its systematization and comprehensiveness across a region. This book is the first comprehensive study on local governance in Japan. It examines issues regarding the sustainability of local governments by exploring their relationships with the national government, other local governments, citizens, and the private sector. Authors from diverse disciplines such as public administration, political science, economics, sociology, and business administration and management have explored local governance in accordance with their unique approaches. In this book, readers will find fascinating insights into how Japan's local governments, which prioritize detailed and uniform services, are attempting to address the challenges of inefficiency.

Finally, we would like to thank Professor Ofer Feldman of Doshisha University for sharing his thoughts on international publications. I sincerely appreciate the Japanese prefectural and municipal government officials for sharing their everyday experiences and challenges in this book. Moreover, I thank each contributor for helping create this remarkable collection amid their busy schedules. Each scientist in this book is an eminent scholar who is simultaneously working on numerous research projects. Many also had to undertake a staggering amount of teaching and university management work. Despite these challenges, they further developed the study of local governance in Japan and systematically compiled it into a book.

We would also like to express our gratitude for the financial support we received from several bodies, including the Japan Society for the Promotion of Science (JSPS) [grant numbers 23K01243, 22K01714, 22K01349, 21K01341, 20K01476, 19K01456, 17K03771, 24530359] and the Short-Term Research Project [grant number 22210, 23209] of the Institute of Economic Research in Aoyama Gakuin University College of Economics.

Kyoto, Japan   Yu Noda

Contents

About the Editor

Yu Noda is Professor at the Faculty of Policy Studies, Doshisha University. He was a Fulbright Visiting Scholar of Public Administration and Policy at Georgetown University in 2014. Since 2024, he has served as Principal of Doshisha Elementary School. In addition, he provided research guidance to graduate students at the Graduate School of Policy and Management at Doshisha University. His educational activities span all age groups from children to older adults. His research focuses on inter-municipal cooperation, performance information and learning effects of citizens, citizen satisfaction with government services, trust in local governments, and governance reforms. His recent articles have appeared in prominent journals, including *Public Administration Review*, *Public Management Review*, *Local Government Studies*, *International Review of Administrative Sciences*, *Asia-Pacific Journal of Public Administration*, and *International Journal of Public Administration*.

List of Figures

List of Tables

Chapter 1
Introduction: Local Government System and the Local Governance in Japan

Yu Noda ⓘ

Abstract This book aims to identify key directions for the sustainability of local governments with severely limited policy resources by examining crucial issues faced by local governments in Japan. Using both quantitative and qualitative methods, we explore how local governments can efficiently and democratically maintain public services in collaboration with diverse stakeholders. The introduction describes how local governments in Japan are large and suffer from population decline and fiscal difficulties in terms of the amount of spending and the scope of services they provide. It then discusses the organizational structure with a clear chain of command and the local fiscal system controlled by the central government. In order for such large local governments with insufficient fiscal discretion to function effectively for local governance, this chapter indicates the need for research that examines cooperation with the national government, other local governments, citizens, nonprofit organizations, and the private businesses. The final section presents the direction of discussion in the chapters related to collaboration with diverse actors.

Keywords Local governance · Local government · Two tier system · Range of services · Seniority-based wage system · Transfer funds

1.1 Objectives of the Study of Local Governance in Japan

The objectives of this volume are to provide the Japanese context of the study of local governance and present key directions for the sustainability of local governments with seriously limited policy resources by examining critical issues for Japanese local governments. The findings provide clues for improving the sustainability of local government's operations and services in relation to various actors, including the central government, other local governments, citizens, nonprofit

Y. Noda (✉)
Faculty of Policy Studies, Doshisha University, Kyoto, Japan
e-mail: ynoda@mail.doshisha.ac.jp

© The Author(s), under exclusive license to Springer Nature   1
Switzerland AG 2024
Y. Noda (ed.), *Local Governance in Japan*, Local and Urban Governance,
https://doi.org/10.1007/978-3-031-77322-8_1

organizations (NPOs), and private businesses. As the political and administrative systems and cultures in Japan differ significantly from those in other Asian countries, a comparative Asian perspective on local governance is less effective. More importantly, the uniformity of Japan's political and administrative systems and size of its government can provide significant insights into how to improve local governance in other countries. This is because whether the uniformity of the system can shift in a direction allowing for diversity, as well as how to change the size of the government, are key issues for any country. The discussion on the exhaustion of policy resources and sustainability of the Japanese government is of particular interest to other countries suffering from fiscal and human resource difficulties.

This book combines quantitative and qualitative methods to examine the effectiveness of local governance, and provides a comprehensive perspective that presents clues and challenges for improving the sustainability of the public services provided by local governments. The intended readership includes scholars and students of public administration, political science, economics, geography, sociology, and business administration and management, as well as policymakers and practitioners. In particular, policymakers and practitioners from other countries can find this book's ideas and innovations valuable for effective governance. This information can guide local government officials and academics, particularly in countries where local governments face human-resource challenges and financial difficulties.

In this chapter, first, basic metrics such as population, economic growth, and the size of local governments in Japan are identified to clarify how Japanese local governments are experiencing policy resource depletion. Next, we discuss Japan's unique environmental context, including the two-tier system of local governments, local organization system, and local fiscal system, to provide a fundamental understanding of the Japanese institutional background. We then discuss the aims of the chapters and their development to capture the key directions for improving the sustainability of local governance.

Japan was the first Asian country to achieve significant economic development and improvement in its citizens' living standards after World War II. Behind the significant economic development achieved by the beginning of the 1990s was the national land development policy of the central government and the implementation of policies by local governments in accordance with national policy. The national government established the Pacific Belt, an east-west development axis connecting the plains on the Pacific Ocean side, linking them via bullet trains and highways, and designating industrial zones and areas. Municipalities also built industrial parks, developed the area in front of the train station, developed the central city area, and built educational, water, sewage, and waste disposal facilities and parks. Alongside this infrastructure development, local governments developed policies to work with the business and third sectors, support community activities, and maintain policies through mergers and collaborations among municipalities, which have helped maintain a well-developed infrastructure and suitable services in every region of the country.

However, Cabinet Office (CAO) data show that Japan's economic growth rate declined numerically from 10.0% in the 1960s, 4.4% in the 1970s, 4.3% in the 1980s, and 1.3% in the 1990s (CAO 2003). Then, Japan experienced the collapse of its bubble economy in the early 1990s and accumulation of government debt. Japan's total population peaked at 128.08 million in 2008 and has since declined, falling to 126.15 million in 2020. It is further estimated that the population will reach 99.65 million in 2056, and the average age will exceed 50 years in 2031 (National Institute of Population and Social Security Research 2023). Additionally, the number of local governments decreased by 46% between 2000 and 2010. Furthermore, two major natural disasters, the Great Hanshin-Awaji Earthquake and the Great East Japan Earthquake, as well as other major earthquakes in Kumamoto and the Noto Peninsula, have exhausted the economy and vitality of local governments.

Once local governments take responsibility for many services, they are faced with a declining population that reduces their tax revenues, leaving them struggling to maintain their capacity to provide these services in the future. Japan's aging rate in 2021 was the highest in the world at 30%, and the situation is becoming more challenging every year. Despite this situation, Japanese local governments are characterized by a very high volume of activity compared to other countries. As of March 31, 2022, there are 47 prefectures, 792 cities, and 926 towns and villages. The average population is 2,679,317 in prefectures, 145,685 in cities, and 11,388 in towns and villages. According to the OECD National Accounts Statistics database, in Fiscal Year (FY) 2021 in Japan, the share of sub-national government revenue in the total revenue of the central government and sub-national governments (state and local governments) was 38.8% in Japan, which was higher than the OECD average of 36.1% (OECD 2023). Japan is a unitary country, with no state government, which leads to this high rate for the local governments alone.

Both the ratio as well as the actual amount spent are among the highest worldwide. A comparison of public investment in 2021 in local government, in U.S. dollars, among OECD member countries is shown in Fig. 1.1. It can be clearly seen that Japan has the second-highest public investment after the U.S. For a unitary state, Japan's local governments are by far the greatest spenders, showing just the scale of the local government in Japan.

I calculated the amount of local government expenditure per local entity using statistics from FY2021 from the Ministry of Internal Affairs and Communications (MIC) (converted at 150 yen to the dollar): The average expenditure was 9,407,682,578 dollars in prefectures, 215,643,171 dollars in cities, and 54,777,484 dollars in towns/villages for each organization (MIC 2023a). As of the end of March 2022, there were 20 ordinance-designated cities that held the most authority in the Japanese city system, with an average expenditure of 5,560,103,285 dollars.

Based on these large expenditure scales, municipalities provide a wide range of services. These include education, welfare for the elderly, child welfare, welfare for the disabled, public assistance, disaster management, firefighting, emergency medical services, bus transportation, crime prevention, park maintenance, road maintenance, waste disposal, agricultural promotion, commercial promotion, industrial

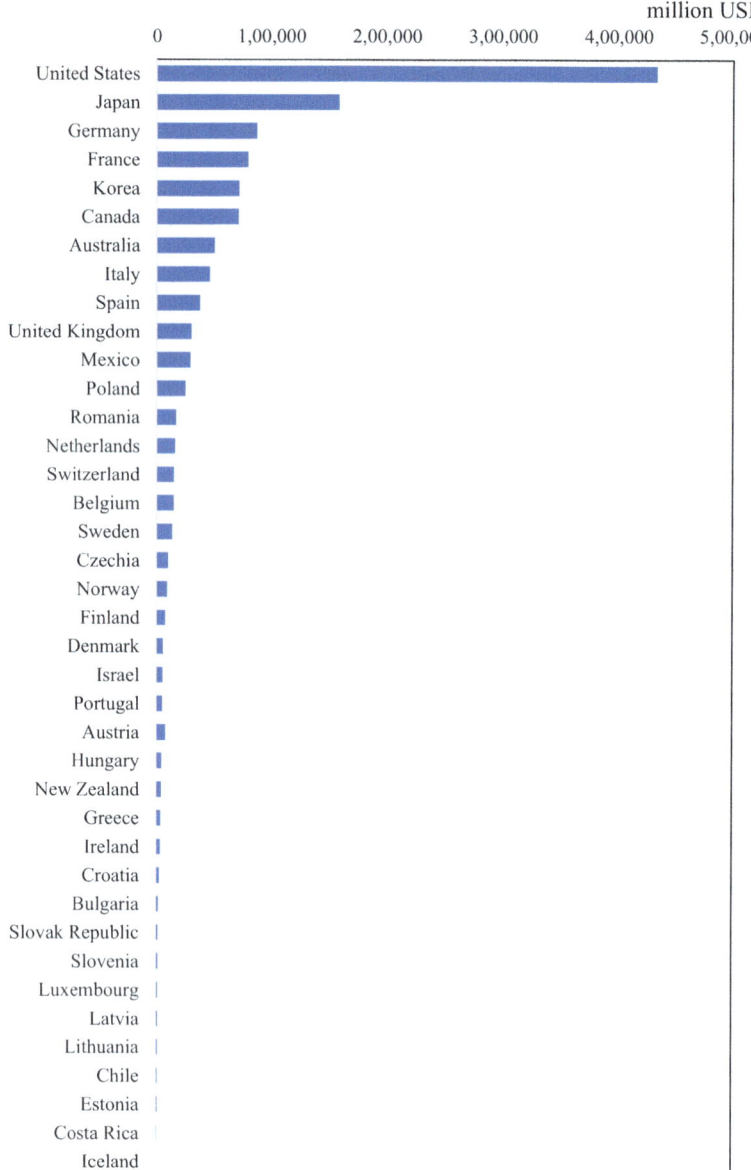

Fig. 1.1 Government investment in 2021. (Notes: Based on the institutional sector classifications in the OECD database, the values for the United States and Australia are for state governments only, the values for Germany, Canada, Austria, Belgium, Mexico, Spain and Switzerland are the sum of state and local government, and the values for all other countries are for local government only. Data for Japan are for the fiscal year. Source: Author's elaboration based on OECD Data Explorer (*Last updated*: January 18, 2024) as an excerpt of indicators published in the 2023 edition of Government at a Glance)

promotion, cultural promotion, sports promotion, recreation, animal control, and community support. Moreover, all regions in Japan have both municipalities and prefectures. Citizens pay taxes to both these local governments. The prefectures carry out large-scale projects such as infrastructure development, industrial policy, and nature conservation, including roads, ports, and airports, over a wide area beyond the municipalities' areas. This book examines how local governments, which have accumulated services in every corner of the country, can efficiently and democratically maintain public services in collaboration with diverse actors in an environment where human and financial resources are depleted.

One could simply assume that for Japanese local governments to manage efficiently and effectively, they need to formulate policies that simultaneously raise tax revenues and reduce unnecessary services. In Japan, however, the local financial system is under the control of the national government, as both national and local governments operate together to maintain uniform services across the country. Furthermore, the national government has failed to seriously correct the trend toward the concentration of population and policymaking authority in Tokyo, which has resulted in an inability to halt the decline of the regions and has led to more serious population declines and tax revenue shortfalls in the regions. To understand this institutional environment, the next section provides an overview of the two-tier system and the local government finance systems. The subsequent sections provide a context for the local governance concepts in this book and their respective chapter developments.

1.2   Two-Tier System and Range of Services

The Japanese local government operates under a two-tier system of prefectures and municipalities, with the same system of local autonomy across the country. Prefectures are regional governments; there are 47 prefectures, ranging from Hokkaido in the north to Okinawa Prefecture in the south (Fig. 1.2). Among the prefectures, the metropolitan district system is used only for the Tokyo Metropolitan Government. Under this system, the 23 special municipalities, called "special wards" in the central area of the Tokyo Metropolitan Government, are internal organizations of the Tokyo Metropolitan Government. Historically, in 1943, near the end of the Second World War, the city of Tokyo, as it existed at that time, was abolished by the national government to centralize the air defense system, resulting in the creation of internal subordinate organizations that are now called special wards. Since then, there has been a movement for the independence of the special wards to implement policies based on tax revenues generated from their own areas, but they have remained subordinate to the Tokyo Metropolitan Government till the present (Noda 2021).

Municipalities other than special wards are not internal organizations of the prefectural government but are independently administered and managed. Municipalities are local governments that provide basic services to residents. In municipalities,

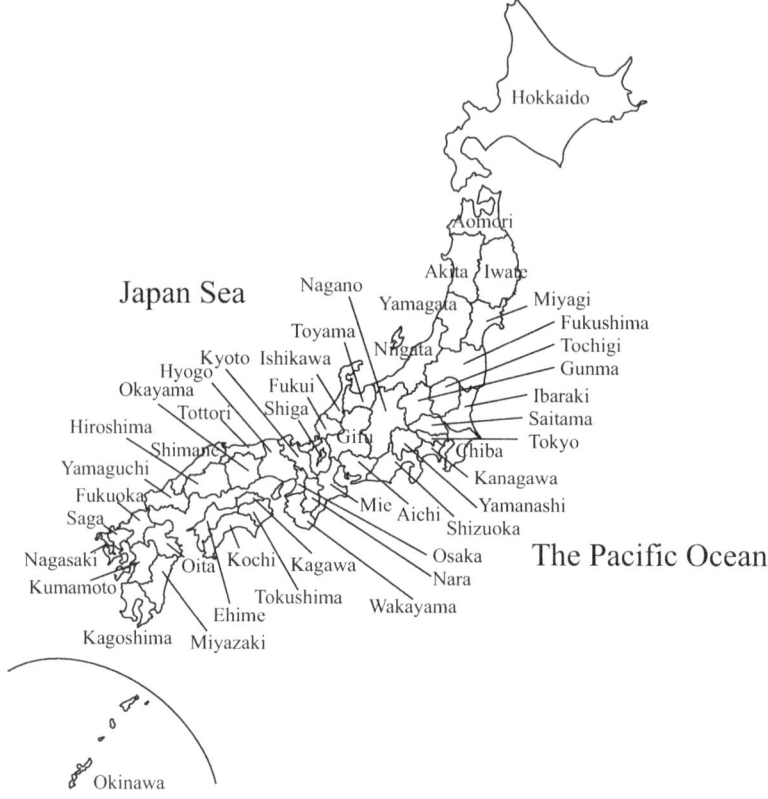

Fig. 1.2 Prefectures in Japan. (Notes: This map omits some islands. Source: Author's elaboration based on the material created by the operator of *Pawapo de dezain* (https://power-point-design. com/ppt-design/japan-map-available-for-powerpoint/), which provides free materials)

ordinance-designated cities have the most authority, followed by core cities, general cities, and towns and villages, in descending order of authority. Ordinance-designated cities are municipalities with a population of 500,000 or more, which are expected to grow to 700,000 or more in the future due to urban development. They have considerable authority over road management, welfare, public health, and land readjustments. They can also establish administrative districts and increase road-specific revenue sources and local tax allocation. Core cities must have a population of 200,000 or more to be designated, and their authority is strong in areas such as welfare, public health, and the environment, as well as in the transfer of financial resources from the national and prefectural governments to the core cities. General cities must have a population of 50,000 or more to be designated as cities; however, there have been no cases of demotion to townships or villages because of population decline. Unlike towns and villages, cities are required to establish welfare offices, enhance welfare services, and perform other land-use projects based on the city-planning areas. Thus, in municipalities, the system of cities has different authorities depending on the size of the population, whereas all prefectures have the same authority. All areas in Japan have a two-tier structure of prefectures and municipalities. All Japanese residents are citizens of both municipalities and prefectures. In this sense, Japan operates a very uniform local government system, which is significantly different from the local system in the U.S., where many areas do not have incorporated municipalities under the county government.

Citizens are often aware of their relationship with the municipal government because they visit the municipal office to have their family registers and certificates of residence issued and to apply for welfare-related benefits. However, it is rare for anyone other than business operators to visit the prefectural office; hence, it is difficult for citizens to imagine a situation in which they interact with the prefectural government. In reality, municipalities, as the government closest to residents, are responsible for the following services: welfare (e.g., for the elderly, children, and the disabled); waste disposal; medical care; health care (in part), maintenance and management of local roads, bridges, rivers, water and sewage systems, parks, community centers, and recreational facilities; loans to small and medium-sized businesses; shopping district promotion; agricultural promotion; support for citizen activities in the community; firefighting; emergency services; crime prevention (excluding police functions); animal control; and education in elementary and junior high schools.

In contrast, prefectures are responsible for the development and management of major roads, ports, and airports; industrial policy (including industrial promotion); land use; health; wide-area medical care; nature conservation; mountain, flood, and pollution control; industrial waste regulation; and wide-area services, such as education in high schools, welfare in town and village areas, and financial support for elementary and junior high school teachers. Additionally, prefectural governments are positioned between the national government and municipalities to coordinate their respective activities. However, in most cases, municipalities request higher levels of government, such as the central government and prefectures, regarding these policies and subsidies. For this reason, much of the coordination work of the prefectures, which stand between the national government and municipalities, is to disseminate national policies to the municipalities.

In Japan, municipalities have maintained this wide range of services at a high cost in accordance with the national philosophy of providing a full set of services. Accordingly, citizens of any municipality can receive the same type of services. In 2014, when the fiscal situation in Japan was difficult nationwide, all municipalities and prefectures were requested by the central government to formulate a comprehensive management plan for public facilities that measured the renewal demand for infrastructure such as roads, bridges, and rivers that had already been developed on a large scale, community centers, schools, and public facilities, and to consolidate, eliminate, or extend the useful lives of these facilities (MIC 2014). Moreover, many municipalities estimate their own administrative and financial plans in addition to such central government requests, promoting the consolidation and elimination of public facilities, transfer of public childcare centers and reception services to the private sector, reduction of municipal officials, transfer of municipal services, such as national health insurance programs, to prefectural governments, use of digital technology, and promotion of wide-area cooperation on their own.

This book discusses how local governments that have maintained such a large scale and wide range of services can explore ways to work with other local governments, businesses, third sectors, and other policy actors.

1.3   Local Government Organization Systems

The local government in Japan is based on a system of dual representation, with a governor or mayor elected by the citizens at the head of the chain of command and a local council made up of members also elected by the citizens. This is the same for both the prefectural and municipal governments. In brief, under this system, the head of a local government has the authority to submit a budget, make decisions in an emergency without passing a motion through the council, request reconsideration when the council opposes a policy proposal, and oversee all administrative organizations, measures affording the head greater authority than the council (Ueda 2012). Although Japan has a dual representation system, very few ordinances are enacted after council members draft policy proposals, and more than 90% of ordinances are drafted by public officials under the direction of the mayor or governor (Noda 2021). In terms of the distribution of authority, the head appears to have greater authority than the assembly. However, as discussed later in Chap. 3, at the prefectural level, there are respects in which the council has a significant influence on the policies and elections of the governor, thus making it impossible to argue uniformly which of the two representatives is in control of the initiative.

The head of the government oversees the administrative organization, which is composed of various departments. Under the head of local government, deputy heads and department managers are the chiefs of the departments in each policy field. Under-department managers are section managers who oversee the divisions, which are the units of each program; and under the chiefs are the section chiefs, forming a pyramid-shaped organization. Operations are usually conducted with each division as the main program unit, and project teams that transcend divisions may be formed for cross-disciplinary themes (Noda 2021). In this pyramidal organizational structure, the mayor or governor sets a major policy direction, the General Affairs Division or Finance Division sets a budgeting policy based on that direction, and then each division formulates individual project proposals. Within each section, the lowest-ranking staff member drafts a policy proposal, which is circulated for approval by the section chief, then the section manager, and finally the department manager. This method of circularization is called the *Ringi* system, a process in which an organization, rather than individual public officials, takes responsibility for policy decisions (Inoue 1981). However, the disadvantage is that decision-making takes longer when many people are involved in the circularization process.

Local governments begin budgeting around October to November based on their budgeting policy, which is deliberated and voted on by the assembly in February to

March of the following year. Policymaking that relies on government subsidies is done through the intermediaries of prefectural and local Diet members, who approach the relevant ministries and agencies, or in the case of ordinance-designated cities and prefectures, the Tokyo Office, which is used by the mayor and senior officials to directly approach the ministry and agency officials.

To eliminate the concentration of authority in an organization headed by a mayor or governor, administrative committees have status and authority independent of the heads. These committees are collegial bodies comprising several members, including the Board of Education, Fairness Committee, Personnel Committee, Election Administration Committee, and Agricultural Committee (Noda 2021). However, the secretariats of these committees are staffed by public officials in organizations that directly report to the mayor or governor and drafts of proposed responses to various issues are prepared by these public officials; thus, they are not completely independent organizations. In addition to the headquarters, branch offices are located in each region of the local government. Furthermore, there is an auditor who audits financial matters for violations of laws and regulations and for the efficient use of government taxes and funds.

The organizational structure of local governments in Japan is a clear pyramid with a clear chain of command and order, which may appear similar to that of other countries, but the organizations are large and staffed by numerous public officials. According to the statistics from the MIC (2023c), only the prefectural and ordinance-designated city averages are confirmed, as the municipal average values are not listed, but they are both quite large. The average for prefectures is 30,530 public officials, of which 5033 are in general administration, 17,243 in education, 6151 in the police, and 1698 in public corporations. The size of the prefectures varies considerably, with the Tokyo Metropolitan Government having the highest number of public officials and general public officials at 175,473 and 19,876, respectively, and Tottori prefecture having the smallest at 11,774 and 2908, respectively. The average for ordinance-designated cities is 17,903, of which 6355 are in general administration, 7744 in education, 1459 in firefighting, and 2345 in public enterprises. Thus, prefectures and large cities employ numerous public officials and are characterized by the prominence of teachers and police officers.

Local government officials are hired through a merit system based on an open competitive examination process that consists of a written application and an interview. They are transferred to different departments every 3 years, including transfers to other organizations, until retirement, while being promoted to higher-level positions. This general style of personnel transfer is adopted to develop generalized human resources with knowledge across policy areas. Conversely, there is also the route of providing early and continuous experience in the finance and human resources departments, which allocate the most important policy resources in the organization (Takeuchi 2019). In addition, salaries for local government officials are based on a seniority-based wage system in which raises are based on years of work experience. For example, when an official is promoted from section chief to section manager, their monthly salary increases, even though the number of years of work experience remains the same. While such a seniority-based wage system promotes stability in the status of public officials, it is problematic because salaries do not vary on a piece-rate basis, thereby reducing motivation for work.

Thus, the budget of the Japanese local government, which is much larger than that of other countries, is expanded into a large organizational structure under a nationwide uniform local system.

1.4   Local Government Finance System

Local government expenditures in Japan used to be dominated by civil work, engineering, and education during the 1990s, but since 2000, costs related to welfare have gradually increased (MIC 2010). The percentage of local government spending by field is the highest for welfare, accounting for 35.4% of the FY2019 budget in ordinary circumstances, before the emergency increase in general administrative and economic spending to cope with the COVID-19 pandemic (MIC 2023b). This is because the Japanese population is aging rapidly. The basic financial resource supporting these expenditures is the inhabitant tax paid by citizens to municipalities and prefectures.

As for the percentage of intergovernmental spending in FY2021, the central government accounted for 17.8%, local governments for 43.3%, social security funds for 34.1%, and public corporations for 4.8%, indicating that local governments had the largest spending scale, but national taxes accounted for 62.9% of tax revenue, compared to only 37.1% for local taxes (MIC 2023b). Regarding major taxes, citizens pay income tax to the national government and resident tax to prefectures and municipalities, in addition to property tax and city planning tax to municipalities for homeowners; moreover, businesses pay business tax in addition to resident tax to prefectures. These are collectively referred to as local taxes. Other revenues for municipalities and prefectures include dues and contributions to joint projects among multiple municipalities, fees and charges for the use of public facilities, property revenue from the sale of owned land, funds to be invested to repay debts or for specific-purpose projects, and local bonds. In municipalities, prefectural disbursements are also a source of funding. The breakdown of local government funding in FY2021 is as follows: for prefectures and municipalities, local taxes accounted for 28.7% and 32.5%, local allocation tax (LAT) for 13.2% and 14.9%, national treasury disbursements for 22.5% and 23.7%, and local bonds for 7.4% and 9.6%, respectively (MIC 2023b). Thus, local taxes, which are a self-financing source of revenue, constitute approximately 30% of the financial resources required to maintain local government services.

As local taxes are proportional to the population and the number of businesses, Tokyo, Kanagawa, and Aichi prefectures have the highest percentage of local taxes in their revenue, while Shimane and Tottori prefectures, with very small populations, have the lowest. As shown in Fig. 1.3, Tokyo is the only prefecture with a fiscal strength index above 1 among prefectural governments, meaning that its revenue exceeds 1 when the revenue generated by its own region exceeds the required

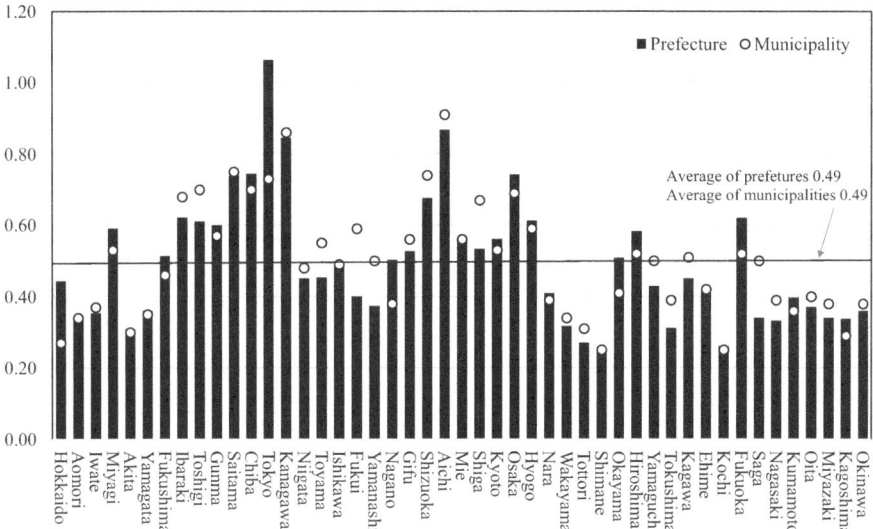

Fig. 1.3 Fiscal strength index of prefectural and municipal governments (FY2022). (Notes: The municipality of Tokyo includes the special wards. Source: Author's own design, based on data taken from the MIC (2024))

demand but falls below 1 when the revenue falls below the required demand (MIC 2023a). Municipalities in better financial condition, however, include those in Aichi Prefecture, where many Toyota Motor Corporation-related companies are located; those in southern Kanto region, which is comprised of the Tokyo, Kanagawa, Saitama, and Chiba prefectures; and many other municipalities that are supplied with a large amount of subsidies provided by central government because of the location of nuclear power plants (MIC 2023a). The financial status of these municipalities by prefecture is indicated by a circle in Fig. 1.3.

Local governments are supposed to implement policies based on the taxes paid. However, because projects cannot be implemented based solely on the local taxes paid by residents in the local government area, LAT subsidies and national treasury disbursements are supplied as sources of funds transferred from the national government. The sources of these transfer funds are collected in higher amounts by national taxes than by local taxes, as discussed earlier; thus, a portion of the national taxes is allocated to the localities.

Of the transfer funds, national treasury disbursements are financial supplements to local government projects by central government ministries which are intended to facilitate local government projects, but at the same time, each ministry and agency also implements its own policies at the local level. Local government spending tends to increase because of national treasury disbursements, as both local governments lacking financial resources and ministries seeking to implement policies are eager to implement infrastructure projects.

LAT is classified by ordinary allocation taxes, which comprise 94% of them, and special allocation taxes, which are allocated according to demand in the event of disasters, comprising 6% of them. In the following section, the ordinary allocation tax, which comprises the majority of LAT, is discussed. This tax is a transfer source of revenue in which the amount of demand generated by a municipality is calculated based on a formula provided by the MIC and compared to 75% of the tax revenue generated by that municipality, resulting in the amount by which demand exceeds the tax revenue contributed to the municipality as a grant. The reason that 75% of tax revenues are counted in the calculation is because if all tax revenues are counted, all the increase in tax revenues from policies to promote business location or population inflow would result in a decrease in LAT, and 25% is a reserved revenue source. While local tax revenues are generated in Tokyo, Kanagawa, Saitama, and Chiba in the southern Kanto region, and Aichi, all of which have high fiscal strength, LAT revenues are allocated to prefectures with small populations, such as Tottori, Kochi, and Shimane, which do not generate sufficient tax revenue. Therefore, the LAT has a fiscal adjustment function.

It should be noted that the national government not only determines and administers the LAT system but also controls financial resources through local fiscal planning. The LAT is financed by the national income tax, corporate tax, liquor tax, consumption tax, and other taxes; however, as these taxes alone are insufficient each year, an additional tax is collected from national budgets and bonds based on the Local Allocation Tax Law. To make these additions to fiscal resources, local fiscal plans are prepared annually by the national government. In establishing the local fiscal plan, the national government estimates the required amount of LAT based on the revenue, expenditure, and public debt of local governments nationwide and clarifies the amount of financial resources secured and the shortfall in this required amount. In other words, the national government assumes and determines the overall picture of local government policies in advance; thus, the LAT also guarantees financial resources, which implies that local finances are managed under the strong control of the central government (Okamoto 2002).

Moreover, the demand in the formula used to calculate the LAT is managed by the central government when guiding its policies. For example, when the central government proposes an 800,000 USD project to be implemented in a city and half of that amount can be added to demand in the following fiscal year's allocation, the amount of demand increases whereas the amount of revenue does not change significantly, resulting in the supply of increased demand as a LAT subsidy. Thus, the LAT, which also has the aspect of a subsidy, increases local government spending (Akai et al. 2003).

Thus, large-scale local government finances are strongly controlled by the central government, making it difficult for local governments to create or reform their own fiscal systems, such as raising tax revenues by creating new taxes themselves. Therefore, it is essential to devise public procurement methods to improve the methods under the existing fiscal system and improve municipal management in cooperation with other entities. The later chapters in this book discuss these issues more in depth.

1.5 Concept of Local Governance and Developments in Each Chapter

Local governance, in contrast to a centralized hierarchy, is a concept in which actors from different areas in a community are linked in a self-organizing manner, transacting and negotiating as a network with their own functions (Rhodes 1996, 2000, 2007). Furthermore, network governance organized by such diverse actors contributes to the production of public purposes through mutual coordination (Torfing 2005). However, local governance itself not only functions in networks among local governments and other community-level entities but also forms part of multilevel governance. Governance does not exclude vertical networks but includes negotiations between governance systems, and vertical governance hierarchies possess horizontal links among various actors in diverse sectors (Pierre and Stoker 2000). The local governance addressed in this book also includes vertical relationships, such as those between local and central governments and between municipalities and prefectures.

Incidentally, local governments are usually the central actors in facilitating effective local governance. This is because they retain public authority to collect taxes from citizens, redistribute them, and supply and regulate services based on financial resources. Both the central and local governments possess public authority. However, local governments, as the governments closest to the people, understand the needs of the citizens and take responsibility for autonomy in accordance with these needs.

The exploration of local governance in this book concerns how local governments, which are central players among diverse actors, can improve the potential for sustainability of services through coordination and collaboration in their relationships with other actors. Figure 1.4 presents the relationships among the different actors, with the local government as the central actor. Central–local relations in Japan are characterized by a fusion type of administration in which authority is concentrated in the central government and both the central and local governments

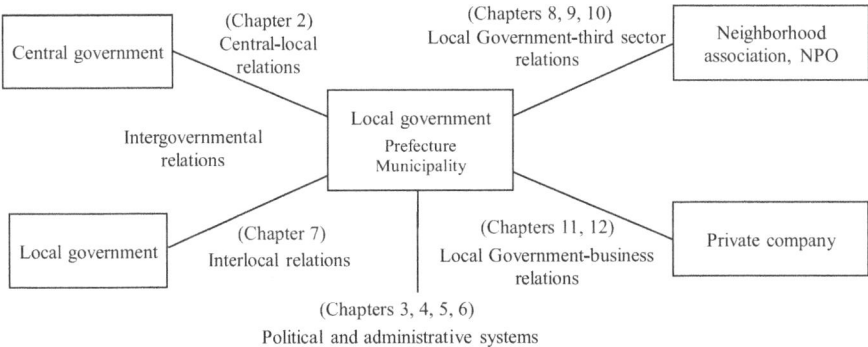

Fig. 1.4 Relationships between actors surrounding local governments. (Source: Author's elaboration)

jointly promote public administration. Chapter 2 examines the historical background of central–local relations in Japan to reveal how decentralization, fiscal transfers, and personnel exchanges have been carried out; how administrative roles have been shared; and to provide a perspective on central–local relations in the future. This chapter presents the local government system from the perspective of continuity, highlighting the characteristics of the two-tier structure, local government powers, and the system of personnel exchange, while from the perspective of transformation, it analyzes the expansion of local government expenditure and the legal framework of local government. Consequently, the author discusses how the national government has maintained local governments to the present day by providing financial support while emphasizing responsiveness to growing local demands. However, with the shortage of human and financial resources required for the provision of government services, the conventional central–local relations through which this problem has been addressed face limitations. A flexible approach to central–local relations is needed in the near future, whereby prefectures actively supplement municipalities, and the national government supports this supplementation.

Chapters 3, 4, 5, and 6 examine the major issues in the political and administrative systems. A major focus in Chap. 3 is outlining the relationship between the electoral system and the dual representation system, which determines how representatives such as political heads (mayors or governors) and council members are chosen. The dual representation system is the most critical factor determining the de facto policies of local governments and impacting their sustainability. This reveals that the problems of this system of dual representation are in fact determined by the electoral system. This chapter discusses how Japan's localities are themselves often considered similar to a presidential form of government but also have a strong parliamentary influence. It also highlights the phenomenon of the splintering of the Liberal Democratic Party (LDP) regarding the future of local politics. In other words, this chapter presents perspectives on local governance in terms of the impact of elections and dual representation systems on local politics. Through this chapter, we recognize the electoral system as a factor in the status quo of existing policies and the lack of reform, raising awareness of the need for institutional change.

Management of municipal organizations using information and communication technology has the potential to improve the shortage of civil servants and the workload of government employees. Chapter 4 quantitatively examines whether the introduction of digital transformation (DX) into municipalities improves management efficiency and productivity. The chapter also verifies whether the impact on municipal management is influenced more by DX or by different factors such as the population agglomeration and vertical cooperation with higher-level governments. DX is a powerful tool for addressing the shortage of qualified staff to serve local governments. However, this chapter reveals that the efficiency effects of public services via DX, which has been considered a means of improving efficiency, have not manifested. In contrast, productivity and efficiency effects can be found as a result of vertical cooperation between the national government, prefectural governments, and municipalities. The conclusion of Chap. 4 highlights the importance of improving workflow efficiency before the introduction of DX. The introduction of a system without consideration of the actual conditions of operations can lead rather to decreasing sustainability.

Chapter 5 clarifies the characteristics of evaluation activities in Japanese local governments, showing that, in addition to Japan-specific administrative evaluations and evaluations of decentralized services, there are also intergovernmental evaluations. The chapter then examines the possibility that central government involvement could disrupt municipal planning and evaluation and hinder self-sustaining administrative management. The institutional challenge of Japan's evaluation activities that Chap. 5 elucidates is the difficulty that local government systems face in responding efficiently to the demands of the central government. While other countries have indicator systems that achieve the systematic evaluation of local governments at the initiative of the central government, evaluation activities in Japan are initiated by local governments in the absence of a unified nationwide evaluation system. This chapter considers the problem of the central government's involvement in local government evaluation activities undermining self-governance.

Although the above public administration and management are for ordinary circumstances, local governance in emergencies requires local governments to retain more top-down authority while collaborating with diverse stakeholders as appropriate, rather than local governance in ordinary circumstances. Chapter 6 explores how Japanese local governments can maintain their crisis management capacity with limited resources in terms of planning, stakeholders, and collaborative management with other governments and the private sector. It also discusses the role of local governments and the effectiveness and challenges of central–local relations in responding to COVID-19. This chapter discusses how intergovernmental cooperation and partnerships with the private sector are essential for local governments to overcome resource constraints during emergencies. In addition, this chapter indicates that the experience of COVID-19 highlights the fact that vertical cooperation between central and local governments will become even more necessary in the future.

There are two types of intergovernmental relations: central–local and interlocal relations. Chapter 7 examines theoretically and empirically the effectiveness of horizontal cooperation between municipalities, which is strongly promoted by the national government. This chapter discusses the integrated forms of intermunicipal cooperation, transaction costs, and collaborative benefits in Japan and identifies the limitations of horizontal cooperation. Moreover, an empirical comparison of areas with and without a national policy of intermunicipal cooperation provides evidence of the ineffectiveness of the policy of horizontal cooperation. Therefore, vertical cooperation between prefectures and municipalities is necessary for local governance.

Chapters 8, 9, and 10 deal with government-third sector relations. Chapter 8 focuses on the relations through co-production with organizations based on local ties. Unlike other countries, Japan is divided into 47 prefectural districts throughout the country, and all areas within each prefecture are incorporated as municipalities. In other words, there are no unincorporated areas. With limited policy resources, local governments in Japan have been efficiently providing public services through the cooperation of local neighborhood associations (NHAs). The nationwide development of a detailed collaboration between citizens and local governments utilizing such NHAs is unique to Japan and has not yet been fully understood. Chapter 8 examines the main characteristics and activities of NHAs and discusses their roles as supplements to public service provision. The chapter also proposes potential research agendas to advance studies on co-production using Japan as a case study.

Exploring the relationship between local governments, NPOs, and civil society organizations contributes to identifying new public policymakers. Chapter 9 focuses on community-level civil society organizations from the perspective of promoting new public commons and a mutually supportive society and discusses the expanding scope of roles that civil society organizations can play in Japanese society. The chapter insists that community-level civil society organizations, such as NPOs, are not only providers of services but also places for citizen participation and innovative practices. Furthermore, they foster social entrepreneurship. With these ideas as a backdrop, in addition to addressing emerging civic needs and challenges, they contribute to moving society in a more positive direction. Community-level civil society has broad potential for improving the sustainability of local governance.

Chapter 10, a unique study in books dealing with local governance, discusses how citizens' intentions of organ donation as a social issue can be changed and lead to behavioral change in collaboration with local governments. Based on this analysis, the chapter discusses how social marketing can contribute to municipal decision-making. Although public policy has proven to be effective, it is not effective unless it actually functions. Citizen cooperation through behavioral changes is vital for effective functioning. In the past, local government policies were based on citizens' demands of the government as recipients of services, but in the future, their role as policy drivers through such behavioral change will become more significant for improving the sustainability of local governance.

Private businesses are partners with whom municipalities may improve public service mobility. The development of facilities based on the procurement of funds at scale, the development of information systems for government organizations, and the production and implementation of various public services such as medical care, welfare, childcare, water supply, and waste disposal can only be fully realized with the support of private companies. In addition, as businesses located within a municipality's jurisdiction are likely to provide significant tax revenue, the municipality has a strong motivation to build good local government–business relations. How best to encourage businesses to locate within a municipality's jurisdiction is a major never-ending challenge. Another major challenge is the creation of institutions that maintain public services smoothly and increase tax revenues in relation to businesses.

Chapter 11 examines the determinants of the increase in the hometown tax donation system, which functions as a tax distribution in the form of donations to municipalities different from their jurisdiction of residence. Furthermore, the mutually beneficial cooperation in local government–business relations based on this system is discussed. The results of the empirical analysis in Chapter 11 demonstrate that a high ratio of spending to tax returns contributes to higher tax revenue. It is a challenge for local governments to develop their marketing ability in terms of what kinds of product combinations and how many products they can offer. The hometown tax donation system changes the local tax collection system, enabling local governments to increase their revenue through strategies that appeal to citizens outside their own cities by combining tax returns with local tax gifts. Cooperation with private companies that develop returned goods can determine local governments' future financial strength. In this sense, the hometown tax donation system strengthens the sustainability of the regional economy and local governance through the effective use of local resources.

Chapter 12 focuses on Japan's public procurement system. It examines how differences in bidding methods, such as competitive and general competitive bidding, are related to the number of participants in the bidding process and whether an increase in the number of participants can be expected to lower the contract price. Local governance depends on institutions to function effectively; however, the chapter addresses the possibility of improving the institution itself, in which local governments procure public services from the business sector. This chapter reveals the importance of discriminating between bidding behavior in designated bidding and in general competitive bidding. For the same bidding method, the contract price ratio is generally lower when there are more participants in the bidding process, suggesting that the more participants there are, the greater the efficiency of the process. Although these institutional changes might seem trivial, they enhance the sustainability of local governments in Japan because local governments make large amounts of public investment, meaning that they can save on construction investment.

The final chapter summarizes the clues to municipal sustainability derived from the relationships among various actors in local governance. The final chapter articulates key directions for the sustainability of local governments with severely limited policy resources.

References

Akai N, Sato M, Yamashita K (2003) The economics of local tax delivery: theory and empirical reform [Chiho kohuzei no keizaigaku: Riron, Jicho ni motoduku kaikaku]. Yuhikaku, Tokyo. (in Japanese)

CAO (2003) 2003 Annual Economic and Fiscal Report [Heisei 15 nenban nenji keizai, zaisei, hokokusyo]. Cabinet Office, Tokyo. (in Japanese)

Inoue S (1981) A study on the critical theory of the circular decision-making system: the actual decision-making process in Japanese administrative agencies [Ringi sei hihanron ni tsuite no ichi kosatsu: Wagakuni gyouseikikan ni okeru ishi kettei katei no jissai]. Institute of Administrative Management, Tokyo. (in Japanese)

MIC (2010) FY2008 settlement white paper on local public finance (illustrated). Ministry of Internal Affairs and Communication, Tokyo

MIC (2014) Guideline for the comprehensive management plan for public facilities [Kokyo shisetsu tou sogo kanri keikaku no sakutei ni atatte]. Ministry of Internal Affairs and Communications, Tokyo. (in Japanese)

MIC (2023a) Annual report of local finance statistics FY 2021 [Chiho zaisei tokei nenpou: 2021 nendo kessan]. Ministry of Internal Affairs and Communications, Tokyo. (in Japanese)

MIC (2023b) FY2021 settlement white paper on local public finance (illustrated). Ministry of Internal Affairs and Communication, Tokyo

MIC (2023c) Survey of local public officials' capacity management in 2022 [Reiwa 4 nendo Chiho kokyodantai teiinkanri chosa kekka]. Ministry of Internal Affairs and Communication, Tokyo. (in Japanese)

MIC (2024) List of major fiscal indicators for local governments in FY2022 [Reiwa 4 nendo chiho kokyo dantai no syuyo zaisei shihyo ichiran]. Accessed June 16, 2024 at: https://www.soumu.go.jp/iken/zaisei/R04_chiho.html. (in Japanese)

National Institute of Population and Social Security Research (2023) Future population projections for Japan (2023 estimates) [Nihon no shorai suikei jinko (Reiwa 5 nen suikei)]. National Institute of Population and Social Security Research, Tokyo. (in Japanese)

Noda Y (2021) What is the issue with local autonomy? Local government studies in practical science [Jichi no doko ni mondai ga arunoka: Jitsugaku no chiho jichiron]. Nihon Keizai Hyuronsha Ltd., Tokyo. (in Japanese)

OECD (2023) Revenues by level of government. In: Government at a glance 2023. OECD Publishing, Paris. https://doi.org/10.1787/3d5c5d31-en

Okamoto Z (2002) Local government finance reform debate: the future of local allocation taxes [Chiho zaisei kaikaku rongi: Chiho kohuzei no shoraizou]. Gyosei. Co., Tokyo. (in Japanese)

Pierre J, Stoker G (2000) Toward multi-level governance. In: Dunleavy P, Gamble A, Holliday I, Peele G (eds) Developments in British politics. Macmillan, London, pp 29–46

Rhodes RAW (1996) The new governance: governing without government. Polit Stud 44(4):652–667. https://doi.org/10.1111/j.1467-9248.1996.tb0174

Rhodes RAW (2000) Governance and public administration. In: Pierre J (ed) Debating governance (Reprint). Oxford University Press, Oxford, pp 54–90

Rhodes RAW (2007) Understanding governance: ten years on. Organ Stud 28(8):1243–1264. https://doi.org/10.1177/0170840607076586

Takeuchi N (2019) Hidden early selection in slow promotion: municipal white collar promotion patterns and organizational functions [Osoi shoshin no nakano kakureta hayai senbatsu: Jichitai howaitokara no shoshin patan to soshiki no kino]. In: Otani M, Kawai K (eds) Civil service personnel in contemporary Japan: how political and administrative reforms changed the personnel system [Gendai nihon no komuin jinji: Seiji gyosei kaikaku ha jinji sisutemu wo dou kaetaka]. Dai–Ichi Hoki. Co., Ltd, Tokyo, pp 157–178. (in Japanese)

Torfing J (2005) Governance network theory: towards a second generation. Eur Political Sci 4:305–315. https://doi.org/10.1057/palgrave.eps.2210031

Ueda M (2012) Functions of dual representative system and councils [Nigendaihyousei to gikai no kino]. In: Mayama T (ed) Local government: the renaissance of local administration [Locaru gobamentoron: Chiho gyousei no runesansu]. Minervashobo. Co., Ltd., Kyoto, pp 40–64. (in Japanese)

Yu Noda is Professor at the Faculty of Policy Studies, Doshisha University. He was a Fulbright Visiting Scholar of Public Administration and Policy at Georgetown University in 2014. Since 2024, he has served as Principal of Doshisha Elementary School. In addition, he provided research guidance to graduate students at the Graduate School of Policy and Management at Doshisha University. His educational activities span all age groups from children to older adults. His research focuses on inter-municipal cooperation, performance information and learning effects of citizens, citizen satisfaction with government services, trust in local governments, and governance reforms. His recent articles have appeared in prominent journals, including *Public Administration Review*, *Public Management Review*, *Local Government Studies*, *International Review of Administrative Sciences*, *Asia-Pacific Journal of Public Administration*, and *International Journal of Public Administration*.

Chapter 2
Historical Overview of the Local Government System and Central–Local Relations

Shunsuke Kimura

Abstract This chapter discusses the *continuity* and *transformation* of the local government system from central–local relations to consider the sustainability of local government. First, the components of *continuity* are the two-tier system, the nature of local government powers, and the personnel exchange system; they can be described as factors that support the stability of administration and the development of functions of local governments. Second, the components of *transformation* are the legal framework of local autonomy, the expansion of local government expenditure through reforms, the establishment of an autonomous local tax system, and the creation of a stable financial transfer system; they can be described as factors that support the direction of strengthening the fragile local autonomy. To sum up these historical facts, Japanese local government system can be assessed as having a history of combining components of continuity and transformation, and of striving to guarantee financial resources while emphasizing stability and the responsiveness of local government to the demands of the citizens. The sustainability of the local government is maintained in this policy fusion. However, new social changes, such as population decline and local resource constraints, require a more flexible approach to the central-local relations. The most crucial aspect is a clearer division of roles among the three tiers of government in terms of responsiveness to the demands of civic life.

Keywords Continuity · Transformation · Two-tier system · General competence type · Fusion type · Personnel exchanges · Local autonomy · Size of local government expenditures · Independent tax · Fund transfer system · Local allocation tax

S. Kimura (✉)
Graduate School of Governance Studies, Meiji University, Tokyo, Japan
e-mail: skimura@meiji.ac.jp

2.1 Introduction

The autonomy of local governments is crucially related to the intergovernmental relationship between the national and local governments. Therefore, by examining the sustainability of the local government, this chapter clarifies the continuity and transformation of local government systems from the perspective of central–local relations in a historical context. The sustainability of the local government in terms of political administration systems and the relationship between governments and other actors, as discussed in Chap. 3 and henceforth, are based on a local government system shaped by its historical context. Thus, it is possible to understand the sustainability of the local government in light of its historical context.

The current Japanese local government system and the central-local relations have several features:

A. The local government structure is the two-tier system.
B. The functional relationship between the central government and local governments is of the general competence and fusion type; local governments can carry out administrative activities in a resilient manner.
C. The personnel exchanges which secure human resources between the central and local governments have been varied.
D. The system of local autonomy is ensured through a legal framework under the post-war 1947 Constitution.
E. The size of the local governments' expenditure is remarkably large because of B above; it is larger than that of the central government.
F. Independent taxation has developed in the local taxation system, and there is a strong decentralized component.
G. The local allocation tax (LAT) has contributed to guaranteeing and equalizing local financial resources by linking its source to a certain percentage of the national taxes, thereby enhancing stability.

These are formulated based on the history of local government system. This chapter recognizes the significance of two factors in understanding the current local government system: *continuity* from the previous era and *transformation* in the system. Each of these factors is made up of several components (See Table 2.1).

Therefore, these features are reviewed from the standpoint of the historical background of the Japanese administration in this chapter. Developments in the system

Table 2.1 Components of continuity and transformation

Continuity	Transformation
Two-tier local government system,	Legal framework of local autonomy
Nature of local government powers (general competence/fusion type)	Expansion of local government expenditure through institutional reform in key administrative areas
	Establishment of an autonomous local tax system
Personnel exchange system	Creation of a stable financial transfer system (LAT)

Source: Author's elaboration

as a modern nation can be divided into two periods. The first period spans from 1868 to 1947 and is referred to as the "Meiji Constitution Era."[1] The second period extends from 1947 to present; the period is referred to as the "Present Constitution Era." This chapter discusses how the sustainability of local government institutions and activities in Japan have been maintained throughout these two periods in terms of central–local relations. These are organized into continuity and transformation.

2.2 Continuity of Local Government System

2.2.1 The Two-Tier Local Government System

What is the of local government system in the Meiji Constitution Era and the Present Constitution Era? The main components of *continuity* are the two-tier local government system, the nature of local government powers, and the personnel exchange system. Here is an overview of those contents.

The primary system is the two-tier system; since the abolition of feudal domains and the establishment of prefectures in 1871, and the enactment of The City Law and The Town& Village Law (Shi-sei, Choson-sei) in 1888, the two-tier local government system, except for a brief period, has basically been maintained to this day (See Table 2.2).

However, the following points should be noted. Originally, when the prefectural system was established in place of feudal domains in 1871 during the Meiji Constitution Era, the governors (chiefs) of prefectures were appointed by the central government from among the ranks of officials in the Ministry of the Interior. Later, with the 1946 amendments, the appointment system was replaced by the direct elections. Through this reform, the prefecture was converted into a local government from the central government's lower mechanism.

Municipalities have been basic local authorities since the Meiji Constitution Era, and because of the principle of subsidiarity, they have been expected to be responsible for administrative services close to the lives of their residents; they have been required to have a population size and administrative functions and structures that are sufficient for the main administrative services, such as tax collection and school education. Under these circumstances, three great municipal merger movements took place throughout the Meiji Constitution Era and the Present Constitution Era: the Great Meiji Consolidation from 1888 to 1889, the Great Showa Consolidation from 1953 to 1956, and the Great Heisei Consolidation from 1999 to 2010.

These great municipal mergers progressed with administrative modernization and decentralization; consequently, the number of municipalities decreased from 71,134 in 1888 to 1724 in 2024 (See Fig. 2.1).

---

[1] Although the year in which the Meiji Constitution was enacted was 1890, in this chapter, "Meiji Constitution Era" refers to the period after 1868, when the Meiji government was established.

Table 2.2 Chronology of the Japanese local government system

Period	Events (Year of enactment of law, etc.)	Japanese	Main contents
1871	The abolition of feudal domains and the establishment of prefectures	Haihan-chiken	Establishment of prefectures
	Prefectural government organization Law	Fuken-kansei	Law providing for the appointment of governors in prefectures.
1878	Three New Laws	San-shin-Pou	First systematic administrative organization laws.
1880	The Ward, Town, and Village Councils Law	Ku-Choson-kai Hou	The associations of wards, towns, and villages were to make decisions on matters of public concern.
1886	Local government administration system	Chihoukan-kansei	Clearly defines the position of governor appointed by the government
1888	The City Law and the Town & Village Law	Shi-sei, Cho-son-sei	Main laws of basic unit (municipalities).
1888~1889	Great Meiji Consolidation	Meiji Daigappei	The number of municipalities decreased from 71,314 to 15,859.
1889	Meiji Constitution promulgated.	Meiji Kenpou	Meiji constitution era starts.
1890	The Prefectural Law and the County Law	Fuken-sei, Gun-sei	Main laws of upper tiers of local government.
1947	Japanese Constitution	Nihonkoku Kenpou	Present Constitution Era starts.
	Local Autonomy Law	Chihou-jichi Hou	Basic law on post-war local governments.
1949	Shoup Recommendations	Shoup Kankoku	Recommendation which proposed fundamental reform of local taxation.
1950	Local Tax Law	Chihou-zei Hou	Modern local tax system developed.
1953~1956	Great Showa Consolidation	Showa Daigappei	The number of municipalities decreased from 9868 to 3975.
2000	Implementation of the Uniform Decentralozation Law	Chiho-Bunken-Ikkatu Hou	The transfer of administrative powers puts seriously on the move.
1999~2010	Great Heisei Consolidation	Heisei Daigappei	The number of municipalities decreased from 3229 to 1727.

Source: Author's elaboration

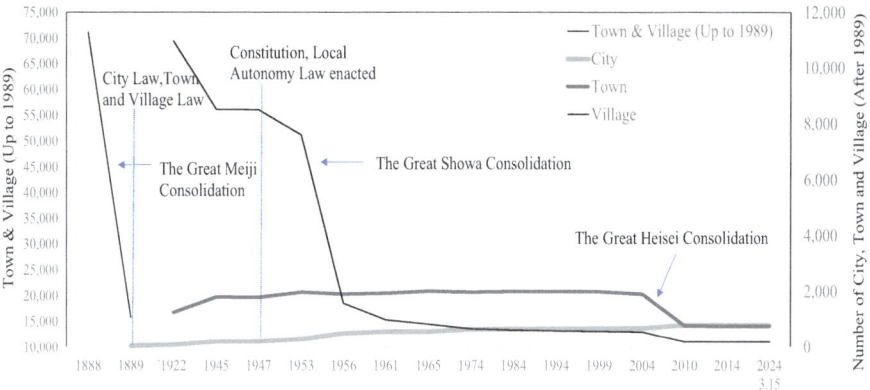

Fig. 2.1 Change of number of municipalities. (Source: Author's elaboration based on the Ministry of Internal Affairs and Communications (MIC) web page, "The Change of Number of Municipalities and the Feature of Meiji & Showa great consolidations")

Table 2.3 Number of municipalities (March 1, 2024)

Local governments		Number
Prefectures		47
Municipalities	Ordinance-designated cities	20
	Cities	772
	Towns	743
	Villages	189

Source: Author's elaboration based on op. cit.

There are two features that distinguish these changes in the number of municipalities:

(a) During the first major merger, the Great Meiji Consolidation, 71,134 towns and villages were consolidated into 15,820 over a period of two years.
(b) During the second and third major mergers, the Showa and Heisei, the number of villages shrank markedly as they merged with neighboring municipalities.

Since 1888, the number of prefectures has remained stable at 47. However, the number of municipalities has been consolidated to one-fortieth through these three merger movements. The number of local governments as a result of these changes is presented in Table 2.3.

2.2.2 Nature of Local Government Powers

The second component of continuity is the Nature of Local Government Powers. The characteristics of the nature of local government powers in the context of intergovernmental relations can be classified along two axes: the scope of responsibility and the vertical relationship between the central government and local government levels.

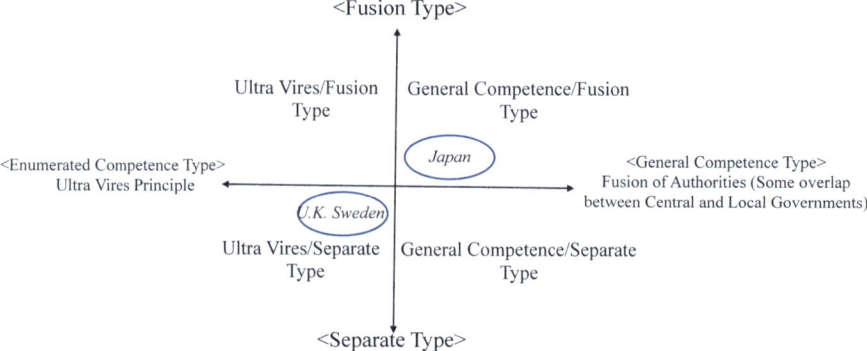

Fig. 2.2 Four types of intergovernmental relations. (Source: Author's elaboration based on Kuhlmann and Wollmann (2019), pp. 25–27)

2.2.2.1   Scope of Responsibility

The first phase is the scope of responsibility, shown on the horizontal axis in Fig. 2.2. The following is a summary of the points made by Kuhlmann and Wollmann (2019)[2]:

Local governments have two types of competencies: The first is the general competence type in which all functions of local-level relevance are assigned to and carried out by local authorities within their respective territories. Many continental European countries have adopted this principle.

The second is the enumerated competence type: local governments carry out competences or responsibilities that are explicitly assigned to them by parliamentary legislation and can virtually be revoked at any time. The Ultra Vires principle is the key term in this type. In Anglo-Saxon countries, which are classified as Ultra Vires type of state, the administrative affairs and the authority that can be exercised by local governments are clearly enumerated in the authorization laws that define the administrative authority of local governments.

2.2.2.2   Vertical Relationship Between the Central Government and Local Governments

The second phase is the relationship between the central and local government levels, which is shown on the vertical axis in Fig. 2.2. The following is a summary of the points made by Kuhlmann and Wollmann (2019)[3]; in the vertical relation between the central and the local government levels, a differentiation in local government system, can be made as to whether central government and local governments execute their responsibilities separately and largely independently from one

---

[2] Kuhlmann and Wollmann (2019), pp. 25–26.

[3] *Op. cit.*, P. 26.

another, or whether the levels interact significantly through a fusion of central and local responsibilities. The former is labeled "Separate type" and the latter "Fusion type." (See Fig. 2.2).

Among these four quadrants, Japan is placed in quadrant 1, the General Competence/Fusion Type. This characteristic of the nature of local government power has been shaped by *continuity*. The historical background of Japan can be summarized as follows:

First, Japan belongs to the general competence type. This characteristic is influenced by historical circumstances. Steiner points out that communities in the Edo period, a feudal era that lasted from the seventeenthd to the nineteenth century, were independent and democratic in the conduct and administration of their municipal affairs (Steiner 1965: 9). The government in the Meiji Constitution Era, which was established in 1868 and began building a modern nation, inherited the village organization of the Edo period, and the Ward, Town, and Village Councils Law (Ku-Choson-kai Hou) enacted in 1880 stipulated that the associations of wards, towns, and villages were to make decisions on matters of public concern. (See Table 2.2). This was the beginning of the rule of general principles in Japan. This was followed by the City Law and Town and Village Law (Shi-sei and Choson-sei) in 1888, which were the basic laws of the local administration until the end of the War. They also stipulated that the councils of cities, towns, and villages had the authority to vote on all cases in their jurisdictions (See Table 2.2). The contribution of Albert Mosse,[4] a German jurist and legal advisor to the cabinet office, to the development of the laws demonstrates the influence of the German legal system in Japan.[5] In this way, Germany influenced Japan in the general competence system.

Through this process, the principle is stipulated in Japan's Local Autonomy Law, which serves as the basic law for local administration, and the general competence is adopted, whereby "ordinary local governments shall handle local affairs and other affairs that are to be handled by law or by a Cabinet order based thereon" (Article 2, paragraph 2 of the Local Autonomy Law).

---

[4] Germany has been a typical country of generalist type. Albert Mosse who was a German jurist, came to Japan in 1886 and worked as a legal advisor to the cabinet office on the drafting of these laws. Steiner describes it as follows: "The General Principles for the Reform of the Local Government System (Chiho Seido Hensan Koryo) drawn up by Mosse were approved by the (Local System Compilation) committee with some amendments central control, and later by the Cabinet … and Mosse drafted a System of Autonomous Entities (Jichi burakusei) dealing with cities, towns, villages. The committee divided Mosse's draft into two parts, one for cities (Shisei), the other for towns and villages (Chosonsei). The draft was submitted to the Cabinet in September, and to the Senate in November 1887." Steiner, *op. cit.*, P. 39.

[5] Steiner (1965) describes it as follows: "(Aritomo) Yamagata (※later to become Prime Minister and an elder statesman in Meiji Constitution Era) was equally fascinated by Prussia, brought Mosse to Japan as an advisor in 1886. He explained this by saying that since Western nations had made institutional modernization in Japan a condition for treaty revision, it was necessary to have the local government system fixed by law, and that the Prussian model was 'the soundest day'." Steiner, *op. cit.*, P. 35. ※ Noted by Author.

Second, Japan belongs to the fusion type; in this type, central and local governments are involved in a single administrative task in a synergistic manner. The historical background is as follows:

(a) In the Meiji Constitution Era, the central government leaders believed that delegating administrative tasks to local governments would lead to greater administrative stability and adopted the policy that it was reasonable to allow local governments to perform a certain amount of work to the extent that it could be controlled by the central government.[6] Considering that this policy was adopted, it can be inferred that the central government envisaged a system in which local governments were controlled by laws enacted by the state to conduct their administrative affairs.

(b) In the Meiji Constitution Era, the prefecture was positioned as an organization with the character of a semi-national agency, and governors were appointed by the central government.[7] They occupied an intermediary position between the central government and municipalities. Therefore, in line with fused intergovernmental relations, the central government appears to have made more effective use of the prefectures, which are semi-state organizations and comprehensive administrative entities, than the branches of the national government, and established a stable system of governance.

The current divisions of administrative duties among the central government, prefectures, and municipalities are presented in Table 2.4. Prefectures and municipalities covered a wide range of administrative duties based on the general competence principle. Furthermore, individual administrative laws were enacted in each administrative field, and a fusion of governance was formed, in which the roles of the central government, prefectures, and municipalities were divided. The intergovernmental relationship between the national and local governments is formed by the reasonable division of roles between the national and local governments through individual administrative laws. In designing the system, an important principle is for the central government to guarantee financial resources so that local governments can perform their administrative duties at an reasonable and standard level.

---

[6] Steiner (1965) describes it as follows: "There were other reasons of somewhat subsidiary nature in Yamagata's (※ an elder statesman) mind. The creation of a modern state would bring a tremendous increase in governmental work. Some of this work could be transferred to the localities so long as there were sufficiently controlled. At the same time, a certain amount of dissatisfaction with the central government could be reflected to the local bodies. Therefore, he stated "the cargo of the government could be lightened and a safe voyage and good speed could be achieved." Steiner, *op. cit.*, P. 38. (※ Noted by Author.)

[7] Steiner (1965) describes it as follows: "The prefectures were different from the other local entities in two ways: as the highest level in the local government structure, they exercised control over the lower levels: and they were 'incomplete autonomous entities,' for their governors were appointed by the central government and has the status of national officials." Steiner, *op. cit.*, P. 140.

Table 2.4 Allocation of responsibilities among three levels of government

Administrative fields	Basic, Safety	Education	Welfare, sanitation	Environment	Social infrastructure	Industry, Economy	Regional development (promotion)	Cultural administration	Tourism
Central Government									
	Enactment and operation of treaties								
	Drafting and operation of individual administrative laws								
	Diplomacy	University	Pension	Climate change action (fulfilment of international commitments)	Highway	Currency	Promotion of National Land Development Plan	Repair, maintenance and utilisation of cultural assets	Implementation of strategic promotion of visits to Japan
	Defense	Subsidy for private school (university)	Social insurance		National road (designated section)	Banking regulation		Strengthening the functions of national cultural institutions	Improvement of the environment for inbound tourism using cultural resources
	Judicature		License for doctor		First-class river	Customs			
	Criminal punishment		Approval of medicine		Airport	Regulation on transportation			
						Regulation on Telecommunication			
						Economic policy			

(continued)

Table 2.4 (continued)

Administrative fields		Basic, Safety	Education	Welfare, sanitation	Environment	Social infrastructure	Industry, Economy	Regional development (promotion)	Cultural administration	Tourism
	Prefecture	Drafting and operation of individual prefectural bylaws								
Local Government		Police	High school	Livelihood assistance (area of town / village)	Decarbonisation measures	National road (other section)	Vocational training	Regional development projects	Sports facility	Improvement of the environment for inbound tourism
			Salary / Personnel of Elementary / Junior high school	Child welfare	Regulation of industrial waste	Prefecture road	Support for small businesses		Cultural facility	
			Subsidy for private school (others)	Elderly welfare		First-class river (designated section)				
				Health center		Second-class river				
						Port				
						Public housing				
						Urban planning				

Municipality	Drafting and operation of individual municipal bylaws								
	Fire defense	Elementary / junior high school	Livelihood assistance (city)	Decarbonisation measures	Municipal road	Regulation on agricultural land use	Regional development projects	Sports facility	Improvement of the environment for inbound tourism
	Family register	Kindergarten	Child welfare	Collection and disposal of general waste (household waste)	Small river			Cultural facility	
	Resident register		Elderly welfare		Port				
			Nursery care insurance		Public housing				
			National health insurance						
			Water supply						
			Sewerage						
			Waste disposal						
			Health center (specific city)						

Source: Author's elaboration

2.2.3 Personnel Exchanges in Historical Circumstances

As discussed in Sect. 2.2.1, prefectural chiefs were originally appointed by the central government in the Meiji Constitution Era. In 1886, the Local Government Official System, an imperial ordinance, was enacted. It clearly stipulated that the governor was an official appointed by the emperor and was responsible for the execution of state affairs. Since 1946, prefectural chiefs have been chosen by direct elections through the reform. Through this reform, the prefecture was converted into a local government from the central government's lower mechanism.

The elected governor system was an essential change in the nature of the prefecture as a local public entity. However, approximately 70% of the prefectures' affairs were positioned as agency delegated affairs,[8] over which the state had direct supervisory authority.[9] Even in the Present Constitution Era, the central government's legal control over local governments through the agency delegated affairs was strong until the Decentralization Law of 1999, and such a fact can be seen as a *continuity* of legal control by the central government throughout the two Eras.

Against this background, the personnel exchanges between the central and the local governments have also been active. The personnel exchanges since 1999 show the following characteristics:

A. The number of officials seconded from the central government to the prefectures has remained largely unchanged (See Fig. 2.3).
B. The number of officials seconded from the central government to municipalities has shown a slight increase.
C. The number of officials seconded from prefectures to the central government has increased markedly; the number of relevant officials in 2022 is 1.6 times higher than that in 1999.
D. There has been a marked increase in the number of officials seconded from municipalities to the state; the number of relevant personnel in 2022 is 6.5 times higher than that in 1999.

It should be noted that those personnel exchanges have been criticized as functioning in some respects as an exercise of influence by central government over local government. Meanwhile, while performing personnel exchanges briskly between the central government and local governments, it leads to mutual exchange of especially talented people on the statute and system side, and talented people with practical administration technology in the field of talented-people reservation and coping with tasks to be done by the administration. The concerned personnel exchanges have achieved the function of a network for policy making. In recent years, an increasing number of transfers from prefectures and municipalities to the central government has been a manifestation of such intergovernmental relationships. The

---

[8] Affairs delegated by the state to a subordinate body, the governor, as a superior body),

[9] This intergovernmental relationship was radically reformed through the Decentralization Law, which was enacted in 1999.

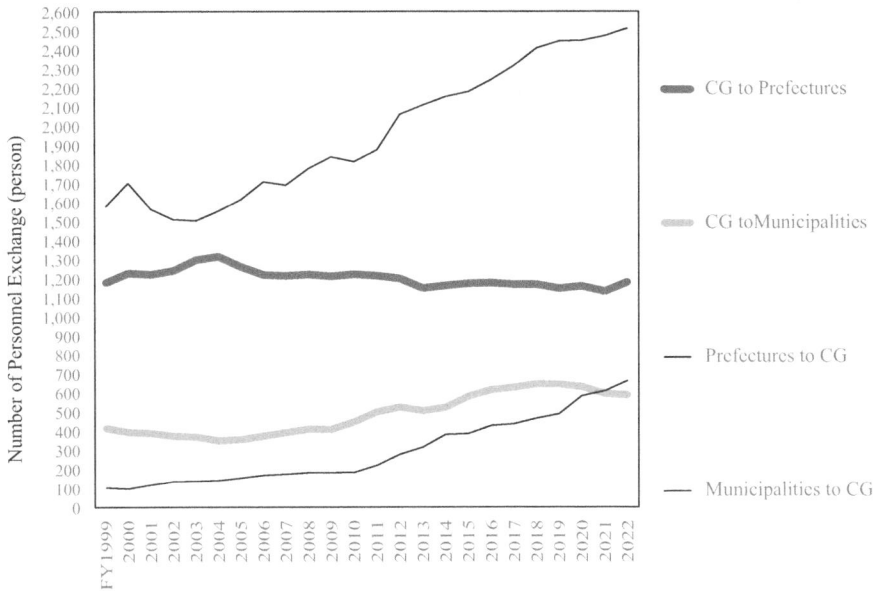

Fig. 2.3 Trend of the personnel exchange between central and local governments. (Source: Author's elaboration based on the "Situation of Personnel Exchange between Central and Local Governments," National Personnel Authority (NPA) (2022))

strengthening of ties between municipalities and central government has become particularly marked in recent years.

2.3   Transformation of Local Government System

2.3.1   Legal Framework of Local Autonomy

What is the transformation of local government system in the Meiji Constitution Era and the Present Constitution Era? In other words, what were the *institutional turning points*? The main components of transformation are the legal framework of local autonomy, the expansion of local government expenditure through institutional reform in key administrative areas, the establishment of an autonomous local tax system, and the creation of a stable financial transfer system. Here is an overview of those contents.

In the process of development of the legal system, the institutional turning point was the foundation of the Constitution,[10] which was enacted in 1947 after the end of

---

[10] In the Constitution of Japan, four Articles, making up one Chapter, prescribe matters concerning local autonomy.

World War II (hereinafter referred to as "the War"). The government system tended to exclude centralization and promote democratization and local autonomy. Consequently, the fundamental legal transformation of local government system is a full-scale introduction of local autonomy in the form of local governments serving citizens. In the present Constitution, a Chapter on "local autonomy" was newly stipulated,[11] and various laws were also enacted in this period, including the Local Autonomy Law. When it came to postwar reforms, the state used the legislative process to ensure that a wide variety of tasks would be carried out by local governments.

The Constitution, Local Autonomy Law, and other related laws established the following points:

A. The main objective of local self-government is institutionally guaranteed.
B. The local government's authority to enact ordinances was provided for in the legal framework. As for the ordinance, the legislative powers of local governments allow them to enact voluntary ordinances[12] as well as delegated ordinances.[13]

2.3.2   Large Size of Local Governments' Expenditure on Historical Changes in the System

2.3.2.1   Current Situation

As discussed in Sect. 2.2.2, general competence is given to the Japanese local government. In this framework, the local government can be responsible for all affairs related to the region. This principle leads to a wide range of public affairs conducted by local governments. Based on this system, which relates to the authority of local governments, the workload of Japanese local government administrative activities

---

Chapter VIII Article 92: Regulations concerning organization and operations of local governments shall be fixed by law in accordance with the principle of local autonomy.

Article 93: The local governments shall establish assemblies as their deliberative organs, in accordance with law. 2) The chief executive officers of all local governments, the members of their assemblies, and such other local officials as may be determined by law shall be elected by direct popular vote within their several communities.

Article 94: Local governments shall have the right to manage their property, affairs and administration and to enact their own regulations within law.

Article 95: A special law, applicable only to one local government, cannot be enacted by the Diet without the consent of the majority of the voters of the local government concerned, obtained in accordance with law.

[11] Meiji Constitution, which was enacted in 1890, did not have a chapter on local autonomy.

[12] Voluntary ordinances refer to the ordinances that are voluntarily enacted by local governments with regard to restrictions not prescribed by the national laws.

[13] Delegated ordinances refer to the ordinances that are delegated by the national laws to prescribe details.

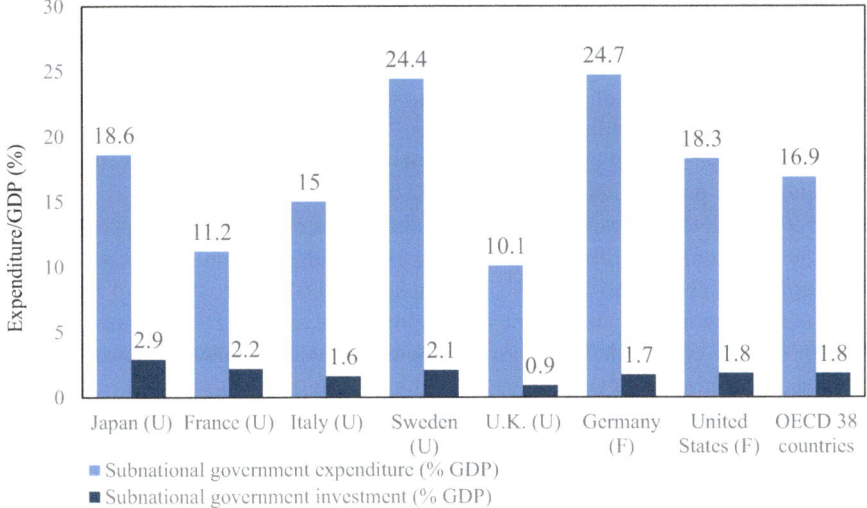

Fig. 2.4 International comparison of size of subnational government expenditure (Percentage of GDP 2021). (Source: Author's elaboration based on subnational governments in OECD countries (OECD 2023))

is high. Due, in part, to differences in Gross Domestic Product (GDP) size and administrative systems, the size of local government expenditures as a percentage of the GDP in Sweden and Germany exceeds that in Japan. However, the size of Japanese local government expenditures as a percentage of GDP (18.6%) is slightly greater than those of 38 Organization for Economic Co-operation and Development (OECD) countries (16.9%). This is true not only for the size of total expenditures but also for the size of operating expenses for administrative investment; that of Japan is 2.9% and that of the OECD 38 countries is (1.8%). This indicates that Japanese local governments play an important role not only in activities such as consumptive expenditures (i.e., spending on benefits equivalent to assistance costs), but also in investment expenditures (i.e., constructing and maintaining infrastructure) (See Fig. 2.4).

2.3.2.2 Historical Background

The current situation is caused by both of *continuity* and *transition*. The continuity is the general competence discipline of local government function. It leads to the expansion of the scope of local government responsibility. The *institutional turning point* is the postwar reconstruction and the rapid economic growth from the 1950s to the 1970s.

This chapter focuses on those turning points: the size of local government spending, with a particular emphasis on postwar history. In the 1940s, just after the end of the War, Japan was faced with loss and devastation throughout the territory, the destruction of the facilities of daily life, and many unemployed people. Under this situation, a Cabinet decision "An outline of emergency employment measures" was made in 1946. Consequently, a public works project was planned and implemented. Moreover, with the aim of providing unemployment support not only for unskilled workers but also for white-collar workers, "broad-based public works projects" were carried out in 1947 and 1948. Local governments were involved in these unemployment projects and borne one-third of the costs.

After the 1950s, the rapid increase in annual expenditure by local governments was due to not only the inflation but also the expansion of administrative services by local governments in various fields. The background is as follows: From fiscal year 1955 to fiscal year 1973, the Japanese economy grew rapidly. During this economic growth period, central and local governments enjoyed an annual increase in tax revenue. LAT boosted revenues dramatically during this period and strongly supported local governments with critical financial difficulties. Additionally, priority was given to administrative investments that contributed to industrial development, and the expenditure scale of local governments increased rapidly. From the 1940s, the size of local government spending (as a percentage of GDP) increased markedly, and by the early 1950s, local government spending exceeded that of the central government. Growth in local government spending continued to exceed central government spending until the 1960s and the mid-1970s (the end of rapid economic growth). (See Fig. 2.5).

The expansion of administrative services was facilitated by the expanded concept of welfare state promoted by the national government. The expansion of administrative services occurred primarily in the following fields:

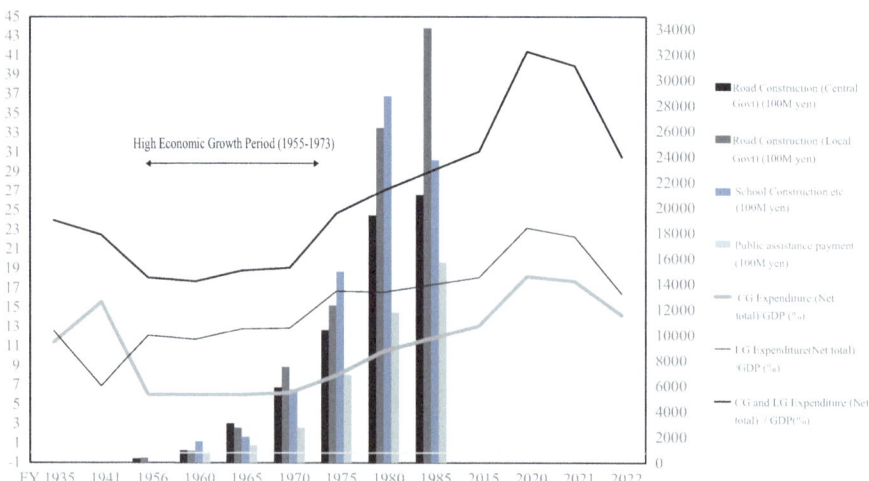

Fig. 2.5 Trends in central and local governments expenditures (Percentage of GDP and expenses by main purpose). (Source: Author's elaboration based on the Local Finance Association (2022) and MIC (1953–1985))

- Public works: Projects such as the construction of roads, bridges, and other social infrastructure.
- Education: Extension of compulsory education by three years (i.e., six years of elementary school plus three years of junior high school), and increase in the number of children and high school students.
- Social welfare: Enactment of the Public Assistance Law, Child Welfare Law, Social Welfare for the Elderly Law, and other laws.

Recently, the role of administrative activities in the national economy has become more significant. The role of local public bodies in administrative activities has also expanded. The historical backgrounds of the main areas are as follows:

A. **Public Works (Constructing Roads)**

Two points are worth mentioning regarding road construction. First, a system of road-specific revenue sources was established by the Temporary Measures for Road Construction Law enacted in 1953. Under this system, certain types of taxes were allocated exclusively to road construction, and central and local governments were able to secure stable financial resources for road construction. This led not only to the central government but also to local governments continuously making large-scale administrative investments in road construction.

Second, a method was established in which the central government formulated a long-term plan for road construction and continuously implemented large-scale administrative investment. The five-year road construction plan based on the Road Construction Emergency Measures Law started in 1958, and since then, this method has been firmly established, and large-scale administrative investment in planned road construction has taken root.

Based on these legal systems, the central and local governments began to invest in earnest in administrative investments for road construction in the 1960s. In the 1970s and 1980s, the scale of road investments by central and local governments increased markedly. Additionally, since the 1970s, the scale of road investments by local governments has markedly exceeded that of the central government (See Fig. 2.5).

B. **Education (Construction Projects)**

In 1947, the Fundamental Law of Education determined the basic principles of education and the central government implemented the School Education Law, which introduced the 6–3–3-4-year schooling system. Compulsory education was extended by three years; six years of elementary school plus three years of junior high school. These changes resulted in an increase in the number of children and high-school students. The system was implemented the following year, and local governments faced an urgent need to move quickly toward school construction projects. Local governments began school construction projects in earnest in the 1960s, and the scale of these projects expanded markedly in the 1970s and the 1980s.

C. Social Welfare (Enactment of the Livelihood Protection Law)

As a result of the steep rise in the number of persons experiencing everyday hardships, the central government implemented a livelihood assistance program aimed at people who were destitute and had extreme problems in their daily lives, providing accommodation, work, treatment for illnesses, clothes, bedding, and other necessities of daily life. In 1945 the central government made a Cabinet decision, "An outline of emergency livelihood assistance for people suffering destitution in their daily lives." Subsequently, the Livelihood Protection Law was enacted, and implemented from 1946. This law clarified the principle of the responsibility of the state to provide livelihood protection to those who needed such protection. The Livelihood Protection Law stipulates that the Minister of Health, Labor, and Welfare (the national government) sets the standard amount for public assistance (Article 8) and that the implementation of public assistance is carried out by prefectural governors, mayors, and mayors of towns and villages where welfare offices are located (Article 19). The central government pays three-fourths of public assistance expenses, public assistance facility office expenses, and commissioned office expenses paid by local governments (Article 75), meaning that local governments pay one-fourth of the expenses.

As indicated in the histories of these public fields, local governments, together with the central government, assume responsibility for public assistance work, as the work of social security for low-income people is a task closely related to the lives of citizens, and local governments bear one-fourth of the public assistance expenditure. In the 1960s, welfare payments by local governments began in earnest and increased markedly in the 1970s and 1980s.

2.3.3 Feature of the Local Tax System Based on Historical Changes in the System

2.3.3.1 Current Situation

The international comparison of the tax revenues of subnational organizations in Fig. 2.6 reveals the following points:

A. Federal states, such as Germany (13.4%) and the U.S. (9.2%), have taxes collected by subnational organizations (states), so this percentage is higher.
B. In unitary states, the size of local tax revenues is determined by the sorting of taxes between the central and local governments. Nordic countries such as Sweden (12.6%) have a large local tax size. Japan (7.8%) also has a larger local tax base than other continental countries and its share is higher than that of the 38 OECD countries (7.2%).

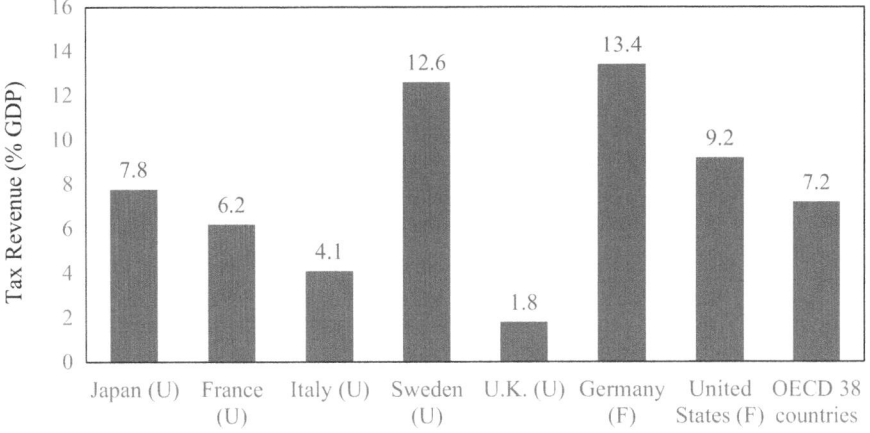

Fig. 2.6 International comparison of subnational government tax sizes (Percentage of GDP: 2021). (Source: Author's elaboration based on OECD (2023))

2.3.3.2 Historical Background

As described in Sect. 2.2.2 Japanese local governments, whose authority belongs to the general competence and fusion types, have jurisdiction over administrative services that are directly related to residents' lives, such as roads, school education, and public assistance. Local governments have expanded their fiscal scale in a structure supported by increased tax revenue from rapid economic growth. Figure 2.6 demonstrates that Japanese local governments' expenditures are larger and that these administrative activities are supported to some extent by these stable local tax revenues. Therefore, the historical background of the local tax system should be considered.

First, the following characteristics can be identified regarding the evolution of the sizes of the national tax, local tax, and LAT (See Fig. 2.7).

The following characteristics of local tax trends can be noted:

A. The basic framework of the current local taxation system was created in 1950; since then, the size of tax revenue has consistently increased (See Table 2.1).
B. Based on the Shoup recommendations, local taxation has been reformed to strengthen its autonomy, for example, by enhancing independent taxation; consequently, the size of national tax revenue has been relatively large in amplitude, while local taxation has been growing steadily.
C. National taxes have continued to increase since the 2010s because of tax reforms, the gradual recovery of the economy, and the expansion of consumption tax revenues.
D. Local taxes have markedly expanded as a result of the 2007 local tax reform (which transferred JPY 3 trillion of tax revenue from the national income tax to the local inhabitant tax), which was implemented as part of the decentralization reform. Consequently, the share of local tax revenues in total taxes reached its peak.

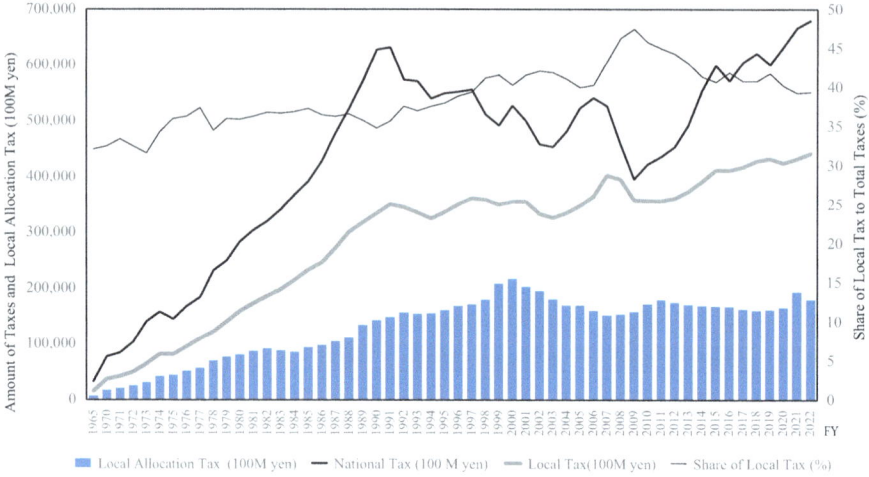

Fig. 2.7 Total amount of national and local taxes. (Source: Author's elaboration based on *the Local Government Finance Handbook* (Dec. 2022))

E. Given that income taxation is a core tax item for not only national tax but also local tax, recessions in the domestic economy, such as the collapse of the bubble economy in 1991 and the Lehman Shock in 2008, have had a significant impact on local tax revenues. This makes tax system reform a serious issue in securing more stable tax revenues.

F. The amount of LAT, whose source is basically a fixed percentage of several national taxes, was introduced in the 1930s and modeled after the German general subsidy for fiscal adjustment among local governments. LAT has been the main source of general revenue for local governments, along with local taxes. Considering that the LAT is funded by a certain percentage of national taxes, its size increases or decreases in tandem with an increase or decrease in national taxes (discussed below). In the 1970s and 1980s, the size of LAT expanded in line with a large increase in national taxes; however, since the Heisei recession of the 1990s, its size has remained flat, with annual fluctuation.

The institutional turning point in the historical background was the Shoup Recommendations. The modern Japanese taxation system dates to the Land Tax Reform of 1873.[14] The local taxes were developed from the 1870s onwards in the Meiji Constitution Era,[15] but they were essentially additional taxes which became a challenge due to the lack of autonomous revenue collection and lack of stability as the role of local finances increased owing to an increase in social problems. For this

---

[14] Under the Land Tax Reform, 3% of land value was collected as a national tax and used to cover national expenses.

[15] The prefectural tax system was legislated in 1878, followed by the municipal tax system in 1888.

reason, the Shoup Recommendations were made in 1949 and 1950, after the War.[16] They pointed out the immaturity of prewar local self-government and stated that it was essential to strengthen the fiscal capacity of local governments to perfect local self-government. Specifically, they called for (a) an enhancement of municipal taxes, (b) the abolition of additional taxes[17] and the establishment of independent taxes, and (c) a reduction in the number of tax types and an increase in tax rates.[18] Based on these recommendations, the current Local Tax Law was enacted in 1950 (See Table 2.1). The 1950 system reform resulted in a systematic enhancement of local taxation, including the expansion of local tax revenues, abolition of additional taxes, and creation of independent taxes such as property taxes. Since then, the Local Tax Law was revised in 1954, and other changes were made, leading to the current Local Tax Law.

Figures 2.8 shows the changes in the local tax before and after 1950. In 1905, during the Meiji Constitutional Era, municipal tax revenues comprised 63% of additional taxes and 37% of independent taxes. In contrast, as a result of the abolition of many additional taxes and the creation of independent taxes, in 2022, the additional tax in a narrow definition accounted for 9%, and the combined ratio of narrow and broad taxes was 45%. Independent taxes accounted for the majority of the total at 55%. Therefore, it can be assessed that the institutionalization of independent taxation has made steady progress in strengthening the autonomy of municipalities with regard to local taxation.

Next, we examine the current system in terms of levying and collecting local taxes. Local and central governments have the right to levy taxes. The specific exercise of this right to taxation, whereby the local governments carry out tax audits, determine the amount of tax themselves, notify taxpayers and collect local taxes, is

---

[16] In the context of Japan's increasingly dire local financial situation, in 1949, a U.S. mission led by Dr. Carl Summer Shoup, a tax expert, visited Japan. The recommendations resulting from their research were issued in August. It identifies a need to increase the independence of local bodies and further emphasizes the need to strengthen the development of local bodies. It goes on to point out that without strengthening the financial capacity of local bodies and, concurrently, further equalizing the imbalance between rich and poor areas, it is difficult to expect the completion of local autonomy.

[17] An additional tax, by a narrow definition, is a tax levied on the amount of tax imposed by another taxing entity as its tax base. For example, the corporate inhabitant tax, a local tax, falls under this category; it is levied on the amount of national corporate tax. If the amount of corporate tax is changed by tax reform, the amount of corporate inhabitant tax is also automatically changed. This means that the tax system is largely affected by changes in the underlying tax system and has little autonomy as a tax system. It should be added that an additional tax, in a broad sense, is a tax levied on the same tax subject as that of the other kinds of taxes. For example, the individual inhabitant tax, a local tax, falls under this category; it is levied on personal income, which is the same tax subject as the income tax. This overlap in taxable subjects leads to a vulnerability in tax revenues.

[18] The contents can be summarized as follows: (a) The enhancement of municipal taxation was requested to strengthen municipalities that are closer to residents in the development of local self-government. (b) The abolition of additional taxes and the establishment of an independent taxation system will clarify the responsibility of local governments as taxing entities for residents. (c) Reducing the types of taxes and raising the tax rate imply simplifying the tax system.

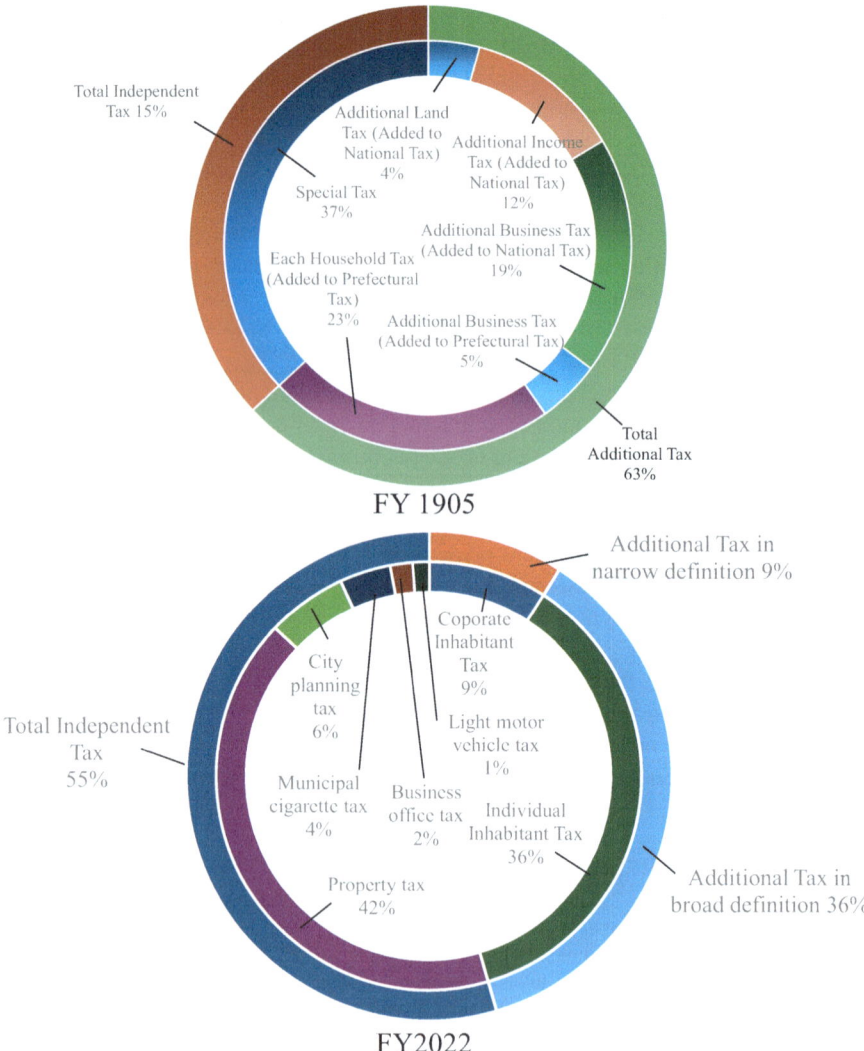

Fig. 2.8 Local taxes in 1905 and 2022. (Source: Author's elaboration based on Ando (2020))

known as "*levying taxation*." In contrast, the method whereby the taxpayer declares the amount of tax due and pays the tax due is known as "*declaration and payment*." In FY 2022, 94% of all local taxes collected were levied taxation. This shows that today's Japanese local governments have a well-established framework for autonomous fiscal management by exercising the taxation rights granted to them to secure financial resources for the administrative services they implement (See Fig. 2.9).

Fig. 2.9 Share of levying taxation type and declaration payment type (Number of cases in FY 2022). (Source: Author's elaboration based on Data by White Paper of Local Finance (2024))

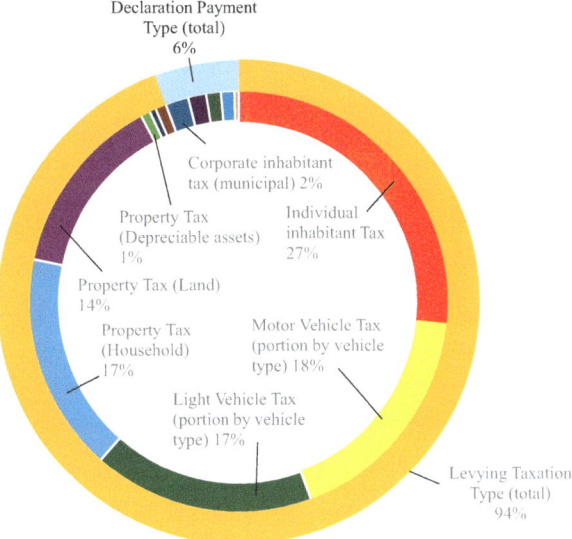

2.3.4   Feature of Local Financial Equalization Based on Historical Changes in the System

2.3.4.1   Current Situation

An international comparison of the revenue compositions of local governments is shown in Fig. 2.10. The characteristics of Japanese local governments are listed below:

A. Federal states, such as Germany and the U.S., have a high share of tax revenues in their revenue. In Japan, the share of local taxes in revenue is not remarkably high for a unitary state.
B. Intergovernmental transfers account for a higher share of revenues in Japan than in other countries. Intergovernmental transfers consist of grants including LAT and government subsidies.

The scale of local government spending in Japan was large, based on the general competence concept. In this circumstance, historically, an urgent agenda for Japanese local government finance systems has been designing a system to finance great fiscal demands. Therefore, based on the Shoup Recommendations, local tax reform became an urgent issue, and funds transferred from the central government played a crucial role.

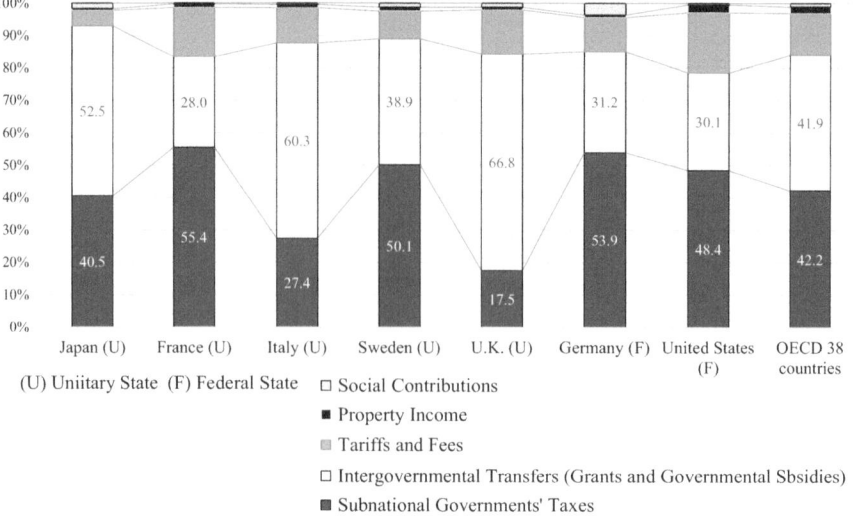

Fig. 2.10 International comparison of the composition of revenue of local governments (2021). (Source: Author's elaboration based on Subnational Governments in OECD (2023))

Funds transferred from the central government to local governments consist of grants, including LAT and national subsidies.[19] In the 2021 settlement, the real size of local tax revenues as a percentage of total national and local taxes is 38.2%. In contrast, the size of local government expenditures accounts for 55.7% of the total expenditures of the national and local governments (See Fig. 2.11). This inversion of the scale of revenue and expenditure between national and local governments is made possible by intergovernmental transfers of funds. In Japan, these transfers play a pivotal role in providing administrative services to the population.

These transfers comprise the National Treasury Expenditure, which amounted to JPY 31,984 billion in 2021, and LAT, which amounted to JPY 19,505 billion. As the transfer fund, not only the former, which has played a role as a source to fulfill specific administrative objectives, but also the latter, has played a unique role in covering the gap between the financial demands faced by local governments and their own financial resources, such as local taxes.

The reason for this ratio in the comparison of real fiscal scale is that the main content of modern public administration is the provision of services to the public, which in Japan is primarily carried out by local governments, which are administrative entities closely connected to the lives of the people. In implementing these services, a large amount of financial resources such as LAT and national expenditures are transferred from the national government to local governments. As shown in Fig. 2.7, the LAT, which is funded by a certain percentage of national tax

---

[19] The national subsidies have played a pivotal role as a source of funds to fulfill specific administrative objectives.

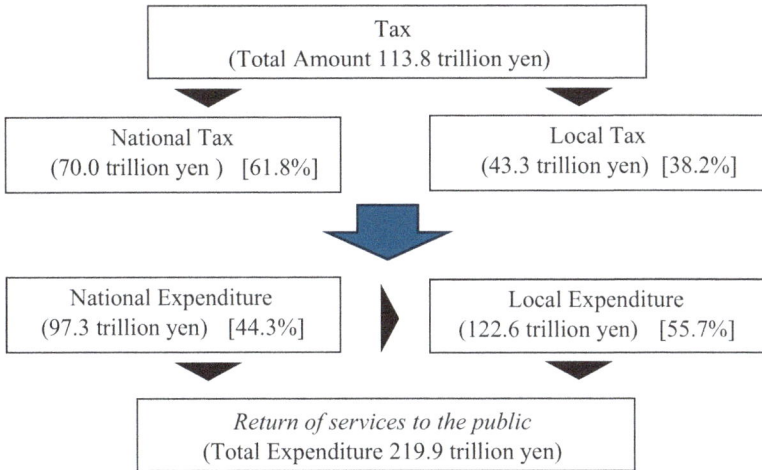

Fig. 2.11 Structure of Revenue and Expenditure of Governments (2021 Settlement). (Source: Author's elaboration based on the data on MIC web page. https://www.soumu.go.jp/main_content/000927758.pdf)

revenues,[20] has been increasing in size in tandem with an increase in national tax revenues since the 1950s.

2.3.4.2   Historical Background

What was the turning point of establishing such stable fund transfers? It was the establishment of the LAT,[21] which dates back to 1954. The predecessor of LAT was the Local Public Finance Equalization Grant System (hereinafter referred to as the "Equalization Grant"), which was established in 1950 in response to the Shoup Recommendations. This system was designed to guarantee the financial resources of individual local governments by calculating their standard fiscal size (base fiscal demand) and covering any shortfalls in their financial resources.[22] However, because the total amount of the annual Equalization Grant was not linked to the national tax

[20] The total amount of LAT was set at 33.1% of income tax and corporate tax (from FY 2015) and 50% of liquor tax (from FY 2015), and was later enhanced to include 19.5% of consumption tax (from FY 2020) and the full amount of local corporate tax (from FY 2014) (Article 6 of the Local Allocation Tax Law).

[21] LAT is collected by the central government on behalf of the local governments and redistributed according to certain reasonable standards to ensure that all local governments can maintain a certain level of financial resources and to adjust the imbalance of financial resources among local governments.

[22] The Shoup Recommendations advocated that local governments should calculate the fiscal demand required to implement standardized administration and compensate the difference between the calculated amount and local tax revenues through equalization grants.

system, it was significantly lower than the local governments' financial resource shortfalls.[23] Consequently, in 1953, the Equalization Grant system was reviewed for a short period of three years because it lacked stability as a source of revenue for local governments.

In 1954, the LAT was established to compensate for the shortcomings of an Equalization Grant. The new method was introduced to link funding to a certain percentage of national taxes. This was a significant transformation in terms of securing independent and stable financial resources.

The situation of fund transfers in recent years is as follows:

The real size of local tax revenues as a percentage of total national and local taxes has generally remained at approximately 38% in recent years. By contrast, the size of local government expenditures has generally remained at approximately 56% in recent years (See Fig. 2.12).

The ratio of national to local tax revenues is 6:4, whereas the ratio of national to local expenditures (net total) on a final expenditure basis is 4:6, indicating that the tax and expenditure ratios are reversed (See Fig. 2.12). In Japan, most administrative tasks are allocated to local governments, and local governments at the same level, even those with weak financial strength, which perform the same administrative tasks. This is made possible by the large transfer of financial resources from the national government to local governments, which redistribute financial resources collected as national taxes to local governments. It can be assessed that one of the significances of LAT is that it has been able to stably fill the gap between the expected administrative demands of local government and the actual weak taxation capacity (See Fig. 2.12). In addition, the sustainability of local governments with increasing responsibilities is supported by this financial system.

2.4   Conclusions

This chapter presents a historical context of the local government system in terms of its continuity and transformation. First, the components of *continuity* such as the two-tier system, the nature of local government powers, and the personnel exchange system, can be described as factors that support the stability of administration and the development of functions of local governments.

Second, when it comes to *transformation*, the local administration system has been experiencing several significant turning points in its history. These are the

---

[23] There is no doubt that the idea of securing the financial resources necessary for fiscal adjustment by anticipating the fiscal demands of local public finances is excellent in terms of establishing the foundation for local autonomy. In practice, however, the Ministry of Finance and the Local Autonomy Agency had to repeatedly negotiate severe budgetary issues over the amount of the Equalization Grant required each fiscal year.

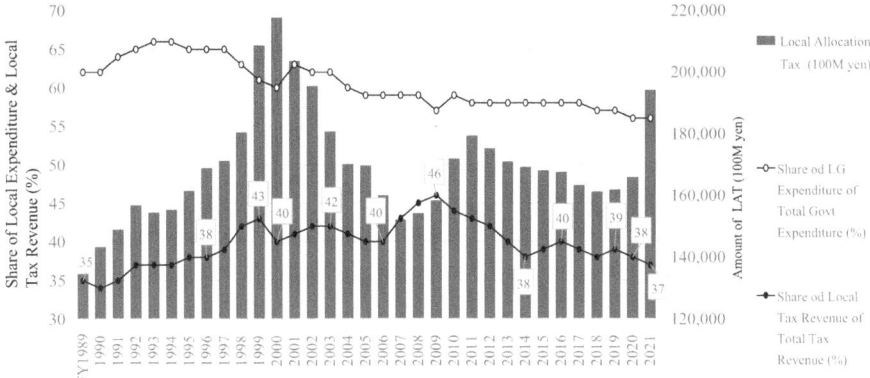

Fig. 2.12 Trend of the share of local expenditure, share of local tax revenue, and amount of LAT. (Source: Author's elaboration based on the data on MIC web page)

enactment of the present Constitution, the remarkable increase in the size of local government expenditure resulting from the institutional reforms in key administrative areas such as public works, education and social welfare, the establishment of an autonomous local tax system based on the Shoup recommendations, and the establishment of a stable fund transfer system through LAT. Considering these institutional turning points, those components of transformation can be described as factors that support the direction of strengthening the fragile local autonomy as much as possible.

To sum up these historical facts, Japanese local government system can be assessed as having a history of combining components of continuity and transformation, and of striving to guarantee financial resources while emphasizing stability and the responsiveness of local government to the demands of the citizens. In other words, local governments have expanded the scope and volume of their policy activities according to policy promotion intentions of national ministries. In this sense, local government institutions have maintained their sustainability in the historical context of cooperation with the central government.

However, when considering the future of the local government system, new social demands have been added in recent years, such as population decline and regional resource constraints: the possibility of a shortage of human and financial resources required for the supply of administrative services.

Therefore, it is considered necessary to take a more flexible view of the roles of prefectures and municipalities than in the past, and to discuss a system in which, for example, it is expected that the central and local governments will plan and operate a system that enables prefectures to fulfil their complementary and alternative functions for municipalities. The most crucial aspect will be the state's insight into and attitude toward the division of roles among the three tiers of government in terms of responsiveness to the demands of civic life.

References

Ando M, Furuichi H, Miyazaki M (2020) Local finance before the introduction of financial equal-
    izing system [Zaiseichouseiseido dounyu izen no chihou zaisei]. Rikyo Keizaigaku Kenkyu,
    Tokyo, pp 59–91. (in Japanese)
Kuhlmann S, Wollmann H (2019) Introduction to comparative public administration. Edward
    Elger Publishing, Cheltenham
Local Finance Association (2022) Local government finance handbook (Dec. 2022) [Chihou
    Zaisei Youran]. Local Finance Association, Tokyo. (in Japanese)
MIC (1953–1985, 2024) White paper of local finance [Chihou Zaisei Hakusho]. Ministry of
    Internal Affairs and Communications, Tokyo. (in Japanese)
MIC Web page. MIC web page. https://www.soumu.go.jp/main_content/000927758.pdf
NPA (2022) Situation of personnel exchange between central and local governments. National
    Personnel Authority, Tokyo
OECD (2023) Subnational governments in OECD countries: key data (2023 Edition). OECD, Paris
Steiner K (1965) Local government in Japan. Stanford University Press, California

Shunsuke Kimura (PhD) is a Professor of the Graduate School of Governance Studies at Meiji
University. He was a visiting professor at the University of Lille in 2023. His areas of expertise are
administrative law and local government finance. He published *Regional Administration in Japan*
(Routledge, 2017). His recent articles include in *Public Organization Review*. He has also contrib-
uted chapters in *Local Finance in Japan, Global Encyclopedia of Public Administration, Public
Policy, and Governance,* and others.

Chapter 3
Political Institutions and Partisan Power in Japanese Local Politics

Yosuke Sunahara ⓘ

Abstract Who holds power in Japanese local politics? This chapter investigates the complexities of local governance in Japan, focusing on the interaction between political heads and local assemblies, with particular attention to the long-term dominant Liberal Democratic Party (LDP). It examines how electoral campaigns, political strategies, and the legislative framework, as influenced by the political system, result in a practice where the LDP's dominance in councils markedly affects the political heads. Although Japan's local government is often equated with a presidential system with a strong political head, this chapter reveals dynamics more akin to a parliamentary system with an influential local council. In this context, the analysis explores the rise of the Osaka Restoration Association (ORA) and the LDP's fragmentation in gubernatorial elections to identify the causes of these remarkable development.

Keywords Electoral systems · Constitutional power · Party competition · Status quo · Party split

3.1 Introduction

Japan has maintained a centralized political system, with traditionally little focus on local politics. This lack of attention stems from the prevailing belief that decisions made by the national government were the most important, and that local governments were merely subject to national directives. However, the 1970s marked a notable exception when governors and mayors backed by leftist parties sought to enact their own policies. During this period, local government leaders, who prioritized social welfare and environmental issues over economic development, were seen as the driving forces to make a difference in local politics, despite many being conservative members of the Liberal Democratic Party (LDP) at both national and

Y. Sunahara (✉)
Graduate School of Law, Kobe University, Kobe, Hyogo, Japan

© The Author(s), under exclusive license to Springer Nature
Switzerland AG 2024
Y. Noda (ed.), *Local Governance in Japan*, Local and Urban Governance,
https://doi.org/10.1007/978-3-031-77322-8_3

47

local levels. Conversely, local councils have often faced criticism for simply rubber-stamping the proposals of governors and mayors.

As decentralization reforms advanced in the late 1990s, local governments began to seek to autonomous and, in some cases, independent decision-making, without being governed by the national government. The leadership roles of governors and mayors were particularly highlighted during the COVID-19 pandemic that began in 2020. Decentralization has enabled local politics to make substantive decisions about their future and sustainability, raising important questions about the distribution of power in the local governments. Although the political head remains a central figure in local governance, as exemplified by the pandemic response, previous studies have explored the significance of local councils (Soga and Machidori 2007; Sunahara 2011). These studies focus on the partisan dynamics within local councils and how council members can influence the political head through their electoral support.

The so-called dual representation system is a critical factor in understanding decision-making within local governments. The complexity of local government decision-making in Japan stems from the fact that both the political head and the local council are elected by the local citizens through separate electoral systems, leading to differing preferences. The structure of Japanese local government is likely considered to resemble a presidential system characterized by an independent chief executive and congress. However, these institutions do not influence policy in isolation. Instead, decision-making occurs through mutual influence between the two. Consequently, the relationship between them may more closely resemble a parliamentary system, where the chief executive reflects the will of the parliament, rather than acting independently.

This chapter explores the power structure in local politics, focusing on the elections of local representatives. It first describes the electoral system that elects political heads and local councils in the so-called dual representation system, and examines the power granted to the head. Although the head has considerable formal authority, this does not necessarily equate to substantial influence over the actions of individual council members. Next, it elaborates on how recent studies of local politics in Japan have highlighted the importance of local council members, especially LDP council members, having influence over their heads through elections. This chapter then discusses two new patterns in the relationship between political heads and councils that have emerged since the 2010s. One is the case of Osaka, where a non-LDP party has gained considerable power under a strong leader, and the other is the LDP split observed in gubernatorial elections across many prefectural governments. The conclusion discusses how these cases, which appear to be deviations from conventional patterns, can be understood in the context of Japanese local politics. While political heads are often the focus of local politics in Japan, it is the local councils that truly forms the core of power.

3.2   The Basic Structure of Japanese Local Governance

3.2.1   Delegation Through Elections

A democratic system is understood as a mechanism by which voters delegate power to a government composed of representatives elected from among themselves (Schumpeter 2013). While voters delegate the exercise of power to the government through elections, the government is accountable to the voters and is expected to realize their interests. This concept of delegation does not imply that only the central government receives delegation from the voters. In local governments, as in the central government, representatives are elected through elections and are tasked with realizing the interests of local residents.

The delegation of authority by voters to their representatives through elections serves as the foundational principle of the theoretical framework because this model is considered appropriate for analyzing the so-called dual representation system that characterizes local governance in Japan. The political head and the local council, delegated by the voters through different electoral systems, tend to have different policy preferences, driven by their aims to win elections and fulfill voter accountable. By analyzing the relationship based on the electoral delegation, Japanese local government can be understood as an arena of political competition between political head and the local council, two representatives who are separately empowered by voters through distinct electoral systems.

The relationship between voters and government through elections can be better understood by referencing studies on parliamentary systems by Strøm (2000) and Huber (2000). These studies conceptualize the parliamentary system as a "chain of delegation" that extends from the voters to the government's end. They highlight the importance of voters choosing politicians who align with their preferences and monitoring the performance. The framework underlines the alignment between the delegation of authority and accountability across the individual relationships: from voter to parliament, parliament to cabinet, and cabinet to ministers. Within this framework, the parliamentary system is perceived as a unified structure of representation, with voters as sovereign delegating authority to their representatives, contrasting with the presidential system, which is characterized by the delegation to multiple representatives.

In a parliamentary system, the primary issue is how the electorate can control their representatives to enhance administrative efficiency under the very simple structure of a "chain of delegation." In contrast, the presidential system lacks a direct mandate connection among the various representatives chosen by the voters, with each required to be accountable to the electorate independently. Therefore, variations in voter-to-representative delegation can incite competition among representatives, each vying to demonstrate their accountability to the voters.

Japanese local governments have the so-called dual representative system, where the head of the local government and the local council coexist, making the structure complex for a single "chain of delegation" explanation. Viewed from the perspective of both institutions being elected, the system appears to be similar to the presidential system depicted by Strøm (2000). In this arrangement, the head and the local council, each delegated by the local population, independently and competitively shape policy, aiming to be accountable to their constituents.

3.2.2 Electoral Systems and Preferences of Representatives

In the local government election process, the political head is elected by plurality voting across the entire local government area. Given the large electoral district, candidates must garner extensive voter support, making it challenging to strongly represent specific regional or industry interests. A candidate for the head of government must appeal to a broad spectrum of community interests to secure election. However, when a candidate for the political head requires the backing of a major political party in the local council to win, they may prioritize the interests of a particular region or industry. In these cases, the local council members supporting the candidate often facilitate the representation of these specific interests.

The local council member, the other representative, is elected via a different electoral system than the political head. Prefectural and municipal elections employ the Single Non-Transferable Voting (SNTV) system, where voters choose a specific candidate and cast a single vote. Votes are tallied for each candidate, with candidates ranked by the total votes received. Election winners are decided based on a predetermined district magnitude, meaning, for instance, if the district magnitude is five, the top five candidates with the most votes will be elected.

Under this voting system, the number of electoral districts and their district magnitude are critical factors in local council elections. Regarding the number of electoral districts, prefectural councils have multiple districts, typically structured around individual municipalities. Similarly, ordinance-designated cities, which are large and possess distinct authorities, also have multiple electoral districts, each corresponding to the administrative wards within these cities. In contrast, municipal councils other than ordinance-designated cities comprise a single electoral district, meaning that all council members are elected from the same district by the SNTV system.

District magnitude varies widely, ranging from 1 to 50. A magnitude of 1 equates to a plurality voting system. In prefectures and ordinance-designated cities with multiple electoral districts, district magnitudes are typically smaller. Prefectures with ordinance- ordinance-designated cities have more districts with smaller magnitudes, while those without ordinance-designated cities see larger magnitudes, often exceeding 10, in their largest cities. Cities designated early as such tend to have smaller magnitudes due to more wards, whereas cities designated after 2000 usually have larger magnitudes. Regarding municipalities, larger municipalities generally have greater district magnitudes, as seen in Setagaya Ward and Funabashi City, each with populations exceeding over 500,000 and 50 seats for local councils.

The electoral system significantly influences local council candidates' campaign strategies. Unlike candidates for the head of government, who aim to mobilize a wide range of voters throughout the local government, council candidates often target specific voter groups due to the low electoral threshold for winning a seat. In settings with multiple districts, candidates must prioritize the interests of their specific constituents over the broader interests of the local government. When the district magnitude is large, the effective strategy for a candidate is to secure the minimum necessary support by mobilizing a specific segment of voters. For instance, in a district with a magnitude of 20, a candidate might emphasize the interests of particular supporters rather than appealing to a broader voter, to garner approximately 5% of the electorate's support, sufficient for winning a seat.

The electoral system results in parties with low cohesion, especially when district magnitudes are large, leading to intense intra-party competition. Due to the intra-party competition, party labels indicating affiliation with a party are not helpful in attracting votes. Therefore, candidates often seek to cultivate personal relationships with voters independently of their parties, advocating public policies that deliver direct benefits to a select voter group. Instead of aligning closely with a political party, individual councilors may seek support by offering specific service to their constituents. As a result, at the municipal level, many council members choose not to disclose their party affiliation during elections (Hijino 2013), except in well-organized parties like Komeito and the Communist Party.

In prefectures and ordinance-designated cities with multiple electoral districts and relatively small district magnitudes, political parties are better developed than in general municipalities. This is attributed to the lower likelihood of intra-party competition in areas with smaller magnitudes. However, the combination of the nature of partisan support and the electoral system's characteristics complicates the party system. In rural areas with small populations and district magnitudes, the LDP often dominates electoral seats. In contrast, urban areas with larger magnitudes experience more active competition among political parties, with their candidates often securing seats by consolidating their support base. The disparity in political competition between urban and rural areas has resulted in the overwhelming dominance of the LDP in prefectural councils and the fragmentation of the opposition (Scheiner 2006). As shown in Fig. 3.1, the LDP continues to hold more than a majority of seats in many prefectural councils.

3.2.3 Constitutional Power and Partisan Power of the Head

Although both the head and the local council are elected by local citizens and operate independently, their powers are not necessarily equal. From a comparative perspective, the constitutional power of the local government head is considered strong (Mainwaring and Shugart 1997; Tsukiyama 2015). Constitutional power refers to the authority granted to executives in governmental decision-making, which includes veto power and the ability to issue executive orders. Japan's Local

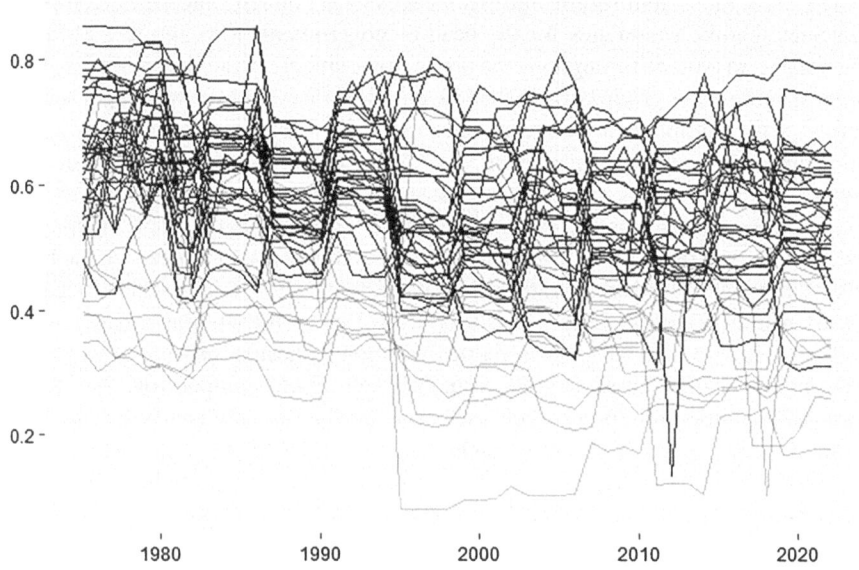

Fig. 3.1 Proportion of LDP seats in 47 prefectures. (Notes: From 1975 to 2022, darker lines represent prefectures where the average seat proportion exceeded 50% throughout this period. Source: Author's elaboration)

Autonomy Act gives the political heads comprehensive veto rights, the power to issue executive orders, and significant control over the budget. Councils are not allowed to propose budgets, nor to make substantial amendments to the budget put forward by the head. Any budget-related decisions within a local government require the head's approval.

Conversely, the local council has the power to pass a vote of no confidence against the head of the local government, adding complexity to their relationship. Although the head and the local council are considered as mutually independent and equal in dual representation, the Local Autonomy Law allows the council to pass a no-confidence vote with the approval of three-quarters of the members present, exceeding two-thirds of the total council membership (Article 178). This provision enables the council to exert pressure on a head who opposes their preferences. However, the thresholds for a no-confidence vote are stringent, and a head facing such a vote can retaliate by dissolving the council, promoting council members to be cautious with no-confidence votes due to the risk of losing their seats.

Conflicts between the two institutions can lead to a local council issuing a vote of no confidence. Governors and mayors with weak support within the local council may face removal from office through another vote of no confidence after reelection, even if the council is dissolved. In such scenarios, they opt to relinquish their positions and seek reaffirmation of voter trust. If a governor or mayor is reinstated by election after being ousted through a no-confidence vote, the local council might experience pressure to align with voter sentiment, even if its composition remains unchanged from the time of the no-confidence vote. This situation can backfire on the local council, undermining its intended effect with the no-confidence vote.

Partisan power is the influence exerted through a party system, where a political head controls the parties that dominate the local council. Mayors in municipalities with underdeveloped political parties find it challenging to exert such power, though more opportunities exist in prefectures. As shown in Fig. 3.1, the LDP often gained a majority of seats in prefectural councils. The LDP predominantly won seats in rural areas, mainly in single-seat electoral districts, while competing with several opposition parties in urban areas. In metropolitan prefectures such as Tokyo and Osaka, the LDP could not secure a majority, but it consistently did so in rural prefectures. In prefectural councils with a stable LDP majority, it has institutionalized decision-making and the allocation of posts, thereby providing incentives for its members to act in unison within the party (Fujimura 2013).

When analyzing the partisan power of chief executives comparatively, the distribution of ministerial positions often indicates whether a government operates as a coalition (Cheibub 2007). However, the absence of a cabinet system in Japanese local governments hinders such comparisons. Tsukiyama (2015) endeavored to distinguish between single-party and coalition governments by examining pre-electoral coalitions in gubernatorial elections, finding that the LDP rarely endorses a candidate as the sole party and wins. In practice, even when the LDP has a dominant presence in a local council, it often supports gubernatorial candidates with other parties. At times, candidates endorsed by opposition parties or independents manage to win. A noteworthy aspect of local politics in Japan is the practice of the LDP supporting gubernatorial candidates along with its national political competitors. This approach, termed "Ainori," has been particularly prevalent since the 1990s (Kawamura 2008).

Despite the LDP often approaching single-party dominance in the prefectural party system, the partisan power of the governor remains limited. Governors rarely align fully with the dominant LDP to retain power and frequently need to navigate the interests of various parties within a coalition government. Sometimes, a governor backed by a minority party faces an LDP majority. Furthermore, as previously discussed, individual council members enjoy significant autonomy due to an electoral system that promotes personal voting. While these LDP members might adhere to institutionalized decision-making within their party, they are less bound by the governor's discipline, which differs from party constraints, thus complicating the governor's exercise of partisan power. This trend is more pronounced in municipal councils, where district magnitudes are large and only a few organized parties have a significant presence.

3.3   Patterns in the Relationship Between the Representatives

Several factors influence local government decision-making. First, the ideology and policy preferences of national political parties, which are linked to local-level counterparts, can shape local government policies. Before the 1990s, national party competition primarily centered on security issues. The right-wing LDP emphasized the U.S.-Japan alliance as well as the importance of economic development, while the left-wing parties consistently opposed military expansion and advocated strengthening social welfare policies. In the 1970s, amidst intense rivalry between these two camps, it was common to see governors and mayors supported by leftist parties adopted policies on social welfare and environmental protection that diverged from those of other local governments (Steiner et al. 1980). Additionally, policy decisions were influenced by not only the political head but the proportion of leftist party representation in the local council (Soga and Machidori 2007). Even after the ideological contention weakened with the end of the Cold War, it has been pointed out that the degree of support for two political parties, the right-wing LDP and the left-leaning Democratic Party of Japan (DPJ) can influence local government decision-making (Soga and Machidori 2008). The competition between the LDP and the DPJ at the local level was not only an ideological conflict, but also a secondary election that punished the national ruling party in local elections (Reif and Schmitt 1980; van der Eijk et al. 1996). This national party influence persisted until the DPJ's fragmentation and exit from power in 2012.

The division of power at the local level suggests that the head and the local council have fundamentally different preferences (Sunahara 2011). The head typically focuses on the broader, unorganized interests of the entire local government area, while council members prioritize organized, specific interests that are unevenly distributed within the territory. The electoral system fosters a significant "Separation of purpose" (Haggard and McCubbins 2001) between these two institutions. Consequently, divided government is likely taking place when the head and the local council have different preferences, potentially causing deadlocks in the policy-making process. Regarding Japan's local government, it's common to find a structure advocating for specific local interests, facilitated by the LDP. Council members tend to prefer incremental decision-making that considers individual interests. Occasionally, a political head not backed by the LDP emerges, attempting policy alterations. While sometimes these changes are successful, it is generally noted that local councils often manage to preserve the status quo.

Despite the "Separation of purpose", the formation of pre-electoral coalitions facilitates decision-making and mitigate divided government effects. Coalitions enable a presidential system to function similarly to a parliamentary system, whereas the division of power view focuses on the "difficult combination" of an independently elected head and a council composed of multiple parties with low cohesion (Mainwaring 1993). It is argued that parties participating in coalitions significantly restrict the head's policy agenda and hinder council deliberations, resulting in static and stagnant local politics (Tsukiyama 2015). The strong influence of party coalitions on the political head is perceived as a "Parliamentarization" of Presidential system (Colomer and Negretto 2005; Chaisty et al. 2014, 2018), a concept with considerable relevance in Japanese local government, where the council has the power to pass a vote of no confidence against the head.[1]

As discussed above, recent studies on local politics in Japan have underscored the significance of the local council, marking a departure from earlier research which, before 2000, primarily examined the authority of the political head and the infrequent cases where the council attempted to modify or reject the head's proposals (Mawatari 2010). These earlier studies often associated the head's wills and capabilities with local government policymaking. However, newer research indicates that political parties within the council significantly impact the head at the prefectural level, where political parties are more developed. Reflecting the LDP's extensive influence across both national and local politics, these studies offer significant insight on the role of the political head amid the inter-party competition dominated by the LDP.

In the 2010s, as the DPJ has collapsed and the LDP's dominance has become even stronger, two significant developments have occurred in Japanese local politics. Firstly, the rise of the Osaka Restoration Association (ORA) in Osaka Prefecture marked a notable change. Secondly, there has been a trend of the LDP splitting in gubernatorial elections across various local governments. These phenomena represent new dynamics in Japanese local politics, deviating from the patterns identified in recent studies, which highlighted the strong influence of LDP-centered party coalitions on the head of government and their tendency towards static policymaking.

3.4 The Case in Osaka: Concentration of Power

3.4.1 The Development of ORA

As Japan's second largest city, Osaka attracted a large number of people and enjoyed prosperity during the country's rapid economic growth period. However, from the 1980s onward, Osaka struggled to adapt to changes in its industrial structure, and its growth remained stagnant. One of the key reasons for Osaka's stagnation has been pointed out as the lack of functioning political coordination between Osaka

---

[1] Some studies contend that the head possesses the capacity not only to make concessions to the coalition but also to wield substantial constitutional powers to influence the parties within the coalition (Takenaka 2022).

Prefecture and the expansive Osaka City within it.[2] Toru Hashimoto, a popular TV celebrity who became the governor of Osaka Prefecture in 2008, advocated for the merger of the two local governments. His proposal aimed to establish unified leadership and transform Osaka into a globally competitive metropolis.[3]

Hashimoto's proposal was so ambitious that its realization in the status quo-oriented local politics appeared challenging. Yet, it received popular support and was successfully approved by the local councils of Osaka Prefecture and Osaka City. Although it was ultimately rejected in a referendum by the Osaka citizens, the councils' approval of such a transformative proposal was notable in the conservative context of Japanese local politics. It was reasonable for Hashimoto, as the political head, to pursue a strategy that emphasizes the interests of Osaka as a whole and propose major institutional reforms. However, local councils, typically dominated by the LDP, are oriented toward maintaining the status quo.

The tactic of leveraging voter support to pressure local councils for reforms has been utilized by numerous governors and mayors. However, Hashimoto's approach set him apart from his predecessors due to his ability to secure a majority within local councils. While earlier "reformers" criticized local councils, they seldom endeavored to win a council majority. Their primary method to rally support was through elections, emphasizing the need to exert pressure on the council with voter backing. In contrast, Hashimoto founded his political party, the ORA, in 2010, and aligning with some ex-members of the local LDP to enhance his influence. This move effectively presented voters with a clear choice regarding their support for his agenda.

In the growth of the ORA, it is important to recognize that its leaders went beyond merely criticizing the status quo of local councils. They managed to position the party as a representative of the broader Osaka region (Zenkyo 2018, 2021). In Japanese local politics, council members as well as governors and mayors typically focus on the interests of their respective local governments. Even though governors and mayors might consider wider interests, the broader concerns spanning multiple local governments, such as those of both Osaka prefecture and Osaka city, are often ignored. The ORA, however, emphasized the interests of the entire Osaka economic zone over those of individual local governments, a stance that resonated with voters. This approach led to the formation of a majority coalition in both the Osaka Prefectural and City Councils, a success seldom achieved by parties other than the LDP.

---

[2] Osaka Prefecture and Osaka City have been embroiled in fierce competition in urban development, often criticized for their lack of coordination. A notable example of this is their rivalry in constructing two high-rise buildings. This competition has led to the construction of two unnecessarily large buildings, drawing significant criticism for the wasteful use of resources and poor planning between the two local governments.

[3] See Sunahara (2012) for details of Hashimoto's proposal described in this section.

3.4.2 Factors Behind the Success of the ORA

As mentioned in the description of the electoral system, the LDP holds significant strength in Japan's local council elections, especially in single-seat districts in rural areas. And in urban areas, the presence of multiple competing parties makes it challenging for non-LDP parties to win substantial seats. Given this context, how did the newly established ORA manage to achieve a majority so swiftly?

A pivotal factor was the unique district magnitude structure of the Osaka Prefectural Council. Compared with other prefectures, Osaka Prefecture includes many municipalities, resulting in a large number of electoral districts. Specifically, Table 3.1 compares Osaka Prefecture with Osaka City, district magnitudes ranging from 2 to 6, and Sakai City (another ordinance-designated city within Osaka Prefecture) with most districts having 7 or more seats. In the 2011 local elections, the Osaka Prefectural Council consisted of 109 members, 33 of whom were elected from one-seat districts, and in total there are 62 districts. The ORA fielded one candidate in almost all of the districts, and 57 of the 60 candidates elected. This indicates that the ORA effectively compelled voters to decide on their support for Hashimoto's proposal, leading to the success in the Osaka Prefectural Council.

Figure 3.2 plots the share of votes received by the ORA in the 2011 prefectural and municipal council elections, arranged by district magnitude. In the Osaka Prefectural Council elections, where the district magnitudes were 1 or 2, the ORA's vote share varied wildly between 30% and 70%, while in the Osaka city and Sakai city council elections, where the district magnitudes were 3 or more, the vote share remained relatively stable at around 30%. These disparities in vote share are not solely attributable to differing levels of support for the ORA across constituencies.

Crucially, the structure of electoral competition changed with the district magnitude. In areas with smaller district magnitudes, the political head's policies often become the focal point, given the limited choices available. However, in municipal

Table 3.1 Results of the 2011 local elections

	District magnitudes	1	2	3	4	5	6	7+	Total
Osaka prefecture	Number of districts	33	21	3	1	3	1	0	62
	Seats	33	42	9	4	15	6	0	109
	ORA candidates	31	21	2	1	3	2	0	60
	ORA winners	28	21	2	1	3	2	0	57
Osaka city	Number of districts	0	6	8	2	6	2	0	24
	Seats	0	12	24	8	30	12	0	86
	ORA candidates	0	8	14	4	12	6	0	44
	ORA winners	0	6	9	3	11	4	0	33
Sakai city	Number of districts	0	0	1	0	1	0	5	7
	Seats	0	0	3	0	5	0	44	52
	ORA candidates	0	0	1	0	2	0	12	15
	ORA winners	0	0	1	0	1	0	11	13

Source: Author's elaboration

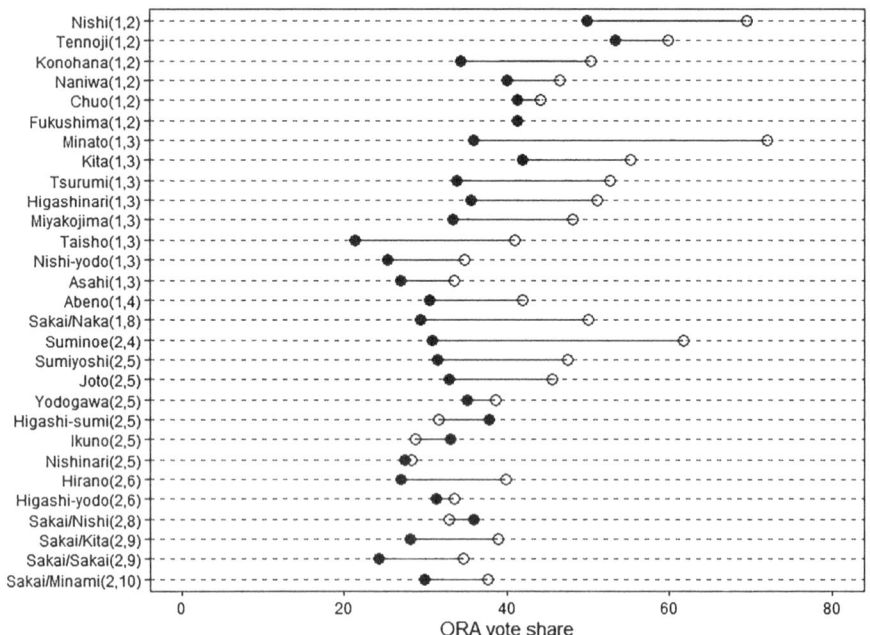

Fig. 3.2 ORA vote share by electoral district. (Notes: Numbers indicate district magnitude for Osaka Prefecture on the left and for Osaka City on the right. Black circles indicate the vote share in Osaka City Council elections; white circles indicate the vote share in Osaka Prefectural Council elections. Source: Author's elaboration)

council elections with larger district magnitudes, the election debate extends beyond the head's policies. In the elections of Osaka City and Sakai City, where candidates from multiple parties, including the ORA, contested, the ORA garnered about 30% of the votes. Yet, in the Osaka Prefectural Council elections, the ORA managed to capture a broader vote range, securing a significant number of seats, by obtaining votes from those who did not vote for the ORA in municipal elections.

In the Osaka Prefectural Council, achieving a majority was possible by winning at least one seat in each district. Hashimoto and his party's strategy, which presented voters with a clear choice of supporting them or not, proved effective, positioning the party label as a favorable option and contributing to his majority win. Table 3.1 indicates that this approach was less effective in the municipal council elections, which has larger district magnitudes. However, the ORA still emerged as the leading party in Osaka City Council. This strategy might have also played a role in instilling discipline among local council members, who generally favored personal voting, aligning them with the ORA's policies. If council members deviated from this discipline and failed to utilize the party label in the next election, their chances of re-election would be reduced. Thus, the ORA managed to impose organized discipline, particularly among prefectural council members.

3.4.3 Consolidation of Dominance

During the 2015 and 2019 local elections, the strategy of the ORA was further accentuated, solidifying its dominance. This was achieved by limiting the choices available to voters before the elections. In Japanese local politics, separate elections occur for the head and the council, and council elections often rely on personal votes. The ORA attempted to unify various issues across multiple elections into one, compelling voters to make a definitive choice regarding their support for the party. Additionally, the ORA demanded exceptional loyalty from council members affiliated with the party, an approach uncommon in local politics. This disciplined method regulated member behavior and enabled the ORA to reintroduce the referendum proposal in 2020, after its initial rejection in 2015.

First, the ORA achieved a strategic alteration in the district magnitude structure of the Osaka Prefectural Council. After the 2011 local elections and the onset of the new session, the ORA proposed a bylaw amendment to reduce council seats from 109 to 88.[4] Although a similar proposal had been presented before the election, it was rejected due to opposition from other parties. Nevertheless, having secured a majority in the 2011 local elections, the ORA adopted a more assertive stance. Despite potential opposition from other council members, the ORA, wielding majority control, succeeded in passing the amendment. Consequently, the number of single-seat districts increased from 33 to 48, representing over half of the 88 council members.

The subsequent election was to be held under this revised system. However, before the 2015 election, the ORA experienced a decline in cohesiveness, resulting in several members departing from the party. This allowed the LDP to pass a proposal merging various single-member districts. While the overall number of council seats remained at 88, single-member districts decreased to 31, and two-member districts doubled from 7 to 15. Although these further changes slightly diluted the advantage, the significant decrease in council seats created a long-term benefit for the ORA.

Secondly, the strategy of holding concurrent elections repeatedly helped to narrow voter choices. Since the 2011 elections for governor and mayor of Osaka with candidates Ichiro Matsui and Hashimoto, followed by the 2015 (Matsui and Hirofumi Yoshimura) and 2019 (Yoshimura and Matsui) elections, the ORA conducted two elections simultaneously, varying the candidates each time. In 2019, the ORA significantly altered the election timing by having both the governor and mayor resign, leading to the Osaka mayor running for governor and the governor for mayor and resulting in four concurrent elections, including those for the Osaka Prefectural and City Councils. Conducting four elections simultaneously in 2019 presented a significant challenge for the opposition, as multiple parties had to

---

[4] The establishment of 88 seats was determined based on Osaka Prefecture's population, which is approximately 8.8 million, leading to a ratio of one councilor per 100,000 people, considered an appropriate representation.

Table 3.2 Results of the 2019 local elections

	District magnitudes	1	2	3	4	5	6	7+	Total
Osaka prefecture	Number of districts	31	15	2	4	1	0	0	53
	Seats	31	30	6	16	5	0	0	88
	ORA candidates	30	15	2	7	1	0	0	55
	ORA winners	26	15	2	7	1	0	0	52
Osaka city	Number of districts	0	5	9	5	4	1	0	24
	Seats	0	10	27	20	20	6	0	83
	ORA candidates	0	6	16	10	8	3	0	43
	ORA winners	0	5	15	10	8	2	0	40
Sakai city	Number of districts	0	1	0	0	1	0	5	7
	Seats	0	2	0	0	5	0	41	48
	ORA candidates	0	1	0	0	2	0	15	18
	ORA winners	0	1	0	0	2	0	15	18

Source: Author's elaboration

coordinate in electing local government heads while competing in council elections. This complex scenario, where parties vying in the Osaka City Council elections formed alliances for the mayoral race, complicated the campaign and confused voters regarding the impact of their votes.

In contrast, the ORA benefited from being a governing party, which simplified campaigning on its track record. In the 2019 elections, the ORA achieved significant success even in the absence of the charismatic Hashimoto, enhancing its support in both the prefectural and city council elections. Notably, the ORA was just two seats short of securing a majority in the Osaka City Council as shown in Table 3.2. Despite the potential for intra-party competition fostered by the SNTV system within the ORA, it is tougher for candidates to defy party discipline than other parties, given their reliance on the party's brand. Although Hashimoto's departure diminished the party's cohesive appeal, the members recognized the challenge of winning elections based solely on individual merit without the party label. This recognition helped them maintain unity and continue as a cohesive political entity.

3.5 LDP Split in Gubernatorial Elections

3.5.1 LDP Split Trends

The LDP, a major player in Japan's local politics, has frequently experienced internal divisions. While these splinter groups often reunite, reunification is not guaranteed. The splits typically arise from disputes over local council management, such as the election of the chairperson, and are commonly ignited by disagreements over gubernatorial election support. Splits during gubernatorial elections are particularly detrimental to the council members involved, as the conflict extends beyond local council powers struggles to include Diet members, intensifying the dispute.

In Ishikawa Prefecture, for example, prominent politicians Yoshiro Mori and Keiwa Okuda, both Diet members, rallied support not only for gubernatorial candidates but also for prefectural and municipal council members aligned with them, causing significant internal strife within the LDP. This strife affected elections beyond the gubernatorial level, influencing House of Councillors elections with prefecture-wide constituencies, and continued for several decades.

Before Japan's national government electoral reform in the 1990s, the LDP was more prone to splits in gubernatorial elections. At that time, the electoral system for the House of Representatives employed the SNTV system, akin to that of local councils, with district magnitudes ranging from 3 to 5. Research on this era indicates a correlation between LDP splits in gubernatorial elections and the dependency of a Diet member on a specific area within their district for vote collection (Sunahara 2017). This correlation suggests that splits were more likely in prefectures with regional disparities in the support structure of Diet members. Additionally, the longer tenure of governors has been identified as a contributing factor to these splits. This indicates that splits often emerge in response to the extended governance of a particular governor, leading to a fixed distribution of benefits.

Following the national electoral system reform in the 1990s, the LDP experienced splits at the local level, aligned with national political realignments (Tsuji 2008; Desposato and Scheiner 2008). Some local LDP members defected to support candidates from other parties in gubernatorial elections. However, as the two-party system between the LDP and the DPJ stabilized after several election cycles, the incidence of LDP splits at the local level diminished (Iwagami 2023). The LDP's strategic focus on countering the DPJ, which was gaining voter support, coupled with the fear that internal divisions could lead to a collective downfall and a DPJ victory, likely mitigated further splits within the LDP.

This trend was underscored when the LDP's local unity weakened following the DPJ's loss of national power at the end of 2012 and its subsequent fragmentation. From 2013 through the 2020s, under the leadership of Prime Minister Shinzo Abe, who maintained high approval ratings, the LDP consistently achieved electoral victories in national politics. However, at the local level, the incidence of splits in gubernatorial elections increased (Iwagami 2023; Hirano 2024). While pre-electoral coalitions commonly formed around the LDP involving multiple parties, the emergence of challengers within the LDP itself became more frequent than those from national opposition parties (Hirano 2024). Additionally, it has been observed that parties outside the LDP are increasingly likely to align with one of the factions resulting from the LDP's internal splits (Iwagami 2023).

3.5.2 What Explains LDP Split?

What might explain the resurgence of LDP splits in gubernatorial elections following the 2012 government change? Insights from previous studies on LDP splits in such elections suggest that the number of LDP Diet members per prefecture impacts the likelihood of splits. As seen in Ishikawa Prefecture, Diet members within a prefecture can organize local politicians loyal to them, leading to internal conflicts. Consequently, the more LDP Diet members in a prefecture, the higher the likelihood of splits.

At the local level, another critical factor is the proportion of LDP seats in prefectural councils. Research on coalition governments suggests that when politicians form coalitions, they often prefer the minimal winning coalitions, which include only as many members as necessary to secure a majority (Riker 1962). This preference stems from the fact that oversized coalitions can dilute the influence of individual politicians. In the context of Japanese local politics, local council members may prefer to establish relationships with the governor when they are part of a smaller group rather than having a large faction support a specific gubernatorial candidate. Therefore, when the LDP's presence in a council becomes excessively large, the motivation to split increases, as individual members or smaller factions may see greater advantage in supporting different gubernatorial candidates and pursuing independent political agendas.

For LDP council members, instigating a split is a strategic decision, especially since losing an election could mean opposing a powerful governor. To understand the behavior, three variables influencing local politicians' strategies are considered. The first is the timing of gubernatorial and council elections. Research on presidential systems has shown that when presidential and congressional elections occur concurrently, voters often rely on the presidential campaign to inform their congressional voting decisions (Samuels 2002; Golder 2006). This dynamic is relevant in Japan's local politics, where governors wield considerable power. Local council members may prefer to support a likely winning candidate, avoiding the risk associated with the gubernatorial contest's competitive nature. Thus, simultaneous elections are expected to reduce the likelihood of splits, as council members are inclined to back candidates expected to win on the same day.

Other considerations include whether the governor is an incumbent and the length of their tenure. Incumbent governors, with their substantial local authority, pose a formidable challenge for council members. If the incumbent is not running, the absence of a clear unifying figure could lead to increased divisiveness. Moreover, the likelihood of division grows under long-serving governors. Such governors, despite their accumulated power, may face underlying dissatisfaction due to a static benefit distribution system. Hence, the longer a governor's tenure, the higher the likelihood of splits. These factors may interact with each other. In case an incumbent governor exits the election, succession contests may grow more intense and divisive, particularly after the extended tenure of a long-serving governor.

Lastly, two factors related to election preparations warrant consideration. The first is whether the governor resigns before the election. A sudden resignation can lead to an election where the LDP may not have sufficient time to consolidate behind a single candidate, increasing the risk of division. Conversely, if there is no resignation and the election proceeds as planned, the four-year term of the governor facilitates better candidate coordination, including the incumbent, thereby reducing the likelihood of a split.

The second factor concerns the incumbent governor's support within the LDP. If the incumbent governor is backed by the LDP, it becomes feasible to manage the party's support, either by running for re-election or by endorsing a successor. In contrast, if the incumbent governor lacks LDP support, it becomes challenging for the LDP to unify around a gubernatorial candidate, diminishing the party's ability to influence the nomination process effectively.

3.5.3 Analysis

Logistic regression analysis will be used to test hypotheses about whether LDP splits occurred in gubernatorial elections since January 2013. The occurrence of splits is determined using data from Hirano (2024). Most election-related data, including the number of LDP Diet members and their seat share in prefectural councils, are sourced from the Ministry of Internal Affairs and Communications (MIC) (2013–2023). However, since the MIC data does not cover the information on whether the former governor was supported by the LDP, data from the Japan Research Institute for Local Government (2013–2023) were utilized.

The logistic regression analysis results are shown in Table 3.3, including models both with and without interaction terms. Interaction terms, as further discussed, did not significantly alter the outcomes. The analysis underlines the significance of the LDP's seat share in prefectural assemblies. The predicted probability of a split notably increases when the LDP seat share exceeds 60%, signifying that the oversize of the party leads to a split. Conversely, the number of LDP Diet members and the former governor's LDP support did not show a significant impact.

Regarding the strategic dynamics between the governor and council members, the governor's tenure length significantly influences the likelihood of splits. The analysis confirms that longer gubernatorial terms increase the probability of splits, suggesting council members' growing dissatisfaction with a static distribution of benefits. The incumbent status of the governor, however, did not exhibit a significant effect. Predicted probabilities for splits, analyzed with interaction terms for both incumbent and non-incumbent scenarios, revealed no notable differences. Surprisingly, concurrent elections had a significant positive effect, contrary to expectations, indicating a higher split probability in such cases.

These findings imply a substantial impact of the council on the governor's elections. In general, a long-serving, incumbent, or concurrently elected governor is perceived to consolidate the power in local politics and mitigate divisiveness.

Table 3.3 Logistic regression for LDP splits		
LDP Diet members	0.024	0.022
	(0.093)	(0.090)
LDP seat ratio	6.780**	6.639**
	(2.924)	(2.904)
Concurrent election	1.459**	1.454**
	(0.704)	(0.708)
Incumbent	1.129	0.876
	(2.772)	(0.764)
Terms	1.086	0.634**
	(0.664)	(0.252)
Incumbent: Terms	−0.530	
	(0.696)	
Resign	0.618	0.037
	(1.650)	(1.373)
LDP support	0.306	0.352
	(0.671)	(0.668)
Constant	−8.761***	−6.889***
	(3.346)	(2.034)
Observations	136	136
Log likelihood	−41.901	−42.232
Akaike Inf. Crit.	101.803	100.465

Note: $*p < 0.1$; $**p < 0.05$; $***p < 0.01$

However, the analysis suggests that such governors do not necessarily diminish the likelihood of split elections but are instead associated with increased divisiveness. Since 2013, with diminishing party competition, particularly in local elections, the LDP has been the primary sponsor of governors. The analysis indicates that splits are more probable when the LDP becomes too large or when escalating conflicts arise between the governor and the LDP.

3.6 Conclusions

This chapter examines the power structure in local politics and reveals the strong influence of local councils and the dominant parties over political heads of local governments. When discussing local politics in Japan, the strong authority of the head often garners significant attention, with the perception that local politics primarily revolves around this figure. The success of heads backed by leftist parties in the 1970s and independent heads in the late 1990s further solidified the view of the head as a central player. While the head undeniably adds dynamism to local politics, this chapter has highlighted the substantial influence of local councils. The dominance of the LDP, holding the majority in many prefectural councils and forming the nucleus of the pre-election coalition for the head, is particularly pivotal.

The emergence of the ORA and the LDP's splits in recent gubernatorial elections might seem like anomalies, yet they align with the analytical framework developed in this chapter. In Osaka, for example, the relatively small district magnitude facilitated a nearly plurality electoral system, enabling the ORA to secure a majority in the councils. Additionally, the concurrent elections of the heads and later councils contribute to party cohesion. While Toru Hashimoto's leadership initially drew focus, the ORA's leadership has evolved, with different candidates for governor and mayor positions post-Hashimoto period. It underscores that the pivotal element is not the individual leader but a unified party under a seemingly majoritarian system, suggesting that Osaka's political dynamics resemble a parliamentary system more than a presidential one.

The split within the LDP reflects similar dynamics. Analysis indicates that splits in the LDP are more likely initiated by council members rather than the governor. Long-term governance and the disproportionate size of political parties contribute to council members' dissatisfaction, which may provoke internal LDP factions to challenge the mainstream, resulting in splits. One contributing factor to LDP splits in gubernatorial elections is the opposition of local council members to candidates promoted by the LDP's national headquarters, a point not thoroughly examined in this chapter. In such cases, there exists a mainstream faction within the LDP that aligns with the national leadership and a faction that opposes it. The splits are primarily instigated by council members, suggesting that the elected governor is likely to be influenced by the faction that endorsed them. This scenario nudges the political system more towards a parliamentary rather than a presidential model.

This chapter, focusing mainly on prefectural and ordinance-designated city elections with distinct party affiliations, recognizes its coverage limitations. Nonetheless, the influence of the LDP is also significant in municipalities where party labels are less evident and warrants further investigation. Future analysis in local politics should explore the dynamics of active inter-party competition, evident to some extent during the late 1990s and 2000s with the DPJ emerging as a national rival to the LDP. While competition at the national level is vital, the lack of consistent inter-party competition at the local level poses a significant challenge. To enhance the vibrancy of local politics and the sustainability of local government, a reform of the electoral system governing local councils is crucial.

References

Chaisty P, Cheeseman N, Power T (2014) Rethinking the 'presidentialism debate': conceptualizing coalitional politics in cross-regional perspective. Democratization 21(1):72–94. https://doi.org/10.1080/13510347.2012.710604

Chaisty P, Cheeseman N, Power T (2018) Coalitional presidentialism in comparative perspective: minority presidents in multiparty systems. Oxford University Press, New York

Cheibub JA (2007) Presidentialism, parliamentarism, and democracy. Cambridge University Press, Cambridge

Colomer JM, Negretto GL (2005) Can presidentialism work like parliamentarism? Gov Oppos 40(1):60–89. https://doi.org/10.1111/j.1477-7053.2005.00143.x

Desposato S, Scheiner E (2008) Governmental centralization and party affiliation: legislator strategies in Brazil and Japan. Am Polit Sci Rev 102(4):509–524

Fujimura N (2013) The position and function of political parties in local politics [Chiho seiji ni okeru seito no ichiduke to kino]. In: Tatebayashi M (ed) Politics of party organization [Seito soshiki no seijigaku]. Toyo Keizai Inc, Tokyo, pp 129–152. (in Japanese)

Golder M (2006) Presidential coattails and legislative fragmentation. Am J Polit Sci 50:34–48. https://doi.org/10.1111/j.1540-5907.2006.00168.x

Haggard S, McCubbins MD (2001) Presidents, parliaments, and policy. Cambridge University Press, Cambridge

Hijino KVL (2013) Liabilities of partisan labels: independents in Japanese local elections. Soc Sci Jpn J 16(1):63–85. https://doi.org/10.1093/ssjj/jys024

Hirano J (2024) Political foundations of heads of local governments: representativeness of the head and electoral politics [Jichitai shucho no seijiteki kiban: Shucho no daihyosei to senkyo seiji]. Toshi Mondai 115(1):51–61. (in Japanese)

Huber JD (2000) Delegation to civil servants in parliamentary democracies. Eur J Polit Res 37:397–413. https://doi.org/10.1111/1475-6765.00519

Iwagami Y (2023) LDP split in election of prefectural governor [Chiji senkyo ni okeru hoshu bunretsu senkyo: sono dōkō to haikei]. Hogaku Kenkyu 96(2):191–213. (in Japanese)

Kawamura K (2008) Local elections and public attitudes in contemporary Japan [Gendai nihon no chiho senkyo to jumin ishiki]. Keio University Press, Tokyo. (in Japanese)

Mainwaring S (1993) Presidentialism, multipartism, and democracy: the difficult combination. Comp Pol Stud 26(2):198–228. https://doi.org/10.1177/0010414093026002003

Mainwaring S, Shugart MS (eds) (1997) Presidentialism and democracy in Latin America. Cambridge, Cambridge University Press

Mawatari T (2010) Local councils in post-war Japan [Sengo Nihon no chiho gikai: 1955–2008]. Minervashobo. Co., Ltd, Kyoto. in Japanese

Ministry of Internal Affairs and Communications, 2013–2023, Survey of the number of council members and heads of local government by party affiliation [Chiho kokyo daitai no gikai no giin oyobi cho no syozoku toha betsu jin'in shirabe]. https://www.soumu.go.jp/senkyo/senkyo_s/data/syozoku/ichiran.html

Reif K, Schmitt H (1980) Nine second-order national elections: a conceptual framework for the analysis of European election results. Eur J Polit Res 8:3–44. https://doi.org/10.1111/j.1475-6765.1980.tb00737.x

Riker WH (1962) The theory of political coalitions. Yale University Press, New Haven/London

Samuels DJ (2002) Presidentialized parties: the separation of powers and party organization and behavior. Comp Pol Stud 35(4):461–483. https://doi.org/10.1177/0010414002035004004

Scheiner E (2006) Democracy without competition in Japan: opposition failure in a one-party dominant state. Cambridge University Press, Cambridge. https://doi.org/10.1017/CBO9780511610660

Schumpeter JA (2013) Capitalism, socialism and democracy. Routledge, London. (originally 1942)

Soga K, Machidori S (2007) Japan's local politics: continuity and change in the presidential system [Nihon no chiho seiji: Nigen daihyosei seifu no seisaku Sentaku]. The University of Nagoya Press. (in Japanese)

Soga K, Machidori S (2008) Changes of Japan's local politics since the 1990s: slowly move toward the two-party competition [Seito saihenki ikou ni okeru seiji no hendou: Chiji ruikei to kaiha gisekiritsu ni miru yuruyaka na nidai seitoka]. Senkyo Kenkyu 24(1):5–15. (in Japanese)

Steiner K, Krauss E, Flanagan S (1980) Political opposition and local politics in Japan. Princeton University Press, Princeton

Strøm K (2000) Delegation and accountability in parliamentary democracies. Eur J Polit Res 37:261–289. https://doi.org/10.1111/1475-6765.00513

Sunahara Y (2011) Democracy in Japanese local governments: an analysis on the dynamics of governance and representation in the presidential system [Chiho Seifu no Minshu shugi: zaisei shigen no seiyaku to chiho seifu no seisaku sentaku]. Yuhikaku Publishing CO., Ltd., Tokyo. (in Japanese)

Sunahara Y (2012) Osaka: can a large city surpass the nation? [Osaka—Daitoshi ha kokka o koeru ka]. Chuokoron-Shinsha, INC, Tokyo. (in Japanese)

Sunahara Y (2017) Party system institutionalization in Japan: between fragmentation and integration [Bunretsu to togo no nihon seiji: Tochi kiko kaikaku to seitou shisutemu no hen'yo]. Chikura Shobo, Tokyo. (in Japanese)

Takenaka Y (2022) Pre-electoral coalitions of governors and legislations in Japan's prefectures [Nihon no todofuken ni okeru shissei chokan no senkyomae rengo to rippou]. Ph.D. dissertation, Graduate School of Law, Kyoto University. (in Japanese)

The Japan Research Institute for Local Government, 2013–2023, National directory of political heads of local governments [Zenkoku syucho meibo], The Japan Research Institute for Local Government

Tsuji A (2008) The "political realignment" and national parties in local assemblies [Seikai saihen to chiho gikai: Keiretsu wa ikiteirunoka]. Senkyo Kenkyu 24(1):16–31. (in Japanese)

Tsukiyama H (2015) The legislative process of local governments in Japan [Nihon no chiho seifu no rippou katei]. Ph.D. dissertation, Graduate School of Law, Keio University. (in Japanese)

van der Eijk C, Franklin M, Marsh M (1996) What voters teach us about Europe-wide elections: what Europe-wide elections teach us about voters. Elect Stud 15(2):149–166. https://doi.org/10.1016/0261-3794(96)00009-1

Zenkyo M (2018) Support for the Ishin: is it a consequence of populism, or rational choice? [Ishin shiji no bunseki: Popyurizumu ka yukensha no gorisei ka]. Yuhikaku Publishing CO., Ltd., Tokyo. (in Japanese)

Zenkyo M (2021) The people's choice: why did the citizens of Osaka oppose the Osaka Metropolis plan again? [Osaka no sentaku: Naze to koso wa futatabi hiketsu sareta no ka]. Yuhikaku Publishing CO., Ltd., Tokyo. (in Japanese)

Yosuke Sunahara is Professor at the Graduate School of Law, Kobe University. His research concerns party politics, central-local government relations with a focus on Japan. He has published several books and articles mainly on Japanese party politics at local level. His recent works appear in *Asian Survey*, *Public Health in Practice*, *Policing and Society*.

Chapter 4
Service Efficiency and Productivity with Digital Transformation in Japanese Local Governments

Koji Adachi 🆔 **and Jun Otahara**

Abstract As the population becomes increasingly concentrated in Tokyo, local regions are experiencing a decline in birth rates, an aging population, and an accelerating labor shortage. These demographic shifts are placing significant financial pressure on these regions. In response, recent technological innovations are transforming the way public services are produced, with the aim of enhancing operational efficiency and collaboration with prefectures. The research question is to ascertain how these transformations in local governments affect the production and efficiency of public services. This chapter examined the production activities of local government in Japanese municipalities regarding service efficiency and productivity. The findings show that most municipalities improved efficiency but slightly decreased productivity across the country. The factor analysis verifies the effects of population agglomeration, the introduction of municipal cloud computing, and vertical cooperation. The results present following three key findings. First, population agglomeration has an inverse U-shaped relationship with municipal efficiency. Second, we could not confirm the effect of introducing the government cloud on improving efficiency, indicating that the productivity of municipalities that introduced the cloud early was relatively low. Finally, enhanced vertical cooperation accompanied by municipalities' efforts to improve their finances could help increase productivity and improve the efficiency of local government services.

Keywords Local government service · Efficiency and productivity · Economy of agglomeration · Digital transformation (DX) · Vertical cooperation

K. Adachi (✉)
Faculty of Policy Studies, Doshisha University, Kyoto, Japan
e-mail: koadachi@mail.doshisha.ac.jp

J. Otahara
Faculty of Commerce, Doshisha University, Kyoto, Japan
e-mail: jotahara@mail.doshisha.ac.jp

4.1 Introduction

In Japan, the birthrate is declining, the population is aging, and labor shortages are becoming more serious. With this situation of limited policy resources, Japanese local governments are also required to promote operational efficiency through digitization and digital transformation (DX), such as by introducing the government cloud and putting public services online. However, whether DX improves the efficiency and productivity of municipal services has never been examined. The research question is to ascertain how these transformations in local governments affect the production and efficiency of public services. This chapter is interested in whether DX can actually be a means to improve the sustainability of local government services. It would be beneficial to investigate the effects of DX with factors that significantly affect the management efficiency of local governments. One of those factors is wide-area cooperation. Local governments are considering wide-area cooperation with other municipalities and vertical cooperation with prefectures and the national government to enhance the sustainability of municipal service provision. Such efforts to improve operational efficiency and productivity are currently underway.

Another important factor in the sustainability of local government services is population agglomeration. The issues facing local governments differ significantly between rural and urban centers. Despite depopulation and labor shortages in rural areas, adverse effects of excessive population concentration exist in urban centers, especially in Tokyo (Mizuno 2020). Hirata et al. (2019) quantitatively implies that intensive investment in road infrastructure in the Tokyo metropolitan area might have led to the concentration of population in Tokyo. They argue that road infrastructure investment in rural areas can effectively correct the concentration of people. Furthermore, Zheng (2001) suggests that excessive population agglomeration result in diseconomies of agglomeration due to congestion, pollution, and rising land prices. Since such diseconomies have the potential to negatively affect the production of local government services, it is necessary to examine whether the recent population agglomeration has affected the production of local government services.

Based on the above background, this chapter examines the effects of the three critical issues to sustain local government services: DX, vertical cooperation, and population agglomeration. The following three hypotheses are investigated in detail: The first hypothesis posits that DX contributes to the efficiency of public service production. The second hypothesis suggests that vertical cooperation between prefectures and municipalities contributes to the improvement of public service production. The third hypothesis posits that while an increase in population density contributes to the efficiency of public services to a certain extent, excessive densification may instead hinder the efficiency of public service production. We examine the efficiency and productivity of local government service production in the 1718 municipalities and the 23 wards of Tokyo, by using data envelope analysis (DEA) and malmquist productivity index. In the next section, we review the discussion on the efficiency and productivity of local government service production. Section 4.3 describes the methodology of analysis, Sect. 4.4 explains the data used, Sect. 4.5 discusses the efficiency and productivity measurement results and its factor analysis, and Sect. 4.6 further discusses efficient production and sustainability of public services in local government. Finally, Sect. 4.7 presents our concluding comments, and provides directions for future research.

4.2 Overview of Related Studies

4.2.1 Local Government Service Reform and DX in Japan

In August 2015, the Japanese central government requested each local government to promote business reforms, such as outsourcing to the private sector and introducing the government cloud, to provide efficient and effective administrative services. Since then, the Ministry of Internal Affairs and Communications (MIC) has compiled data and reported on the status of administrative reform efforts by each local government.

In December 2020, the Japanese government adopted the "Basic Policies for Reform toward the Realization of a Digital Society" by Cabinet decision, setting forth a policy to promote DX in local governments (MIC 2020). The government aims to utilize digital technology and data to improve convenience for residents and operational efficiency, leading to further improvement of administrative services. The policies are also expected to advance administrative sophistication through evidence-based policy making by standardizing data formats and promoting the smooth distribution of data by various entities (MIC 2020). One priority issue is the standardization and commonization of municipal information systems, and the introduction of the government cloud which increases every year (Fig. 4.1). As of April 2021, about 80% of the 1718 municipalities have implemented some form of government cloud computing.

Countries and regions with advanced digitalization, such as the United States and the European Union (EU), began initiatives related to eGovernment around the mid-1990s. Cross-agency organizations have recently taken the lead in promoting the establishment of digitally-based administrative services (MIC 2021b). For instance, the EU's "eGovernment Benchmark" measure evaluates each member state's digital government efforts from four perspectives: (1) user centricity, (2) transparency, (3) key enablers, and (4) cross-border mobility (EU 2023).

Iida (2022) discusses the possibility that DX will significantly change how people's opinions are gathered and consequently influence policy decisions. Indeed, Japanese local governments are undergoing a period of change through DX; however, the status of DX is not evaluated from multiple perspectives, as is the case in the EU. In addition, quantitative measurement of the effects of DX promotion and feedback on the results is necessary.

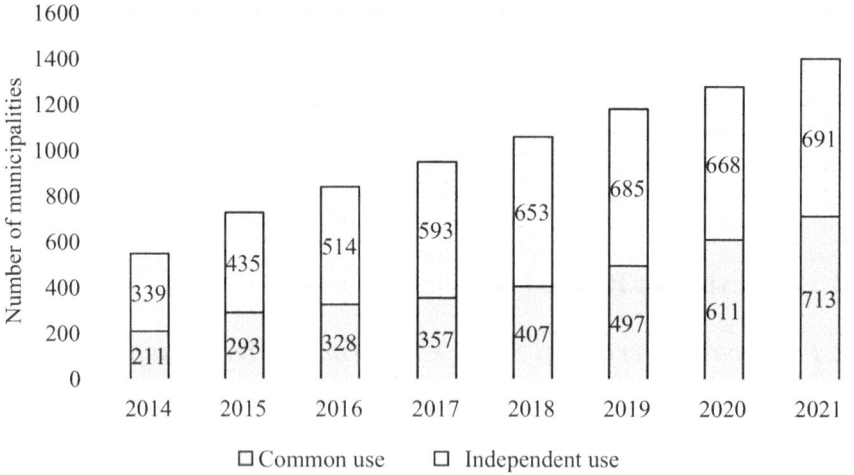

Fig. 4.1 Status of government cloud adoption by local governments. (Source: Author's design, based on data taken from the MIC (2021a))

4.2.2   Vertical Cooperation of Local Governments

Since the 2000s, various MIC study groups discuss new measures for vertical sup-plementation by prefectures and horizontal supplementation among municipalities. Additional actions have included decentralization reforms, municipal mergers, the transfer of authority to municipalities, such as special exceptions for administrative processing, and increased subsidies directly granted to municipalities. Noda (2011) conductes a pioneering study on the subsidiarity of Japanese municipal administra-tion by prefectures, and found that vertical cooperation does not necessarily contrib-ute to expenditure efficiency in some areas. Ichikawa (2013) discusses the need to promote cooperation among municipalities and the necessity of subsidiarity by pre-fectures, especially for small municipalities, in the absence of significant progress in merging municipalities. Yamazaki (2022) states that since the 2000s, subsidies directly granted to municipalities have increased; however, the complementary function of prefectures has not shrunk, and their position as wide-area municipali-ties has been stably maintained. Furthermore, he concludes that, in general, prefec-tures are executing a wide range of projects in cooperation, complementation, and support with municipalities through their own diverse and flexible methods.

In one of the few quantitative studies on vertical cooperation, Noda (2023) finds that a vertical relationship with a higher-level government (i.e., prefecture and national government) contributes to higher financial efficiency and that public offi-cials perceive the benefits of collaboration more strongly in the case of a partial administrative association. Nonetheless, to the best of our knowledge, the extant literature has not quantitatively tested how this vertical cooperation affects the pro-duction of a public service.

4.2.3 Efficiency and Productivity of Local Governments

Empirical studies have examined the efficiency of local governments from various perspectives over the past 30 years, and systematic reviews have been conducted (Worthington and Dollery 2000a; Narbón-Perpiñá and De Witte 2018a, b; Daraio et al. 2020). Studies on the efficiency of local governments can be divided into two broad categories: (1) research focusing on the evaluation of specific local services, for example, waste collection (Worthington and Dollery 2000b; Suzuki 2012), libraries (Stevens 2005), and road maintenance (Kalb 2014). (2) Studies on the evaluation of the performance of local governments include comprehensive indicators of the level of services and facilities (education, health, road infrastructure, social services, sports, culture, garbage collection, water supply, etc.) that must be provided by municipalities (Afonso and Fernandes 2006; Nijkamp and Suzuki 2009; and Yusfany 2015). Furthermore, for factor analysis of efficiency, Drew et al. (2015) identifies the determinants by Tobit regression on the measured efficiency of local governments.

Previous empirical studies have reported both positive and negative aspects of the effect of population agglomeration on efficiency (Narbón-Perpiñá and De Witte 2018b). A positive effect of cost advantages exists due to economies of scale (Sung 2007; Geys et al. 2010; Yusfany 2015), and a negative effect of higher costs of providing public services arises due to increased complexity caused by agglomeration (Kalb et al. 2012; Geys et al. 2013). For municipal productivity, Raiher (2020) finds that agglomeration economies (location and urbanization effects) positively impact industrial productivity and spillover effects on neighborhood and regional groups.

Several studies examine the relationship between the economic status of each municipality and its efficiency. For example, Sousa and Stošić (2005) uses average income as a proxy variable for poverty, finding that poor cities tend to be more efficient. Conversely, some studies have shown a negative relationship with efficiency, determining that providing public services in disadvantaged areas is particularly difficult (Revelli 2010; Andrews and Entwistle 2015). Moreover, positive relationships have been reported between the level of technology and the efficiency of municipalities. For example, Ibrahim and Karim (2004) and Sousa and Stošić (2005) find that using computers facilitates administrative tasks, improving decision-making efficiency. The authors also find that using computers in decision-making is more efficient since it facilitates administrative tasks. Sung (2007) and Seol et al. (2008) constructs an index that includes variables such as investment, equipment, percentage of information technology technicians, and application of information technology to administrative processes, and uncovers a positive and significant correlation between "information technology" and efficiency. Few empirical studies are related to digital transformation in the public sector (Mergel et al. 2019); untill now, no empirical studies have been found on the relationship between municipal efficiency and DX.

Studies on the service efficiency of local governments in Japan have developed rapidly since the 2000s, focusing on three issues: (1) financial evaluation (Yamashita et al. 2002; Hayashi 2017), (2) verification of the effects of municipal amalgamation

(Munakata et al. 2009; Nakazawa 2014), and (3) evaluation of public services and residents' satisfaction (Itaba 2007; Suzuki 2008; Suzuki et al. 2008). Adachi et al. (2021) presents a comprehensive review of these studies. Our study attempts to examine the impact of the ongoing promotion of DX, vertical cooperation, and population agglomeration on the efficiency of local governments in Japan, which has not been empirically investigated.

4.3 Methodology

We measure technical efficiency and the Malmquist productivity index in Japanese local governments and analyzes its factors. This section explains the basic concepts of DEA and the productivity index.

4.3.1 Data Envelopment Analysis (DEA)

There are several basic models for DEA. The two most commonly used include the constant returns to scale (CRS) model of Charnes et al. (1978), which assumes constant harvest concerning scale, and the variable returns to scale (VRS) model of Banker et al. (1984), which assumes variable harvest for scale. DEA further requires setting an orientation type (output-oriented or input-oriented). The output-oriented model evaluates how much output can be produced under a specific input factor. An input-oriented model, alternatively, evaluates how much of a given product can be produced with how few inputs. Since local governments consider how much administrative services they can provide given their finances and the number of employees, this study selects the output-oriented model for analysis.

We assume that the local government produces M outputs with K inputs. Let X denote the input vector and Y denote the output vector. The following linear programming can express both output-oriented models.

Output-oriented CRS Model:

$$\max_{\delta, \lambda} \delta$$

$$\text{s.t.} \quad \delta y_o - Y\lambda \leq 0$$
$$X\lambda \leq x_o$$
$$\lambda \geq 0$$

Output-oriented VRS Model:

$$\max_{\delta,\lambda} \delta$$

$$\text{s.t.} \quad \delta y_o - Y\lambda \leq 0$$

$$X\lambda \leq x_o$$

$$\lambda \geq 0$$

$$\Sigma \lambda = 1$$

The value of δ is the inverse of the efficiency value θ and is greater than or equal to 1. A value of 1 indicates that the most efficient municipality is located (relatively) on the frontier. A value of δ greater than 1 indicates that it would be efficient to increase the production level by a factor of δ while maintaining the current input level. The inverse of δ ($\delta = 1$) is also used. The reciprocal of δ ($1/\delta$) corresponds to the efficiency value θ (taking values between 0 and 1) as measured by the input-oriented model. λ is a vector of unknown weights.

4.3.2 Malmquist Productivity Index

Caves et al. (1982) defines the Malmquist productivity index (MI) used in productivity analysis as an index for measuring changes in productivity. This index isbased on the concept of an index proposed by Malmquist (1953), who conducts consumption analysis using an input distance function. Färe et al. (1994) decomposes the index into two components (efficiency change and technological progress), making it more versatile and applicable in various fields.

The DEA distance function is used to measure the MI. First, the output distance function at the technology level in period t is defined as follows:

$$D_O^t\left(x^t,y^t\right) = \min\left\{\theta : \left(x^t,y^t / \theta\right) \in P^t\right\}. \tag{4.1}$$

The change in productivity between period t and period $t + 1$ is expressed using the distance function according to Caves et al. (1982) as follows:

$$M\left(x^t,y^t,x^{t+1},y^{t+1}\right) = \left[\frac{D_O^t\left(x^{t+1},y^{t+1}\right)}{D_O^t\left(x^t,y^t\right)} \times \frac{D_O^{t+1}\left(x^{t+1},y^{t+1}\right)}{D_O^{t+1}\left(x^t,y^t\right)}\right]^{\frac{1}{2}}. \tag{4.2}$$

The subscript O in the distance function indicates that it is an output-oriented distance function.

Next, we examine the decomposition of the MI. The Färe et al. (1994) model, which is widely adopted, decomposes Eq. (4.2) into "technological efficiency change" and "technological change" using an output distance function based on the production frontier under the CRS assumption.[1] However, this does not correspond to the VRS; therefore, we adopt the model developed by Ray and Desli (1997), which can be expressed in the following equation.

$$
M\left(x^{t},y^{t},x^{t+1},y^{t+1}\right) = \frac{D_{VO}^{t+1}\left(x^{t+1},y^{t+1}\right)}{D_{VO}^{t}\left(x^{t},y^{t}\right)} \cdot \left[\frac{D_{VO}^{t}\left(x^{t+1},y^{t+1}\right)}{D_{VO}^{t+1}\left(x^{t+1},y^{t+1}\right)} \cdot \frac{D_{VO}^{t}\left(x^{t},y^{t}\right)}{D_{VO}^{t+1}\left(x^{t},y^{t}\right)}\right]^{\frac{1}{2}}
$$

$$
\cdot \left[\frac{\dfrac{D_{CO}^{t}\left(x^{t+1},y^{t+1}\right)}{D_{VO}^{t}\left(x^{t+1},y^{t+1}\right)}}{\dfrac{D_{CO}^{t}\left(x^{t},y^{t}\right)}{D_{VO}^{t}\left(x^{t},y^{t}\right)}} \cdot \frac{\dfrac{D_{CO}^{t+1}\left(x^{t+1},y^{t+1}\right)}{D_{VO}^{t+1}\left(x^{t+1},y^{t+1}\right)}}{\dfrac{D_{CO}^{t+1}\left(x^{t},y^{t}\right)}{D_{VO}^{t+1}\left(x^{t},y^{t}\right)}}\right]^{\frac{1}{2}} \tag{4.3}
$$

$$
= PTEC \cdot TC \cdot SEC.
$$

The subscripts CO and VO in the distance functions indicate that they are output-oriented distance functions when the production technology is assumed to be CRS and VRS, respectively. Productivity change can be decomposed into three components: technological efficiency change (*PTEC*), technological change (*TC*), and scale efficiency change (*SEC*).

4.4   Data

4.4.1   Input and Output Variables

We measure changes in the efficiency and productivity of public service production from FY2015 to FY2020. This chapter examines Japan's 1718 municipalities and 23 special wards of Tokyo and analyze the factors behind these changes. Note that four towns in Fukushima Prefecture (Tomioka, Okuma, Futaba, and Namie) are excluded from the analysis because the entire area was designated as an evacuation zone due to the nuclear disaster of the Great East Japan Earthquake and the 2015 census was not conducted. The sample size uses in this study is 1737. Table 4.1 presents the list of variables used. We use two input factors for public services (general expenditures and the number of employees) and three output factors (population, local taxes, and an overall public service level indicator). Expenditure, population, and local taxes are obtained from "Statistics of Municipalities [Toukei de miru shikuchouson no sugata] (each year)" by the Statistics Bureau of MIC. The number of employees is obtained from "Capacity Management of Local

---

[1] This model assumes that the frontiers in each period do not intersect and require the assumption of CRS, so the decomposition of the components may not make sense if actual productivity is changing concerning scale.

Table 4.1 Definitions and summary statistics of variables

Variable		Definition	Unit	Mean	SD
Input	MS	Number of municipal staff (2014 and 2019)	Persons	657.50	1648.94
	EXLG	Annual constant expenditures (2014 and 2019)	Million Yen	32819	88414.11
Output	POP	Population (2015 and 2020)	Persons	72895	189535.10
	TRLG	Annual tax revenue of local government (2015 and 2020)	Million Yen	11355	37951.79
	SLGS	Score of local government service (2015 and 2020)	Number	49.91	3.73
Environment	POPD	Population density	Persons per km^2	1383.82	2556.03
	SUP	Share of expenditures by the national and prefectural governments in revenues (2014 and 2019)	Ratio	0.19	0.07
	SUPD	Difference in the share of expenditures by the national and prefectural governments in revenues between 2014 and 2019	Ratio	0.0003	0.05
	FCI	Finantial capability index (2014 and 2019)	Number	0.50	0.28
	FCIA	Average of 2014 and 2019 finantial capability index	Number	0.50	0.28
	FCID	Difference between 2014 and 2019 finantial capability index	Number	0.02	0.05
	EAGC	Early adoption of government cloud	Dummy		
	AGC	Adoption of government cloud after 2015	Dummy		
	GODC	Government-ordinance-designated cities	Dummy		
	CC	Core cities	Dummy		
	TSW	Tokyo special wads	Dummy		

Governments [Chihou koukyou dantai teiinn kanri kankei] (each year)." The overall administrative service level index is an independently calculated value based on the data from the "Statistics of Municipalities [Toukei de miru shikuchouson no sugata] (each year)" of the Statistics Bureau of MIC; its calculation method will be explained later. Regarding the production of public services, since input and output are considered to have a time lag rather than simultaneous, data from the previous year are used for each input variable. Therefore, the data for FY2020 are almost unaffected by COVID-19.

Factor analysis includes regression analysis using population density (POPD), degree of vertical cooperation (SUPD), municipal financial status (FCIA and FCID), DX progress (EAGC and AGC), and municipal classification (government-designated cities (GODC), core cities (CC), and Tokyo special wards (TSW)). The data for EAGC and AGC are compiled using data from the "Survey on the Status of

Table 4.2 Indicators to measure the level of public service in each field

Field	Indicator
Education	Number of kindergartens per thousand students
	Number of elementary schools and teachers per thousand students
	Number of junior high schools and teachers per thousand students
	Number of high schools and teachers per thousand students
Amenity	Percentage of people without flush environment
	Number of stores per 100,000 pop
	Dining establishments per 100,000 pop
Culture	Number of community centers and libraries per 100,000 pop
	Number of community centers and libraries per inhabitable land
Medical care	Number of general hospitals, General Clinics and gingivals clinics per 100,000 pop
	Nunber of Doctors, Gingual doctors, and Pharmacists per 100,000 pop
Welfare	Number of nursing homes, child welfare facilities, and nursery schools per 100,000 pop.

Notes: The larger the value of each indicator, the more favorable it is; however, for negative factors (percentage of people without flush environment), the larger the value, the less favorable it is (i.e., the sign is reversed)

Local Administration Service Reform Efforts [Chihou gyousei service kaikaku no torikumi jyoukyou ni kansuru chousa] (each year)." All other data are compiled from the "Statistics of Municipalities [Toukei de miru shikuchouson no sugata] (each year)."

4.4.2   Local Government Service

We quantify the overall public services following Suzuki et al. (2008). First, standard scores are calculated for each of the selected indicators (Table 4.2) in each of the five public service fields (education, amenity, culture, healthcare, and welfare); the average of these scores is used as the service level for each field. In addition, we define the overall level of public services by averaging the service level values for each of the five areas.

4.5   Results

4.5.1   Efficiency Change

First, we discuss the results of the measured efficiency of the production of public services in the municipalities. Figure 4.2 presents the distribution of efficiency values for 1738 municipalities each year, indicating that most municipalities with an

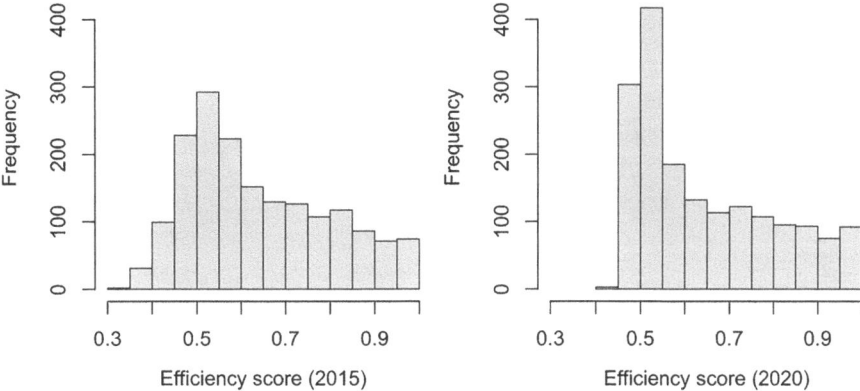

Fig. 4.2 Distribution of efficiency scores

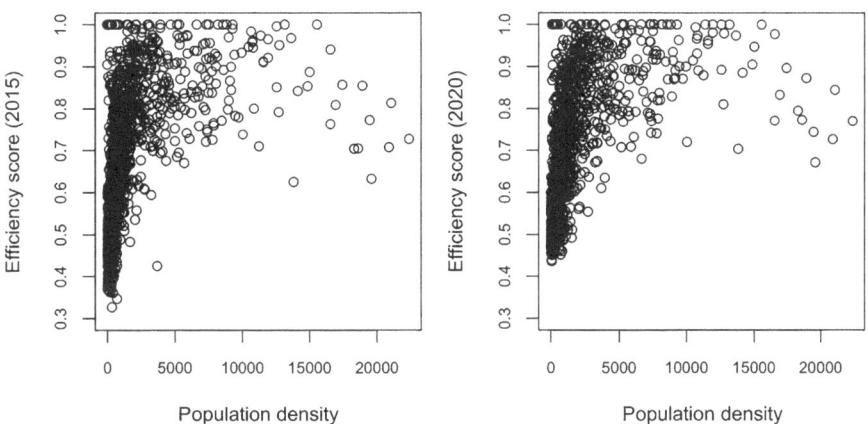

Fig. 4.3 Efficiency scores and population density

efficiency value of less than 0.5 for the production of public services have improved their efficiency over 2020. In contrast, the distribution of municipalities with high-efficiency values has not changed significantly. In other words, we can infer that a relative bottom-up has been achieved. Figure 4.3 reveals the relationship between efficiency values and POPD, indicating two aspects: inefficiency due to overcrowding and efficiency in producing public services due to increased POPD. The effect of inefficiency due to overcrowding is more pronounced in FY2015, and a slight improvement occurs in efficiency even in overpopulated municipalities toward FY2020.

Figure 4.4 shows the distribution of efficiency values by prefecture. Overall, the values are high in the Tokyo metropolitan area (Tokyo, Kanagawa, Saitama, and Chiba), while Aichi and Osaka are at the same level. The efficiency of public service production is higher on average in the surrounding areas of Kanagawa and Saitama

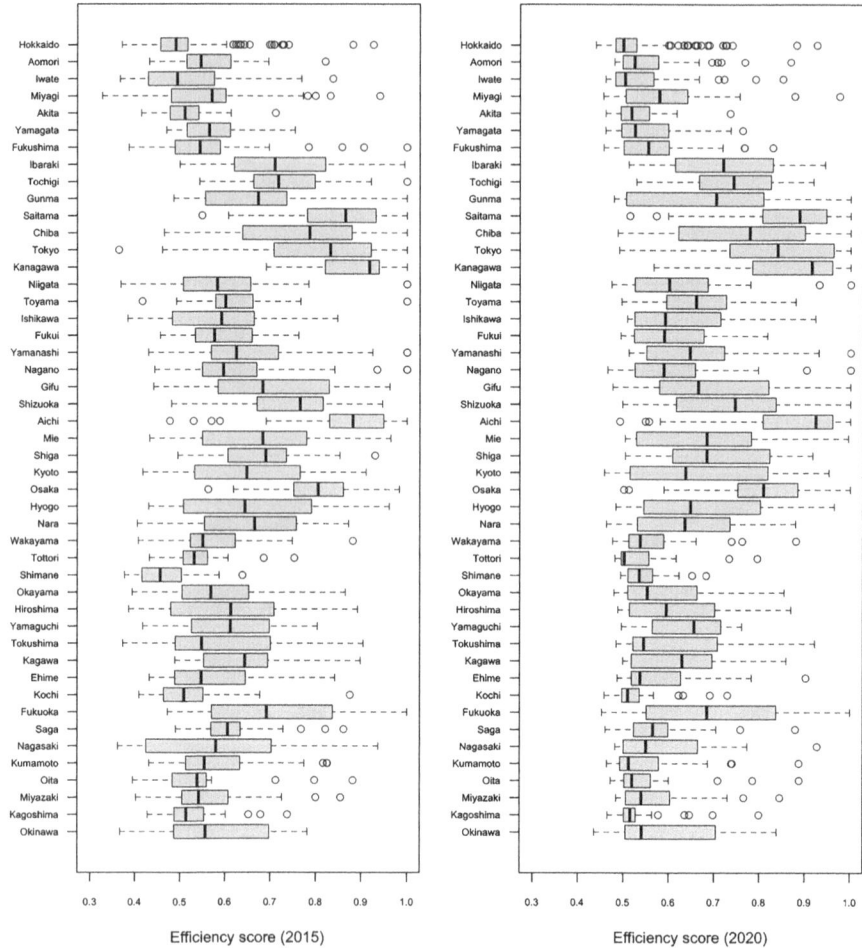

Fig. 4.4 Distribution of efficiency scores by prefecture

than in Tokyo, where the population is most concentrated. Conversely, the efficiency of municipalities in northern Japan, such as Hokkaido and the Tohoku region, is generally lower, and the variation is relatively small.

4.5.2 Productivity Change

Table 4.3 shows each prefecture's average change values in productivity and components. The productivity level in 2015 is set to 1. If MI is above 1, productivity will increase through 2020; if MI is below 1, productivity will decrease.

Table 4.3 Productivity change and component change (Average by prefecture)

Prefecture	MI	PTEC	TC	SEC
Hokkaido	0.926	1.037	0.929	0.965
Aomori	0.944	0.982	0.982	0.980
Iwate	0.976	1.062	0.936	0.990
Miyagi	0.996	1.068	0.946	0.990
Akita	0.984	1.028	0.970	0.990
Yamagata	0.886	0.968	0.972	0.942
Fukushima	1.009	1.033	0.978	1.001
Ibaraki	0.945	0.989	0.960	0.995
Tochigi	0.965	1.012	0.956	0.998
Gunma	0.966	1.022	0.967	0.982
Saitama	0.965	1.026	0.946	0.995
Chiba	0.930	0.991	0.962	0.977
Tokyo	0.978	1.041	0.965	0.976
Kanagawa	0.904	0.973	0.948	0.983
Niigata	0.977	1.054	0.935	0.995
Toyama	1.022	1.064	0.954	1.011
Ishikawa	1.015	1.086	0.937	0.998
Fukui	0.983	1.016	0.977	0.991
Yamanashi	0.970	1.001	0.977	0.992
Nagano	0.960	0.992	0.993	0.977
Gifu	0.927	0.996	0.945	0.986
Shizuoka	0.918	0.980	0.956	0.978
Aichi	0.941	1.016	0.940	0.985
Mie	0.950	1.018	0.952	0.980
Shiga	0.966	1.034	0.952	0.982
Kyoto	0.963	1.028	0.957	0.982
Osaka	0.940	0.998	0.951	0.989
Hyogo	0.946	1.021	0.938	0.988
Nara	0.919	0.978	0.977	0.963
Wakayama	0.938	0.989	0.977	0.973
Tottori	0.951	1.001	0.986	0.964
Shimane	0.978	1.186	0.850	0.979
Okayama	0.936	1.036	0.937	0.971
Hiroshima	0.942	1.059	0.913	0.983
Yamaguchi	0.965	1.053	0.934	0.983
Tokushima	0.954	1.056	0.937	0.973
Kagawa	0.917	0.978	0.963	0.972
Ehime	0.909	1.021	0.927	0.963
Kochi	0.903	1.021	0.934	0.951
Fukuoka	0.937	0.989	0.961	0.985
Saga	0.882	0.939	0.969	0.965

(continued)

Table 4.3 (continued)

Prefecture	MI	PTEC	TC	SEC
Nagasaki	0.916	1.069	0.888	0.977
Kumamoto	0.857	0.947	0.963	0.941
Oita	0.889	1.024	0.913	0.955
Miyazaki	0.879	1.009	0.929	0.939
Kagoshima	0.883	1.013	0.922	0.947
Okinawa	0.976	1.041	0.952	0.988
Average	0.942	1.017	0.951	0.977

Notes: The average value in the last line on the right side shows the average values for all municipalities

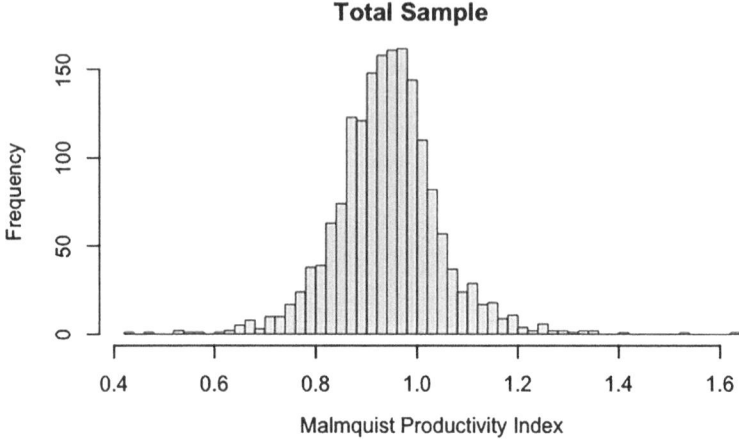

Fig. 4.5 Distribution of MI (Total)

This interpretation also holds for the other components. Only three prefectures (Fukushima, Toyama, and Ishikawa) increased their productivity on average between 2015 and 2020, while Kumamoto had the lowest mean MI. Although technical efficiency improved slightly (up 1.7%), the technology and scale efficiency levels declined by 4.9% and 2.3%, respectively.

Figure 4.5 presents histograms of MI. Most of the municipalities have MI values below one, indicating a decrease in the productivity of public services. Focusing on Tokyo, which has an enormous population concentration, we find that among the 23 wards, only 5 increased productivity (MI is more than 1), while productivity decreased in many wards (Fig. 4.6).

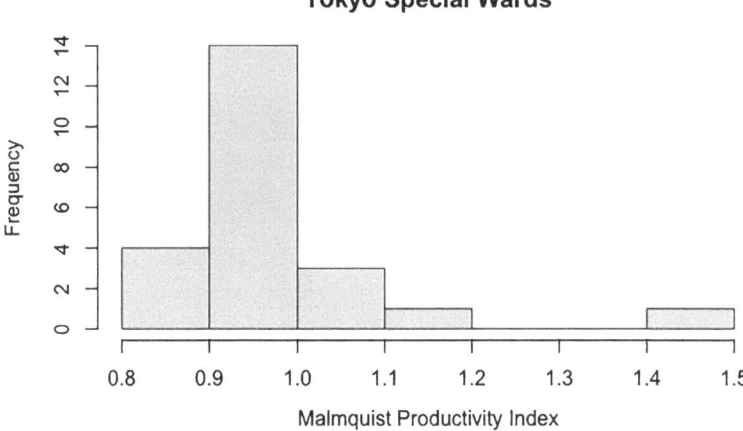

Fig. 4.6 Distribution of MI (Tokyo special wards only)

4.5.3 Regression Results

Factor analysis is conducted to determine the impact of DX, vertical cooperation, and population agglomeration on municipal service efficiency and productivity. Table 4.4 presents the results of the Tobit regression with the efficiency values measured by the VRS model for each year as the explained variable. The three dummy variables representing administrative divisions, GODC, CC, and TSW are mostly positive and statistically significant. Figure 4.3 confirms that inefficiency due to overcrowding and efficiency due to population agglomeration coincide; therefore, a quadratic term for POPD was set as an explanatory variable. This coefficient was negative and statistically significant in all models. In other words, an inverse U-shaped relationship exists between POPD and efficiency.

In contrast, none of the two dummy variables employed as proxy variables for DX were statistically significant. It may take some time for the government cloud to be introduced to improve the technical efficiency of public service production. Since we used data from 2015 and 2020 (a short period of 5 years), the efficiency of public service production gains could not be detected.

We examine the effect of enhanced vertical cooperation on efficiency values in FY2020 using control variables representing the financial status of municipalities (FCI and FCID); the results are robustly positive in all models. In other words, the results suggest that enhanced vertical cooperation by municipalities and support from the national government and prefectures can improve the efficiency of administrative service production.

Table 4.5 displays the results of the ordinary least squares regression with MI as the explained variable. In both models, the coefficient of POPD is not statistically significant. Regarding the municipality category, the robust and positive values for ordinance-designated cities and TSW indicate a high average productivity.

Table 4.4 Tobit regressions on efficiency scores

Independent variables	Dependent variable: Efficiency score (2015)				Dependent variable: Efficiency score (2020)			
	(1)		(2)		(3)		(4)	
	Estimate	S.E.	Estimate	S.E.	Estimate	S.E.	Estimate	S.E.
Constant	0.425^{***}	0.005	0.426^{***}	0.005	0.551^{***}	0.006	0.426^{***}	0.005
Local government class								
GODC	0.016	0.021	0.039^{**}	0.018	0.045^{*}	0.026	0.042^{**}	0.018
CC	0.006	0.012	0.024^{**}	0.010	0.039^{***}	0.015	0.023^{**}	0.010
TSW	0.115^{***}	0.037	0.187^{***}	0.034	0.156^{***}	0.051	0.187^{***}	0.034
Population agglomeration								
POPD	$4.5.\text{E-}05^{***}$	2.7.E-06	$4.4.\text{E-}05^{***}$	2.3.E-06	$9.4.\text{E-}05^{***}$	3.E-06	$4.4.\text{E-}05^{***}$	2.E-06
POPD^2	$-2.4.\text{E-}09^{***}$	2.1.E-10	$-2.4.\text{E-}09^{***}$	1.9.E-10	$-5.0.\text{E-}09^{***}$	3.E-10	$-2.4.\text{E-}09^{***}$	2.E-10
Government cloud								
EAGC	0.017^{***}	0.004	0.006	0.005	−0.005	0.006	0.006	0.005
AGC			−0.004	0.005	−0.006	0.007	−0.004	0.005
Financial								
FCI	0.332^{***}	0.010	0.340^{***}	0.009	0.370^{***}		0.337^{***}	0.009
FCID						0.053	0.104^{***}	0.039
Vertical cooperation								
SUPD			0.135^{***}	0.035	0.228^{***}	0.049	0.141^{***}	0.035
Log-likelihood	1657.039		1932.014		1376.223		1939.549	
Observations	1737		1737		1737		1737	

Note: *, **, *** implies statistical significance at 10, 5 and 1% level, respectively

Table 4.5 Regressions on MI

Independent variables	Dependent variable: MI					
	(1)		(2)		(3)	
	Estimate	S.E.	Estimate	S.E.	Estimate	S.E.
Constant	0.920***	0.007	0.920***	0.007	0.920***	0.007
Local government class						
GODC	0.061***	0.023	0.059**	0.023	0.061***	0.023
CC	0.019	0.014	0.018	0.014	0.019	0.013
TSW	0.045	0.031	0.064*	0.038	0.046**	0.021
Population agglomeration						
POPD	7.6.E-08	1.5.E-06	2.2.E-06	3.0.E-06		
POPD^2			−1.9.E-10	2.3.E-10		
Government cloud						
EAGC	−0.013**	0.006	−0.012	0.006	−0.013**	0.006
AGC	0.004	0.006	0.004	0.006	0.004	0.006
Vertical cooperation						
SUPD	−0.547***	0.056	−0.548***	0.056	−0.547**	0.056
FCID	0.062	0.051	0.061	0.051	0.062	0.051
SUPD×FCID	2.168**	0.968	2.130**	0.969	2.170**	0.966
FCIA	0.047***	0.010	0.044***	0.011	0.047***	0.009
Adjusted R-squared	0.079		0.079		0.079	
Observations	1737		1737		1737	

Note: *, **, *** implies statistical significance at 10, 5 and 1% level, respectively

The results for the DX proxy variable (EAGC and AGC) show unexpected results—the productivity of municipalities that implemented a municipal cloud in 2015 is significantly lower than the others. Notably, the promotion of digitalization in its infancy shows the opposite result instead of contributing to the increase in productivity of municipalities. Several hypotheses can be considered to interpret these results. For example, productivity may be relatively low because the organizations are not mature enough to adapt to the early introduction of new technology. A time lag exists for organizations to adapt to new technology, and achieving positive effects in 5 years may be challenging. Another hypothesis is that the effect may be due to the gap between technological innovation and the speed at which organizations adapt to new technologies. Digital technology has advanced remarkably in recent years, and the speed of technological development of cloud systems could be faster than the speed at which local governments adapt to digitalization and increased productivity. This disparity may have resulted in relatively low productivity in the initial group of cloud adopters. Regardless, DX is an ongoing policy issue that is changing, and further effectiveness verification is required, since we can not conclude the policy outcomes of DX only with this study.

For vertical cooperation, the analysis is conducted with a cross-term to control for the municipalities' financial situation and examine the relationship between the self-help efforts of each municipality concerning its finances. The results show that the enhanced vertical cooperation (SUPD) coefficient is negative, but the cross-term (SUPD × FCID) with changes in fiscal conditions is positive. The results suggest that enhanced vertical cooperation can contribute to productivity growth under conditions where the fiscal capacity index improves by 0.25 or more. Conversely, strengthening cooperation may not improve productivity if the financial situation does not increase.

4.6   Sustainability and Efficiency of Public Service

What should local governments do in the future to provide public services in an efficient and sustainable manner? The answer to this question can be summarized in the following two clues, based on the suggestions obtained from the empirical analysis of this chapter.

The first is to review whether DX promotion efforts are really being implemented in a way that is appropriate for each local government. Certainly, DX itself is important and may contribute to local efficiency. However, the results of the factor analysis reveals that DX does not necessarily improve the service efficiency of local governments. Uniform attempts to digitize tasks that do not require DX may result in more labor and inefficiencies. Introducing DX without a detailed analysis of the workflow in a local government may result in the application of DX to tasks that are not appropriate, contributing to inefficiencies. Each municipality benefit from imprementing DX with constatnt consideration of the optimum scale and situation which is potentially lead to greater efficiency and productivity.

Second, a well-balanced combination of financial self-help and public assistance is needed. Unless the financial situation improves, it will be difficult to provide better public services. However, there is a limit to the self-help efforts of each municipality alone. In addition to self-help efforts, vertical cooperation with prefectures and the national government could be strengthened to increase the sustainability of public services in each municipality.

4.7   Conclusions

This chapter investigates the effects of the three critical issues to sustain local government (DX, vertical cooperation, and population agglomeration), with the objective of providing insight into the impact of these transformation in local government on the production and efficiency of public services. To test the three hypotheses stated in the introduction, we examine Japan's 1738 municipalities and 23 wards of Tokyo regarding the efficiency and productivity of local government service production using DEA and MI. The results provide three essential findings. First, we could not confirm the effect of the DX promotion on improving efficiency, indicating relatively low productivity for municipalities that introduced the government cloud early. Second, enhanced vertical cooperation accompanied by municipalities' efforts to improve their finances could contribute to increased productivity and improved efficiency of local government services. Finally, population agglomeration has an inverse U-shaped relationship with municipal efficiency, indicating that the efficiency benefits of population agglomeration and the flight rate due to overcrowding occur simultaneously.

Limitations of this research include the fact that administrative reform efforts are only partially quantified. Outsourcing receptionist services and public facility management need to be considered. Second, in-depth exploration of effects of DX is not sufficient. DX efforts are related to the government cloud, various organizational structures, and policy implementation capabilities; thus, it is necessary to quantify these aspects and conduct a more multifaceted evaluation. Finally, the period after the COVID-19 pandemic was not included in the analysis; therefore, the actual impact of the pandemic on the production of public services could not be examined. These are future challenges in examining sustainability of local governments.

Despite these limitations, the findings of this chapter contribute to the existing literature on productivity and efficiency in local government. Furthermore, the results can inform the policy decisions of policymakers and officials, enabling them to assess and potentially modify the state of public services at different levels of local government.

References

Adachi K, Otahara J, Noda Y (2021) Review of efficiency analysis on local government [Chihou jichitai no keiei kouritsusei ni kansuru kenkyuu no tenbou to kadai]. Doshisha Bus Rev 72(4):595–616. (in Japanese). https://doi.org/10.14988/00027860

Afonso A, Fernandes S (2006) Measuring local government spending efficiency: evidence for the Lisbon region. Reg Stud 40(1):39–53. https://doi.org/10.1080/00343400500449937

Andrews R, Entwistle T (2015) Public–private partnerships, management capacity and public service efficiency. Policy & Politics 43(2):273–290

Banker RD, Charnes A, Cooper WW (1984) Some models for estimating technical and scale inefficiencies in data envelopment analysis. Manag Sci 30(9):1078–1092. https://www.jstor.org/stable/2631725

Caves D, Christensen L, Diewert WE (1982) The economic theory of index numbers and the measurement of input, output and productivity. Econometrica 50:1393–1414. https://doi.org/10.2307/1913388

Charnes A, Cooper WW, Rhodes E (1978) Measuring the efficiency of decision making units. Eur J Oper Res 2(6):429–444. https://doi.org/10.1016/0377-2217(78)90138-8

Daraio C, Kerstens K, Nepomuceno T, Sickles RC (2020) Empirical surveys of frontier applications: a meta-review. Int Trans Oper Res 27(2):709–738. https://doi.org/10.1111/itor.12649

Drew J, Kortt M, Dollery B (2015) What determines efficiency in local government? A DEA analysis of NSW local government. Econ Papers J Appl Econ Policy 34(4):243–256. https://doi.org/10.1111/1759-3441.12118

EU (2023) eGovernment Benchmark 2023 Insight Report

Färe R, Grosskopf S, Norris M, Zhang Z (1994) Productivity growth, technical progress, and efficiency change in industrialized countries. Am Econ Rev 84(1):66–83. https://www.jstor.org/stable/2117971

Geys B, Heinemann F, Kalb A (2010) Voter involvement, fiscal autonomy and public sector efficiency: evidence from German municipalities. Eur J Polit Econ 26(2):265–278. https://doi.org/10.1016/j.ejpoleco.2009.11.002

Geys B, Heinemann F, Kalb A (2013) Local government efficiency in German municipalities. Raumforsch Raumordn 71(4):283–293. https://doi.org/10.1007/s13147-012-0191-x

Hayashi R (2017) Efficiency of local governments and determinants of management: A multilevel model approach for urban municipalities [Jichitai keiei no kouritsusei to kettei youin—Tadannkai moderu apurochi wo mochiita toshi jichitai no kensho—]. Joint J Nat Univer Kyushu Educ Humanit 4(1, 2):27. (in Japanese)

Hirata M, Kawabata Y, Fujii S (2019) A study on the effect of investment in road infrastructures on the population concentration into Tokyo. J Jpn Soc Civil Eng Ser D3 (Infrastruct Plan Manag) 75(5):I_967–I_978. (in Japanese). https://doi.org/10.2208/jscejipm.75.I_967

Ibrahim F, Karim M (2004) Efficiency of local governments in Malaysia and its correlates. Int J Manag Stud 11(1):57–70. https://doi.org/10.32890/ijms

Ichikawa Y (2013) Basic municipalities, regional municipalities, and the national government: "collaboration" and "complementation" of public services by municipalities [Todouhuken ni yoru shichouson no Hokan wo kangaeru]. Community Gov 20:27–34. (in Japanese)

Iida T (2022) The impact of evidence-based policymaking and digital transformation on planning administration [EBPM to DX ha keikakugyosei wo dou kaeruka]. Plan Public Manag 45(1):27–32. (in Japanese). https://doi.org/10.14985/jappm.45.1_27

Itaba Y (2007) Fiscal bankruptcy of a local government: the case of Yubari city [Chihou jichitai no zaisei hatan: Yubarishi no kesu]. Doshisha Univ Econ Rev 59(1):51–72. (in Japanese). https://doi.org/10.14988/pa.2017.0000012327

Kalb A (2014) What determines local governments' cost-efficiency? The case of road maintenance. Reg Stud 48(9):1483–1498. https://doi.org/10.1080/00343404.2012.731044

Kalb A, Geys B, Heinemann F (2012) Value for money? German local government efficiency in a comparative perspective. Appl Econ 44(2):201–218. https://doi.org/10.1080/00036846.2010.502110

Malmquist S (1953) Index numbers and indifference surfaces. Trab Estad 4(2):209–242. https://doi.org/10.1007/BF03006863

Mergel I, Edelmann N, Haug N (2019) Defining digital transformation: results from expert interviews. Gov Inf Q 36(4):101385. https://doi.org/10.1016/j.giq.2019.06.002

MIC (2020) Municipal digital transformation (DX) promotion Plan [Jichitai dejitaru toransufomeisyon (DX) suishin keikaku] (in Japanese)

MIC (2021a) Cloud introduction status [Curaudo dounyu jyoukyou (Reiwa 3 nen genzai)]. Accessed at: https://www.soumu.go.jp/main_content/000855084.pdf

MIC (2021b) White paper on information and communications FY2021 [Reiwa 3 nenban jyouhou tsushin hakusyo] (in Japanese)

Mizuno M (2020) Why do firms concentrate in Tokyo? An economic geography perspective. Jpn Inst Labour Policy Train:29–39. (in Japanese)

Munakata M, Honma S, MIyano T (2009) Local public administration and finance towards sustainable development in remote islands: comparison among Iki, Tsushima, and Goto islands [Rito jichitai ni okeru kankyou gyouzaisei no kenkyuu – Iki, Tsushima, Goto retto no hikaku bunseki]. J Ind Manag Ind Manage Inst 41:107–129. (in Japanese)

Nakazawa K (2014) Does the method of amalgamation affect cost inefficiency of the new municipalities? Open J Appl Sci 4(4):143–154. https://doi.org/10.4236/ojapps.2014.44015

Narbón-Perpiñá I, De Witte K (2018a) Local governments' efficiency: a systematic literature review—Part I. Int Trans Oper Res 25(2):431–468. https://doi.org/10.1111/itor.12364

Narbón-Perpiñá I, De Witte K (2018b) Local governments' efficiency: a systematic literature review—Part II. Int Trans Oper Res 25(4):1107–1136. https://doi.org/10.1111/itor.12389

Nijkamp P, Suzuki S (2009) A generalized goals-achievement model in data envelopment analysis: an application to efficiency improvement in local government finance in Japan. Spat Econ Anal 4(3):249–274. https://doi.org/10.1080/17421770903114687

Noda Y (2011) Evaluating the impact of vertical subsidiarity on municipalities in Japan [Kiso jichitai ni taisuru suichoku hokan no kouka]. Ann Jpn Society for Public Adm 46:126–143. (in Japanese). https://doi.org/10.11290/jspa1962.2011.46_126

Noda Y (2023) Intermunicipal cooperation, integration forms, and vertical and horizontal effects in Japan. Public Adm Rev 83(3):654–678. https://doi.org/10.1111/puar.13569

Raiher AP (2020) Economies of agglomeration and their relation with industrial productivity in Brazilian municipalities. Pap Reg Sci 99(3):725–747. https://doi.org/10.1111/pirs.12487

Ray SC, Desli E (1997) Productivity growth, technical progress, and efficiency change in industrialized countries: comment. Am Econ Rev 87(5):1033–1039. https://www.jstor.org/stable/2951340

Revelli F (2010) Spend more, get more? An inquiry into English local government performance. Oxf Econ Pap 62(1):185–207

Seol H, Lee H, Kim S, Park Y (2008) The impact of information technology on organizational efficiency in public services: a DEA-based DT approach. J Oper Res Soc 59(2):231–238. https://doi.org/10.1057/palgrave.jors.2602453

Sousa M, Stošić B (2005) Technical efficiency of the Brazilian municipalities: correcting nonparametric frontier measurements for outliers. J Prod Anal 24(2):157–181. https://doi.org/10.1007/s11123-005-4702-4

Stevens PA (2005) Assessing the performance of local government. Natl Inst Econ Rev 193:90–101. https://doi.org/10.1177/0027950105058565

Sung N (2007) Information technology, efficiency and productivity: evidence from Korean local governments. Appl Econ 39(13):1691–1703. https://doi.org/10.1080/00036840600675620

Suzuki S (2008) Efficiency evaluation and improvement of city administration management by means of data envelopment analysis: a development and an application of the distance friction minimization model. Sapporo Univ J 25:35–47. (in Japanese)

Suzuki J (2012) Productivity analysis of refuse disposal service by DEA [DEA ni yoru gomi shori sabisu no seisannsei bunseki]. Kwansei Gakuin Econ Rev 43:17–28. (in Japanese)

Suzuki S, Nijkamp P, Rietveld P (2008) Efficiency improvement of city administration management by means of distance friction minimization in data envelopment analysis: application to government ordinance designated cities in Japan [DEA ni okeru DFM moderu wo mochiita toshi gyousei keiei no kouritsusei kaizenn—Nihon ni okeru seirei shitei toshi heno tekiyou]. Stud Reg Sci 38(4):1041–1053. (in Japanese). https://doi.org/10.2457/srs.38.1041

Worthington AC, Dollery BE (2000a) An empirical survey of frontier efficiency measurement techniques in local government. Local Gov Stud 26(2):23–52. https://doi.org/10.1080/03003930008433988

Worthington AC, Dollery BE (2000b) Measuring efficiency in local governments' planning and regulatory function. Public Product Manag Rev 23(4):469–485. https://doi.org/10.2307/3380564

Yamashita K, Akai N, Sato M (2002) Incentive effects hidden in the local allocation tax system: an examination of the soft budget constraint problem by frontier cost functions [Chihou kouhuzei seido ni hisomu insenteibu Kouka-Furonteia hiyou kansu ni yoru sofuto na yosann seiyaku mondai no kensho-]. Financ Rev 61:120–145. (in Japanese)

Yamazaki, M. (2022). Cooperation, complementation, and support by prefectures with municipalities [Todouhuken ni yoru shichouson tono renkei, Hokan, shien]. Japan Municipal Research Center (ed) Urban municipalities in an era of declining population – Prefectural relations, pp 57–72 (in Japanese)

Yusfany A (2015) The efficiency of local governments and its influence factors. Int J Technol Enhanc Emerg Eng Res 4(10):219–241

Zheng XP (2001) Determinants of agglomeration economies and diseconomies: empirical evidence from Tokyo. Socio Econ Plan Sci 35(2):131–144. https://doi.org/10.1016/S0038-0121(00)00008-2

Koji Adachi is an Associate Professor at the Faculty of Policy Studies, Doshisha University. His research interests include the efficiency of public organizations, such as local governments and airports. His recent work has been published in *Public Utilities and Public Policy: Empirical Studies Focusing on Japan.*

Jun Otahara is a Professor at the Faculty of Commerce, Doshisha University. He was also a Visiting scholar at Reischauer Institute of Japanese Studies at Harvard University from 2013 to 2015. His research focuses innovation and entrepreneurship. His recent articles have been published in *Doshisha Business Review.*

Chapter 5
Program and Project Evaluation Systems in Local Governments

Keita Hashimoto ⓘ

Abstract This chapter examines the characteristics and overall landscape of policy evaluation activities in assessing the sustainability of local government management in Japan. It is widely recognized that local government evaluation activities are typically conducted independently of central government oversight. However, recent years have seen a growing level of central government intervention in these evaluations. Consequently, previous research that has exclusively focused on the evaluation activities of local governments has become increasingly narrow in its scope. This chapter explores the following research question: How has central government intervention influenced the evaluation activities of local governments? This chapter categorizes the evaluation of local governments in Japan into three categories: (1) administrative evaluations, (2) evaluations of decentralized services, and (3) intergovernmental evaluations. The first half of the chapter provides an overview of the historical background and systems associated with each evaluation type. The latter half offers a qualitative analysis of the content of 204 basic principles of the central government and includes a graphical representation of intergovernmental evaluations conducted by central government ministries. The analysis reveals that certain ministries are mandating local governments to formulate and evaluate plans for implementing national policies. This trend suggests an increase in evaluation activities by local governments, which may impact their autonomy and sustainability.

Keywords Administrative evaluations · Comprehensive plan · Performance measurement · Decentralized services · Intergovernmental relations

K. Hashimoto (✉)
Faculty of Law, Kobe Gakuin University, Kobe, Hyogo, Japan
e-mail: hashimoto@law.kobegakuin.ac.jp

© The Author(s), under exclusive license to Springer Nature Switzerland AG 2024
Y. Noda (ed.), *Local Governance in Japan*, Local and Urban Governance, https://doi.org/10.1007/978-3-031-77322-8_5

5.1 Introduction

Japan has a unitary system of governance, with the involvement of the central government in the administration of local governments. While the central government enacted the Government Policy Evaluations Act in 2001 and began to engage in policy evaluation, local governments began to engage in evaluation in the late 1990s, thus preceding the introduction of evaluation by the central government. As a result, evaluation by local governments in Japan has developed as an independent effort without the involvement of the central government. Evaluations undertaken by local governments in Japan are generally based on performance measurement methods. Prior research on local government performance measurement has indicated that performance measurement has been introduced by local governments not only in Japan but also in other countries, contributing to the efficiency of public management and responding to citizens' demand for accountability (Poister and Streib 1999). In performance measurement, public sector managers work to achieve a variety of goals, including supporting strategic planning, controlling subordinates, and managing budgets (Behn 2003).

In recent years, performance management has been addressed not as a separate local government initiative but rather as a means of central government involvement with local governments. In response to decentralization and greater local government autonomy, higher-level governments require or encourage local governments to use performance management to properly manage policies and programs (Ateh et al. 2020). Researchers in the field of federalism have also pointed out that the pursuit of local representation may be a tradeoff for the pursuit of efficiency and equity. That is, while federalism promotes democratic representation, it also leads to inefficient administrative operations and inequities in public services due to policy differences across states (Weissert and Jones 2015). In contrast, in Japan, because of its unitary system, the central government has jurisdiction over the local fiscal system and has emphasized uniform service delivery throughout the country through laws, ordinances and public notices. Decentralization reform in the late 1990s was a move toward regional representation, and the introduction of evaluation by local governments was a key tool in this effort. In recent years, however, a trend toward central government involvement in local governments has again formed. Prior research has pointed to the existence of a "devolution paradox", in which citizens want local governments to assume more responsibility than the central government while, at the same time, wanting policies to be implemented uniformly and fairly across the country (Henderson et al. 2013).

There may be costs associated with intergovernmental performance management compared to management by a single government entity. Investing human, monetary, and time resources in the operation of a performance management system creates opportunity costs and consumes resources that could have been invested in other policies (OECD 2009). It has also been noted that the extensive performance evaluation process associated with performance management causes "overload" among staff (Oh 2023). In Japan, the massive amount of evaluation materials that must be prepared may also hinder efficient administrative evaluation. In addition, to ensure accountability to higher-level government, local governments collect performance information as evidence and develop administrative rules and procedures for implementation. These factors increase the internal opportunity costs of local governments as well as the "administrative burden" placed on employees associated with service delivery. This administrative burden not only sacrifices program effectiveness and administrative efficiency but also increases the material and psychological costs of those seeking public services (Moynihan et al. 2015). Moreover, this administrative burden affects the behavior of street-level workers implementing government programs and citizens' comprehension of and motivation to participate in such programs (Doughty and Baehler 2020).

Although all of the above issues are relevant to the evaluation practices of local governments, they have not been well researched in Japan. In particular, no previous research has discussed how central government control has affected the nature of local government evaluation. In addition, while several English-language studies have described the evaluation system of Japan's central government (Kikuchi 2017; Koike et al. 2007; Yamamoto 2008), there has been no comprehensive discussion of the evaluation system of local governments in the English-language literature. Therefore, this chapter organizes the evaluations undertaken by Japanese local governments into several typologies and examines how recent intergovernmental relations have affected local government evaluations.

5.2 Internal Measurements Within Local Governments

5.2.1 Types of Local Government Evaluations

Central governments have established indicator systems in other countries to measure and monitor public services and control local governments' activities (Mizell 2008). The extent to which intergovernmental performance reporting systems are used in each country depends on institutional factors and administrative culture, with differences in legal, social, and administrative systems in Anglo-Saxon, Nordic, and Southern European countries affecting the implementation of central government performance reporting systems for local governments (Brusca and Montesinos 2016). For example, in the United Kingdom, local governments are overburdened with a myriad of obligations, such as submitting reports to ministries, due to top-down intervention by the central government, whereas the French government shows a bottom-up pragmatism that allows for local autonomy regarding performance measurement (Kuhlmann 2010).

In contrast, evaluations conducted by Japanese local governments are characterized by the fact that they were initially developed as initiatives by local governments. While local governments in Japan are controlled by the central government based on the legal system and the local finance system, there is no institutional

involvement of the national government in evaluations conducted by local governments because local governments established their evaluation systems in the late
1990s, prior to the national policy evaluation system. Evaluations conducted by the
central government under the Government Policy Evaluations Act in 2001 cover
only central government programs and projects and not those conducted by local
governments. As a result, a nationwide integrated performance measurement system has yet to be developed in Japan. In the 2000s, however, the central government
became more involved legally and financially, and new public management reforms
spilled over into local governments nationwide.

This section describes the following three categories of evaluations undertaken
by Japanese local governments: (1) administrative evaluations, (2) evaluations of
decentralized services, and (3) intergovernmental evaluations. Performance measurement is distinguished by whether it is intraorganizational (an internal measurement) or interorganizational (an external measurement) and whether it is vertical or
horizontal (Kuhlmann 2010). Administrative evaluation, which arose spontaneously
from local government initiatives in the late 1990s, began as an internal/horizontal
measurement of local governments. In the 2000s, central government initiatives led
to the agencification and privatization of local governments and the development of
internal/vertical measurements between administrative units and decentralized services. In addition, since 2000, the laws and ordinances enacted by the central government have increasingly required local governments to create plans and measure
progress, leading to the development of external and vertical measurements between
central and local governments. In other words, local government evaluation activities, which began as a process for learning and improvement, today function as a
process for monitoring different levels of government and strengthening
accountability.

5.2.2 Administrative Evaluations

In general, evaluations undertaken by local governments in Japan are called "administrative evaluations." While the detailed methods used to conduct administrative
evaluations vary from one local government to another, the overall main characteristic is the evaluation of the local government's comprehensive plan. A comprehensive plan is a document that systematically outlines the goals to be realized by the
local government and the corresponding projects that it will undertake to realize
those goals. A comprehensive plan generally consists of the following three components: a basic concept that outlines the future vision of the municipality and the
system of measures through which to achieve it, a basic plan that outlines the direction and major projects in each policy area, and an implementation plan that outlines
the schedule and budget for all subprojects under the major projects.

Comprehensive plans are formulated for the purpose of comprehensive and systematic administrative management by local governments. Municipalities were
once required by the Local Government Act to formulate comprehensive plans. In

2011, the Local Government Act was amended to eliminate the legal obligation for municipalities to formulate comprehensive plans, and municipalities can now do so on their own initiative. However, many local governments still formulate comprehensive plans. Japan has a unitary system of governance, and the structure and functions of local governments are defined by the Local Government Act. Local governments conduct affairs specific to their area or those entrusted to them by the central government in accordance with the Local Government Act and other national laws and ordinances. Therefore, comprehensive plans are still utilized by many local governments as a means through which to comprehensively manage their own projects.

Since the late 1990s, local governments across Japan have engaged in administrative evaluation. Mie Prefecture was the first prefecture in Japan to introduce administrative evaluation. At the time, the newly appointed governor of Mie Prefecture promoted administrative reform. The background to this reform effort was the revelation that employees were misusing budgets within the prefectural government, and the central objective was to improve the efficiency of public services. In 1996, Mie Prefecture introduced an evaluation system for projects, identifying approximately 3000 projects, creating an evaluation table, and consolidating these projects into approximately 500 basic projects for evaluation (Umeda 2000). Mie Prefecture's evaluation system has spread to other local governments throughout Japan.

The Ministry of Internal Affairs and Communications (MIC) released a survey in 2024 that revealed the introduction rate of administrative evaluations in local governments nationwide (MIC 2024). Although all 47 prefectures had introduced administrative evaluations, the rate of adoption was 85.0% for cities and only 48.3% for towns and villages with smaller populations. The survey also revealed that many local governments evaluate all or part of their administrative activities by dividing them into the following hierarchical categories: policies, programs, and projects. While administrative evaluation is a unique initiative of each local government, the design and implementation of the evaluation system are similar for many local governments.

Based on the above history, several characteristics of administrative evaluation by local governments can be identified. First, in administrative evaluations, local governments design evaluation systems for comprehensive plans. The basic concept, basic plan, and implementation plan of the comprehensive plan are evaluated in correspondence with policies, programs, and projects, respectively. The comprehensive plan comprehensively presents the principles, activities, and goals of the local government. Therefore, administrative evaluation is used as a means to annually determine whether the goals of the comprehensive plan are being achieved. In the evaluation of programs and projects, evaluation indicators are described, and an annual check is performed to determine whether the indicators are being achieved.

Second, a vast number of projects are evaluated. As a characteristic of the Japanese budget structure, the unit of a project coincides with the unit of the budget and often coincides with the department in charge. Therefore, projects serve as the most basic unit of evaluation. In addition, a wide range of administrative tasks are delegated to local governments by national ministries. Since the national ministries are divided by jurisdiction, one local government must address the affairs of all central government ministries. As a result, the number of local government projects tends to increase in proportion to the number of central government projects.

Third, programs are defined in a bottom-up manner. Under normal circumstances, policies and programs are top-down concepts and key units in translating government strategies into concrete goals and measures. For Japanese local governments, however, programs are perceived as bundles of projects. One program contains goals that are common to multiple projects, and a list of indicators for each project and their status is included in the programs. When the number of projects subject to evaluation is too large, evaluating a relatively small number of programs has the advantage of allowing for many projects to be reviewed. In addition, since the programs include a variety of projects under the control of different departments, there is no department that leads the program. Programs are only abstract concepts for evaluation purposes, and projects that coincide with budgetary and organizational units are regarded as effective evaluation units.

Fourth, administrative evaluation is conducted as a performance measurement. In Japanese, the word "evaluation" is an abstract and broad concept that tends to refer to a variety of activities, including performance measurement, program evaluation, preassessment, and surveys. In Japan, performance measurement is widespread and is considered synonymous with evaluation. All projects are evaluated using the same standardized evaluation form, which allows for the progress of each project within the comprehensive plan to be compared with that of other projects. Another unique feature is that a grade is assigned to each project and program according to the level of achievement of the indicators. It is expected that obtaining a high rating will serve as an incentive for staff members, and conversely, obtaining a low rating will encourage staff members to make improvements. These evaluation forms are generally created in an Excel file, and the staff member in charge fills in the cells. Many local governments publish these evaluation forms on their websites.

Fifth, the evaluation is a self-evaluation. Based on the method of performance measurement, each staff member of the department in charge completes an evaluation form. These evaluation forms are consolidated and sent to the general affairs department, which then publishes them as evaluation documents. Some local governments may establish an external evaluation committee of experts to discuss this evaluation form. However, the purpose is only to confirm the internal evaluation after the fact and to obtain comments from experts to partially improve the content of these projects and programs. Notably, external evaluation experts do not lead the evaluation. Administrative evaluation is characterized by the accumulation of self-evaluation results by the department in charge.

The characteristics of administrative evaluation described above are only general trends. Some local governments have unique approaches that differ from these characteristics, while others have abolished administrative evaluation. The approach to administrative evaluation varies from one local government to another. Many local governments publicize the results of administrative evaluation along with their comprehensive plans, which contributes to greater transparency for citizens. Conversely, nearly a quarter of a century has passed since administrative evaluation began, and the evaluation system has become a routine task for many local governments.

5.2.3   Evaluations of Decentralized Services

In addition to administrative evaluations by local governments, local governments evaluate the status of their contractors' administration and management. Typical examples are evaluations of local incorporated administrative agencies and designated administrators. The basis for evaluating local incorporated administrative agencies is the Local Incorporated Administrative Agency Act, while the basis for evaluating designated administrators is the Local Government Act. Since both are based on the laws and ordinances of the central government, local governments that have established local incorporated administrative agencies or designated administrators and outsourced their administrative operations to them conduct these evaluations.

Local incorporated administrative agencies are a form of decentralized service that separates some of the policy implementation divisions of local governments and gives them corporate status.[1] Such decentralized service was introduced in a law enacted in 2003, modeled after the central government's incorporated administrative agency system. Like the central government system, this decentralized system requires performance management and evaluation based on midterm targets and plans. It is said to allow for more flexible financial and personnel management than when local governments directly execute projects. As of 2023, a total of 165 local incorporated administrative agencies had been established by local governments nationwide, of which the largest number was 84 for universities, followed by 66 for local public corporations (public hospitals) (MIC 2023). Although local incorporated administrative agencies are intended to cover all public services, in reality, the system is intended for local public universities and public hospitals.

The Local Incorporated Administrative Agency Act requires local incorporated administrative agencies to establish an evaluation committee and conduct periodic evaluations.[2] During the midterm goal period, evaluation must be conducted every fiscal year or immediately before and immediately after the end of the goal period. The results of these evaluations are reflected in future goals and plans and in the improvement of operations, and the status of such reflection is made public each year. In the case of local incorporated administrative agency evaluations, the central government designs an evaluation system based on laws and ordinances, and local governments formulate midterm goals and manage local incorporated administrative agencies based on this system. The evaluation is intended to improve the

---

[1] Local Incorporated Administrative Agency Act, Section 1 https://elaws.e-gov.go.jp/document?lawid=415AC0000000118

[2] Local Incorporated Administrative Agency Act, Article11, 28, and 29 https://elaws.e-gov.go.jp/document?lawid=415AC0000000118

performance of local incorporated administrative agencies by evaluating the progress of their midterm and annual plans formulated in response to these midterm goals.

Although the operational performance report, which corresponds to the evaluation report, differs across agencies, it actually shares many points in common with administrative evaluations. In local incorporated administrative agency evaluations, each responsible department conducts a self-evaluation of its individual operations corresponding to its midterm plan. These are basically conducted as performance measurements using a standardized evaluation form. In addition, the grades assigned according to the degree of achievement of the goals are emphasized. Midterm plans and operational performance reports comprehensively describe each agency's activities and are used as a means through which local governments can control agencies.

The designated administrator is a system introduced by the 2003 amendment of the Local Government Act with the objective of outsourcing the management of public facilities to private organizations. Prior to the introduction of the designated administrator system, the management of public facilities was legally restricted to public organizations. With the introduction of the designated administrator system, it is now possible for a variety of organizations, including private companies and nonprofit organizations, to take charge of facility management. There are various types of public facilities that can be broadly classified into the following five categories: recreation and sports, industrial promotion, infrastructure, educational, and social welfare facilities. According to a survey by the MIC, a total of 77,537 public facilities are managed by designated administrators nationwide, of which 6721 are in prefectures, 8063 are in ordinance-designated cities, and 62,753 are in municipalities, with the introduction rate for prefectures reaching 59.5% (MIC 2022). Thus, the management of public facilities owned by local governments is now being carried out by private organizations.

The evaluation of designated administrators can be divided into two major categories. The first is evaluation during the selection process. Local governments usually establish a designated administrator selection committee consisting of outside experts to ensure fairness in the designation of administrators. To be designated as an administrator, an applicant organization must be selected in a competitive process. Evaluation criteria are established in advance to determine whether the applicant organization's work plan and income/expenditure plan are appropriate. The applicant organization with the highest total score is then selected. In many cases, strict rules are established by each municipality during the selection process. After selection, the designated administrator must submit an annual project report to the local government.[3]

The second is the evaluation of the management and operation of public facilities. Local governments evaluate the activities of their respective public facilities, including each facility's occupancy rate and revenue, to understand how well they

---

[3] Local Government Act, Article 244-2 https://elaws.e-gov.go.jp/document?lawid=322AC000 0000067

are operating. According to a survey by the MIC, 6721 (100.0%) facilities in prefectures, 7817 (96.9%) facilities in ordinance-designated cities, and 48,885 (77.9%) facilities in municipalities nationwide have implemented these evaluations, for a total of 63,423 (81.8%) facilities. In addition, 3910 (58.2%) facilities in prefectures and 4907 (60.9%) facilities in ordinance-designated cities have implemented evaluations by outside experts (MIC 2022). In the evaluation of the management and operational status of designated administrators, each department usually evaluates the facilities under its jurisdiction within the local government. In general, evaluation forms are prepared for each facility using a standardized format that includes indicators such as facility occupancy rates, user satisfaction, financial and revenue information, and reasons for the evaluation and rating. Since designated administrators are subject to periodic evaluation by the department in charge, they may have established their own system for conducting self-evaluations.

5.3 External Controls by the Central Government

5.3.1 Intergovernmental Evaluations

Internal measurements such as administrative evaluations and evaluations of decentralized services are left to local governments to decide, at their discretion, whether to conduct and how to design the evaluations. In contrast, local governments are required to evaluate projects at the request of the central government. Although these evaluations are carried out as local government affairs, the central government establishes the responsibilities and planning obligations of local governments. The central government stipulates a certain level of involvement based on laws and ordinances and subsidies, which limits the discretion of local governments. To receive national subsidies, local governments are required to conduct evaluations that show the results of their subsidized projects. In recent years, this type of evaluation has been on the rise, straining local government resources. Since this type of evaluation is very diverse, this section is divided into basic acts and other laws.

5.3.2 Evaluation Under the National Basic Act

Numerous Japanese laws and ordinances contain the term "basic act" in the title. The oldest basic act is the Basic Act on Education enacted in 1947. Many basic acts were enacted in the 1960s, and many more were enacted beginning in 1989 (Nishikawa 2015). Compared to ordinary laws, the main characteristics of a basic act are as follows: (1) the provisions of a basic act are enlightening to the public, (2) a basic act does not function by itself but requires legislative and financial measures for implementation, (3) almost all basic acts require the government to formulate a plan, (4) a basic act exhibits the characteristic of being cross-ministerial, and (5) the content of a basic act is abstract and has little legal normative character for the public (Shiono 2008).

Due to the abstract nature of the content of basic acts, the government needs to take measures to implement these laws. Most basic acts establish the responsibilities of the central government and local governments and often require these governments to develop plans to carry out their responsibilities. The laws and ordinances search database on the government's e-government portal site indicates that 53 laws include "basic act" in their titles.[4] Of these, all but three (Atomic Energy Basic Act, Basic Act for the Reform of Central Government Ministries and Agencies, and Basic Act for the Reform of National Public Service System) stipulate the responsibilities of local governments, and some require prefectures and municipalities to formulate plans.

For example, the Basic Act for Gender Equal Society enacted in 1999 stipulates the responsibilities of the central government and local governments, requiring the central government and prefectures to formulate plans and municipalities to at least make efforts to formulate plans.[5] Based on this provision, the Gender Equality Bureau of the Cabinet Office formulates and publishes a Basic Plan for Gender Equality every five years. The central government's Basic Plan comprehensively describes specific programs for realizing gender equality and their promotion systems. The central government's Basic Plan also sets performance targets for each program and monitors the percentage of women in the public sector, private sector, and local communities. Local governments formulate plans based on the central government's Basic Plan. The central government annually tabulates the status of the formulation and implementation of local government gender equality plans. According to the survey, all 47 prefectures and 1509 (86.7%) municipalities have formulated plans (Cabinet Office 2022). Except for small towns and villages, nearly all local governments have plans in place.

Most local governments have established a system for evaluating their gender equality plans to monitor their implementation and whether they achieve their goals. This evaluation is conducted in a similar manner to the administrative evaluation described in the previous section. Many local governments have established a gender equality section, which has cross-departmental control over the programs undertaken by these local governments. The Gender Equality Section monitors not only the implementation status of the projects under its jurisdiction but also whether gender equality is being realized in projects under the jurisdiction of other departments. The department in charge of a project completes the evaluation of the status of the implementation of the project and the progress of the indicators in a unified format, and in the gender equality section, the results are compiled. In this way, the evaluation of local gender equality plans is used as a means through which to

---

[4] e-Gov Laws and Ordinances Search https://elaws.e-gov.go.jp/

[5] Basic Act for Gender Equal Society, Article 13 and 14 https://www.japaneselawtranslation.go.jp/ja/laws/view/2526/en

manage the progress of plans based on performance measurements, similar to administrative evaluations.

In the case of gender equality policies, the Cabinet Office, which has jurisdiction over the policy, has no direct policy instruments; thus, the implementation of the policy requires the cooperation of other ministries and local governments. The Cabinet Office controls these institutions indirectly through the use of planning and evaluations to promote the policy. In addition to gender equality policies, many other policy issues based on a basic act affect all central government ministries and agencies and local governments, and planning and evaluation are used as means of ex ante and ex post control, respectively. New basic acts are enacted as new policy issues emerge; therefore, it is expected that the workload of planning and evaluation by local governments will continue to increase.

5.3.3 Evaluation Based on Laws Other Than the Basic Act

In addition to the basic act, many other laws established by the central government require local governments to formulate plans. In many cases, local governments develop individual plans and evaluate them based on national laws. As new laws are enacted, local governments increase their workload to meet the demands of the central government, as the central ministries provide subsidies to local governments to implement their policies. Although the Japanese government promoted decentralization reforms in the late 1990s, local government activities are still controlled by laws, ordinances and public notices enacted by the central government. In Japan's legal system, after the central government enacts laws, the government generally enacts cabinet orders and ministerial orders that specifically state how the laws are to be enforced based on delegations from the law. Based on these laws and ordinances, ministries formulate public notices (e.g., guidelines) that describe their interpretation of laws and ordinances and their policies for administrative operations.

The central government stipulates the responsibilities and duties of local governments in terms of laws and ordinances. In addition, the central government issues detailed public notices to specify what local governments should work on. Since the Japanese government adopts a unitary system rather than a federal system, the cooperation of local governments is essential for the central government to implement its policies uniformly throughout the country. Although central government ministries may have regional bureaus and offices in prefectures, their roles and human resources are limited. Local governments in Japan are autonomous governing bodies in their respective regions, but at the same time, they serve as implementing bodies for central government policies. Since the decentralization reform, instead of the central government directly directing and ordering local governments, it has increasingly exercised indirect control over them through laws, ordinances and public notices.

In the text of the law, the central government has stipulated that local governments formulate their own plans. To date, such laws have been enacted in increasing numbers, and the workload for local governments in formulating plans and managing their progress continues to increase. According to a report by an expert panel established in the Cabinet Office, the number of articles in laws on planning was 514 as of the end of December 2021, an increase of approximately 1.5 times over the previous decade (Cabinet Office 2023a). In its Basic Policy on Economic and Fiscal Management and Reform, which lays out the basic direction of state management, the central government instructs ministries not to require local governments to develop new plans.[6]

While the central government leaves the planning process to local governments, it has established basic principles that indirectly suggest the planning framework to be developed by local governments. The central government's basic principles and local government plans correspond, and plans developed by local governments are required to substantially follow the central government's basic principles. These principles may require local governments to evaluate the progress of their plans. Evaluations are used by the central government to control local government planning. Since the implementation system for these evaluations is determined by individual laws, ordinances and basic principles, there is no overall picture of how much evaluation is being conducted.

The method through which the central government directs local governments based on plans was originally widely observed in regional development in Japan. For example, since the United States returned administrative authority over Okinawa to Japan in 1972, the central government has financed regional development in Okinawa through legislation and planning. While the central government was responsible for formulating the basic principle, Okinawa Prefecture was responsible for setting the basic plan. The content of the plan established by Okinawa Prefecture must conform to the central government's basic principles, and if the central government finds that the plan does not do so, then it can request that the governor of Okinawa Prefecture make changes to the plan.[7] The basic principles require evaluation of the plan's progress as well as the status of the use of subsidies granted to the prefecture by the central government.

The Promotion of Regional Revitalization Act enacted in 2014 requires the central government, prefectures, and municipalities to develop a "comprehensive strategy" that describes programs to address the declining birthrate and aging population.[8] Comprehensive strategies are required to set numerical targets and key performance indicators and to evaluate whether they are achieved. Although the formulation of a comprehensive strategy by local governments is voluntary, as of April 2023, 47 (100%) prefectures and 1739 (99.9%) municipalities, excluding two entities, had formulated a comprehensive strategy, and 808 (45.2%) local governments had for-

---

[6] Basic Policy on Economic and Fiscal Management and Reform 2022 https://www5.cao.go.jp/keizai-shimon/kaigi/cabinet/honebuto/2022/decision0607.html

[7] Act on Special Measures for the Promotion and Development of Okinawa, Paragraph 7 of Article 4 https://elaws.e-gov.go.jp/document?lawid=414AC0000000014

[8] Promotion of Regional Revitalization Act, Article 8, 9, and 10 https://elaws.e-gov.go.jp/document?lawid=426AC0000000136_20210901_503AC0000000036

mulated a comprehensive plan and a comprehensive strategy in an integrated manner (Cabinet Secretariat 2023).

Thus, evaluations began in the late 1990s as a means through which local governments could verify and improve their own activities, and today, it is used by local governments to report to the central government on the progress of their plans so that they can receive subsidies. The number of plans that the central government requires local governments to develop in accordance with laws and ordinances has been increasing, resulting in a proliferation of different plans. While this situation has the potential to bring diversity to the uniform evaluation practices of local governments, it also puts pressure on local governments' administrative resources and affects their sustainability.

5.4   Effects of Intergovernmental Evaluations

5.4.1   Characteristics of Internal Measurements

Local government evaluation activities are essential for improving policy quality and strengthening accountability. These activities are conducted to improve administrative activities and outcomes, increase the efficiency of administrative operations, and ensure accountability (MIC 2017). Local governments conduct administrative evaluations and evaluations of decentralized services (local incorporated administrative agencies' evaluations and designated administrators' evaluations) as internal measurements, which are discretionary for each local government. In contrast, in intergovernmental evaluations, the evaluation activities of local governments are legally and financially controlled by the central government since the evaluations are conducted as a form of external measurement between the two levels of government. The excessive burden of evaluation work in internal measurement and the tightening of central government control in external measurement affect the sustainability of local governments.

Since 2017, Mitsubishi UFJ Research and Consulting has conducted a nationwide questionnaire survey of local governments and published reports annually. In the 2023 report, 80.3% of local governments responded that the workload for administrative evaluation was burdensome, accounting for the highest percentage of all issues (Mitsubishi UFJ Research and Consulting 2023). The Japanese public sector, including the central government and agencies, shares the perception that evaluation work is overbearing. A characteristic of Japanese public sector evaluation is that it exhaustively evaluates all projects within an organization. Since the evaluation targets are not narrowed down or prioritized, there is a tendency to produce an enormous number of evaluation sheets. The human and time costs and workload involved in the evaluation burden the division in charge, leading to operational inefficiencies.

Most local governments use performance and financial information in a coordinated manner. The report shows that an increasing number of local governments are using the results of administrative evaluations in their budgeting process, with 37.9% of local governments reflecting evaluation results in their budgeting process in principle and 50.9% using the results as a reference for budgeting (Mitsubishi UFJ Research and Consulting 2023). The MIC has also developed financial and performance reporting guidelines for evaluations by local incorporated administrative agencies, encouraging evaluation results to increase fiscal efficiency.[9] In addition, designated administrators are also evaluated with a focus on savings and efficiency, and evaluation results can lead to negative incentives such as further reductions in outsourcing costs or sanctions such as the nonrenewal of the next contract. Vertical measurement for decentralized services reinforces financial dependence and reduces the quality and responsiveness of service delivery to citizens.

In intergovernmental evaluations, the central government uses guidelines and subsidies to control local governments. Increasingly, the central government requires local governments to develop plans to implement their policies nationwide and use evaluations to verify performance. Therefore, this section presents data on the extent to which local governments are required to conduct this type of evaluation.

5.4.2   The Overall Picture of Intergovernmental Evaluation

As mentioned in the previous section, a report published by the Cabinet Office revealed that the number of provisions in laws and ordinances requiring ministries and local governments to develop plans has been on the rise in recent years. Along with this report, the Cabinet Office has published survey data on such plans (Cabinet Office 2023b). These survey data, based on responses from each ministry, provide comprehensive information on the jurisdiction of the law, the name of the plan established by the local government, the name of the law, the provisions on which the plan is based, and the basic principles established by the central government. The report published by the Cabinet Office is based on these survey data. However, these survey data do not include information on the status of evaluation implementation, and whether the central government conducts evaluations in conjunction with its plans is not clear.

Therefore, the author collected the central government's basic principles listed in these survey data and conducted a qualitative study to determine whether the principles contained statements that called for evaluation. When the central government requires local governments to conduct evaluations, the instructions are generally

---

[9] Basic Guideline for Financial Reporting by Local Incorporated Administrative Agencies, August 31, 2022 https://www.soumu.go.jp/main_content/000833120.pdf;

Guideline for Business Reporting by Local Incorporated Administrative Agencies, August 31, 2022 https://www.soumu.go.jp/main_content/000833121.pdf

contained in the central government's basic principles or in guidelines that embody those principles. Therefore, plans for which only legislation exists but no central government basic principles have been formulated were excluded from the data. In addition, to eliminate duplication of data, the data were organized by law. As a result, 204 plans for which evaluation may be needed were identified.[10] A comprehensive survey of the central government's basic principles for these plans was conducted, and 111 plans for which evaluation was required were ultimately identified.

Figure 5.1 shows how many basic principles are under the jurisdiction of each ministry of the central government and what percentage of these principles require evaluation by local governments.[11] This chart shows the extent to which each

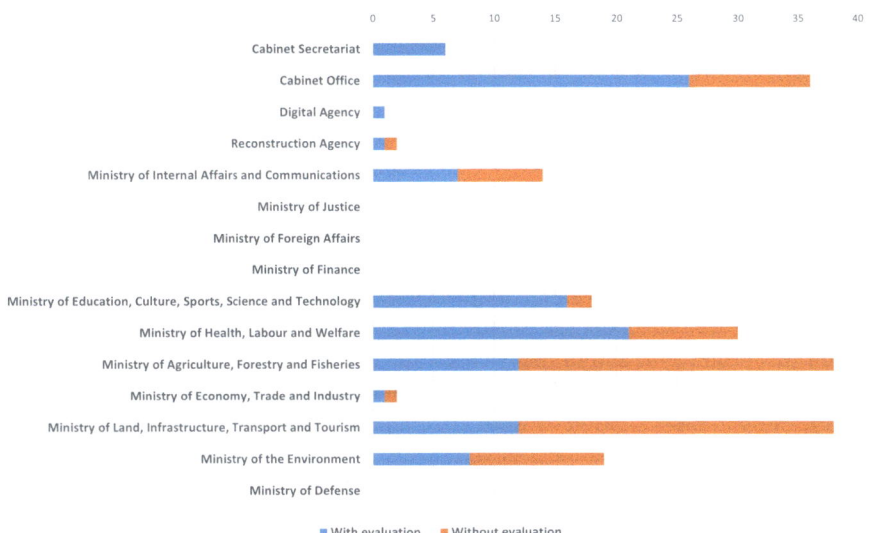

Fig. 5.1 Number of basic principles of each ministry. (Source: Author's elaboration based on the data of the Cabinet Office (2023b))

---

[10] In cases where the same law has multiple articles requiring prefectures and municipalities to formulate plans, survey data were compiled for each of these different articles. In other cases, a single law may require the formulation of several plans with different names in order to subdivide the content of the plan. In these cases, the data were tabulated as a single data set. In addition, several plans may be developed on the basis of the same law but different basic principles. In such cases, the data were tabulated as different data for each case because the purpose of formulating the plan was different. Therefore, the actual number of laws or national basic principles is slightly less than 204.

[11] These data include laws under the joint jurisdiction of several ministries, 50 of 204. For convenience, these laws are included in the ministry that has primary jurisdiction over the law. One case of data from the Headquarters for Promoting Development of Specified Complex Tourist Facilities Areas was integrated into the Cabinet Secretariat, two cases of data from the National Public Safety Commission (National Police Agency), and three cases of data from the Consumer Affairs Agency, and six cases of data from the Children and Families Agency were integrated into the Cabinet Office, but all of them required the implementation of evaluation. For the basic act, 21 data items were included, of which 18 basic principles required the implementation of evaluation.

ministry utilizes evaluation. Based on the results of qualitative research, the following below five characteristics of the central government's involvement with local
governments regarding evaluation activities were identified.

First, while the Ministry of Agriculture, Forestry and Fisheries and the Ministry
of Land, Infrastructure, Transport and Tourism have the most extensive requirements for local governments to develop plans, these ministries do not require local
governments to conduct evaluations to the same extent as other ministries. The
plans that these ministries require are often routine in terms of operation, such as
pest control, forest management, and national land surveys; thus, less uncertainty is
associated with policy implementation. This trend was also observed in other ministries and was often found in plans related to the implementation of operations such
as firefighting, food hygiene monitoring and guidance, and infrastructure management of water supply and utility poles. Although some of these basic principles
included evaluation languages, they were used mostly in a technical and scien-
tific sense.

Second, the Ministry of Health, Labour and Welfare (MHLW) and the Ministry
of Education, Culture, Sports, Science and Technology (MEXT) were the organizations that most commonly required local governments to implement evaluation.
Since the welfare and education sectors target people, the greater degree of uncertainty in policy implementation compared to that in public works and routine operations may be another reason for the frequent use of evaluations by these organizations.
In the field of welfare under the jurisdiction of MHLW, the implementation of evaluation was prominent, and in many cases, the method of implementation was also
stipulated in detail in the basic principles and guidelines. In the area of welfare
policy, while implementation by local governments is fundamental, the central government sets standards for local governments and public health centers to ensure
uniform service delivery throughout the country. The policies of MEXT are influenced by Japan's education policy. In Japan, local governments hold primary
responsibility for educational administration to reduce the direct involvement of the
central government in educational content. As a result, educational evaluation and
school evaluation are frequently used in education policy in Japan, and there are
many situations in which the central government is indirectly involved with local
governments through evaluation. Despite decentralization reforms, the central government remains heavily involved in education policy.

Third, many of the basic principles formulated by the Cabinet Office and Cabinet
Secretariat required local governments to conduct evaluations. The Cabinet Office
and Cabinet Secretariat have jurisdiction over cross-sectoral policies that span multiple ministries and agencies, such as gender equality policies, science and technology policies, and regional policies. Cooperation from other ministries and local
governments is essential for implementing these policies, and evaluation is used to
manage policy progress. In some cases, the effectiveness of policy measures is
tested. Examples include the special economic zone system, which has been dereg-
ulated in certain areas, or subsidies allocated to specific local governments. However,
evaluations tend not to be conducted in the field of disaster management because

tsunami evacuation plans and disaster business plans are defined as emergency operations and are not suitable for postevent verification.

Fourth, the MIC and the Ministry of the Environment (MOE) have formulated many basic principles, approximately half of which require evaluation. In the case of the MIC, evaluation is used in programs related to regional development targeting specific regions (e.g., peninsular regions and regions with heavy snowfall) and region-related programs such as land use and vacant house measures. In the case of the MOE, evaluation tends to be used in environmental fields such as climate change and biodiversity, which are international issues and need to be addressed nationwide, as well as in operations exclusively carried out by local governments, such as waste disposal. Conversely, evaluation is not used for projects that are less uncertain, such as environmentally friendly procurement promotion by local governments, or for purely technical performance standards or environmental standards, such as industrial waste treatment facilities or water quality conservation.

Fifth, ministries with jurisdiction over legal and budgetary systems, such as the Ministry of Justice and the Ministry of Finance, and ministries with jurisdiction over foreign affairs and security—which are the exclusive responsibility of the central government—such as the Ministry of Foreign Affairs and the Ministry of Defense, have few opportunities to ask local governments to implement their policies. In addition, ministries with regional bureaus and offices in each of Japan's prefectures have little incentive to seek evaluation from local governments when they can implement their policies through those agencies. For example, the Prefectural Human Resource Development Plans and Regional Employment Development Plans under the jurisdiction of MHLW do not require local governments to conduct evaluations. The reason for this is that unlike in the welfare sector, policies in the labor and employment sectors can be implemented through regional bureaus and offices established in each prefecture.

5.4.3 Factors of Central Government Involvement

As more plans are developed by local governments based on national legislation, local governments are also required to conduct evaluations. Since these evaluations must be carried out by local governments rather than by the central government, the increased burden of evaluation work puts pressure on local government resources. Two major factors have influenced the central government to require local governments to develop their own plans.

The first factor is decentralization; following the decentralization reforms of the late 1990s, the relationship between the central government and local governments was revised to a horizontal rather than a traditional vertical relationship. Many of the affairs that had been delegated by the central government were then reorganized as the affairs of local governments. Instead of the central government implementing policies through local governments, it began to work indirectly with local governments through planning. Since the 2000s, the central government has engaged local governments by evaluating subsidies instead of giving them more discretion in the use of funds and the selection of projects. Subsidies are often granted on the basis of laws and basic principles, and local governments are required to formulate plans and conduct evaluations of their plans and projects as a prerequisite for receiving subsidies.

The second is the increase in administrative demand and diversification of needs. Japan's social structure and global environment are rapidly changing, as evidenced by the decline and aging of the population, the decline of local communities, and environmental issues such as climate change. In addition, needs for public administration are becoming more diverse in areas such as social welfare and school education. There are also an increasing number of policy areas in which cross-sectoral efforts by multiple ministries and local governments are essential, such as gender equality policy, children's policy, immigration policy, and the promotion of e-government. While planning and evaluation are effective tools for implementing policies outside the organizational framework of administrative agencies, they also increase the administrative burdens on local governments, which are responsible for policy implementation. However, the central government's requirement that local governments formulate plans and conduct evaluations puts pressure on the limited amount of human resources.

Since individual plans need to be developed separately from comprehensive plans, local governments can conduct other evaluations in addition to administrative evaluations, which results in the duplication of evaluation activities and the workload of local governments. The comprehensive plans traditionally developed by local governments have been used as a means to comprehensively manage administrative affairs that are carried out through a division of labor. However, as the central government requires local governments to formulate plans based on the law, the number of plans to be managed by local governments has increased. In some cases, local governments have positioned these plans as sectoral plans under the comprehensive plan, but there is concern that as a result, the comprehensive plan may become a mere skeleton.

5.5   Conclusions and Prospects

This chapter focuses on the classification of the evaluation of local governments in Japan. It provides a detailed account of the historical background and systems associated with each type of evaluation, with particular emphasis on intergovernmental evaluations to elucidate their current state. The qualitative analysis reveals that the central government is increasingly influencing local governments' evaluation activities by mandating the formulation and evaluation of plans for implementing national policies based on basic principles. This trend is especially pronounced in certain ministries and is shaped by the decentralization reforms of the late 1990s, along with the recent rise in administrative demands and the diversification of needs. In Japan, evaluation activities initially began as local government initiatives, but the central government involvement has gradually increased, affecting local evaluations through measures such as agencification, privatization, and the implementation of government plans. However, the lack of overall coordination among ministries has led to an increased burden on local governments and has undermined their autonomy.

In light of these considerations, it is crucial to develop a revised evaluation process between local governments and the central government. Currently, local government evaluation has become an exhaustive measurement activity covering all projects, reducing the utility of evaluation results. Therefore, it is necessary to clarify the issues facing local governments and then construct an evaluation system that addresses these issues. In addition, for policy issues that require nationwide efforts, such as climate change and gender equality policies, the central government needs to establish an integrated indicator system for systematic comparison and monitoring among local governments. To realize sustainable government and society, the bottom-up evaluation system for local-level issues and the top-down evaluation system for national-level issues should be redesigned, and optimization between the two processes should be achieved by eliminating unnecessary evaluation activities and reviewing overlapping activities.

References

Ateh MY, Berman E, Prasojo E (2020) Intergovernmental strategies advancing performance management use. Public Perform Manag Rev 43(5):993–1024. https://doi.org/10.1080/1530957 6.2020.1736588

Behn RD (2003) Why measure performance? Different purposes require different measures. Public Adm Rev 63(5):586–606. https://doi.org/10.1111/1540-6210.00322

Brusca I, Montesinos V (2016) Implementing performance reporting in local government: a cross-countries comparison. Public Perform Manag Rev 39(3):506–534. https://doi.org/10.108 0/15309576.2015.1137768

Cabinet Office (2022) Status of formation of a gender-equal society or promotion of programs related to women in local governments (FY2022) [Chiho kokyo dantai ni okeru danjo kyodo sankaku shakai no keisei mataha josei ni kansuru shisaku no suishin jokyo (Reiwa 4 nendo)] (in Japanese). https://www.gender.go.jp/research/kenkyu/suishinjokyo/2022/report.html

Cabinet Office (2023a) Toward an efficient and effective planning administration [Koritsu teki koka teki na keikaku gyosei ni mukete] (in Japanese). https://www.cao.go.jp/bunken-suishin/ keikaku/gyouseikeikaku.pdf

Cabinet Office (2023b) Survey table 1: duration and basis of the central government's basic principles for local government planning (as of April 1, 2023) [Chosa hyo 1: Chiho kokyo dantai no keikaku to ni kakaru kuni no kihon hoshin to no kikan oyobi sono konkyo ni tsuite (Reiwa 5 nen 4 gatsu 1 nichi jiten)] (in Japanese). https://www.cao.go.jp/bunken-suishin/keikaku/ chousahyou1.xlsx

Cabinet Secretariat (2023) Results of survey on formulation of local comprehensive strategies [Chiho ban sogo senryaku no sakutei jokyo to ni kansuru chosa kekka] (in Japanese). https:// www.chisou.go.jp/sousei/about/chihouban/pdf/sakuteijoukyou231020.pdf

Doughty M, Baehler KJ (2020) "Hostages to compliance": towards a reasonableness test for administrative burdens. Perspect Public Manage Gov 3(4):273–287. https://doi.org/10.1093/ ppmgov/gvaa010

Henderson A, Jeffery C, Wincott D, Wyn Jones R (2013) Reflections on the 'devolution paradox': a comparative examination of multilevel citizenship. Reg Stud 47(3):303–322. https://doi.org/1 0.1080/00343404.2013.768764

Kikuchi M (2017) Performance management reforms in Japan. In: Berman EM, Moon MJ, Choi H (eds) Public administration in East Asia: mainland China, Japan, South Korea, and Taiwan. Routledge, New York. https://doi.org/10.4324/9781315089317

Koike O, Hori M, Kabashima H (2007) The Japanese government reform of 2001 and policy evaluation system: efforts, results and limitations. Ritsumeikan Law Rev 24:1–12

Kuhlmann S (2010) Performance measurement in European local governments: a comparative analysis of reform experiences in Great Britain, France, Sweden and Germany. Int Rev Adm Sci 76(2):331–345. https://doi.org/10.1177/0020852310372050

MIC (2017) Status of administrative evaluation efforts in local government (as of October 1, 2016) [Chiho kokyo dantai ni okeru gyosei hyoka no torikumi jokyo (Heisei 28 nen 10 gatsu 1 nichi genzai)] (in Japanese). https://www.soumu.go.jp/iken/02gyosei04_04000062.html

MIC (2022) Results of a survey on the introduction of a designated administrator system for public facilities [Oyake no shisetsu no shitei kanrisha seido no donyu jokyo to ni kansuru chosa kekka no gaiyo] (in Japanese). https://www.soumu.go.jp/main_content/000804851.pdf

MIC (2023) Status of establishment of local incorporated administrative agencies (as of April 1, 2023) [Chiho dokuritsu gyosei hojin no setsuritsu jokyo (Reiwa 5 nen 4 gatsu 1 nichi genzai)] (in Japanese). https://www.soumu.go.jp/main_content/000879644.xlsx

MIC (2024) Status of administrative evaluation efforts in local government (as of April 1, 2023) [Chiho kokyo dantai ni okeru gyosei hyoka no torikumi jokyo (Reiwa 5 nen 4 gatsu 1 nichi genzai)] (in Japanese). https://www.soumu.go.jp/main_content/000939449.xlsx

Mitsubishi UFJ Research and Consulting (2023) Report on the survey on local government management reform in FY2022 [Reiwa 4 nendo jichitai keiei kaikaku ni kansuru jittai chosa hokoku] (in Japanese). https://www.murc.jp/wp-content/uploads/2023/07/seiken_230728_01.pdf

Mizell L (2008) Promoting performance: using indicators to enhance the effectiveness of sub-central spending. OECD Publishing, Paris. https://doi.org/10.1787/5k97b11g190r-en

Moynihan D, Herd P, Harvey H (2015) Administrative burden: learning, psychological, and compliance costs in citizen-state interactions. J Public Adm Res Theory 25(1):43–69. https://doi.org/10.1093/jopart/muu009

Nishikawa A (2015) Discussion on basic acts' purposes and issues [Kihon ho no igi to kadai]. The Reference 65(2):43–54. (in Japanese)

OECD (2009) Governing regional development policy: the use of performance indicators. OECD Publishing, Paris. https://doi.org/10.1787/9789264056299-en

Oh Y (2023) Exploring the dysfunctional consequences of performance evaluation systems: how does 'evaluation overload' affect organizational performance? Public Manag Rev 1–20:2260–2279. https://doi.org/10.1080/14719037.2023.2189900

Poister TH, Streib G (1999) Performance measurement in municipal government: assessing the state of the practice. Public Adm Rev 59(4):325–335. https://doi.org/10.2307/3110115

Shiono H (2008) On "basic acts" [Kihon ho ni tsuite]. Trans Jpn Acad 63(1):1–33. (in Japanese). https://doi.org/10.2183/tja.63.1_1

Umeda J (2000) Experiences in the introduction of policy evaluation: Systematic resistance within the Mie prefectural government to the introduction of the project performance evaluation system [Seisaku hyoka donyu no taiken: Jimu jigyo hyoka shisutemu no donyu ni taisuru Mie kencho nai no soshiki teki teiko]. Public Policy, 2000, 2000-1-009 (in Japanese). https://doi.org/10.32202/ppsaj.2000.0_2000-1-009

Weissert CS, Jones DB (2015) Devolution paradox and the US South. Reg Federal Stud 25(3):259–276. https://doi.org/10.1080/13597566.2015.1054281

Yamamoto K (2008) Has agencification succeeded in public sector reform? Realities and rhetoric in the case of Japan. Asian J Polit Sci 16(1):24–40. https://doi.org/10.1080/02185370801962317

Keita Hashimoto is an Associate Professor in the Faculty of Law, Kobe Gakuin University. His research focuses on organizational management and accountability systems in the public sector, particularly in the areas of strategic planning, public budgeting, policy and program evaluation, and performance management.

Chapter 6
Local Government and Crisis Management in Japan

Masao Kikuchi

Abstract This chapter examines how Japanese local governments manage crises and disasters with limited resources. Local governments in Japan are primarily responsible for disaster management and resource mobilization. However, the decentralized approach faces significant challenges due to depopulation, an aging society, and the COVID-19 pandemic. The chapter addresses the following questions: How should the scarcity and uneven distribution of resources be managed? How do local governments collaborate with other local governments and sectors in crisis management? To answer these questions in line with the concept of collaborative management, the chapter analyzes the institutional and collaborative aspects of crisis management through qualitative analysis using multiple case studies. The analysis reveals that Japanese local governments extensively use inter-municipal cooperation mechanisms, such as agreements, fire districts, and nationwide rescue teams, to address resource limitations. They also seek collaboration with other local entities, including private companies, community groups, and civic sectors. In light of COVID-19 and demographic shifts, there is an increasing expectation for enhanced vertical collaboration among local governments and with the central government. Effective and sustainable crisis management by local governments necessitates both horizontal cooperation with the private and civic sectors and vertical cooperation with the central government to ensure the effectiveness of their efforts.

Keywords Inter-municipal cooperation · Crisis management · Collaborative management · Public health response · COVID-19

M. Kikuchi (✉)
Department of Public Management, Meiji University, Tokyo, Japan
e-mail: kms@meiji.ac.jp

© The Author(s), under exclusive license to Springer Nature Switzerland AG 2024
Y. Noda (ed.), *Local Governance in Japan*, Local and Urban Governance,
https://doi.org/10.1007/978-3-031-77322-8_6

6.1   Introduction

Japan faces a high risk of natural disasters, including earthquakes, typhoons, and heavy snowfall. Situated in the Pacific Ring of Fire, Japan covers just 0.25% of the Earth's total land area, yet hosts approximately 10% of the world's active volcanoes (Cabinet Office 2021). With frequent seismic and volcanic activities in the region, Japan experiences a notable number of earthquakes and ongoing volcanic activity. Additionally, due to its geographical and meteorological conditions, the country is prone to regular natural hazards such as typhoons, heavy rainfall, and substantial snowfall.

The foundational institutional structure and policy framework for disaster management were established in 1961 through the implementation of the Disaster Countermeasures Basic Act. This act outlines a comprehensive and strategic system for managing disasters. The enactment of this act followed the significant devastation caused by the Ise-wan Typhoon in 1959, which resulted in extraordinarily high surges and left some of the worst damage in Japan's history, leading to more than 5000 casualties (Cabinet Office 2021). The disaster management system has been further reinforced based on the lessons and insights gained from major disasters like the Great Hanshin-Awaji Earthquake in 1995, and the Great East Japan Earthquake in 2011. The Act specifies the roles and responsibilities of both national and local governments and identifies relevant stakeholders in the public and private sectors for effective disaster management throughout all phases of a disaster (OECD 2009).

While immediate responses through top-down policy implementation are crucial in crisis management, there is also an emphasis on decentralized resource allocation to address specific and unevenly distributed local disaster response needs (Liu et al. 2021; Nakamura and Kikuchi 2011). Due to Japan's extended north-south geography and archipelago structure, the natural environment, disaster risks, and population density, key factors in crisis management, vary significantly among communities. As a result, beyond national responsibilities like defense, the approach to crisis management is not uniformly directed by the central government. Instead, municipalities play a pivotal role, tailoring their crisis management strategies to the unique regional circumstances of each area (Kikuchi 2020).

In Japan, when an actual disaster occurs, prefectures and municipalities are responsible for implementing necessary emergency measures. Their role is to safeguard the lives, well-being, and property of citizens, along with ensuring the overall safety of the local community. Specifically, municipalities, serving as the fundamental local government, are mandated to establish evacuation orders, define hazard areas, and organize teams for fire and flood prevention (Cabinet Office 2021; OECD 2009). The Disaster Countermeasures Basic Act designates municipalities as the unequivocal leaders in disaster prevention, with prefectures and the central government serving as backup and support organizations in Japan. Municipalities bear the primary responsibility for handling disasters and mobilizing firefighting organizations to respond effectively. Also, Japanese local governments have been based on a full-set self-sufficiency orientation by themselves. However, the decentralized nature of crisis management in local government faced significant challenges amidst depopulation, as well as the COVID-19 pandemic and the enforcement of public health measures (Moon et al. 2021). In a crisis management, collaboration is one of the main research agendas as it is key for the effective crisis management (Waugh and Streib 2006). Based on this recognition, this chapter aims to illustrate the distinctive aspects of crisis management in local government in Japan, especially examining from the collaborative management perspective (Agranoff and McGuire 2003). The concept of collaborative management is similar to Institutional Collective Action (ICA), which attempts to solve problems by building relationships among actors and focuses on service implementation networks among actors such as local governments (Feiock 2013). In this context, collaborative management can be considered a concept included in ICA.

The primary objective is to comprehend how Japanese local governments have managed crises and disasters with limited resources, particularly in the context of a super-aging society and depopulation situations. In essence, this chapter seeks to answer the following questions: What are the unique features of crisis management in local government in Japan? How should the scarcity and uneven distribution of resources be addressed? How do local governments collaborate with other local governments and other sectors in managing crises? This chapter aims to analyze the institutional and collaborative features of crisis management in local government in Japan to provide insights into these questions. Depending on the necessary resources, local governments in Japan utilize both vertical and horizontal collaborative management to address crises. Therefore, in line with the concept of collaborative management, qualitative analysis will be conducted based on multiple case studies. From this purpose, this chapter is divided into four folds. The following section illustrates the intuitional arrangement of crisis management in Japan, with special attention to inter-municipal cooperation. The third section delineates the collaborative management of local government with the community and civic sectors in crisis management. The fourth section focuses on the crisis management of local government in dealing with the COVID-19, and it is followed by the conclusions.

6.2 Crisis Management Capacity in Local Government in Japan

6.2.1 Institutional Arrangement of Crisis Management in Japan

As safeguarding citizens' lives and property is the government's top priority, the disaster management system, outlined in the Act, adopts a top-down governance style in its institutional arrangements within the central government (OECD 2009). The Central Disaster Management Council, chaired by the prime minister, oversees comprehensive disaster countermeasures and formulates the Basic Disaster

Management Plan and Earthquake Plan. It is administered by the Minister of State for Disaster Management and the Cabinet Office's disaster management section, that was established in 2001 with the central government reform (Cabinet Office 2021).

The Basic Disaster Management Plan broadly categorizes disasters into two types: (A) Natural Disasters (Earthquake, Storms and Floods, Volcano Disaster, Snow Disaster), and (B) Accident Disasters (Maritime Disaster, Aviation Disaster, Railroad Disaster, Road Disaster, Nuclear Disaster, Hazardous Materials Disaster, Large-Scale Fire, Forest Fire). The plan outlines tangible countermeasures for all these disasters, involving stakeholders like national ministries, local governments, public corporations, and other entities, across different phases: prevention and preparedness, emergency response, recovery, and rehabilitation. Relevant ministries with disaster management responsibilities include the National Police Agency, Fire and Disaster Management Agency, Ministry of Land, Infrastructure, Transport, and Tourism, Geographical Survey Institute, Meteorological Agency, Ministry of Education, Culture, Sports, Science, and Technology, Ministry of Health, Labour and Welfare, and Ministry of Defense. Notably, the Fire and Disaster Management Agency is a primary agency for implementing emergency measures to protect citizens' lives and property.

As one of the primary agencies in implementing emergency measures at the central level, the mission and role of the Fire and Disaster Management Agency is basically coordinating fire service administration and providing the headquarters for disaster response when a large-scale disaster occurs. The agency only has 174 employees, including the fire and disaster management college, as of April 2023. The agency maintains and drafts necessary laws and regulations for fire and disaster management. During natural disasters that cannot be overcome by local firefighting forces, such as large-scale earthquakes and typhoons, the disaster countermeasures headquarters headed by the commissioner of the Fire and Disaster Management Agency are promptly established in the agency to implement the disaster response through information collection and operation of emergency fire response teams coordinated by the commissioner. In response to the Great East Japan Earthquake, the first call out order to the emergency fire response teams by the Commissioner for Fire was at 15: 40 on March 11, 2011, which was 54 min after the earthquake occurred.

If a disaster actually occurs, prefectures and municipalities are called upon to implement the necessary emergency measures to protect the lives and property of citizens, as well as to ensure the safety of the community they live. In particular, as the fundamental local public body, municipalities are required to establish evacuation orders and hazard areas, and to take measures for dispatching teams for fire and flood prevention (OECD 2009). In Japan, municipalities are unambiguously in charge of disaster management, while prefectures and the central government are positioned as backup and support organizations. Municipalities have the primary obligation to deal with disasters and provide firefighting organizations to perform duties (Kikuchi 2020).

6.2.2   Professional Fire Service and Fire Corps in Local Government

As the Municipalities have the primary obligation to deal with disasters, they provide firefighting organizations to perform appropriate duties. With very few exceptions such as island municipalities, each municipality provides two types of firefighting organizations: full-time professional firefighting organizations, and part-time firefighting organizations (Fire Corps). In addition to the full-time professional firefighting organizations parti-time firefighting organizations (Fire Corps) in in each municipality, there are also community based voluntary disaster prevention organizations set up mainly at the neighborhood/resident association level, functioning as fully voluntary mutual aid organizations. In total, three organizations are involved in crisis management in local government. In many cases, within a municipality, there exists one full-time professional firefighting organizations, one part-time firefighting organizations (Fire Corps), and multiple community based voluntary disaster prevention organizations. During actual disaster response, these three organizations engage in collaborative management. Section 6.4.1 will provide detailed coverage of the community based voluntary disaster prevention organizations.

Full-time firefighting organizations are fire department headquarters and fire stations established by municipalities where full-time staffs are employed. As of fiscal year 2022, there are 167,510 full time officials working in 1714 fire stations under 723 fire departments in each jurisdiction (Fire and Disaster Management Agency 2022b). The number of full-time officials includes more than 6100 female officials as well.

In terms of the capacity for crisis management, the number of full-time officials has been on a gradual increase in the last twenty years, following a series of crisis events, including the Great East Japan Earthquake in 2011 (Fig. 6.1). However, during the same period, the number of local government employees in all categories decreased by about 10% due to depopulation and fewer children, as the major local government employee category is public school teachers.

In contrast to the gradual increase of full-time firefighting officials, the number of volunteer (part-time) fire corps, which has a much longer history originating in the eighteenth century, has been declining in recent years. As of April 2023, there are 763,000 volunteer firefighters in Japan, which is a decrease of over 20,000 compared to the previous year, reflecting depopulation and an aging society in each community (Fire and Disaster Management Agency 2022b). Based on the mentality of "protecting our own land by ourselves," volunteer firefighters have other livelihoods while being part-time local public employees with the authority and responsibility to carry out firefighting activities. In tradition, the majority of part-time fire fighters making up the fire corps have been business or shop owners in each community. As the number of employees who commute to their workplace outside of their home community has been on the increase, traditional community-based participation in fire corps has decreased over a time. All municipalities in Japan have

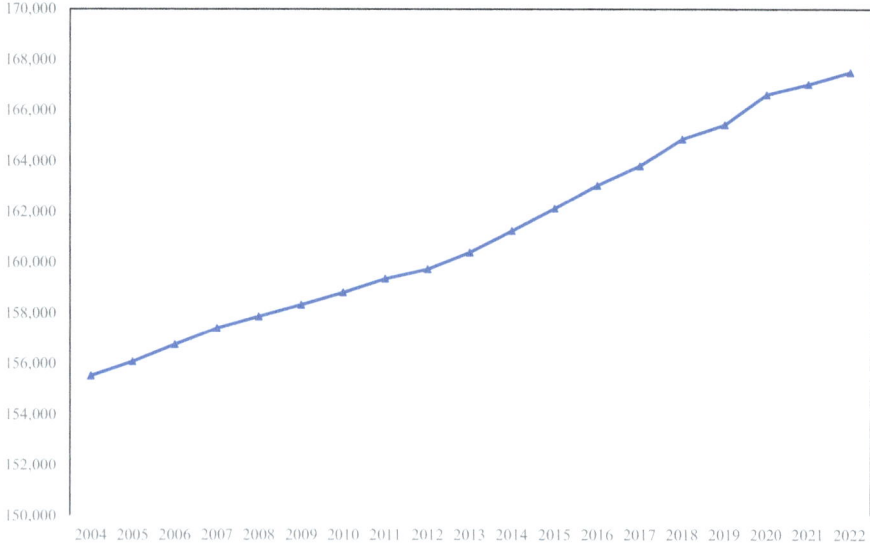

Fig. 6.1 Number of full-time firefighting and ambulance staff between 2004 and 2022. (Source: Author's elaboration based on Fire and Disaster Management Agency (2022a))

own volunteer fire corps, and the number is 2196 as of April 2022. The number of municipalities in Japan is 1718 as of 2022, and the larger number of volunteer fire corps than the number of municipalities is because even after the municipality is merged with neighbors, some volunteer fire corps keep their activity based on the former municipality jurisdiction, independent from the newly merged municipality.

Historically, professional firefighting organizations with full time staff originated, mainly in large cities, under the police organization before the World War II period. In many places, firefighting activities at disaster scenes were primarily carried out by the volunteer (part-time) fire corps. Even after the war period, the number of volunteer fire corps exceeded that of fulltime firefighting staff, relying on these volunteer fire corps for disaster management with limited resources. This was evident in the response to the Great East Japan Earthquake in 2011, where the number of volunteer firefighters who sacrificed their lives was nearly ten times higher than that of fulltime fighting staff, highlighting the reliance on volunteer fire corps for disaster response (Fire and Disaster Management Agency 2011).

6.3   Inter-Municipal Cooperation

6.3.1   Inter-Municipal Cooperation Agreement

While natural disasters can occur anywhere globally, the extent of their impacts varies based on the government's capacity to manage such crises. Additionally, peripheral regions of a nation or local government may experience more frequent occurrences of natural disasters than central areas, given that geographical features like high mountains, rivers, and oceans often delineate jurisdictional boundaries. As a result, there are inherent constraints on the ability of individual local governments to promptly respond to large-scale disasters. In the case of a small-sized local government, dealing with a large-scale disaster becomes more challenging. Identifying the extent of damage and offering necessary assistance to the affected area becomes more difficult, especially when the entire community, including government officials, is damaged. Inter-municipal cooperation efforts between municipalities, serving as an interdependence mechanism for sharing resources among governments, play a crucial role in a disaster response (Aoki 2015; Hulst and van Montfort 2007). Local governments in Japan have been making inter-municipal cooperation agreements in crisis management as a horizontal style of collaborative management. Especially after the Great Hanshin-Awaji Earthquakes in 1995 and the Mid-Niigata Prefecture Earthquake in 2004, the number of agreements has been on the increase. Similarly, after the Great East Japan Earthquake in 2011, local governments made agreements with geographically disconnected local governments to prepare for large-scale natural disasters (Table 6.1).

Effective inter-municipal cooperation is imperative for dealing with large scale disasters that extend beyond borders. Typical agreement elements are: (1) Providing food, water and other necessities of life, and necessary materials and equipment. A prime example is to send stockpiled food, water, blankets and other necessary goods, or to send a water tank truck to the affected suffered area. (2) Providing materials and equipment for the rescue of the victims, medical supplies, materials and equipment for control of epidemics, materials and equipment for emergency rehabilitation of facilities, such as sending emergency kits, public nurse teams,

Table 6.1 Number of municipalities with inter-municipal cooperation agreements in crisis management

2010	1571 (89.8%)
2011	1476 (91.2%)
2012	1645 (94.4%)
2013	1650 (94.7%)
2014	1697 (97.4%)
2015	1705 (97.9%)
2016	1699 (97.6%)
2017	1698 (97.5%)
2018	1701 (97.7%)
2019	1708 (98.1%)
2020	1708 (98.1%)
2021	1704 (97.9%)
2022	1692 (97.2%)

Notes: Proportion of Municipalities with agreements in parentheses. The number excludes the inter-municipal cooperation agreements that cross prefectural boundaries
Source: Author's elaboration based on Fire and Disaster Management Agency (2022a)

septic tank trucks and other support of this nature. (3) Providing vehicles for rescue activities, such as fire trucks and ambulances. (4) Providing necessary staff to assist local government activities. (5) Coordinating volunteers. (6) Taking care of children and the seniors from the affected area. (7) Providing temporary housing for victims.

Once a local government in a cooperation agreement receives a request from another affected local government, the agreement is activated. If the affected local government is unable to make requests due to communication interception, the other local governments involved can voluntarily send materials and equipment without formal requests. While the general principle is that the receiving local government covers the cost of received goods, materials, and equipment, sending local governments often, especially if the recipient is small, bear either the full or partial cost.

More recently, as part of the efforts of inter-municipal cooperation in crisis management, an increasing number of local governments are formulating the "Receiving Assistance Plan." This plan, designed for disaster-affected local governments to solicit support from others, involves a strategic framework outlining the process and measures for seeking assistance. It delineates the specific needs and challenges faced by the affected community, along with the types of aid required. Serving as a guide for coordinating assistance from assisting local governments and organizations, the plan often incorporates provisions for personnel deployment, resource sharing, and collaborative efforts to effectively address the aftermath of the disaster. The ultimate objective is to establish a coordinated and efficient system that facilitates the timely and appropriate provision of support from other local governments during crises. As of April 2022, 97.9% of prefectures and 67.3% of municipalities had already developed the receiving assistance plan (Fire and Disaster Management Agency 2022a).

Moreover, in response to the lessons learned from the 2008 Sichuan Earthquake in China, what is referred to as counterpart assistance, or paired assistance among local governments based on mutual agreement, has become prevalent (Tang 2020). In many cases, such agreements are rooted in sister city relations among local governments located remotely from each other within Japan.

6.3.2 Fire District and Contract Out

In the absence of establishing any institutional arrangement, inter-municipal cooperation agreements rely solely on mutual agreement, resulting in a relatively loose and informal form of cooperation among municipalities (Noda 2023). Compared to this, the cooperation with the institutional development or with the legal contract is "hard" or formal cooperation and that is the Fire District and contract out of fire service. In Japan, there are two types of inter-municipal cooperation institutional arrangement. One is the partial service associations, and the other is broad service associations (Hijino 2021; Kimura 2016). Both are with the corporate status as a special local government, which is closer to the special district government in the U.S. Of the 1690 municipalities with the full-time professional fire service in 2022, only 434 operate own independent fire headquarters, representing about 26%. The remaining approximately 74% of municipalities (1256 municipalities) either engage in inter-municipal cooperation through partial service associations or broad service associations, or outsource their fire service operations to the other neighboring municipalities (Fire and Disaster Management Agency 2022b). Especially among towns or villages, municipalities with smaller populations and capacities, the utilization of fire districts (such as partial service associations or broad service associations) or outsourcing is more common. Among 736 towns, only 49 towns (6.7%) have their own independent fire headquarters, while the remaining 687 towns (93.3%) rely on fire districts or outsourcing. Similarly, among 161 villages, only 1 village (0.62%) has its own independent fire headquarters, with the remaining 160 villages (99.38%) using fire districts or outsourcing.

More recently, there has been a noticeable increase in the adoption of joint operation models for fire command centers, where multiple municipalities collaborate to operate a single command center while member municipalities keep own fire station operation. This approach aims to enhance resource efficiency and promote information sharing, ultimately improving responsiveness during emergencies and crisis.

6.3.3 Emergency Response Teams: Nationwide and Top-Down Approach

Apart from municipal cooperation, which facilitates mutual support among local government services, Japan established nationwide emergency response teams of firefighting organizations in 1995 after learning from the Great Hanshin-Awaji Earthquake. These teams enable efficient and rapid survivor rescue operations during large-scale disasters like earthquakes. In such events, each fire department nationwide is called upon by the commissioner of the Fire and Disaster Management Agency to converge on the disaster area and provide relief operations. Unlike other forms of inter-municipal cooperation such as agreements, fire districts, or contracting out, this scheme represents a top-down collaborative management approach from the national government and is therefore a nationwide system, although each emergency response team comprises the fire headquarters of each local government (Caruson and MacManus 2012). Since 1995, there have been 33 cases of forming emergency response teams to address various disasters, including the 2011 Great East Japan Earthquake, which was the largest mobilization order (Fire and Disaster Management Agency 2022b).

Immediately after the 2011 earthquake struck, emergency response teams from the remaining 44 prefectures were instructed to deploy to the directly affected areas: Iwate, Miyagi, and Fukushima. Over a span of 88 days, from March 11 to June 6, 2011, a total of 30,684 personnel were dispatched, equivalent to about one in every five or six firefighters nationwide. The rescue efforts resulted in the saving of 5064 individuals, including those rescued in collaboration with local fire departments (Fire and Disaster Management Agency 2013).

6.4   Collaboration with Community and Civic Sector

There are certain limits to the ability of government acting alone to have effective disaster management. Disaster management is a complex process, and there needs to be collaborative management with non-governmental actors in civil society. In the Japanese context, local governments, which are the primary agent for managing disasters, are under severe financial challenge due to socio-economic change in the communities. In order to sustain effective disaster management, it is crucial to establish collaborative relations with private and civil society actors.

6.4.1   Community Based Voluntary Disaster Prevention Organizations

In contrast with the declining number of fire corps, there are a number of Voluntary Disaster Prevention Organizations that are organized based on community and various social groups including schools, companies, neighborhood associations and others. Their numbers have been steadily increasing (Fig. 6.2). As of 2021, its number is 169,804, and it covers about 84.4% of whole households (Fire and Disaster Management Agency 2022a).

Unlike fire corps, which consist of part-time civil servants and are integrated into firefighting organizations operating under local fire department authority, these groups are purely private voluntary organizations founded on the principles of

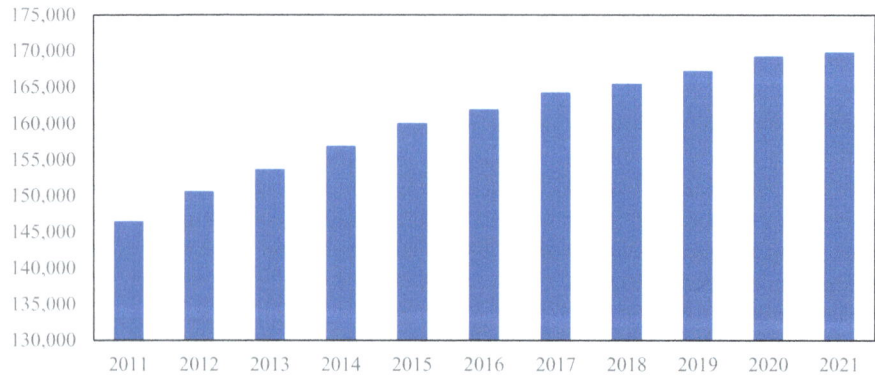

Fig. 6.2 Number of voluntary disaster prevention organizations between 2011 and 2021. (Source: Author's elaboration based on Fire and Disaster Management Agency (2022a))

mutual aid and community support, operating independently of government control. These organizations are typically established and run at the neighborhood or resident association level, serving as grassroots initiatives to empower communities, and the scope of activities and the size of the communities are much smaller than those of municipalities where fire crops are located.

Activities of these voluntary disaster prevention organizations are critical for providing self-help and co-help (mutual assistance) when the government organizations are struggling with rescue operations especially in a large-scale disaster (Bajek et al. 2008). During the 1995 Great Hanshin-Awaji Earthquake, about 98% of people who were trapped or buried managed to free themselves or were helped by family, neighbors, or friends (Fire and Disaster Management Agency 2022b). This highlights the importance of self-help and assistance from others in the immediate aftermath of a disaster. The basis of voluntary disaster prevention organizations extends beyond neighborhood/resident associations to include schools and companies, creating diversified and layered structures within communities. Both national and local governments are promoting organizations, providing financial assistance for operational costs, and aiding in the acquisition of resources and equipment.

6.4.2 Collaborating with Social and Civic Sectors

In the event of a natural disaster, governments depend on other key stakeholders in the conduct of rescue and crisis management activities. Especially in the case of small local governments, due to financial difficulties and low capacity, the government collaborates with companies, local resident groups, professional groups, and others. In response to the Great East Japan Earthquake, the Japan Medical Association, which is a professional organization of medical doctors in Japan, sent more than 6000 medical staff to the affected area to support medical activities. The Japanese Red Cross sent about 900 emergency rescue units as well. In addition, a total of 2200 pharmacists were dispatched under the coordination of the Japan Pharmaceutical Association coordination (Ministry of Health Labour and Welfare 2011). As these prime cases in the Great East Japan Earthquake imply, collaboration with private groups is key to effective rescue activities in a crisis (Okada 2022; Waugh and Streib 2006). Such public-private partnership is imperative in the local government's crisis management. Lessons from the Great Hanshin–Awaji Earthquake, local governments are promoting the collaborative agreement with private sector organizations in crisis management in a verity of area (Fig. 6.3).

Among the municipalities in Japan, the most common cooperation agreement with the private sector in crisis management is the supplies agreement. It mainly involves food chain stores, factories, and supermarkets to ensure food supply in times of crisis. Agreements with postal services include: sharing of post office buildings and land during disasters, using the postal service network for distributing disaster information, establishing temporary mail services at evacuation shelters,

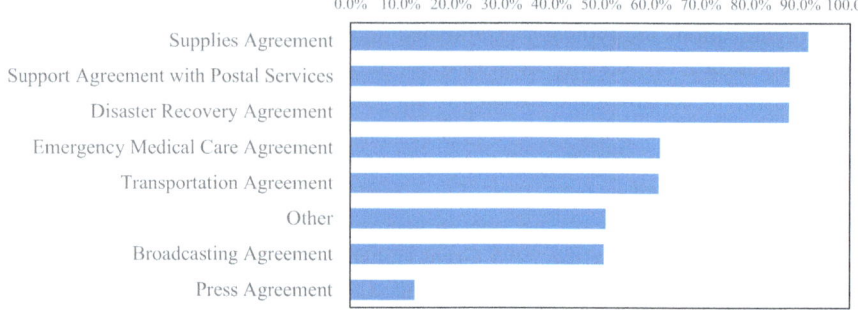

Fig. 6.3 Ratio of municipalities making cooperation agreements with private companies and non-profit organizations as of April 2022. (Notes: Proportion of municipalities that have agreements with private sector organizations in each field. Source: Author's elaboration based on Fire and Disaster Management Agency (2022a))

and others. Disaster recovery agreements involve utilities suppliers and construction companies' associations to provide essential utilities such as gas, electricity, water, roads, bridges, and others. Another crucial aspect involves agreements with local gas stations to supply fuel to rescue and relief vehicles. Transportation agreements are made with the local trucking association and various freight suppliers to support the transportation of rescue and relief goods and provide vehicles for delivering food and relief materials to evacuation shelters. Broadcasting and press agreements entail information dissemination between local governments and local television and radio stations, cable TV, and local newspapers to distribute disaster information and evacuation orders to citizens in the community.

Voluntary activities for disaster management first received special attention among Japanese when the Great Hanshin–Awaji Earthquake occurred in 1995. Many people, especially the youth, admired the volunteer rescue operations and restoration assistance to help the earthquake victims. This later led to legislation to support the volunteer and nonprofit organizations, called the NPO (specified Non-Profit Corporation) law, in 1998. Currently, there are more than 4000 registered NPOs those main activity is the disaster relief. In the event of the Great East Japan Earthquake in 2011, many individuals and nonprofit organizations went to the affected area to provide volunteer services. For better collaboration between local governments and NPOs, and among NPOs and volunteers, since the 2016 Kumamoto earthquake, in the event of large-scale disasters, it has become well-established practice to set up information sharing meetings among them to share information on support activities and coordinate the activities. In the event of large-scale disaster, the JVOAD (Japan Voluntary Organizations Active in Disaster) coordinates the NPOs and volunteer groups in collaboration with the national government and affected local governments (Cabinet Office 2021).

6.5 Public Health Response of Local Government During the COVID-19

6.5.1 Features COVID-19 Response in Japan

Despite having a higher proportion of elderly people per capita compared with other countries, Japan is regarded as one of the few countries that effectively controlled the spread of COVID-19, especially in the early stage in 2020 (OECD 2020). Indeed, the data reveal that there was no excess mortality in 2020, when the spread of COVID-19 was rampant spreading globally. Many governments implemented strict measures to control and contain COVID-19. Stay-at-home orders were intended to limit civil liabilities and were justified on the grounds that it saved lives. In many countries, the police were given authority through new laws in order to enhance the effectiveness of such policies. For instance, in the UK, the 2020 "Coronavirus Act" gave police the authority to issue fines to citizens who violated stay-at-home restrictions. Such violations were deemed a criminal offense punishable by fines, arrests, and even prison sentences. While most non-pharmaceutical policy measures aimed to change the behavior of citizens, the central role of policies involved the use of force against citizens for the sake of common good, necessitating the utilization of police resources. However, in many countries, police responses to the pandemic have resulted in further militarization and created deeper divides between the authority and the communities they serve (Jones 2020). The loss of procedural justice leads to the loss of public trust, resulting in the loss of institutional legitimacy of the policies.

In contrast, the Japanese government did not implement a "hard" lockdown, but instead requested the cooperation of citizens and urged them to follow its recommendations during several declared states of emergency (OECD 2020; Moon et al. 2021). Even though the state of emergency was enacted by law, most of the policies aimed at preventing the spread of COVID-19 were based on guidance and requests rather than orders, fines, or arrests. In a state of emergency, prefectural governors, rather than central government authorities, can appeal to the public to stay at home and request temporary closures of stores and other commercial activities to prevent disease spread. However, this remains a request and not a mandate.

6.5.2 Roles of Local Government in COVID-19 Response

Local governments in Japan have indeed played crucial roles in controlling the pandemic crisis beyond issuing stay-at-home requests. Its activities extend to implementing vaccination measures, conducting infectious disease surveillance, and supporting various government economic measures. In monitoring and controlling pandemic, the Japanese government heavily relied on the public health center at each local government. The Community Health Act stipulates that all prefectural and city governments with a certain population should establish a public health center. These centers are regarded as bases for responding to public health emergencies in each locality and are expected to play a leading role in public health prevention work, including disease control. The Infection Disease Control Law specifies the infectious disease category and gives the local government (i.e., the public health center director) the authority to issue "recommendations for hospitalization" to patients. Those who flee from their designated hospital or who fail to justify reasons for refusing hospitalization are subject to a fine. Although in the pre-war period the police were granted coercive power for disease control, today the director of the public health center in the local government, who is also a medical doctor, has the authority to control patient liberty. In the early stages of the COVID-19 crisis, particularly in early 2020, staff at public health centers experienced significant overwork. As the public health center is the hub of contact tracing, outbreak management, and enforcement of preventive measures, a staff union report highlighted that more than 20% of the surveyed staff experienced more than 80 h of monthly overwork, which is considered a threshold that could raise the risk of death from overwork. (Japan Times 2022).

Municipalities faced significant challenges in both vaccine distribution and the administrative process for specific relief payments during the pandemic. The coordination and logistics required for mass vaccination campaigns, along with the complex application process for specific relief payments for all citizens, placed considerable strain on local governments. With limited resources, staffing shortages, and the urgency of the COVID-19 pandemic, preparations for specific relief payments and vaccination campaigns at the municipal level became a daunting task. It took much longer than anticipated, exceeding the expected timeframe.

6.5.3 Central Local Relations and Challenges in COVID-19

The relationship between the central government and local governments in public health response was characterized by confusion, akin to many other countries experiencing a state of emergency declaration. Prefectural governors and governments were granted authority to issue requests to citizens without clear guidelines from the central government (Shiroyama 2020). For instance, in Tokyo, the largest urban area in Japan, the governor attempted to issue a shutdown request, but the central government insisted on prior consultation. Following such incidents, local governments urged the central government to establish a clear division of roles and responsibilities. Criticisms focused on information sharing between the central government and local governments, as well as among local governments. This inadequacy led to the creation of the Digital Agency in the central government in 2021, aiming to standardize core information systems developed and maintained by each local government by 2026. While this standardization facilitates information sharing, it also implies coercive standardization led by the central government. More recently, the central government seeks to revise the Local Autonomy Law, the fundamental legislation defining central-local relations, to enhance the comprehensive directive authority of the central government over local governments during large-scale crises.

6.6 Conclusions

The Japanese government has faced various disasters throughout its history, given the country's vulnerability to natural calamities like earthquakes. Each disaster has provided valuable lessons, helping the government improve its crisis response. As discussed, local government plays a primary role in disaster management and safeguarding the Japanese public's lives and property, rather than central government agencies. Most of the crisis management capacity resides within local governments rather than the central government. However, these aspects of Japan's institutional arrangements and disaster management capacities face sustainability challenges. Japan is experiencing depopulation, and regional disparities in the pace and scale of aging are making the situation more challenging. While urban areas maintain robust economies, rural areas are witnessing accelerated depopulation and aging due to the migration of working-age populations. With most welfare policies falling on local governments, an aging population in areas with limited financial resources undermines the self-sufficiency principle of local public finance, affecting crisis management and policy.

In light of the situation described above, this chapter has tried to answer the following questions by analyzing the institutional and collaborative features of crisis management in local government in Japan: What are the unique features of crisis management in local government in Japan? How should the scarcity and uneven distribution of resources be addressed? How do local governments collaborate with other local governments and other sectors in managing crises? Qualitative analysis through multiple case studies reveals that local governments in Japan are exploring sustainable approaches to maintaining service standards through collaborative management with other local governments, the national government, as well as private, community, and civic sectors.

Specifically, inter-governmental cooperation among both the same and different levels of government takes various forms, including agreements, fire districts, nationwide rescue teams, and others. Recently, there has been a trend towards more functional integration among local governments, including vertical cooperation and integration. Examples include joint operation of command centers while individual local governments maintain fire stations, or the integration of fire academy functions between prefectures and ordinance-designated cities (big cities). In inter-governmental relations, particularly horizontal collaboration between municipalities, or local governments and the private sector, enhances policy implementation capacity by sharing respective resource deficiencies (Miyashita and Sumi 2023). Collaboration with the private sector presents both longstanding and emerging challenges. While the number of volunteer firefighters (fire corps), traditional community-based firefighting organizations, is sharply declining due to socioeconomic changes, collaboration with private companies, voluntary disaster prevention organizations, and disaster management NPOs has become mainstream.

In addition, the COVID-19 experience in Japan has highlighted the need to further strengthen vertical collaborative management between the central government and local governments. It raised questions about local government-based crisis management and the effectiveness of inter-municipal cooperation. As urban areas with greater capacity suffered more, urban areas expected mutual support from rural areas where resources are scarcer. Confusion regarding the division of roles and responsibilities in public health responses prompted revisions to clarify the roles between the central and local governments, moving towards more centralization. With ongoing depopulation and an unevenly aging population structure, there is an expectation of increased vertical collaboration among local governments and with the central government. Such vertical collaborative management ensures resource allocation through subsidies and other forms provided by the central government, while horizontal cooperation fosters synergy and resource-sharing among local governments and private sectors. As explained in Sect. 6.4.2, in the event of large-scale disasters, information-sharing meetings among stakeholders including local governments, private sectors, and volunteer groups to facilitate coordination of support activities have become instrumental. These feedback mechanisms enhance information flow, enabling timely adjustments to responses more strategically.

In essence, it has been found that collaborative management beyond organizational boundaries can optimize crisis response capabilities more effectively, leveraging diverse expertise and resources to address increasingly complex challenges in an era of resource scarcity. Effective and sustainable crisis management by local governments requires both horizontal cooperation with the private and civic sectors and vertical cooperation with the central government to ensure the effectiveness of their efforts. While this chapter employs qualitative analysis based on multiple case studies, it has certain limitations in generalizing the findings, although local governments in Japan are more uniform as Japan employs a unitary state in its central-local relation and thus has smaller variation than other countries such as federal countries. Further empirical research is necessary to understand how local governments employ different kinds of collaborative management under different environmental conditions and resource constraints for a better understanding of the strategies local governments in Japan use to deal with collaborative crisis management beyond organizational boundaries over resource constraints.

References

Agranoff R, McGuire M (2003) Collaborative public management. Georgetown University Press, Washington, DC

Aoki N (2015) Wide-area collaboration in the aftermath of the March 11 disasters in Japan: implications for responsible disaster management. Int Rev Public Adm 81(1):196–213. https://doi.org/10.1177/00208523145415

Bajek R, Matsuda Y, Okada N (2008) Japan's Jishu-bosai-soshiki community activities: analysis of its role in participatory community disaster risk management. Nat Hazards 44:281–292

Cabinet Office (2021) Disaster management in Japan. Cabinet Office, Tokyo

Caruson K, MacManus SA (2012) Interlocal emergency management collaboration: vertical and horizontal roadblocks. Publius 42(1):162–187. https://doi.org/10.1093/publius/pjr024

Feiock RC (2013) The institutional collective action framework. Policy Stud J 41(3):397–425. https://doi.org/10.1111/psj.12023

Fire and Disaster Management Agency (2011) White paper on fire service [Syoubou hakusyo]. Fire and Disaster Management Agency, Tokyo. (in Japanese)

Fire and Disaster Management Agency (2013) White paper on fire service [Syoubou hakusyo]. Fire and Disaster Management Agency, Tokyo. (in Japanese)

Fire and Disaster Management Agency (2022a) Current status of local fire and disaster management administration [Tihou bousai gyousei no genkyo]. Fire and Disaster Management Agency, Tokyo. (in Japanese)

Fire and Disaster Management Agency (2022b) White paper on fire service [Syoubou hakusyo]. Fire and Disaster Management Agency, Tokyo. (in Japanese)

Hijino K (2021) Local government in Japan. In: Pekkanen RJ, Pekkanen SM (eds) The Oxford handbook of Japanese politics. Oxford University Press, New York, pp 134–158. https://doi.org/10.1093/oxfordhb/9780190050993.013.16

Hulst R, van Montfort A (eds) (2007) Inter-municipal cooperation in Europe. Springer, Dordrecht

Japan Times Newspaper (2022) 20% of Japan's public health center staff overworked with COVID-19 duties. February 18, 2022

Jones DJ (2020) The potential impacts of pandemic policing on police legitimacy: planning past the COVID-19 crisis. Policing 14(3):579–586. https://doi.org/10.1093/police/paaa026

Kikuchi M (2020) Living on a disaster-prone country: institutional arrangements and capacities of disaster management in Japan. In: Brown D, Czaputowicz J (eds) Dealing with disaster: public capacities for crisis and contingency management. International Institute of Administrative Sciences, Brussel, pp 325–344

Kimura S (2016) Regional administration in Japan. Routledge, New York

Liu Z, Guo J, Zhong W, Gui T (2021) Multi-level governance, policy coordination and subnational responses to COVID-19: comparing China and the US. J Comp Policy Anal Res Pract 23(2):204–218. https://doi.org/10.1080/13876988.2021.1873703

Ministry of Health, Labour and Welfare (2011) Annual health, labour and welfare report 2011–2012. Ministry of Health, Labour and Welfare, Tokyo

Miyashita T, Sumi E (2023) Policy evaluation of wide-area cooperation between municipalities: empirical analysis with "self-support settlement region framework" as the case study. Public Policy Rev 19(2):1–57. https://doi.org/10.57520/prippr.19-2-6

Moon MJ, Suzuki K, Park TI, Sakuwa K (2021) A comparative study of COVID-19 responses in South Korea and Japan: political nexus triad and policy responses. Int Rev Adm Sci 87(3):651–671. https://doi.org/10.1177/00208523219975

Nakamura A, Kikuchi M (2011) What we know, and what we have not yet learned: triple disasters and the Fukushima nuclear fiasco in Japan. Public Adm Rev 71(6):893–899. https://doi.org/10.1111/j.1540-6210.2011.02437.x

Noda Y (2023) Intermunicipal cooperation, integration forms, and vertical and horizontal effects in Japan. Public Adm Rev 83(3):457–717. https://doi.org/10.1111/puar.13569

OECD (2009) OECD reviews of risk management policies Japan: large-scale floods and earthquakes. OECD Publishing, Paris

OECD (2020) The territorial impact of COVID-19: managing the crisis across levels of government. In: OECD Policy responses to coronavirus (COVID-19). OECD. https://doi.org/10.1787/d3e314e1-en

Okada A (2022) Facilitating citizens' voluntary commitment: Japan's cooperation-based approach. In: Comfort LK, Rhodes ML (eds) Global risk management: the role of collective cognition in response to COVID-19. Routledge, New York, pp 84–102

Shiroyama H (2020) Japan's response to the COVID-19. In: Joyce P, Maron F, Reddy PS (eds) Good public governance in a global pandemic. International Institute of Administrative Sciences, Brussel, pp 195–204

Tang G (2020) Research on transformation from "paired assistance" to "collaborative networks" in post-disaster recovery of 2008 Wenchuan Earthquake, China. Nat Hazards 104(Suppl 1): 31–53. https://doi.org/10.1007/s11069-019-03598-0

Waugh WL, Streib G (2006) Collaboration and leadership for effective emergency management. Public Adm Rev 66:131–140. https://doi.org/10.1111/j.1540-6210.2006.00673.x

Masao Kikuchi is a Professor of Public Policy and Management in the Department of Public Management at the School of Business Administration, Meiji University, Tokyo. He has published articles in *Public Administration Review, Journal of Asian Public Policy, Environmental Policy and Governance, Lex localis—Journal of Local Self-Government*, and others. He has also contributed chapters in the *International Handbook on Civil Service Systems, Handbook of Public Administration in East Asia, Global Encyclopedia of Public Administration, Public Policy, and Governance, Patronage Politics in Asian Bureaucracies,* and others.

Chapter 7
Regional Governance in Japan

Yu Noda ⓘ

Abstract This chapter explores the effectiveness of horizontal and vertical cooperation among local governments for the sustainability of local governments in Japan's regional governance structure. Local governments in Japan encompass both prefectures and municipalities. While prefectural governments have remained unchanged since 1888, municipalities have undergone three significant mergers and, recently, have been promoting shared services through horizontal cooperation with other municipalities. Despite the widespread adoption of shared services, a substantial number of municipalities in Japan face notable deficiencies in policy resources, raising uncertainties about the actual enhancement of local government sustainability. Currently, the central government promotes intermunicipal cooperation (IMC) as a means of enhancing municipal sustainability; however, to the best of our knowledge, the effectiveness of this approach has not been thoroughly explored. Leveraging the institutional collective action (ICA) framework for municipal relations in Japan, this chapter discusses integration forms, transaction costs, and collaborative benefits for IMC, and identifies the limitations of IMC. In addition, the chapter empirically examines the limitations of the effectiveness of prevailing measures aimed at fostering horizontal IMC among local governments. It delves into emerging trends in vertical IMC, such as the support provided by prefectural governments to municipalities, offers insights into the prospective landscape of Japan's regional governance.

Keywords Local government · Regional governance · Horizontal cooperation · Vertical cooperation · Institutional collective action

Y. Noda (✉)
Faculty of Policy Studies, Doshisha University, Kyoto, Japan
e-mail: ynoda@mail.doshisha.ac.jp

7.1 Introduction

Local governments, facing substantial citizen demands and constrained policy resources, require appropriate administrative arrangements to effectively govern the region. This chapter discusses the sustainability of local governments through horizontal and vertical cooperation among local entities, analyzing the configuration of local governance in Japan and its benefits. The discussion is anchored in the theory of institutional collective action (ICA), a framework developed by Feiock's studies (Feiock 2007, 2013; Kim et al. 2022). ICA posits that two or more governments collaborate based on the mutual benefits of producing or providing services within a region. Regional governance is a collaborative, self-steering form of governance among organizations across administrative boundaries that addresses regional responsiveness, as distinguished from a top-down planning approach (Böcher 2008). In public administration, regional governance has been discussed in intermunicipal cooperation (IMC) arrangements, such as municipal mergers, consolidation of local and regional governments, and shared services, to address regional issues.

Traditionally, debates have revolved around the preference for either a consolidated or a fragmented system of local government (Lyons and Lowery 1989). Consolidated government systems aim to eliminate the inefficiencies associated with fragmentation, reduce the cost of delivering government services, and enhance technical efficiency through economies of scale and scope (Downs 1994; Lowery 2000). Recent studies have examined the positive effects of municipal mergers on fixed cost reduction and economies of scale (Bikker and van del Linde 2016; Drew et al. 2016). However, under fragmented environments, citizens move to municipalities with services and tax combinations compatible with their preferences, thus, rendering each municipality more competitive and, thus, more efficient (Tiebout 1956). Within such fragmented settings, effects of polycentrism emerge in which multiple central municipalities involve surrounding municipalities (Ostrom et al. 1988). The demand for IMC increases particularly in fragmented environments because not many services can be produced by small municipalities individually.

Municipal merger policies have been implemented several times in Japan, advocating a consolidated government. However, only the preparation of a policy for either consolidation or fragmentation of the local government system is not sufficient to ensure efficient and effective provision of public services. In Japan, there are no unincorporated areas, that is, all the regions have prefectures and municipalities. Small municipalities, facing operational difficulties, have maintained their services either through vertical subsidiarity, where the higher government, the prefectures, complement them, or through horizontal IMC, where they either integrate or collaborate with neighboring municipalities. The latter has been the preferred method of regional governance in Japan, which is promoted strongly by the national government.

However, can horizontal IMCs promoted by the central government maintain the services of municipalities with insufficient financial and human resources? Horizontal IMC is possible as municipalities utilize the resources of other municipalities, in cases when they lack such resources. This chapter examines the effectiveness of national policy in promoting horizontal cooperation among municipalities, based on ICA theory and quantitative datasets.

As discussed in Chap. 1, few regions, such as the southern Kanto and Aichi prefectures, can absorb a large amount of local taxes, while most municipalities are financially vulnerable. Therefore, although most municipalities are willing to collaborate horizontally, maintaining service production is challenging due to weak finances on both sides. This results in a national policy to promote horizontal cooperation among municipalities that is expected to fail. This chapter identifies the limitations of horizontal cooperation based on the ICA theory and empirically clarifies the ineffectiveness of the Collaborative Central City-Region (CCCR) as a national government-led policy through a difference-in-differences (DID) analysis.

The next section introduces the ICA framework and reviews the national IMC promotion measures. Based on the ICA framework, the limitations of the integrated forms of IMC in relation to collaborative benefits are then clarified. In addition, this chapter quantitatively examines the limitations of the effectiveness of the current measure of CCCR, which promotes horizontal IMCs. Finally, we consider the initiatives by prefectural governments to make regional governance function while coordinating between municipalities. The chapter identifies the prospects and future challenges for regional governance in Japan.

7.2 ICA Framework and Regional Governance System

7.2.1 ICA and Inter-municipal Conditions for Collaboration

In the ICA framework by Kim et al. (2022), the requirements for collaboration among municipalities to be realized are determined by a combination of risk and benefits variables. These variables include the context of the issue to be addressed through collaboration, actor preferences, and the existing institutions in the collaboration, leading to the determination of the degree of collaboration risk based on these three variables. The collaboration benefits are compared with the collaboration risks and if the expected net benefits are positive, each municipality chooses to collaborate.

Even though collaboration among municipalities is realized, mechanism costs are incurred in operating the collaboration. High mechanism costs are conditions in which the reduction in the autonomy of the municipality and the transaction costs of negotiating during collaboration are perceived by the municipality to be high (Kim et al. 2022). The high cost motivates municipalities to withdraw from collaboration. Factors that influence mechanism costs include intermunicipal conditions and integration forms. Regarding intermunicipal conditions, the desirable conditions for increasing the probability of cooperative orientation include a small number of municipalities (Feiock 2013), low heterogeneity in sociodemographic characteristics, such as race and income (Gerber et al. 2013), large disparities in economic status among municipalities (Yi et al. 2018), and high political homogeneity, such as partisanship (Gerber et al. 2013; Shaowei et al. 2016).

The probability of collaboration is higher when previous collaboration and trust between municipalities is high (Klok et al. 2018; Percoco 2016). Trust among Japanese municipalities minimizes the transaction costs associated with horizontal IMC, enabling collaboration and ensuring that the positive benefits are acknowledged by public officials (Noda 2023). In other words, even though population and economic disparities exist between large cities and small municipalities, which may offer little benefit to the large cities, relationships of trust facilitate such collaborations.

In addition, the Japanese government has promoted IMC on grounds of financial incentives across the country, resulting in relatively successful collaboration among municipalities, including those with socioeconomic disparities. However, the central government's inducement of cooperative performance among municipalities, which leads to trust building among municipalities, does not extend to their authority to compel municipalities to cooperate. This is because, according to the Law on Decentralization enacted in 2000, the relationship between the central government and municipalities is legally equal in Japan. Thus, the decision to collaborate is voluntary, based on the positive net benefits expected among the municipalities. Therefore, intermunicipal trust has a positive impact on the promotion of collaboration, even in the presence of municipal disparities. When collaboration is accomplished, the collaboration performance further increases the likelihood of reinforcing intermunicipal trust.

7.2.2   Reform Strategies for Regional Governance in Japan

The institutional environment in Japan that encourages municipalities to voluntarily collaborate and amalgamate has been guided by the government's four reform strategies for regional governance—promoting IMC, promoting municipal mergers, urban system reforms, and prefectural system reforms. Except for prefectural reforms, the strategies have employed methods to improve the financial incentives for collaboration and amalgamation. Regarding promoting municipal mergers, a consolidated government has been advocated thrice in the past. In the Great Meiji Consolidation of 1888, the number of entities was reduced from over 70,000 to about 15,000 when the municipal system came into effect. In the Great Showa Consolidation of the 1950s, the municipalities were facilitated to be larger than 8000 in size to manage services, such as school administration, health, and welfare, resulting in approximately 3500 municipalities in the 1960s. The Great Heisei Consolidation, which began just before the turn of the millennium, was promoted based on tremendous financial incentives to strengthen the financial base of the municipalities that had difficulty securing financial resources. By 2010 the number of municipalities had been reduced by half to 1790.

Urban system reforms include the ordinance-designated city system, which was established in 1956 to reconcile the interests of the prefectures with those of major cities, such as Osaka and Kobe, that sought independence from the prefectural governments, and the core city system, which was created in 1995 to promote decentralization. Japanese cities operate under a system in which authority is delegated by the national and prefectural governments based on population size. Those authorities are various, such as roads, land use, and health and sanitation. As of April 1, 2024, there are 20 cities in the ordinance-designated city system and 67 cities in the core city system. Regarding prefectural system reforms, the concept of establishing regional governments larger than the prefectural governments, known as the *doshu* system, has been under discussion since before World War II. However, there has not been significant progress, except for a comprehensive examination by a national advisory committee, which resulted in two reports in 1957 and 2006.

Of these strategies, this chapter focuses on promoting IMC. The Japanese government has promoted a policy scheme for IMC across every region by subsidizing municipalities if they develop a plan for cooperation. The policy, known as the Wide-Area Administrative Region Policy (WARP), was initiated in the 1960s and continued until 2008, just before the declaration of the end of the Great Heisei Consolidation. Under WARP, a large number of special service districts requiring incorporation were established as a form of IMC to implement services, such as firefighting and waste management. The policy covered the entire country, including cooperation between metropolitan areas and their suburbs, and areas away from the metropolitan areas.

The Ministry of Internal Affairs and Communications (MIC) has been implementing the CCCR Policy since 2014 to promote collaboration at a stage that does not necessarily require the establishment of a corporation. According to the policy, the national government extends financial support when the central city and neighboring cities enter a partnership agreement and devise a plan for prospective joint projects. The objective is to assist small municipalities in sustaining services through collaborative efforts with central cities in a horizontal cooperation framework. The Ministry of Land, Infrastructure, Transport and Tourism (MLIT) implemented a policy called the Settling Independence Zone Initiative (SIZI) before the CCCR, almost identical to the CCCR, thus, enforcing the adverse effects of sectionalism in the central ministries. However, due to the substantial subsidy allocated by the MIC for the CCCR, it has become the prevailing policy for promoting IMC.

With three rounds of merger facilitation measures implemented and a declaration of merger closure issued by the national government in 2010, the main reform strategy for regional governance in Japan is centered around the facilitation of IMC, particularly the CCCR. Although Japanese municipalities had been based on a full-set orientation, managing all the policy areas, including welfare, education, waste disposal, and road maintenance, they gave up on that orientation by promoting IMC.

Behind this strategy is the trust among municipalities that has been fostered through past experiences of cooperation induced by the central government. A causal relationship, guided by the ICA, is that trust among municipalities promotes collaboration (Klok et al. 2018; Noda 2023). However, the CCCR is merely a coordination of policies, with specific forms of coordination to be explored after the plan is formulated. Therefore, it is necessary to elucidate how transaction costs and cooperative benefits are related to the integration forms.

7.2.3 Integration Forms

Currently, the remaining integration forms of IMC for regional administration are classified into the following three types. The first is the serviced by a partner organization (SPO). This includes contracted services in which services are purchased by the partner municipality under a contract, and an alternative execution system, in which other local governments are responsible for providing services on behalf of the smaller municipality. In the former, the contracted municipality is the managing entity, while in the latter, the contracting municipality is the managing entity. In the latter case, the prefectural government performs the administrative work on behalf of the smaller municipality.

The second is collaboration-based organization formation (CBOF). This includes partial service associations and broad service associations with a juridical personality, and joint organizations and councils of governments (COGs) without a juridical personality. Partial service associations are special district governments, and only municipalities can be members of these associations. In broad service associations, municipalities, prefectures, and special wards can become members. When a partial service association is generally composed of a large city with a strong voice and other municipalities, the strong city's policies take precedence over the association's own policies. To address these issues, broad service associations have the authority to orient the member municipalities to conform to the policies of the associations. However, the differences between the two forms are not very significant, hence, the number of partial service associations, which is an older system, is greater.

Regarding the establishment of organizational units without juridical personality, joint organizations are those in which municipalities jointly establish a board of education and professional personnel. COGs are organizations that consider broad-based plans related to tourism and industrial policies, and their board of directors consists of several municipalities, however, they do not have a structure for implementing the operations. For COGs, there are similar organization names such as the Planning Commission and Economic Development District. Inter-municipal organizations called COGs tend to be established in the same region with many similar entities, resulting in the organizations not necessarily recognized by the national government as representative of the region. To address these issues, recent studies have called intermunicipal organizations that function as political entities explicitly recognized by higher governments as regional intergovernmental organizations (RIGOs) (Miller et al. 2019). This covers the largest geography of organizations established across boundaries that are comprised of general-purpose local governments and have a broad policy agenda, a legitimacy recognized by higher governments, and an agenda that allows the local voice to be expressed to higher governments, and representativeness (Miller et al. 2019: 85). According to this definition, Japan's COGs are not RIGOs because they cannot promote policies beyond the purview of their constituent local governments and are not recognized by the higher government as decision-making bodies like other local governments.

The third is the involving policy coordination (IPC), which corresponds to the coordination agreement scheme. This is based on CCCR in which the central city and neighboring cities sign an agreement to collaborate on various policies, such as industry and welfare, with a division of roles. This scheme is limited to a design in which the collaboration direction is included in the contract and the progress of the target outcome is presented to the government several years later. After this scheme is completed, certain administrative tasks may be outsourced or a special district government may be established, however, such specific cooperation is not necessarily undertaken.

7.2.4   Transaction Costs and Collaborative Benefits of Horizontal IMC by Integration Forms

In the ICA framework, even though the net expected benefit of collaboration is positive, if the mechanism cost is high enough to sacrifice the autonomy of each government in favor of the process of arrangements to integrate collective action, feedback is provided for the context surrounding the issue and the actors, leading to a new calculation of the collaboration risk and possible disruption (Kim et al. 2022). In the integration mechanism choice, how to adopt integration forms is an important issue (Noda 2023). SPOs, such as contracted services, have lower political costs in countries, such as Japan, that adopt a system that does not require voting among the municipalities involved over CBOF with a juridical personality, such as district governments, that set up a coordinated organization (Holzer and Fry 2011). An unincorporated council is easier to establish because the authority of the constituent municipalities is not constrained. IPC is the agreement system before the organization is established. Thus, the political costs in the integration forms are low.

Based on the ICA framework, when comparing the transaction costs among the municipalities and the collaborative benefits obtained from the IMC, the benefits are clear because the responsibility of the services provided by the IMC can be ensured. However, the transaction costs before and after the IMC are difficult to understand in advance given that no one can determine the conditions that the municipalities expect before the IMC is realized, and whether any of the constituent municipalities may leave the IMC. The easiest form of IMC in such a situation is contracted services.

Services with large investments, such as water and fire facilities, have high asset specificity, leading to higher transaction costs for IMCs (Shrestha and Feiock 2011; Williamson 1979). Therefore, given that CBOF has higher transaction costs (Holzer and Fry 2011), outsourcing a service that the counterparty has already implemented is less expensive. In policy collaboration, transaction costs are lower than in CBOF because the organization is not necessarily established to promote a specific project. However, the responsibility of policy collaboration is lower than that of contracted services and CBOF. This is because a partnership agreement is an arrangement that focuses on the policy-making stage and does not commit to the implementation of specific projects. Transparency is necessary for the democratic operation of municipal organizations, however, IMCs are opaque from the perspective of citizens because they produce services where multiple municipalities are involved and rarely explain their structure to the citizens.

For example, transaction costs are higher when an organization is established to constrain the discretion of the constituent municipalities, as in the case of CBOF with a juridical personality. Conversely, transaction costs are lower in cases where the establishment of an organization is not mandatory, such as the IPC, represented by CCCR, currently being promoted by the central government. However, IPC has the disadvantage of low service responsiveness because it is an agreement without any coercive power to implement the project. This responsibility can be discussed in a detailed breakdown as collaborative benefits. The coordination benefits are discussed by Giacomini et al. (2018) who examined service effectiveness and institutional legitimacy, however, these variables are the result of the quality of services, capacity, and fiscal efficiency of the cooperating municipalities. Following Noda (2023), this chapter focuses on four benefits—(1) maintaining and improving the quality of services in a municipality, (2) improving the financial efficiency of a municipality, (3) improving the capacity of a municipality to solve its issues, and (4) improving the capacity to solve issues of the entire region.

Horizontal cooperation among municipalities improves the service quality and the capacity to provide services in the municipality or region concerned, while vertical cooperation between the national and prefectural governments and municipalities provides increased fiscal efficiency for the municipalities (Noda 2023). This is because the financial subsidies from the national and prefectural governments are the drivers for the realization of IMCs and their collaborative benefits, given the fragile financial situation of several municipalities across the country. However, this discussion on collaborative benefits is based on the assumption that IMCs in a CBOF with a juridical personality between municipalities do not provide the same benefits in all types of integration forms.

Contracted services improve the service quality for the outsourcing municipality because the services are maintained by the partner municipality. Moreover, CBOF with a juridical personality increases the service quality because the service is maintained in a cooperative organization. However, in cases without juridical personality or in the cooperative agreement system, the service quality is low due to services not necessarily being maintained. CBOFs with legal personality and IPCs are more fiscally efficient compared to other forms because they are subsidized by the central government when they formulate plans for collaboration among municipalities.

However, these subsidies cannot last long because the term of the plan is finite. Compared with the situation in which projects are implemented in continuous collaboration with the prefectural government (i.e., a higher-level government), the fiscal efficiency benefits gained through municipal collaboration are considerably lower. Municipal and regional capacities increase when IMCs set up organizations and create new services, thus, CBOF with a juridical personality. Table 7.1 summarizes the characteristics of the integration forms, transaction costs, and collaborative benefits based on the ICA framework.

In summary, the transaction costs and collaborative benefits of horizontal cooperation among municipalities differ depending on the form of integration. Although a CBOF with legal personality and an SPO can improve quality as collaborative benefits, financial efficiency cannot be expected to increase compared to vertical cooperation in any of the integration forms. The consequence derived from the ICA's analytical frame of reference is that neither collaboration benefit is obtainable in the integration forms of IPC, including CCCR, which are currently strongly promoted by the national government. The next section identifies problems with horizontal IMCs by empirically detecting the CCCR policy effects.

Table 7.1 Transaction costs and collaborative benefits of horizontal IMC by integration forms

Typologies of integration forms		SPO	CBOF		IPC
			With a juridical personality	Without a juridical personality	
Examples of integration forms		Contracted services, replacement of administrative functions	Special service districts, broad service associations, co-establishment of agencies	COG	CCCR, SIZI
Policy process		Implementation	Implementation	Plan	Plan
Transaction costs		Low	High	Low	Low
Responsibility		High	High	Middle	Low
Collaborative benefits	The quality of services in a municipality	High	High	Low	Low
	The financial efficiency of a municipality	Low	Low	Low	Low
	The capacity of a municipality	Low	High	Low	Low
	The capacity of the entire region	Low	High	Low	Low

Source: Author's elaboration

7.3   Effectiveness of CCCR as Horizontal IMC

7.3.1   CCCR Policy

The CCCR policy aims to promote horizontal IMCs and shared services among municipalities. The effects of IMC are likely to be observed in the improvement of fiscal efficiency (Dollery et al. 2009). The efficiency varies depending on the type of service (Holzer and Fry 2011; Maher 2015). However, as a result of the broad progression of IMC by the national government, as in Japan, municipalities collaborate, yet do not reform their municipalities or improve their fiscal efficiency. Thus, in Hokkaido and Nagano Prefecture, where a large number of partial service associations have been established, wide-area cooperation has increased per-population expenditures, causing fiscal inefficiencies (Noda 2017). In addition, no effect of SIZI, a collaboration scheme similar to CCCR, on increasing the population of municipalities has been demonstrated (Miyashita and Sumi 2022).

After terminating the WARP in 2008, CCCR, as the reform strategy for horizontal IMC, was made the central measure to be promoted nationwide, starting in 2014. In 2015, four regions, two spanning Okayama and Hiroshima prefectures, one in Hyogo Prefecture, and one in Miyazaki Prefecture, were the first to develop a vision for collaboration and were certified by the national government as CCCR targets. CCCR is included in IPC as an integration form. The central cities are Fukuyama, Kurashiki, Himeji, and Miyazaki, all of which are core cities that possess the second strongest authority after ordinance-designated cities. Excluding duplications, whereby, the same municipality is involved in multiple CCCRs in these four regions, 29 municipalities adopted CCCRs in 2015. As of March 31, 2024, CCCRs are certified and promoted in 197 municipalities (excluding duplications) in 38 regions throughout Japan.

The 38 regions are operated by the municipalities in the horizontal cooperation framework, with the central city and neighboring municipalities forming agreements with each other. The promotion of the entire region is monitored by Key Performance Indicators, which are measured by changes in statistical indicators that have been ascertained from the perspective of economic growth of the entire region, the concentration and strengthening of higher-order urban functions, and the improvement of life-related functional services. These indicators are set by the number of employees, research grants, and projects implemented, and promote a high level of urban strengthening and concentration. The prerequisite is the concentration of human and financial resources, which indicates a steady increase in the population and taxable base.

Despite this promotion of CCCR, the central city in the region area is suffering from economic exhaustion and sluggish financial strength, reflecting the nationwide situation, except in the Tokyo metropolitan area and Aichi Prefecture. The Tokyo metropolitan area is the location of central government ministries and agencies that have regulatory authority over industries, including finance and construction-related industries, leading to a concentration of headquarters for major corporations. As a result, the population moves into the Tokyo metropolitan area for job opportunities from rural areas of Japan. In addition, Aichi Prefecture is the center of automobile-related industries, except for a few regions, which have sufficient population and tax income.

Therefore, we need to verify whether the CCCR policy benefits regions other than the Tokyo metropolitan area and Aichi Prefecture where there are several municipalities with great fiscal strength.

7.3.2   Data and Methods

This section quantitatively examines the IMC's failure to ensure regional sustainability through CCCR, one of its current major policies, and an integration form of IPC. In particular, we detect differences in the status of regional development between municipalities that have and have not adopted the CCCR. CCCR is an agreement between a central city and surrounding municipalities to develop industrial policies and lifestyle infrastructure to increase tax revenues associated with population growth and industrial revitalization. Thus, municipalities that implement CCCR are expected to increase their population and taxable income per capita compared to municipalities that do not implement CCCR. Taxable income is an indicator based on the linkage between the stimulation of industry, the increase in income of people working in firms, and the increase in the amount of taxes.

Based on the above, the DID analysis was conducted with population and taxable income per capita as the dependent variables. The dependent variables were logarithms. In the DID analysis, the presence or absence of policy effects is derived by comparing before and after policy implementation for the treatment group that adopted the policy and the control group that did not. The treatment group consisted of municipalities that adopted the CCCR, which included the central city and the peripheral cities.

The period from FY2012–FY2021 was used in consideration of the latest available statistical data. Basic Resident Registration population, expenditure per capita, and local taxes per capita were used. Because the most recent fiscal statistics available were for FY 2019 (March 2020), the central cities and six surrounding cities whose urban visions were formulated in 2019 or later were excluded from the analysis.

The control group, that is, the municipalities that have not introduced CCCR, consisted of selected metropolitan areas around the candidate municipalities identified by the central government based on the following criteria. First, according to the national guidelines for the Promotion of the CCCR Policy,[1] candidate central

---

[1] In Japan, Metropolitan Area has not been established as in the U.S., however, UEA was established by Kanemoto and Tokuoka (2002) based on the following criteria: (1) the central city is set by Densely Inhabited Districts population, (2) suburban cities are defined as municipalities with a commuting rate of 10% or more to the central city, and (3) the metropolitan area setting allows for

cities must be located primarily in areas outside the three metropolitan areas of Tokyo, Osaka, and Nagoya. If they are within these three metropolitan areas, less than 10% of their residents should be commuting to the metropolitan areas. Among the cities that met these conditions, 24 cities did not apply for CCCR. With these as the central cities, the municipalities in the Urban Employment Area (UEA), established by Kanemoto and Tokuoka (2002), were defined as a metropolitan area.[2]

Other points considered in the data preparation include the following—In cases where the same municipality is included in two separate CCCRs, the municipality in the area where the CCCR was formed first was included. In the case of separate UEAs that include the same municipalities, only one of the municipalities was included. In cases where the same municipality was included in both the central urban area and the UEA, both municipalities were excluded.

Based on the above steps, 172 municipalities were selected as the control group. The changes in the dependent variable for the 197 municipalities that adopted CCCR till 2018 and the 172 municipalities that are candidate areas but had not adopted CCCR are as follows. The change in population from 2012 to 2021 and the average taxable income per capita from 2012 to 2019 are—3717 persons and 13,235 yen, respectively, in 197 municipalities that adopted the CCCR, and—1584 persons and 18,492 yen, respectively, in the 172 municipalities that did not adopt CCCR. The results show that the population has decreased in both cases, the taxable income per capita has increased slightly, and the areas that did not adopt CCCR had a lower degree of population decrease and a higher increase in taxable income per capita.

However, given that these comparisons do not allow us to detect a causal relationship between CCCR adoption and non-adoption, verification by DID is performed. Assuming that changes in population and taxable income are affected by environmental factors in the municipality, this analysis examined both models with and without considering the area (log-transformed) of the municipality and the fiscal strength index as independent variables in DID testing. In addition, due to the different dates of adoption of CCCR, the DID analyses were performed for 2015, 2016, 2017, and 2018. Descriptive statistics are shown in Table 7.2.

---

the presence of multiple central cities within the same metropolitan area. A metropolitan employment area is defined as a metropolitan area with a Densely Inhabited Districts population of 50,000 or more in the central city, while a micropolitan employment area is defined as a metropolitan area with a Densely Inhabited Districts population of 10,000–50,000. Densely Inhabited Districts are defined by the national government as areas with a population density of 4000 or more people per square kilometer, adjacent to each other within the boundaries of a municipality, and where the population of the adjacent areas is 5000 or more at the time of the census. See the following URL for the guideline: https://www.soumu.go.jp/main_content/000757551.pdf

[2] See the following URL for UEA. https://www.csis.u-tokyo.ac.jp/UEA/uea_code.htm

Table 7.2 Descriptive statistics

	Observations				Mean				SD			
	2015	2016	2017	2018	2015	2016	2017	2018	2015	2016	2017	2018
Population	2010	2650	2120	2070	93,317	97,602	94,885	84,961	168,544	182,768	173,714	162,000
Taxable income per capita	1608	2120	1696	1656	146.9	140.5	144.0	144.3	79.7	72.3	79.5	79.5
Treat	2010	2650	2120	2070	0.09	0.18	0.08	0.05	0.28	0.38	0.26	0.22
Area	2010	2650	2120	2070	20,191	21,125	21,229	19,561	25,475	26,123	25,912	25,635
Fiscal strength index	1608	2120	1696	1656	0.62	0.60	0.60	0.60	0.25	0.24	0.25	0.26

	Min				Max			
	2015	2016	2017	2018	2015	2016	2017	2018
Population	1636	1636	1636	832	1,568,265	1,568,265	1,568,265	1,568,265
Taxable income per capita	67.1	63.2	67.1	65.5	854.9	854.9	854.9	854.9
Treat	0	0	0	0	1	1	1	1
Area	0.32	0.32	0.32	0.32	155.806	155.806	155.806	155.806
Fiscal strength index	0.14	0.13	0.12	0.12	1.53	1.53	1.53	1.53

7.3.3 Findings

Table 7.3 presents the results of the test of policy differences between the control group and the municipalities in the region that received CCCR approval from 2015 to 2018. For each year, we estimated two patterns, one with and one without area and fiscal strength index as control variables. In DID, the parallel-trend assumption must hold between the treatment and control groups. Parallel trends are met for models P1, P2, P3, P4, and P8, while P5 is rejected at the 5% level, and P6 and P7 are rejected at the 10% level. Regarding P6, the average treatment effect on the treated (ATET) has a significant negative impact at the 5% level if the parallel trend is assumed to be fulfilled. In other models, where parallel trends are expected to be satisfied, the effects are not statistically significant, however, they are all negative in sign.

The fiscal strength index, which is included as a control variable, significantly increases the population. Although CCCR is based on the assumption that the target regions do not include the three largest metropolitan areas, even among municipalities outside the three largest metropolitan areas, fiscal strength contributes to population boost, indicating that CCCR's policy effects are not realized.

Table 7.4 provides estimates of CCCR's impact on taxable income per capita. The parallel trend test results are not rejected in either model. However, the coefficients of ATET are not significant across all the models. In addition, in many models, the negative signs of ATET suggest a lack of evidence for an increase in taxable income per capita. It is noteworthy that the fiscal strength index demonstrates a consistently significant positive impact in each model presented in Table 7.4.

In summary, the findings indicate that in regions where CCCR policies were implemented, there was a general decline in population. In addition, per capita taxable income has declined in some areas. There is no evidence suggesting that CCCR policies have increased population or taxable income. In essence, achieving sustainable municipal governance through CCCR, which has become the primary vehicle for horizontal IMCs among municipalities, appears challenging. As vertical IMCs are necessary for improving sustainability of municipalities, the next section discusses the methods and examples of prefectural support for municipalities.

7.4 Developing Vertical IMC

7.4.1 Municipal Support Options by Prefectures

Vertical IMCs provide for the sharing of policy resources between prefectures and municipalities. Ordinance-designated cities, which have the greatest authority among the municipalities, have more services and facilities than prefectures. In such cases, prefectures have an incentive to share city resources, for instance, Aichi Prefecture uses Nagoya City's fire academy. In most cases, however, municipalities

Table 7.3 Effects of CCCR on population

	2015		2016		2017		2018	
	P1	P2	P3	P4	P5	P6	P7	P8
ATET								
CCCR (Treatment vs control)	−0.013 (0.008)	−0.007 (0.006)	−0.008 (0.006)	−0.004 (0.005)	−0.021*** (0.007)	−0.013** (0.006)	−0.149 (0.010)	−0.010 (0.008)
Controls Log(Area)		0.402 (0.483)		0.339 (0.484)		0.196 (0.510)		0.400 (0.496)
Fiscal strength index		0.255*** (0.063)		0.272*** (0.063)		0.248*** (0.060)		0.257** (0.062)
Year								
2013	−0.002*** (0.001)	−0.003*** (0.001)	−0.002*** (0.001)	−0.003*** (0.001)	−0.002*** (0.001)	−0.003*** (0.001)	−0.003*** (0.001)	−0.003*** (0.001)
2014	−0.008*** (0.001)	−0.010*** (0.001)	−0.009*** (0.001)	−0.010*** (0.001)	−0.009*** (0.001)	−0.010*** (0.001)	−0.009*** (0.001)	−0.010*** (0.001)
2015	−0.014*** (0.002)	−0.018*** (0.002)	−0.015*** (0.002)	−0.019*** (0.002)	−0.0015*** (0.002)	−0.018*** (0.002)	−0.015*** (0.002)	−0.019*** (0.002)
2016	−0.018*** (0.003)	−0.025*** (0.003)	−0.021*** (0.002)	−0.027*** (0.002)	−0.021*** (0.003)	−0.026*** (0.003)	−0.021*** (0.003)	−0.027*** (0.003)
2017	−0.025*** (0.004)	−0.033*** (0.004)	−0.025*** (0.004)	−0.034*** (0.004)	−0.029*** (0.003)	−0.035*** (0.003)	−0.028*** (0.004)	−0.035*** (0.004)
2018	−0.033*** (0.005)	−0.042*** (0.005)	−0.033*** (0.004)	−0.042*** (0.004)	−0.032*** (0.004)	−0.041*** (0.004)	−0.035*** (0.004)	−0.043*** (0.004)
2019	−0.049*** (0.006)	−0.050*** (0.005)	−0.041*** (0.005)	−0.051*** (0.005)	−0.041*** (0.005)	−0.050*** (0.005)	−0.041*** (0.005)	−0.051*** (0.005)
Constant	10.634*** (0.003)	6.758 (4.479)	10.640*** (0.003)	7.326 (4.514)	10.639*** (0.003)	8.665 (4.765)	10.484*** (0.003)	6.655 (4.567)
Parallel-trends test	0.125	0.141	0.125	0.288	0.013**	0.060*	0.086*	0.188
Observations	2010	1608	2650	2120	2120	1696	2070	1656

Notes: ATET estimate adjusted for group effects and time effects. *$p < 0.1$; **$p < 0.05$; ***$p < 0.01$

Table 7.4 Effects of CCCR on taxable income per capita

	2015		2016		2017		2018	
	T1	T2	T3	T4	T5	T6	T7	T8
ATET								
CCCR (Treatment vs control)	−0.010 (0.007)	−0.007 (0.006)	0.006 (0.006)	0.008 (0.005)	0.004 (0.008)	0.009 (0.008)	−0.001 (0.010)	0.002 (0.009)
Controls Log(Area)		−0.113 (1.871)		0.018 (1.589)		0.188 −1.862		−0.369 (1.757)
Fiscal strength index		0.294* (0.167)		0.311** (0.156)		0.296* (0.166)		0.297* (0.167)
Year								
2013	0.016*** (0.002)	0.015*** (0.003)	0.015*** (0.002)	0.014*** (0.002)	0.017*** (0.002)	0.017 (0.002)	0.016*** (0.002)	0.016*** (0.002)
2014	0.046*** (0.005)	0.044*** (0.005)	0.043*** (0.004)	0.041*** (0.004)	0.046*** (0.005)	0.044 (0.005)	0.046*** (0.005)	0.044*** (0.005)
2015	0.043*** (0.006)	0.039*** (0.005)	0.04*** (0.005)	0.036*** (0.004)	0.043*** (0.006)	0.039 (0.005)	0.042*** (0.006)	0.038*** (0.005)
2016	0.057*** (0.006)	0.050*** (0.006)	0.057*** (0.005)	0.050*** (0.005)	0.058*** (0.005)	0.052 (0.005)	0.058*** (0.005)	0.052*** (0.005)
2017	0.081*** (0.006)	0.073*** (0.006)	0.079*** (0.005)	0.070*** (0.005)	0.082*** (0.005)	0.075 (0.005)	0.081*** (0.006)	0.073*** (0.005)
2018	0.093*** (0.006)	0.083*** (0.006)	0.092*** (0.005)	0.082*** (0.006)	0.094*** (0.006)	0.084 (0.006)	0.096*** (0.006)	0.087*** (0.006)
2019	0.112*** (0.006)	0.102*** (0.007)	0.112*** (0.006)	0.101*** (0.007)	0.113*** (0.006)	0.102 (0.007)	0.112*** (0.006)	0.102*** (0.007)
Constant	4.855*** (0.004)	5.724 (17.367)	4.817*** (0.003)	4.467 −14.836	4.830*** (0.004)	2.900 (17.429)	4.832*** (0.004)	8.053 (16.215)
Parallel-trends test	0.163	0.181	0.377	0.521	0.814	0.779	0.773	0.496
Observations	1608	1608	2120	2120	1696	1696	1656	1656

Notes: ATET estimate adjusted for group effects and time effects. $^{*}p < 0.1$; $^{**}p < 0.05$; $^{***}p < 0.01$

lacking policy resources have a greater need for a share of the prefectural government's human and financial resources. Thus, vertical IMCs differ from horizontal IMCs in that the prefectures are predominantly supplemental to or substitute for the services of the municipalities.

Except for cases where a municipality goes bankrupt[3] and the financial revitalization is managed by the national and prefectural governments, there are three ways in which prefectures can support municipalities—prefectures can perform projects on behalf of municipalities, specific administrative municipal operations are transferred to prefectures simultaneously throughout Japan, and prefectures can serve as coordinators among municipalities. When a prefecture performs a project on behalf of a municipality, it includes contracted services, which are performed nationwide, and prefectural agency projects, which are performed in depopulated areas. In addition, an administrative agency system was introduced in FY2014, under which other local governments perform administrative services in the name of the municipality that submits them to outsourcing. Under this system, the legal responsibility for services rests with the outsourcing municipality, and there is no transfer of administrative and executive authority. For example, the prefectures are substituting for water supply and pollution control services that are difficult for municipalities to implement alone.

Regarding specific municipal operations being transferred to prefectures, the National Health Insurance, which had been operated by municipalities, was operated by prefectures, starting in 2018. National Health Insurance is a medical insurance system for those who are not covered by workplace medical insurance and people over 75 years, operated by the local government as the insurer. Because maintaining the insurance system was not feasible in municipalities with small populations, prefectures became the insurers to cover large populations. Development of wide-area services and infrastructure that would be difficult for municipalities with vulnerable finances to provide include industrial policy, water supply and sewerage, and road maintenance, which could be transferred to the prefectural governments in the future.

Prefectures function as coordinators between municipalities when most municipalities are facing financial and human resource difficulties. For example, Nagano Prefecture has established regular meetings to share policy issues with municipalities in the prefecture. Based on the discussions, necessary prefectural support is considered. In Nara Prefecture, the prefectural government has established a system to identify the intentions of the national government and the issues faced by municipalities and is creating the core services needed by the municipalities, such as water supply services and medical centers (Nara Prefecture 2017).

---

[3] When a municipality goes bankrupt, the government formulates a fiscal revitalization plan, with the consent of the Minister of MIC and the support of the national and prefectural governments, to cut municipal services significantly and issue exceptional bonds. In 2009, the Law Concerning the Financial Soundness of Local Governments was enacted, which requires that local governments be designated as fiscal rehabilitation entities or fiscal soundness entities based on financial indicators that show the ratio of deficits and public debt costs.

Even in prefectures where large cities are located, specific efforts are underway to promote horizontal IMCs in areas with financially distressed municipalities. For instance, Osaka Prefecture and 10 municipalities established the study group in 2020. In 2022, Osaka Prefecture, jointly with the Minami Kawachi region consisting of Taishi Town, Kanan Town, and Chihaya Akasaka Village, considered measures to address regional public issues (Osaka Prefecture, Taishi Town, Kanan Town, and Chihaya Akasaka Village 2023). In March 2024, Osaka Prefecture enacted Ordinance on the Enhancement and Strengthening of Basic Autonomy Functions, establishing a mechanism to provide more human resources and subsidies to maintain municipal services and facilities based on a thorough understanding of municipal demands. In addition, Aichi Prefecture is working on a vertical IMC in which the prefecture commits to the Higashi-Mikawa region to promote further cooperation among municipalities. Thus, support for municipalities by prefectures is becoming more assertive, and vertical IMC is solidifying the sustainability of local governments.

7.4.2 Vertical IMC Based on Strong Prefectural Leadership

In certain cases, such a coordinating role is actively played by the prefectural government, even in prefectures with relatively large policy resources. In Aichi Prefecture, most municipalities have ample tax revenues due to the concentration of the automobile industry. However, this is not the case for the small municipalities in the Higashi-Mikawa region. This region consists of the core city of Toyohashi, with a population of about 370,000, Toyokawa, with a population of about 180,000, three other cities with populations ranging from 40,000–80,000, and three small towns and villages with tight finances—Shitara Town (less than 4000 residents), Toei Town (less than 3000 residents), and Toyone Village (less than 900 residents). The total population of the Higashi-Mikawa region is approximately 750,000, which is 10% of the population of Aichi Prefecture. Therefore, in 2015, eight municipalities created the Higashi-Mikawa broad service association to jointly carry out programs for regional development, such as the promotion of industry and tourism, and welfare programs. Decision-making by the association is made by the assembly of Higashi-Mikawa broad service association. In general, the establishment of such a broad service association, with towns and villages with a weak financial base, does not offer much benefit to Toyohashi and other cities.

However, behind the establishment of the broad-based association was a prefectural-led initiative to establish the Higashi Mikawa Vision Council with the Higashi-Mikawa Prefectural Government, an agency of Aichi Prefecture, in 2012, to discuss promotion measures for the region (Higashi-Mikawa Vision Council 2021). The Higashi-Mikawa Prefectural Government is staffed by the deputy governor of Aichi Prefecture, and the deputy governor exerts a strong influence on the disbursement of subsidies for road maintenance projects and various other projects. in the Higashi-Mikawa region (Toda 2022). The Higashi-Mikawa Vision Council is an organization composed of the business community, universities, and mayors and association heads of the eight municipalities. The results of the exchange of information at the council has resulted in giving the de facto legitimacy to the projects of the broad service association. In other words, a scheme was established to be implemented by the broad service association based on the legitimacy of the cooperative experience of the council and congress, and the subsidy provided by the Higashi-Mikawa Prefectural Government. This organizational arrangement is sometimes regarded as multi-level governance in which each entity manages each other toward a common policy agenda (Imasato 2017). However, due to the strong prefectural initiative, we can reasonably regard it as a regional governance, based mainly on prefectural coordination in vertical IMC arrangements.

A broad service association is an organization with a legal personality. Hence, it is a form of collaboration with high political costs associated with transactions between municipalities. Cities, such as Toyohashi and Tahara, value water services for the promotion of industry and agriculture, which is the background for cooperation, because the water sources for these cities are located in the three towns and villages mentioned above, which have small populations and financial difficulties. Therefore, Aichi Prefecture supports an environment of cooperation in securing high-quality water resources, which is the key to industrial policies. In addition, unique to the Higashi-Mikawa case is the existence of a higher-level government, Aichi Prefecture, which provides financial and human support for intermunicipal relations. Herein lies the vertical cooperation that facilitates horizontal cooperation.

7.5 Conclusions and Prospects for Regional Governance

In Japan, municipal mergers have been promoted in most regions. The current strategy of promoting horizontal IMCs is aimed at having functional regional governance to maintain sustainable local governments, the core method of which is CCCR. Japanese local governments have a culture of cooperation based on trust and past collaboration experiences, even though there are economic, population, and other disparities among the municipalities. The transaction costs indicated by the ICA are relatively low among Japanese municipalities based on trust, which facilitates horizontal cooperation among them.

However, the analyses based on the ICA framework and empirical examination in this chapter find that the regional reform strategy through the CCCR has little effect on increasing the population or tax revenues of municipalities. The answer to this chapter's research question is that central government-led horizontal IMCs cannot sustain municipal services with inadequate policy resources.

Meanwhile, there could be other definitions for the control group of metropolitan areas when conducting DID. In addition, if the number of adopted CCCRs increases, the accuracy of the analysis can be improved by validation using a larger sample. Despite these limitations, the robustness of the analytical results is high, given that this analysis also used a certain number of samples and that most of the models do not find positive policy effects.

All the regions in Japan have prefectures, under which municipalities are established, leaving no areas without a local government. This structure of the local system encourages prefectures to establish vertical IMCs by subsidizing municipalities. Because horizontal IMC is the basic administrative arrangement of shared services to promote regional governance, collaboration among municipalities needs to be maintained in feasible regions. However, horizontal IMCs alone are no longer sufficient to maintain municipal sustainability, hence, vertical IMCs represent the primary approach to securing scarce policy resources. Strengthening vertical IMCs is being explored in Aichi and Osaka prefectures through proactive prefectural leadership. It is expected that prefectural governments will provide more municipal services on behalf of the municipalities in the future, however, citizens remain in the dark about which entity provides the services.

Japanese municipalities are democratic governments. They need to avoid becoming governments that cannot be monitored by citizens through vertical IMCs. Fortunately, prefectures have systems for citizen participation, however, compared to municipalities, prefectures are less active in citizen participation meetings and forums. Therefore, as vertical IMCs become widespread, it is necessary to enhance the participation procedures that allow citizens to monitor and voice their opinions on projects that involve cooperation between prefectures and municipalities.

References

Bikker JA, van del Linde D (2016) Scale economies in local public administration. Local Gov Stud 42(3):441–463. https://doi.org/10.1080/03003930.2016.1146139

Böcher M (2008) Regional governance and rural development in Germany: the implementation of LEADER+. Sociol Rural 48(4):372–388. https://doi.org/10.1111/j.1467-9523.2008.00468.x

Dollery BE, Akimov A, Byrnes J (2009) Shared services in Australian local government: rationale, alternative models and empirical evidence. Aust J Public Adm 68(2):208–219

Downs A (1994) New visions for metropolitan America. The Brookings Institution, Washington, DC

Drew J, Kortt MA, Dollery B (2016) Did the big stick work? An empirical assessment of scale economies and the Queensland forced amalgamation program. Local Gov Stud 42(1):1–14. https://doi.org/10.1080/03003930.2013.874341

Feiock RC (2007) Rational choice and regional governance. J Urban Aff 29(1):47–63. https://doi.org/10.1111/j.1467-9906.2007.00322.x

Feiock RC (2013) The institutional collective action framework. Policy Stud J 41(3):397–425. https://doi.org/10.1111/psj.12023

Gerber ER, Henry AD, Lubell M (2013) Political homophily and collaboration in regional planning networks. Am J Polit Sci 57(3):598–610. https://doi.org/10.1111/ajps.12011

Giacomini D, Sancino A, Simonetto A (2018) The introduction of mandatory inter-municipal cooperation in small municipalities. Int J Public Sect Manag 31(3):331–346. https://doi.org/10.1108/IJPSM-03-2017-0071

Higashi-Mikawa Vision Council (2021) Higashi-Mikawa promotion vision 2030: creating the future through cooperation and collaboration Higashi-Mikawa continues to shine [Higashi mikawa shinko bijyon 2030: Renkei to kyodo de mirai wo tsukuru kagayaki tsuzukeru Higashi mikawa]. Aichi Prefecture, Nagoya. (in Japanese)

Holzer M, Fry JC (2011) Shared services and municipal consolidation: a critical analysis. Public Technology Institute, Alexandria

Imasato K (2017) Optimizing local resources: various phases of multi-level governance in the Higashi-mikawa region [Chiiki shigen no saitekika o hakaru: Higashi-mikawa chiiki ni okeru maruchi reberu gabanansu no shoso]. In: Shiraishi K, Matoba N, Abe D (eds) Local governance through a collaborative approach: building a theory of regional resilience [Renkei aporochi ni yoru rokaru gabanansu: Chiiki rejiriensu]. Nippon Hyoronsya Co., Ltd, Tokyo, pp 90–112. (in Japanese)

Kanemoto Y, Tokuoka K (2002) The criteria for establishing metropolitan employment areas in Japan. J Appl Area Stud 7:1–15

Kim SY, Swann WL, Weible CM, Bolognesi T, Krause RM, Park AYS, Tang T, Maletsky K, Feiock RC (2022) Updating the institutional collective action framework. Policy Stud J 50(1):9–34. https://doi.org/10.1111/psj.12392

Klok P, Denters B, Boogers M, Sanders M (2018) Intermunicipal cooperation in The Netherlands: the costs and the effectiveness of polycentric regional governance. Public Adm Rev 78(4):527–536. https://doi.org/10.1111/puar.12931

Lowery D (2000) A transaction costs model of metropolitan governance: allocation vs. redistribution in urban America. J Public Adm Res Theory 10:49–78

Lyons WE, Lowery D (1989) Governmental fragmentation versus consolidation: five public-choice myths about how to create informed, involved, and happy citizens. Public Adm Rev 49(6):533–543

Maher CS (2015) A longitudinal analysis of the effects of service consolidation on local government expenditures. Public Adm Q 39(3):393–425

Miller D, Nelles J, Dougherty G, Rickabaugh J (2019) Discovering American regionalism: an introduction to regional intergovernmental organizations. Routledge, New York

Miyashita T, Sumi E (2022) Policy evaluation of wide–area cooperation between municipalities: empirical analysis with "self–support settlement region framework" as the case study. Financ Rev (Policy Research Institute, Ministry of Finance, JAPAN) 149:158–201. (in Japanese)

Nara Prefecture (Nara Model Study Committee) (2017) The Nara model: a concerted effort by the prefecture and municipalities to confront a population decline, declining birthrate, and aging society [Nara moderu no arikata kento iinkai hokokusho Nara moderu: Jinko gensho shoshi korei shakai ni tachimukau ken to shichoson no soryokusen]. Nara: Nara Prefecture. (in Japanese)

Noda Y (2017) Forms and effects of shared services: an assessment of local government arrangements in Japan. Asia Pac J Public Adm 39(1):39–50. https://doi.org/10.1080/23276665.2017.1290903

Noda Y (2023) Intermunicipal cooperation, integration forms, and vertical and horizontal effects in Japan. Public Adm Rev 83(3):457–717. https://doi.org/10.1111/puar.13569

Osaka Prefecture, Taishi Town, Kanan Town, & Chihaya Akasaka Village (2023) Report on the study of measures to address future issues in the Minami–Kawachi region [Minami–Kawachi chiiki shorai kadai no taio hosaku no kento houkokusho]. Osaka Prefecture, Osaka. (in Japanese)

Ostrom V, Bish R, Ostrom E (1988) Local government in the United States. Institute for Contemporary Studies, San Francisco

Percoco M (2016) Strategic planning and institutional collective action in Italian cities. Public Manag Rev 18(1):139–158. https://doi.org/10.1080/14719037.2014.969758

Shaowei C, Rui L, Youqiang W (2016) Role and significance of political incentives understanding institutional collective action in local inter-governmental arrangements in China. Asia Pac J Public Adm 38(4):211–222. https://doi.org/10.1080/23276665.2016.1258890

Shrestha MK, Feiock RC (2011) Transaction cost, exchange embeddedness, and interlocal cooperation in local public goods supply. Polit Res Q 64(3):573–587. https://doi.org/10.1177/10659129103706

Tiebout CM (1956) A pure theory of local expenditures. J Polit Econ 64(5):416–424. https://doi.org/10.1086/257839

Toda T (2022) Remote collaboration and municipalities [Enkaku gata renkei to Jichitai]. Local Finance [Chiho zaimu] 6:186–195

Williamson OE (1979) Transaction-cost economics: the governance of contractual relations. J Law Econ 22(2):233–261

Yi H, Suo L, Shen R, Zhang J, Ramaswami A, Feiock RC (2018) Regional governance and institutional collective action for environmental sustainability. Public Adm Rev 78(4):556–566. https://doi.org/10.1111/puar.12799

Yu Noda is Professor at the Faculty of Policy Studies, Doshisha University. He was a Fulbright Visiting Scholar of Public Administration and Policy at Georgetown University in 2014. Since 2024, he has served as Principal of Doshisha Elementary School. In addition, he provided research guidance to graduate students at the Graduate School of Policy and Management at Doshisha University. His educational activities span all age groups from children to older adults. His research focuses on inter-municipal cooperation, performance information and learning effects of citizens, citizen satisfaction with government services, trust in local governments, and governance reforms. His recent articles have appeared in prominent journals, including *Public Administration Review*, *Public Management Review*, *Local Government Studies*, *International Review of Administrative Sciences*, *Asia-Pacific Journal of Public Administration*, and *International Journal of Public Administration*.

Chapter 8
Local Government and Citizen Co-production Through Neighborhood Associations

Kohei Suzuki ⓘ

Abstract This chapter explores co-production practices of local governments, focusing on the role of neighborhood associations (NHAs) in Japan. This chapter investigates the overall research question of this book: how to enhance government performance under resource constraints, by focusing on the concept of citizen co-production. Historically, NHAs have played a significant role in supplementing municipal service provisions as co-producers for local governments. Despite the rich history of NHAs and their contributions to public service delivery at the municipal level, theoretical and empirical studies on NHAs and co-production practices remain limited. This chapter aims to address this research gap by exploring the following research questions: What are NHAs from a perspective of citizen co-production? What are the potential contributions of studying NHAs to the broader theory of co-production? What are the future research agendas? The chapter provides an overview of the origin and evolution of the co-production concept. It then examines the main characteristics and activities of NHAs and discusses their roles in supplementing local public service provision. Finally, the chapter proposes potential research agendas to advance studies on co-production using Japan as a case study.

Keywords Citizens · Local governments · Co-production · Neighborhood associations · Collaborative governance

8.1 Introduction

Despite limited administrative resources, Japanese local governments have handled a greater volume of administrative activities and tasks compared to their counterparts in other OECD countries, as discussed in Chap. 1. The financial crisis since the

K. Suzuki (✉)
Institute of Public Administration, Leiden University, The Hague, The Netherlands
e-mail: k.suzuki@fgga.leidenuniv.nl

Y. Noda (ed.), *Local Governance in Japan*, Local and Urban Governance,
https://doi.org/10.1007/978-3-031-77322-8_8

late 2000s and demographic changes have further strained local governments' finances while increasing demands for public services. For many OECD member countries' governments facing fiscal challenges, one solution to maintain public services in the face of declining resources is to strategically devolve responsibility for these services to local actors, including voluntary organizations and communities (Suzuki 2020). However, what may be less known outside of Japan is that entrusting government roles and functions, including the provision of public services, to local private organizations such as neighborhood associations (NHAs) has been a key feature of Japanese public administration since the post-war period (Hidaka 2015; Mori 2008; Muramatsu 1997; Pekkanen 2009). This practice has been deeply rooted in the Japanese administrative system for decades, serving as a crucial strategy for local governments to effectively manage their responsibilities and maintain public service delivery.

Local governments in Japan have actively collaborated with NHAs to supplement their human and financial resources and carry out various administrative tasks and public service delivery activities. Despite the long-standing practice of collaboration between local governments and NHAs in Japan, English language research on this topic remains limited (Pekkanen 2009; Van Houwelingen 2012). Furthermore, although the concept of co-production was introduced in Japan as early as 1990 and has been extensively studied in Japanese research and practice (Kotagiri 2018), there is a scarcity of English language studies that utilize Japanese cases in the field of public administration and management, with only a few exceptions.[1] This suggests a need for greater communication and exchange of ideas between Japanese and English language research communities on these topics.

The limited exchange of ideas between Japanese and English language research communities is unfortunate, particularly in light of the growing academic interest in the significance of contextual factors and the development of global public administration and management knowledge (Beagles et al. 2019; Bhuiyan and Perry 2024; Milward et al. 2016; O'Toole Jr and Meier 2015; Peci and Fornazin 2017; Roberts 2018, 2021; Suzuki and Hur 2020). By incorporating insights from understudied countries, researchers can refine and further develop established theories and concepts while also testing their external validity (Toshkov 2016). This lack of dialogue represents a missed opportunity to advance our understanding of co-production in diverse contexts and to build a more comprehensive and globally relevant body of knowledge in the field.

---

[1] Several studies (written in English) have considered related concepts such as citizen volunteering and civil society (Avenell 2010; Haddad 2006, 2011, 2020; Schoppa 2012), social capital at the local level (Aldrich 2012; Fraser 2021; Fraser and Aldrich 2021; Van Houwelingen 2012), citizen participation (Aoki 2018; Uddin et al. 2019), and grassroots groups and non-profit organizations (Okada et al. 2017; Pekkanen 2006, 2009; Pekkanen and Tsujinaka 2008). However, comparatively little effort has focused on the application of co-production concept in the Japanese context. Examples of studies on co-production or collaborative governance include but are not limited to Aoki (2014, 2015), Ben-Ari (1990), Dollery et al. (2020), Kinoshita et al. (2020), Ohta (2020), Pestoff (2021), Suzuki (2017), Suzuki et al. (2021), Yamazaki et al. (2022).

This chapter focuses on NHAs, which have played a significant role in supporting local governments to sustain public service provisions and local communities. The primary purpose of this chapter is to expand the collective knowledge of co-production by connecting Japan's experience with the scholarly discussions on this concept in the international academic community. This chapter aims to address this research gap by exploring the following research questions: What are the NHAs from a perspective of citizen co-production? What are the potential contributions of studying NHAs to the broader theory of co-production? What are the future research agendas? The chapter consists of three parts. First, it provides a brief overview of the origin and development of the concept of co-production. Second, it reviews the main characteristics and activities of NHAs and discusses their roles in supplementing local public service provisions. Finally, the chapter discusses potential research agendas for theory development and testing of co-production using Japan as a case study.

8.2 Co-production Research

8.2.1 Origins and Development of Co-production

Coproduction is a concept that describes the collaboration between citizens and government in the joint production of public services. The concept was developed and first applied in the late 1970s and early 1980s by Dr. Elinor Ostrom, Dr. Vincent Ostrom, and their colleagues at Indiana University's Workshop in Political Theory and Policy Analysis in the United States (Brudney 1984; Nabatchi et al. 2017; Ostrom and Ostrom 1979; Parks et al. 1981; Percy 1983; Sharp 1980; Whitaker 1980). During this period, many large central cities in the United States faced various challenges, including demographic shifts, land-development trends, economic downturns, stagflation, and political issues (Justice and Scorsone 2013). State and local governments experienced pressure to provide more services while dealing with budget constraints, leading to a shift in budgeting practices and the emergence of research on cutback management and organizational decline (Levine 1978, 1979; Plerhoples and Scorsone 2013; Raudla et al. 2015).

Amidst these developments, co-production gained popularity as an innovative approach to public service delivery. By involving citizens in the production of public services, co-production was seen as a way to address the challenge of providing more services with limited resources (Brudney and England 1983). Engaging citizens as partners in service delivery offered a means to maintain or even improve service levels while effectively managing costs. The emergence of co-production as a topic of interest in public administration research during this period can be attributed to its potential to address the challenges faced by state and local governments. As scholars and practitioners sought new ways to deliver public services in an era of fiscal constraints and increased demands, co-production presented a promising alternative to traditional service delivery models.

Since its introduction, scholarly interest in co-production has fluctuated (Nabatchi et al. 2017). While co-production quickly gained momentum and inspired ground-breaking research in the late 1970s and 1980s (Brudney and England 1983; Percy 1984; Sharp 1980; Whitaker 1980), its progress seemed to stall in the 1990s and early 2000s due to several factors, including the rise of New Public Management (NPM) as the dominant paradigm in public administration (Brudney 2021; Nabatchi et al. 2017). NPM, which focuses on improving the efficiency and effectiveness of public organizations, views citizens as clients or customers of public services rather than partners of government, as the co-production approach does. Under NPM, governments were advised to view their citizens as customers and to aim for more professional, efficient, effective, and customer- and result-oriented public management (Brudney 2021; Hood 1991; Lapuente and Van de Walle 2020). This shift in how citizens were perceived under the NPM framework likely diverted scholarly attention away from co-production during the 1990s, even if it did not entirely suppress interest in the concept (Brudney 2021; Nabatchi et al. 2017).

However, in recent years, there has been a resurgence of interest in co-production among scholars and practitioners due to several factors. The emergence of "new governance" (Rhodes 1996; Salamon 2000) and "collaborative governance" (McGuire 2006; Ansell and Gash 2008) approaches has played a significant role in this revival. These approaches emphasize a pluralistic model of public service that relies on interorganizational relationships, networks, collaborative partnerships, and other forms of multi-actor policy making and public action. Additionally, the global financial crisis has compelled governments worldwide to reduce public services and spending, leading scholars to re-examine co-production as a potential avenue for cost savings. Furthermore, the weakening notion of citizenship and the associated decline in social capital have prompted a search for innovative public service delivery mechanisms that aim to reinvigorate the role of citizens in their communities, moving beyond their limited roles as voters and customers (Nabatchi et al. 2017).[2]

8.2.2 Roles of Citizens as Co-producers of Public Services

The concept of co-production emphasizes the proactive roles of citizens as producers of public services rather than treating them as passive recipients or clients (Ostrom 1996). In the late 1960s and 1970s, when co-production was first conceptualized, the dominant approach to urban service delivery treated citizens as mere consumers of public services, not as active participants. Conceptually, this model consisted of two distinct spheres: regular producers (service agents and bureaucrats) and consumers (clients, citizens, interest groups, and neighborhood associations). Producers operated within a service delivery environment shaped by public demands

---

[2] See also Brudney (2021) for history of co-production research. See also Sicilia et al. (2019), Palumbo and Manesh (2023), and Voorberg et al. (2015) for systematic reviews and recent development in the co-production literature.

and support, using standard procedures to allocate goods and services. Consumers responded to the adequacy of service delivery through various means, such as making new demands, supporting or rejecting service patterns, or providing feedback (Brudney and England 1983).

While the dominant model at that time emphasized a clear distinction between producers and consumers of public services, the co-production model envisions an overlap between these two spheres of activities and "the conjoint responsibility of lay citizens and professional government agents for the delivery of public services" (Sharp 1980, 105). Co-production, therefore, involves "a mixing of the productive efforts of regular and consumer producers" (Parks et al. 1981, 1002). In the co-production model, citizens are considered not only consumers of public services but also active consumer-producers in public service delivery. This model recognizes that citizens have the ability to actively participate in and contribute to the delivery of local services, thereby improving both the quantity and quality of services provided by local agencies (Ostrom 1996; Percy 1984). In the municipal realm, co-production can be accomplished by community groups or individual residents (Bovaird and Loeffler 2012). Bovaird (2007, 847) defines user and community co-production as "the provision of services through regular, long-term relationships between professionalized service providers (in any sector) and service users or other members of the community, where all parties make substantial resource contributions".

8.2.3 Benefits of Co-production

Co-production is a distinctive approach that goes beyond traditional citizen participation methods by directly engaging citizens in the implementation of public policy alongside professionals. This approach seeks to bridge the democratic deficit in public service provision, foster greater trust in government, and ultimately result in more effective and efficient public services and programs (McMullin 2021b). Additionally, co-production has the potential to lead to better individual well-being and citizen empowerment (Bovaird and Loeffler 2012; Fledderus et al. 2014; Levine and Fisher 1984; McMullin 2021b; Ostrom 1996; Percy 1984). The quality of public services is expected to improve through citizen inputs as co-producers of services.[3]

---

[3] For example, when it comes to police services, crime prevention can be more effective when it involves not only the efforts of the regular service provider, the police, but also the contributions of citizens. These citizen inputs can include participating in neighborhood watch and patrol programs, alerting the police when they witness suspicious activities, investing in self-defense equipment, and engaging in community organizations focused on safety and security. By working together, the police and the community can create a more comprehensive and efficient approach to crime prevention (Ostrom 1978).

However, despite the premise that co-production offers various benefits, empirical evidence supporting these claims is surprisingly scarce (Bovaird and Loeffler 2021; Brix et al. 2020). For instance, Voorberg et al. (2015) conducted a systematic review of 122 articles on co-production and found that only 24 studies reported concrete outcomes. The majority of the studies included in their review did not even aim to identify or evaluate the results of co-production. Instead, most of them focused on identifying influential factors for co-production or finding a typology of co-production, somewhat assuming that co-production leads to better outcomes.

8.2.4   Co-production and National Contexts

To the best of the author's knowledge, there is no reliable data on the coverage of studied countries in co-production research. However, the majority of existing studies still seem to focus on the United States or European countries, with studies focusing on Asia and other non-Western countries being very limited. Although there has been a growing body of research on co-production from various countries, the theoretical exploration of how co-production manifests and operates across different sectors and countries has been relatively limited. In particular, we still do not know how different institutional arrangements, administrative traditions, and cultural factors play out in the implementation of co-production activities (McMullin 2019, 2021a, b). For example, from a comparative perspective, in what country context or institutional arrangements is co-production more likely to take place? To what extent can the concept of co-production, which has been theoretically developed in a few OECD member countries, be applied to public management practice in other countries? Are there any countries with more suitable conditions for co-production? With the goal of theory development, researchers need to increase the number of countries studied and conduct more theoretical and empirical research (Toshkov 2016).

In fact, the skewed focus on specific regions, particularly the lack of studies on the Asia-Pacific region, is not unique to co-production research but is a broader issue in the public administration and management field.[4] By conducting co-production studies using Japan as a case, researchers can contribute to the development and testing of co-production theories while addressing the need for context-specific research and the critiques of West-centric approaches (Beagles et al. 2019; Gulrajani and Moloney 2012; Milward et al. 2016; O'Toole Jr and Meier 2015; Roberts 2018, 2021; Peci and Fornazin 2017).

---

[4] See several recent scholarly efforts to build more global public administration and management knowledge by incorporating studies focusing on the Asia-Pacific region (Chen et al. 2022; Chen et al. 2023; Lapuente and Suzuki 2022; van Der Wal and Demircioglu 2020; Van der Wal and Mussagulova 2023).

8.3   The Role of Local Neighborhood Associations in Supplementing Government Resources

Co-production has been understood as the devolution of service responsibility to neighborhood organizations, individual service consumers, and public/private partnerships, with citizens and public agencies jointly providing public services (Levine and Fisher 1984). Examples include citizens carrying out garbage collection, parent participation in education, and voluntary organization of recreation programs using local government facilities. Along with the deprofessionalization of bureaucracies, which involves replacing professionals with non-specialists in formal government positions, utilizing volunteers, and employing part-time staff, the devolution of service responsibilities to citizen organizations and service users presents a promising approach to public service delivery in times of fiscal stress (Levine and Fisher 1984).

In fact, although not widely recognized by researchers outside of those specializing in Japan, the devolution of service responsibilities to local citizen groups and service consumers, as well as the reliance on community groups' networks and human resources, has been a key characteristic of post-war Japanese bureaucracies (Muramatsu 1997; Hidaka 2015; Ohta 2020). In the aftermath of World War II, the Japanese government faced severe resource constraints, including limited personnel and budgets. To achieve its post-war reconstruction and economic development goals, the government chose not to expand its own organizational size and agencies. Instead, it created networks, including private organizations, to mobilize resources from society as a whole to accomplish its policy objectives. Muramatsu characterized this distinctive feature of post-war Japanese administration as the "maximum mobilization system" (Muramatsu 1997). For example, the central government delegated administrative tasks and activities to local governments and monitored their progress, enabling it to achieve its policy goals without increasing its own size. At the local level, local governments have maintained relationships with community organizations and effectively utilized their human resources, ideas, and assets to supplement scarce resources and carry out administrative activities (Hidaka 2015; Ohta 2020). Local neighborhood associations (NHAs) have played a key role in complementing the lack of administrative resources of local governments.

8.4   Local Neighborhood Associations in Japan

There are differing views regarding the origins of NHAs, with some researchers tracing their roots back to the seventh century. However, many scholars argue that NHAs emerged during or after the Meiji era (1868–1912), which marked the beginning of Japan's modernization (Torigoe 1994). NHAs in their current form developed during the twentieth century (Pekkanen 2006, 2009). Although there are several definitions of NHAs by Japanese scholars (Torigoe 1994), recent NHA studies in English often rely on Pekkanen's (2009, 29) definition: "voluntary groups whose membership is drawn from a small, geographically delimited, and exclusive area (a neighborhood), and whose activities are multiple and are centered on that same area".

NHAs are a ubiquitous form of civil society organization in Japan, far more prevalent than in other advanced industrialized democracies (Pekkanen 2009). These associations are formed based on residential proximity, typically comprising 100 to 300 households. Members pay dues, elect leaders, and engage in various community activities together (Pekkanen 2009). NHAs are called *jichikai, chonai-kai, choukai, burakukai, kukai, ku*, and other names in Japanese, depending on the area. According to the Ministry of Internal Affairs and Communications (2024a), there were 295,838 NHAs in Japan as of April 1, 2023, compared to 293,227 in August 1996 (Ministry of Internal Affairs and Communications 1997), indicating no major change in the total number of NHAs in recent years.[5] Out of 1741 municipalities in Japan, 85.0% (1479 municipalities) reported having NHAs in their jurisdiction, confirming that NHAs are present in most municipalities.

The unit of membership in an NHA is the household, and each association is restricted to a specific geographic area, with only one NHA per area. To acquire legal status, all individuals with a domicile in the area must be eligible for membership, and a substantial number of them should be current members (Ministry of Internal Affairs and Communications 2024a). Although nationwide data on household membership rates in NHAs is not available, the Ministry of Internal Affairs and Communications (2024a) provides membership rates for 5050 legally recognized NHAs. Among these, 45.9% (2320 NHAs) have a 90–100% household membership rate, 31.0% (1563 NHAs) have a 70–90% rate, 16.7% (843 NHAs) have a 50–70% rate, and 6.4% (324 NHAs) have less than 50% membership rate. As previously mentioned, NHAs are the most pervasive form of residents' association in Japan, present in most municipal areas and encompassing a considerable portion of households as members. In fact, the prevalence of NHAs throughout Japan and the longstanding relationships between municipalities and NHAs are considered comparative advantages that Japanese local governments have in practicing and promoting coproduction at the local level (Dollery et al. 2020). These associations have been instrumental in providing and implementing a range of local public services, including fire protection, flood warnings, cultural festivals, and various community activities (Pekkanen 2006, 2009).

NHAs have been described as "state-society straddler organizations" or "ambiguous organizations" (Pekkanen 2009, 28). Some Japanese public administration experts view NHAs as quasi-public entities or quasi-municipalities rather than voluntary associations (Kanai 2004; Nishio 2000), while others consider them "embedded organizations" that engage in frequent, habitual interactions with the bureaucracy and participate in policy-making and implementation processes alongside bureaucrats (Haddad 2006). Hidaka (2021) refers to NHAs as "informal players in the local governance system", lacking a formal legal foundation. In contrast, some

---

[5]These numbers are limited to those NHAs which have acquired legal status.

scholars regard NHAs as civil society organizations, emphasizing their voluntary and independent nature (Pekkanen 2006, 2009).

Although not explicitly stated, co-production literature in English seems to assume co-production with purely independent resident associations and does not elaborate on co-production with associations of an ambiguous nature such as NHAs. Ostrom (1996, 1973) defines co-production as "the process through which inputs used to produce a good or service are contributed by individuals who are not 'in' the same organization". Therefore, the ambiguous nature of NHAs, whether they are considered public organizations or external entities, is a key issue when exploring their role in co-production.

Another characteristic of NHAs is their engagement in various service activities for the common benefit of local residents (Hidaka 2021). Neighborhood associations are involved in activities that encompass various aspects of community life, including fire and crime prevention, education, welfare, sanitation, and ceremonies such as weddings and funerals (Torigoe 1994). According to Ministry of Internal Affairs and Communications (2024a), the top activities performed by legally recognized NHAs are: (1) environmental beautification and cleaning activities in the area (93.3%), (2) communication among residents (circular notices, newsletters, etc.) (92.5%), (3) maintenance and management of community facilities (85.8%), (4) disaster and fire prevention (48.5%), (5) traffic safety and crime prevention (37.4%), (6) cultural and recreational activities (31.5%), (7) other activities (28.4%), (8) sports and recreational activities (26.0%), (9) organizing events such as bon dance, festivals, elderly appreciation day, and adulthood celebration day (25.8%), (10) social welfare activities (mainly for the elderly) (22.0%), (11) maintenance, repair, and improvement of roads and street lights (20.9%), (12) social welfare activities (mainly for children) (19.8%), (13) requests and petitions to administrative agencies (16.0%), and (14) celebrations and condolences (10.2%).[6]

NHAs work in close collaboration with local authorities, enabling them to enhance the efficiency and effectiveness of government services while simultaneously reducing expenses (Pekkanen and Tsujinaka 2008). In addition to their voluntary activities, NHAs have been extensively involved in local governments' administrative activities as informal actors. For instance, they have been responsible for disseminating administrative information to local residents, acting as intermediaries between residents and local governments by conveying residents' requests to the authorities, and supplementing or carrying out administrative services on behalf of the government. This system, in which local governments entrust NHAs with the execution of various administrative tasks, is referred to by Japanese scholars as the "administrative cooperation system" (gyōsei kyōryoku seido) (Hidaka 2015; Mori 2008). In fact, while some activities of NHAs are purely resident-led independent activities, a significant portion of their activities involves supporting, supplementing, and acting as an extension of municipal administrative functions (Hidaka 2015).

---

[6] The percentages of NHAs show the proportion of approved NHAs that were granted legal status between the fiscal years 2018 and 2022.

Many local governments engage in various administrative cooperation tasks with NHAs. According to Hidaka (2022), which collects survey data from 730 city-level municipalities in 2020, 86.6% of the responding local governments work with NHAs on irregular and emergency information distribution, circulation, and posting of notices. Collection of donations and fundraising is carried out by 85.4% of the surveyed local governments in collaboration with NHAs. Additionally, 83.5% of the local governments involve NHAs in the recommendation and selection of community committee members and in channeling local needs to the local government. Road beautification and environmental maintenance are undertaken by 80.8% of the surveyed local governments in partnership with NHAs. Furthermore, 79.9% of the local governments distribute, circulate, and post regular government bulletins through NHAs, while 79.5% manage crime prevention lights, curved mirrors, and community centers with the help of NHAs. Lastly, 75.3% of the surveyed local governments conduct disaster prevention drills and implement measures for vulnerable people during disasters in cooperation with NHAs.

Several studies have documented co-production activities between local governments and NHAs. For instance, Suzuki et al. (2021) shows how a local government collaborates with NHAs to tackle the issue of social isolation among elderly citizens in the Adachi ward. The Adachi ward encourages neighborhood associations to engage in activities that support and monitor senior citizens who may be at risk of isolation. These associations carry out various initiatives to connect with and assist the elderly population in their communities. Kinoshita et al. (2020) documents the synergistic relationships between local government and local community groups fostered by these co-production programs and the significant roles that NHAs play in creating operational manuals for evacuation centers in Sendai city. Although the term "co-production" is not explicitly used, Van Houwelingen (2012) describes how NHAs' activities contribute to enhancing social capital at the community level.

Population declines and government service cuts, especially in rural areas of Japan, have become critical issues. Suzuki (2017) empirically analyzes how local government spending cuts are associated with co-production activities primarily by NHAs, complementing declining administrative resources. Recently, the Japanese government, especially the Ministry of Internal Affairs and Communications, has been promoting the establishment and activities of regional management organizations (RMOs) to solve local issues and supplement public service provisions at the local level (Jentzsch 2024). RMOs are resident organizations that operate in a wider area than NHAs and include more local groups such as NPOs and private companies as members in addition to NHAs. For example, RMOs are engaged in various activities for the benefit of local residents, such as maintenance of public facilities, operation of community buses, snow shoveling and snow removal, interaction with the elderly, and childcare support (Ministry of Internal Affairs and Communications 2024b). Although like NHAs, RMOs are considered straddler organizations (Jentzsch 2024), they perform a number of significant activities in the context of co-production.

8.5   Conclusions

This chapter has provided a concise overview of the origin and evolution of the co-production concept, as well as the key features of Neighborhood Associations (NHAs) and their co-production activities in Japan, addressing the first research question: What are NHAs from a citizen co-production perspective? The idea of co-production primarily emerged and evolved as an alternative approach to service delivery for U.S. municipalities confronting financial hardship. Interestingly, Japanese local governments, which have consistently faced constraints in human and financial resources, have historically utilized and mobilized the resources of community-based organizations, particularly NHAs, to provide public goods and services in a similar manner. Despite this established practice of co-production, Japanese local governments' co-production efforts with NHAs have been under-studied in the research on co-production, particularly in terms of testing and developing existing theories.

Another significant point is to examine how accumulated co-production research in the Japanese language makes theoretical and empirical contributions to the broader field of co-production research, addressing the second research question. As discussed earlier, existing ideas and theories of co-production have made limited efforts to examine co-production practices outside North America and particular European countries, with little focus on comparative research. For example, how does co-production practice in Japan differ from that in other countries? From a comparative perspective, does Japan have advantages in co-production due to the existence of NHAs? Is co-production with ambiguous organizations such as NHAs unique to Japan? What insights can we gain from Japan's experience? Can findings from Japanese research fill the gaps in English-language research on co-production? Systematic reviews of Japanese-language research on co-production, as seen in Cho et al. (2020) for Korean language studies on participatory budgeting, should serve as a bridge between academic discussions in the international community and those in the Japanese community, leading to a greater contribution to the development of global knowledge on co-production.

Finally, to answer the third research question, the chapter concludes by proposing several significant potential research questions for future study. One such question involves examining the impacts of co-production with NHAs on public service quality, efficiency, effectiveness, and citizen-government relationships. As explained earlier, despite the large volume of theoretical studies on co-production, empirical work aimed at analyzing the effects of co-production remains limited (Bovaird and Loeffler 2021; Brix et al. 2020). For example, to what extent does co-production with NHAs help municipalities improve their fiscal efficiency and the quality of public services? To what extent does the presence of NHAs increase residents' trust in their local government? How much do residents' satisfaction with and trust in government services differ between municipalities or areas where NHAs are active and those where they are not? These questions highlight promising directions for future research, given the limited empirical work on this topic.

References

Aldrich DP (2012) Building resilience: social capital in post-disaster recovery. University of Chicago Press, Chicago

Ansell C, Gash A (2008) Collaborative governance in theory and practice. J Public Adm Res Theory 18(4):543–571. https://doi.org/10.1093/jopart/mum032

Aoki N (2014) Wide-area collaboration in the aftermath of the march 11 disasters in Japan: implications for responsible disaster management. Int Rev Adm Sci 81(1):196–213. https://doi.org/10.1177/0020852314541563

Aoki N (2015) Collaborative manpower support for restoring hope in the aftermath of the march 11 disasters in Japan. In: Brassard C, Howitt AM, Giles DW (eds) Natural disaster management in the Asia-Pacific: policy and governance. Springer, Tokyo, pp 101–117

Aoki N (2018) Sequencing and combining participation in urban planning: the case of tsunami-ravaged Onagawa Town, Japan. Cities 72:226–236. https://doi.org/10.1016/j.cities.2017.08.020

Avenell SA (2010) Facilitating spontaneity: the state and independent volunteering in contemporary Japan. Soc Sci Jpn J 13(1):69–93. https://doi.org/10.1093/ssjj/jyq001

Beagles JE, Schnell S, Gerard C (2019) Overcoming parochialism in American Public Administration. Perspect Public Manag Gov 2(4):255–266. https://doi.org/10.1093/ppmgov/gvz009

Ben-Ari E (1990) A bureaucrat in every Japanese kitchen? On cultural assumptions and coproduction. Adm Soc 21(4):472–492. https://doi.org/10.1177/009539979002100405

Bhuiyan S, Perry JL (2024) Building global public administration knowledge: leveraging the power of collaboration. Public Adm Rev 84(3):426–431. https://doi.org/10.1111/puar.13768

Bovaird T (2007) Beyond engagement and participation: user and community coproduction of public services. Public Adm Rev 67(5):846–860. https://doi.org/10.1111/j.1540-6210.2007.00773.x

Bovaird T, Loeffler E (2012) From engagement to co-production: the contribution of users and communities to outcomes and public value. Volunt Int J Volunt Nonprofit Org 23:1119–1138. https://doi.org/10.1007/s11266-012-9309-6

Bovaird T, Loeffler E (2021) Developing evidence-based co-production: a research agenda. In: The Palgrave handbook of co-production of public services and outcomes. Palgrave Macmillan, Cham, pp 693–713

Brix J, Krogstrup HK, Mortensen NM (2020) Evaluating the outcomes of co-production in local government. Local Gov Stud 46(2):169–185. https://doi.org/10.1080/03003930.2019.1702530

Brudney JL (1984) Local coproduction of services and the analysis of municipal productivity. Urban Aff Q 19(4):465–484. https://doi.org/10.1177/004208168401900405

Brudney JL (2021) Co-production in political science and public administration. In: Loeffler E, Bovaird T (eds) The Palgrave handbook of co-production of public services and outcomes. Palgrave Macmillan, Cham, pp 61–77

Brudney JL, England RE (1983) Toward a definition of the coproduction concept. Public Adm Rev:59–65. https://doi.org/10.2307/975300

Chen W, Donga B, Hsieha C, Liua N, Walker RM, Wanga Y, Wen B, Wua P, Zhang J (2022) Experimental research in the Asia-Pacific region: review and assessment of regional capacity. Asia Pac J Public Adm 44(1):4–25. https://doi.org/10.1080/23276665.2021.1945470

Chen C, Kim S, Ma L (2023) Special issue introduction: integrating Asia Pacific influences and public management research. Asia Pac J Public Adm 45(2):115–117. https://doi.org/10.1080/23276665.2023.2172438

Cho BS, No W, Park Y (2020) Diffusing participatory budgeting knowledge: lessons from Korean-language research. Asia Pac J Public Adm 42(3):188–206. https://doi.org/10.1080/23276665.2020.1789481

Dollery B, Kinoshita Y, Yamazaki K (2020) Humanitarian co-production in local government: the case of natural disaster volunteering in Japan. Local Gov Stud 46(6):959–978. https://doi.org/10.1080/03003930.2019.1702531

Fledderus J, Brandsenand T, Honingh M (2014) Restoring trust through the co-production of public services: a theoretical elaboration. Public Manag Rev 16(3):424–443. https://doi.org/10.108 0/14719037.2013.848920

Fraser T (2021) Japanese social capital and social vulnerability indices: measuring drivers of community resilience 2000–2017. Int J Disaster Risk Reduct 52:101965

Fraser T, Aldrich DP (2021) The dual effect of social ties on COVID-19 spread in Japan. Sci Rep 11(1):1596. https://doi.org/10.1038/s41598-021-81001-4

Gulrajani N, Moloney K (2012) Globalizing public administration: today's research and tomorrow's agenda. Public Adm Rev 72(1):78–86

Haddad MA (2006) Civic responsibility and patterns of voluntary participation around the world. Comp Pol Stud 39(10):1220–1242. https://doi.org/10.1177/0010414005281937

Haddad A (2011) A state-in-society approach to the nonprofit sector: welfare services in Japan. Volunt Int J Volunt Nonprofit Org 22(1):26–47

Haddad MA (2020) Civil society in Japan. In: Takeda H, Williams M (eds) Routledge handbook of contemporary Japan. Routledge, London, pp 102–117

Hidaka A (2015) An empirical study on the "administrative cooperation system": the "collaborative" relationship between basic local governments and neighborhood associations ["Gyōsei kyōryoku seido" ni kansuru jisshō kenkyū - Kiso-teki jichitai to chōnaikai jichikai to no "kyōdō" kankei]. Yamanashigakuin Law Rev:1–64. (in Japanese)

Hidaka A (2021) The future developments of the local government community policy focusing on the relationship between municipalities and community Organisations [Jichitai komyuniti seisaku no yukue: Chōnaikai jichikai to no kankei wo chūshin ni]. Yamanashigakuin Law Rev 87:87–151. (in Japanese)

Hidaka A (2022) How are the relationships between municipal governments and neighborhood associations changing?: a comparative analysis of the 2008 local government survey and the 2020 urban survey [Toshi jichitai to chōnaikai jichikai to no kankei ni dono yō na henka ga shōjite iru ka: 2008-nen jichitai chōsa to 2020-nen toshi chōsa no hikaku bunseki]. Yamanashigakuin Law Rev:89–153. (in Japanese)

Hood C (1991) A public management for all seasons? Public Adm 69(1):3–19. https://doi.org/10.1111/j.1467-9299.1991.tb00779.x

Jentzsch H (2024) Regional management organizations as institutional compromises: renegotiating state-society relations in Japan's aging peripheries. The international conference "compromise in plural worlds: comparing Japan and Europe", Essen, Germany, March 7–8, 2024

Justice JB, Scorsone EA (2013) Measuring and predicting local government fiscal stress. In: Levine H, Jonathan BJ, Scorsone EA (eds) Handbook of local government fiscal health. Jones & Bartlett Learning, Burlington, pp 43–74

Kanai T (2004) Local government administration and citizen activities in post-war Japan [Sengo Nihon no jichitai gyōsei to jūmin katsudō]. In: Nishio M, Jinno N (eds) Jichitai kaikaku 9: Jūmin/komyuniti to no kyōdō. Gyousei, Tokyo. (in Japanese)

Kinoshita Y, Dollery B, Yamazak K (2020) Creating institutional advantage: local government co-production with community groups. Asia Pac J Public Adm 1–18. https://doi.org/10.1080/23276665.2020.1776624

Kotagiri Y (2018) Research trend of collaboration theory [Kyodo ron no kenkyu doukou to kadai: gyousei gaku wo chushin toshita gakusaiteki shiten kara]. Soc Sci Res [Shakai Kagaku Kenkyu] 32:97–124. (in Japanese)

Lapuente V, Suzuki K (2022) Quality of government in the Asia Pacific region. Asia Pac J Public Adm 44(2):101–105. https://doi.org/10.1080/23276665.2022.2062400

Lapuente V, Van de Walle S (2020) The effects of new public management on the quality of public services. Governance 33(3):461–475. https://doi.org/10.1111/gove.12502

Levine CH (1978) Organizational decline and cutback management. Public Adm Rev 38(4):316–325. https://doi.org/10.2307/975813

Levine CH (1979) More on cutback management: hard questions for hard times. Public Adm Rev 39(2):179–183. https://doi.org/10.2307/3110475

Levine CH, Fisher G (1984) Citizenship and service delivery: the promise of coproduction. Public Adm Rev 44:178–189

McGuire M (2006) Collaborative public management: assessing what we know and how we know it. Public Adm Rev 66:33–43. https://doi.org/10.1111/j.1540-6210.2006.00664.x

McMullin C (2019) Coproduction and the third sector in France: governmental traditions and the French conceptualization of participation. Soc Policy Adm 53(2):295–310. https://doi.org/10.1111/spol.12482

McMullin C (2021a) Challenging the necessity of new public governance: co-production by third sector organizations under different models of public management. Public Adm 99(1):5–22. https://doi.org/10.1111/padm.12672

McMullin C (2021b) Co-production of public services: institutional barriers to the involvement of citizens in policy implementation. In: The Palgrave handbook of the public servant. Springer, Cham, pp 651–667

Milward B, Jensen L, Roberts A, Dussauge-Laguna MI, Junjan V, Torenvlied R, Boin A, Colebatch HK, Kettl D, Durant R (2016) Is public management neglecting the state? Governance 29(3):311–334. https://doi.org/10.1111/gove.12201

Ministry of Internal Affairs and Communications (1997) Survey Results on the Status of Approval Procedures for Community-Based Organizations [Chien ni yoru dantai no ninka jimu no jōkyō-tō ni kansuru chōsa kekka]. Accessed June 5, 2024. https://www.soumu.go.jp/main_content/000901478.pdf. (in Japanese)

Ministry of Internal Affairs and Communications (2024a) Survey Results on the Status of Approval Procedures for Community-Based Organizations [Chien ni yoru dantai no ninka jimu no jōkyō-tō ni kansuru chōsa kekka]. Accessed June 5, 2024. https://www.soumu.go.jp/main_content/000938670.pdf. (in Japanese)

Ministry of Internal Affairs and Communications (2024b) FY2023 Research Project Report on the Formation and Sustainable Operation of Regional Management Organizations [Reiwa 5-nendo Chiiki Unei Soshiki no Keisei oyobi Jizokutekina Unei ni kansuru Chosa Kenkyu Jigyo Hokokusho]. Accessed June 13, 2024. https://www.soumu.go.jp/main_content/000874295.pdf. (in Japanese)

Mori H (2008) The reality of partnerships: issues in the relationships between local governments and community-based organizations and the administrative cooperation system [Pātonāshippu no genjitsu: Chihō seifu · chiensoshiki kan kankei to gyōsei kyōryoku seido no kadai]. Ann Jpn Soc Public Adm 43:170–188. (in Japanese)

Muramatsu M (1997) Post-war politics in Japan: bureaucracy versus the party/parties in power. In: Muramatsu M, Naschold F (eds) State and Administration in Japan and Germany. De Gruyter, Berlin/Boston, pp 13–38

Nabatchi T, Sancino A, Sicilia M (2017) Varieties of participation in public services: the who, when, and what of coproduction. Public Adm Rev 77(5):766–776. https://doi.org/10.1111/puar.12765

Nishio M (2000) Adinistrative activities [Gyosei no katsudou]. Yuhikaku, Tokyo. (in Japanese)

O'Toole Jr LJ, Meier KJ (2015) Public management, context, and performance: in quest of a more general theory. J Public Adm Res Theory 25(1):237–256. https://doi.org/10.1093/jopart/muu011

Ohta K (2020) Challenges and efforts towards local governance capacity development in the era of austerity in Japan. In: Edelenbos J, Molenveld A, van Meerkerk I (eds) Civic engagement, community-based initiatives and governance capacity. Routledge, New York, pp 156–176

Okada A, Ishida Y, Nakajima T, Kotagiri Y (2017) The state of nonprofit sector research in Japan: a literature review. Voluntaristics Rev 2(3):1–68

Ostrom E (1978) Citizen participation and policing: what do we know? J Voluntary Action Res 7(1–2):102–108. https://doi.org/10.1177/089976407800700110

Ostrom E (1996) Crossing the great divide: coproduction, synergy, and development. World Dev 24(6):1073–1087. https://doi.org/10.1016/0305-750X(96)00023-X

Ostrom V, Ostrom E (1979) Public goods and public choices. In: Savas ES (ed) Alternatives for delivering public services: toward improved performance. Routledge, New York, pp 7–49

Palumbo R, Manesh MF (2023) Travelling along the public service co-production road: a bibliometric analysis and interpretive review. Public Manag Rev 25(7):1348–1384. https://doi.org/1 0.1080/14719037.2021.2015222

Parks RB, Baker PC, Kiser L, Oakerson R, Ostrom E, Ostrom V, Percy SL, Vandivort MB, Whitaker GP, Wilson R (1981) Consumers as coproducers of public services: some economic and institutional considerations. Policy Stud J 9(7):1001–1011. https://doi.org/10.1111/j.1541-0072.1981.tb01208.xh

Peci A, Fornazin M (2017) The knowledge-building process of public administration research: a comparative perspective between Brazil and North American contexts. Int Rev Adm Sci 83(1_suppl):99–119. https://doi.org/10.1177/0020852316637660

Pekkanen R (2006) Japan's dual civil society: members without advocates. Stanford University Press

Pekkanen R (2009) Japan's neighborhood associations: membership without advocacy. In: Local organizations and urban governance in East and Southeast Asia. Routledge, pp 37–67

Pekkanen R, Tsujinaka Y (2008) Neighbourhood associations and the demographic challenge. In: Coulmas F, Conrad H, Schad-Seifert A, Vogt G (eds) The demographic challenge: a handbook about Japan. Brill, Leiden, pp 707–720

Percy SL (1983) Citizen coproduction: prospects for improving service delivery. J Urban Aff 5(3):203–210. https://doi.org/10.1111/j.1467-9906.1983.tb00035.x

Percy SL (1984) Citizen participation in the coproduction of urban services. Urban Aff Q 19(4):431–446. https://doi.org/10.1177/004208168401900403

Pestoff V (2021) Co-production and Japanese healthcare: work environment, governance, service quality and social values. Routledge, New York

Plerhoples C, Scorsone EA (2013) Fiscal stress and cutback management among state and local governments. In: Levine H, Justice JB, Scorsone EA (eds) Handbook of local government fiscal health. Jones & Bartlett Learning, Burlington, pp 253–283

Raudla R, Savi R, Randma-Liiv T (2015) Cutback management literature in the 1970s and 1980s: taking stock. Int Rev Adm Sci 81(3):433–456. https://doi.org/10.1177/0020852314564313

Rhodes RAW (1996) The new governance: governing without government. Polit Stud 44(4):652–667. https://doi.org/10.1111/j.1467-9248.1996.tb01747.x

Roberts A (2018) The aims of public administration: reviving the classical view. Perspect Public Manag Gov 1(1):73–85. https://doi.org/10.1093/ppmgov/gvx003

Roberts A (2021) How to bridge east and west. Asia Pac J Public Adm 43(2):63–66. https://doi.org/10.1080/23276665.2020.1869046

Salamon LM (2000) The new governance and the tools of public action: an introduction. Fordham Urb LJ 28:1611–1674

Schoppa L (2012) Residential mobility and local civic engagement in Japan and the United States divergent paths to school. Comp Pol Stud 46(9):1058–1081. https://doi.org/10.1177/0010414012463896

Sharp EB (1980) Toward a new understanding of urban services and citizen participation: the coproduction concept. Midwest Rev Public Adm 14(2):105–118. https://doi.org/10.1177/027507408001400203

Sicilia M, Sancino A, Nabatchi T, Guarini E (2019) Facilitating co-production in public services: management implications from a systematic literature review. Public Money Manag 39(4):233–240. https://doi.org/10.1080/09540962.2019.1592904

Suzuki K (2017) Government expenditure cuts and voluntary activities of citizens: the experience of Japanese municipalities. Asia Pac J Public Adm 39(4):258–275. https://doi.org/10.108 0/23276665.2017.1403179

Suzuki K (2020) Government retrenchment and citizen participation in volunteering: a crossnational analysis of OECD countries. Public Policy Adm 35(3):266–288. https://doi.org/10.1177/0952076718796097

Suzuki K, Hur H (2020) Bureaucratic structures and organizational commitment: findings from a comparative study of 20 European countries. Public Manag Rev 22(6):877–907. https://doi.org/10.1080/14719037.2019.1619813

Suzuki K, Dollery BE, Kortt MA (2021) Addressing loneliness and social isolation amongst elderly people through local co-production in Japan. Soc Policy Adm 55(4):674–686. https://doi.org/10.1111/spol.12650

Torigoe H (1994) Study of local neighborhood associations [Chiiki Jichikai no Kenkyu]. Mineruva Shobo, Kyoto. (in Japanese)

Toshkov D (2016) Research design in political science. Macmillan International Higher Education

Uddin S, Mori Y, Adhikari P (2019) Participatory budgeting in a local government in a vertical society: a Japanese story. Int Rev Adm Sci 85(3):490–505. https://doi.org/10.1177/0020852317721335

van Der Wal Z, Demircioglu MA (2020) Public sector innovation in the Asia-pacific trends, challenges, and opportunities. Aust J Public Adm 79(3):271–278. https://doi.org/10.1111/1467-8500.12435

Van der Wal Z, Mussagulova A (2023) Developing public service motivation in the non-Western world. Asia Pac J Public Adm 45(3):244–247. https://doi.org/10.1080/23276665.2023.2237619

Van Houwelingen P (2012) Neighborhood associations and social capital in Japan. Urban Aff Rev 48(4):467–497. https://doi.org/10.1177/1078087411434906

Voorberg WH, BekkersLars VJJM, Tummers LG (2015) A systematic review of co-creation and co-production: embarking on the social innovation journey. Public Manag Rev 17(9):1333–1357. https://doi.org/10.1080/14719037.2014.930505

Whitaker GP (1980) Coproduction: citizen participation in service delivery. Public Adm Rev:240–246. https://doi.org/10.2307/975377

Yamazaki K, Dollery B, Kinoshita Y (2022) Local factors sustaining co-production: two case studies from the city of Yokohama, Japan. J Urban Aff:1–14. https://doi.org/10.1080/07352166.2022.2095916

Kohei Suzuki is assistant professor in the Institute of Public Administration, Faculty of Governance and Global Affairs at Leiden University, the Netherlands. He obtained his PhD from the Paul H. O'Neill School of Public and Environmental Affairs at Indiana University, Bloomington. He also holds the title of docent (Associate Professor) in Political Science at the Department of Political Science, University of Gothenburg, Sweden. He studies bureaucracy from a comparative perspective with a focus on bureaucratic structure, personnel policy, and gender representation. His work has been published in *Public Administration Review*, *Journal of European Public Policy*, *Governance*, *Public Management Review*, and several other peer-reviewed academic journals.

Chapter 9
Communities and NPOs

Aya Okada (ORCID)

Abstract Recent Japan has observed a rising expectation towards community-level civil society organizations as key actors in local governance. Ranging from neighborhood associations (NHAs), voluntary groups, to formally incorporated nonprofits, these organizations are to take active part in provision of public goods and services. What roles are they expected to play and do those expected roles make the most of civil society organizations? This chapter conducts document analysis of two policy initiatives that served as key momentum for these organizations to step into the spotlight of local governance: "New Public Commons" and "Promoting the Society of Mutual Assistance." Identified are traits of neoliberalism and participatory/associative democracy. The chapter argues that these policies take a rather narrow view on the roles of civil society organizations as service deliverers with enhanced citizen participation. Such understanding overlooks the wide range of roles that these organizations play in the Japanese society, such as offering space of innovative practices, for citizens to have their voices heard, and for citizens to express their beliefs and values. Expanding the understanding of the roles of communities and nonprofit organizations (NPOs) opens broader channels through which these organizations contribute to sustainable local governance.

Keywords Communities · NPOs · Mutual assistance · Citizen participation · Neoliberalism

9.1   Introduction

In the past three decades, there has been rising expectation towards community-level civil society organizations in Japan. Policies on local governance mostly favor these organizations and encourage their activities. Subsidies are often available for

A. Okada (✉)
Graduate School of Information Sciences, Tohoku University, Sendai, Japan
e-mail: aya.okada.e3@tohoku.ac.jp

© The Author(s), under exclusive license to Springer Nature
Switzerland AG 2024
Y. Noda (ed.), *Local Governance in Japan*, Local and Urban Governance,
https://doi.org/10.1007/978-3-031-77322-8_9

local community groups and organizations, and many local governments contract out provision of public goods and services to these civil society organizations. Local governments across the country have in place an ordinance that facilitates collaboration with citizens, and many also house a division focused on citizen collaboration. Today, institutions pursuing citizen participation and partnerships have become common place among many local governments in Japan (Kotagiri 2014).

Expectation towards community-level civil society organizations—neighborhood associations (NHAs), residents' associations, nonprofit organizations (NPOs), just to name a few—became explicit in Japan particularly after the Great Hanshin Awaji Earthquake in 1995. Often known as the Kobe Earthquake, volunteers and community organizations played a major role in responding to this crisis. The disaster served as a momentum for the Japanese government to take active measures to consider them as key actors in local governance (Homma and Deguchi 1995). It was in 1998, three years after the earthquake, that the first legislation exclusively on nonprofits was enacted in Japan (Act on Promotion of Specified Non-profit Activities). This act enabled volunteer groups to obtain legal status with less difficulties than before. Doing so allows them to make contracts as an organization and to enjoy tax exemption (more to be described in Sect. 9.2.3).

Given the increasing spotlight on community-level civil society organizations in recent Japan, this chapter critically examines key aspects emphasized in policies that reflect this trend. What roles are civil society organizations expected to play and do those expected roles make the most of these organizations?

To explore the questions, the chapter conducts document analysis of two policy initiatives that served as key momentum for civil society organizations to step into the spotlight of local governance: "New Public Commons" and "Promoting the Society of Mutual Assistance." Identified are traits of neoliberalism and participatory/associative democracy. Analysis reveal that these policies understand civil society organizations narrowly as service deliverers with enhanced citizen participation. This chapter argues that such narrow view overlooks the wide range of roles that these organizations play in the Japanese society. By introducing the framework on the role of nonprofit organizations org proposed by Frumkin (2002), the chapter shows how civil society organizations go beyond such conventional roles to offer space of innovative practices, for citizens to have their voices heard, and for citizens to express their beliefs and values.

The chapter proceeds as follows. After a brief overview of different types of organizations, two key policy initiatives—"New Public Commons" and "Promoting the Society of Mutual Assistance" are introduced. Close examination of these policies reveals the use of the logic of neoliberalism and participatory/associative democracy, manifesting a narrow view of civil society organizations as service deliverers with enhanced citizen participation. To argue for the need to expand such view, the chapter then introduces a framework proposed by Frumkin (2002). Expanding the understanding of the roles of communities and NPOs opens broader channels through which these organizations contribute to sustainable local governance.

9.2   Types of Community-Level Civil Society Organizations

9.2.1   Two Categories

Japan has a rich tradition of associations and voluntary groups in communities (Fujiwara 2006). Several types of citizen organizations exist with the potential to contribute to local governance. This section presents these organizations in two broad categories: those bounded by geographical boundaries and those organized under a specific mission.

9.2.2   Groups Bounded by Geographical Boundaries

As seen in a typical example of NHAs (*chonaikai or chokai*) and residents' associations (*jichikai*), groups bounded by geographical boundaries are commonly observed across Japan. These organizations consist of citizens with residential address in a bounded region. Participation is fundamentally voluntary. As neighbors, members of these groups engage in a wide range of community activities. Some organize street clean-ups regularly to maintain clean neighborhood, while others organize disaster drills to prepare the community to natural disasters. Collecting recyclable wastes is also quite common. Some NHAs collaborate with school districts to host community festivals or organize morning exercises during the summer. Each group is unique in their activities, but all share a common characteristic that their members and activities remain within a bounded geographic region. Article 26 of The Local Autonomy Law defines these groups as "organizations based on local ties (*chien ni yoru dantai*)." In 2019, Ministry of Internal Affairs and Communications reported a total of 296,800 of these groups bounded by geographical boundaries (MIC 2019). Specific numbers with wide range of names in Japanese are presented in Table 9.1.

Observing the Japanese civil society from an American perspective, Pekkanen (2006) highlighted NHAs as vibrant part of Japanese civil society. He argues that in comparison to the limited number of large professionalized groups that shape public debates and influence public policy, these local grassroots organizations have been promoted by the state and are widespread across the country. These groups "form a

Table 9.1 Types of organizations bounded by geographical boundaries

Jichikai	131,679
Chonaikai	67,869
Chokai	17,937
Burakukai	4960
Kukai	3426
Ku	37,098
Others	33,831
TOTAL	296,800

Source: MIC (2019)

crucial base of social life" in Japan that "help build up stocks of social capital and perhaps improve the performance of local governments" (Pekkanen 2006: 9). Participation to these organizations bounded by geographical boundaries is voluntary. Despite the fact that these groups are found all across Japan, participation has been on a declining trend. In 2022, Research Group on Regional Communities (2022) reported 71.8% as the rate of participation by household, with steady decline since 78.0% in 2010. Indeed, a survey by the Cabinet Office Gender Equality Bureau (2017) found that 53.3% of these groups saw declining rate of participation as issues they face. Additional concerns were lack of board members and those who engage in management (86.1%), aging of board members (82.8%), and dilution of NHAs (59.2%).

Among these groups bounded by geographical boundaries, some choose to go beyond being a voluntary group to obtaining a legal status. Doing so enables organizations to behave as legal entities. For example, they will be able to rent or purchase real estates under the organization name. There are range of possible legal status to which these organizations can apply including Approved Territorial Assembly (*ninka chien dantai*). In 2017, there were 51,030 organizations under this specific legal status (MIC 2019). Groups bounded by geographical boundaries may also choose to obtain other legal status as will be presented next for groups organized under a specific mission.

9.2.3   *Groups Organized Under a Specific Mission*

In addition to community-level civil society groups bounded by geographical boundaries, there are groups organized under a specific mission. They groups operate to advance a specific aim or a vision shared among people to gather around the group. Missions range in a diverse field of society—from child care, education, elderly care, community revitalization, disaster preparedness, sports, minorities and LGBTQs, just to name a few. Some missions are set to solve particular social issues, but others focus on enhancing well-beings of the citizens, sometimes even animals.

As with groups bounded by geographical boundaries, these groups organized under a specific mission can choose to operate as a voluntary group or with a legal status. Available legal statuses are presented in Table 9.2. Historically, obtaining a legal status had not been an easy task for these voluntary groups. While there had been a system of Public Interest Corporation (PIC) since 1898 under the Civil Code (*Minpo*), conditions to be met for eligibility were strict and the applying organizations had to go through rigorous examination by the national and local governments. Even after granted a permission for a legal status, authorities maintained those organizations under strict supervision.

More relaxed systems were introduced in the late 1990s and onwards, particularly after the aforementioned Act on Promotion of Specified Nonprofit Activities enacted in 1998. The new system made it easier these groups to incorporate as long as the purpose of their activities is related to public interest. Currently, there are

Table 9.2 Legal status for groups organized under a specific mission

Name of legal status in English	In Japanese	Extant number
Specified Nonprofit Corporation	*Tokutei hieiri katsudo hojin (or NPO hojin)*	50,021 (as of March 25, 2024)
Public Interest Incorporated Association	*Koeki shadan hojin*	4171 (as of May 30, 2022)
Public Interest Incorporated Foundation	*Koeki zaidan hojin*	5487 (as of May 30, 2022)
General Incorporated Association	*Ippan shadan hojin*	68,949 (as of May 30, 2022)
General Incorporated Foundation	*Ippan zaidan hojin*	7547 (as of May 30, 2022)

Source: Author's elaboration based on Cabinet Office (2024) and The Japan Foundation Center (2022)

about 50,000 organizations that have obtained the legal status of Specified Nonprofit Corporation (*Tokutei Hieiri Katsudo Hojin* or NPO *Hojin*). The traditional Public Interest Corporation (PIC) system also underwent reform in 2008, relaxing the conditions to be met to obtain four different types of legal status. Many organizations today choose to incorporate under the legal status General Incorporated Association (*Ippan Shadan Hojin*) as requirements are the most relaxed among available legal status for the groups organized under a specific mission. Overall, legislations for groups organized under a specific mission has become more flexible over the years. For a comprehensive list of available legal status and detailed information, see Okada et al. (2017).

9.2.4   Encouraging Collaboration

While groups bounded by geographical boundaries and groups organized under a specific mission operate independently, they are encouraged to work together in respective communities. Ministry of Internal Affairs and Communications (MIC) has pushed forward an initiative for collaboration with an establishment of Region Management Organization (*Chiiki Unei Soshiki*). Abbreviated as RMO, this is "an organization that continuously implements initiatives to resolve regional issues based on regional management guidelines established by a consultative organization formed mainly by people living in the region and involving various related entities in the region, in order to protect the livelihood of the region." In FY 2023, there were 7710 RMOs in 874 municipalities (MIC Group for Regional Vitalization 2024).

9.3 Policy Initiatives

A range of policies in the recent decades in Japan favor and support the above two types of organizations as active actors in local governance in Japan. This section reviews policy initiatives that place community-level civil society organizations into the spotlight of local governance. After a brief prehistory in the 1990s, two nation-wide policies—"New Public Commons (*Atarashi Kokyo*)" and "Promoting the Society of Mutual Assistance (*Kyojo Shakai Zukuri*)" are examined.

9.3.1 Prehistory

Momentum to recognize community-level civil society organizations as key actors of local governance first began to be seen around the 1990s at the level of local governments. It was in the questions and answers at local councils and assemblies that reference to these organizations began to be seen (Makise 2020). In December 1990, the then director of the welfare department made the following statement in the local assembly of Hyogo Prefecture, referring to the importance of community-level action:

> We aim to form a welfare society with a good balance of public, self-assistance and mutual assistance, including the promotion of mutual assistance activities such as mutual help campaigns in the community (Quoted in Makise 2020).

In 2004, the prefectural government of Mie released a report "Research Report on the Promotion of 'Public in a New Era'" and proceeded to a formulation of "Promotion Policy of the Public in the New Era" in 2005. Here, the idea of the "Public in the New Era" was described as a society in which diverse actors participate in activities in the public sphere and the activities that contribute to forming such a society (Prefectural Government of Mie 2005: 6). In 2004, a similar idea of the "New Public" was also referenced in the *White Paper on the National Lifestyle* in 2004. These developments at the level of local government led to emergence of nation-wide policies. Below, the chapter introduces two representative examples of such policies.

9.3.2 New Public Commons

The policy initiative of the "New Public Commons (*Atarashi Kokyo*)" was advocated by the Democratic Party of Japan between 2009 and 2012. The party overthrew the long-governing Liberal Democratic Party (LDP) in the national election in August 2009 and took office. This was a historical change of government where non-LDP parties took power of the Cabinet. As such, policies proposed and implemented by the new Cabinet highlighted contrasting shift from those led by the LDP

Cabinets. One of such was to feature the importance of civil society and communities.

Forty days after taking office, Yukio Hatoyama, then Prime Minister, laid out basic ideas of the Cabinet with the concept "New Public Commons (*Atarashi Kokyo*)." In his very first policy statement speech to the Diet in October 2009, Hatoyama described the basic vision of this policy initiative. He began by illustrating what he envisions as an ideal society, where public goods and services are provided not only by the public agencies, but by people themselves. Citizens are to take active role in provision of public services.

> What I am seeking is a "new public commons", under which people support and are of service to each other. It consists of a new set of values that sees the supporting role being played not just by people in the bureaucracy but also by each person in local communities who is involved in such activities as education or child-rearing, community-building, crime and disaster prevention, medical care and welfare. Such efforts ought to be supported by society as a whole. (Cabinet Office 2009)

Hatoyama went on to stress that in a society where citizens support each other to fulfill the needs of everyday lives, the role of public sector is limited. He criticized the regulations that had been in place for citizen activities—established by the LDP—and advocates to remove them.

> The role of politics may not be very large at the level of people's daily lives. In fact, the only role politics can play may be to remove those excessive regulations that hinder the launching of initiatives among citizens and NPOs or do little else but increase the workload and budgets of government offices. I believe, though, that lending such indirect support to civic and NPO activities is exactly the role that politics should play in the twenty-first century. (*ibid.*)

With the belief that citizens have the power and ability to engage and to contribute to community issues, Hatoyama saw citizens as key actors in tackling social issues. He stated clearly that the public sector is not equipped with sufficient resources to deal with all problems in the society. Hatoyama saw further benefits of having more active citizen participation in provision of public services that it will lead to nurturing bonds and trust among the citizens.

> Building a new nation is certainly not a matter that can be consigned to others. Neither can all problems be resolved merely through political or administrative efforts to increase the budget. Only by having each individual citizen foster and develop the ideal of self-support and co-existence can we revive the bonds within society and recover the relationships of trust among people. (*ibid.*)

Hatoyama concluded the "New Public Commons" section of the speech that in a society of mutual help, every citizen counts. Everyone has a place in the society and that there is no single citizen who cannot contribute to the society.

> I will stand at the forefront of the efforts by the nation, local authorities and people to come together as one, dedicating all my strength to bringing about a "Japanese society whose members offer mutual support" in which all people recognise the existence of all other people as invaluable and in which each person can discover a "place he or she belongs" and his or her own "role to play". (*ibid.*)

In June 2010, the Cabinet was succeeded by Naoto Kan, also of the Democratic Party of Japan. The new Cabinet continued on with the initiative of "New Public Commons" with a document titled "Declaration of 'New Public Commons'" (Cabinet Office 2010). Confirming the ideal society where every citizen plays an active role in supporting each other, the document introduced an economic perspective to the initiative. An ideal society is to bring about economic benefits to the citizens. A vibrant society of mutual help, the declaration states, will lead to emergence of new markets, gains of which are to be given back to citizens' everyday lives.

> The traits promoted by the "New Public Commons" are mutual support and social vibrancy. In this society, everyone has a place to go and a role to play. People value the pleasure of helping others, and by generating new markets and services they allow economic activity to thrive. When the fruits of such activities are properly returned to society, people can live better lives. Thus, such a society develops in a virtuous cycle. (Cabinet Office 2010)

"Declaration of 'New Public Commons'" also confirms that the public sector alone cannot solve issues that exist in the Japanese society. The document saw citizens and communities as key actors and highlighted multi-faceted benefits that the vibrant society can bring about. Not only will social capital be nurtured with trust and confidence among the citizens, but with less costs and more happiness. More interactions among citizens are assumed to bring about innovation, leading to new markets and economic growth.

> With a declining birth rate, the Japanese population is rapidly aging. This demographic shift will create new challenges and new social issues, and these issues cannot be resolved by the government alone or by simply injecting money and goods into the community. However, a society of mutual support and vibrancy, realized through the "New Public Commons," can create communities that are rich in social capital and that enjoy a high level of mutual confidence, low social costs and a great degree of happiness. In such communities, new ideas can emerge from the bonds among people, triggering social innovations that will lead the way to fresh growth. (*ibid.*)

9.3.3   Promoting the Society of Mutual Assistance

The Democratic Party of Japan did not stay long in power. They were struck by the triple disasters of earthquake, tsunami, and nuclear accident in Northeastern Japan in March 2011 and gradually lost support as they were scrutinized for their responses to the crisis. In December 2012, the LDP came back in power. However, the momentum to feature community-level civil society organizations did not cease, but rather continued. An example of such is the initiative of "Promotion of the Society of Mutual Assistance (*kyojo shakai zukuri*)" led by the then-Prime Minister Shinzo Abe of LDP. This section reviews the document outlining the initiative titled "*Promoting the Society of Mutual Assistance: Aiming to Build New 'Ties'*."

As with the "New Public Commons," this initiative envisions a society where local residents take an active role in provision of public services. It acknowledges that resources currently available for social issues in communities are not sufficient.

The following paragraph from the document clearly states that such was the case in responding to the disaster, most likely to recall citizens of the situations experienced in the 2011 disaster.

> There are growing concerns about the future among local residents, including concerns over shortages of human resources that will support the community, as well as facilities for medical and long-term care, and concerns over weakened local economies. On the other hand, the majority of people believe that voluntary efforts made by local residents are important to address these social needs and challenges. In fact, in the event of a major disaster, mutual aid between local residents plays an important role in things like living assistance and this in turn largely depends on the degree of relationships or ties that neighbors have established in daily lives. (Council for Promotion of the Society of Mutual Assistance 2015)

It is acknowledged, that relying on individual citizens for active involvement, is not realistic today with declining population and social capital. Mutual support among local residents does not emerge naturally. As such, the initiative turns attention to the active roles local-level community organizations such as NPOs can take in provision of public services.

> However, it is difficult to expect residents alone to support each other in the community in a traditional manner, considering a current situation, where the population is rapidly declining and aging while fewer babies are being born, and relationships or community-based ties are weakening, particularly in urban areas.

> Meanwhile, diverse agents, such as the NPOs and general/public interest corporations, etc. (NPOs, etc.), private companies, social enterprises operators, financial institutions, educational institutions and the government, have started to take part in activities aimed to solve local challenges and involved in the promotion of the society of mutual assistance. (*ibid.*)

Not only are these organizations encouraged to work together, but individual citizens are also encouraged to take part in these organizations in their respective communities.

> We expect that more diverse actors will participate in such efforts and vitalize their activities in the future. In the society of mutual assistance, it is important that such diverse actors cooperate with each other to support local residents and the residents themselves also choose to participate as an actor in activities that fit their values and living situation. (*ibid.*)

Interestingly, "Promoting the Society of Mutual Assistance" takes over the same emphasis the "New Public Commons" made in stating that every citizen counts. The document gives examples of youth, elderly, and women who might feel isolated or left out from the communities, encourages them to take active role to have their voices heard. It is believed that doing so will contribute to nurturing relationships and to re-energizing communities.

> In particular, it is significant that people such as youth who could not find their place in the community, the elderly who tend to be isolated, and women who could hardly raise their voice, all participate actively, not passively, in the promotion of the society of mutual assistance in their community. As they start to have opportunities or places to participate in the community, it is expected that the unheard voices of vulnerable people will be reflected in the local community.

> This will help to vitalize the communities and create new "ties" among the people, which leads to the revitalization of new regional communities. (*ibid.*)

Mutual assistance that involves community-level civil society organizations are believed to bring about positive impact not only for individuals, but also for the communities, regions, and even for the country. Not only will the society be stronger and vibrant with individuals having their voices heard, but also become a society that grow.

> Furthermore, the ties between people and the capacity of the community will be a base for the resilience and vitalization of the community. Similarly, by participating in the society in a meaningful manner, all people can make their life more active which in turn will lead to the realization of robust growth in our country.

> From that perspective, we believe that the image of the society of mutual assistance that we should aim for is: The society built up by all, where new "ties" are established, while the various values and wills of individuals are respected. (*ibid.*)

9.4 Logics of Neoliberalism and Democracy

9.4.1 Underlying Logics

A brief look at these policy initiatives reveals that community-level civil society organizations are pushed into the spotlight of local governance. The chapter will now take a closer look to examine the logics used to legitimize these policy initiatives. Building on scholars who have examined "New Public Commons" and other related policies on collaboration in Japan (Abe 2013; Ogawa 2009), two angles are considered: neoliberalism and participatory/associative democracy.

9.4.2 Neoliberalism

In the context of communities and NPOs, neoliberalism refers to a school of economic and political thoughts that promote market-based reforms (Evans et al. 2005). While definitions vary by disciplines, scholars, and policies (Springer et al. 2016), for the purpose of understanding Japanese policies related to community-level civil society organizations, the chapter understands neoliberalism in two regards. First, neoliberalism favors small government, leading to shrinking governmental responsibilities. Second, neoliberalism advocates efficiency and effectiveness in provision of public services. Involved is a strong push for cutting costs and an orientation towards achieving results. Proposed aim is to be met in a manner that satisfies the clients or those who receive the service. As follows, a close examination of the aforementioned policies reveals traits of neoliberalism. For purpose of simplification, this section refers to the "New Public Commons" as the first policy and "Promoting the Society of Mutual Assistance" as the second policy.

The first trait observed in the two policy initiatives is its inclination towards limited government engagement. "New Public Commons" explicitly stated the limited role of politics and bureaucracy in dealing with citizens' everyday lives, that problems cannot be solved "*by the government alone or by simply injecting money and goods into the community*" or "*merely through political or administrative efforts to increase the budget.*" Assumed here is a small government with public agencies having a moderate and passive role of offering support to community-level citizen groups.

The second trait of neoliberalism found is citizens bearing more responsibilities. "New Public Commons" is again quite explicit in this regard, stating that "*building a new nation is certainly not a matter that can be consigned to others*" and that individuals are to "*foster and develop the ideal of self-support and co-existence.*" "Promoting the Society of Mutual Assistance" refers to the fact that "*mutual aid between local residents*" are already being observed in Japan and that residents are expected to "*choose to participate as an actor in activities that fit their values and living situation.*"

The third trait is its inclination towards efficiency. "New Public Commons" argues that a vibrant society realizes "*less social cost.*" While what is meant by "social cost" in unclear in the document, it mostly likely means decreased transaction costs in the process to figure out how to solve social issues in the communities. In terms of achieving efficiency, "New Public Commons" even goes on to say that less regulations on activities by citizens and NPOs will lead to less "*workload and budgets of government offices.*"

Inclination towards achieving effectiveness in development and growth is the fourth trait of neoliberalism found in the two policy initiatives. "New Public Commons" states that with active and vibrant participation of non-governmental actors such as community-level civil society organizations, there emerges "*new markets and services*" that lead to "*economic activity to thrive.*" Active engagement of citizens is considered to lead to emergence of "*new ideas*" and trigger "*social innovations that will lead the way to fresh growth.*" "Promoting the Society of Mutual Assistance" also argues that such a society will "*lead to the realization of robust growth in our country.*"

9.4.3 Participatory/Associative Democracy

Another logic used in the two policies is participatory democracy. This school of political thought advocates the importance and benefits of ensuring an opportunity for individual citizens to engage and participate in decision-making and implementation of public policies. The notion contrasts a form of democracy against representative democracy. (Barber 2014). Two traits of participatory democracy are observed in the two aforementioned policy initiatives.

The first trait is their assumption that every citizen has a role to play. Both initiatives ensure that all citizens belong to the society with a possibility to make contributions. "New Public Commons" states that *"everyone has a place to go and a role to play"* and "Promoting the Society of Mutual Assistance" states *"each person can discover a 'place he or she belongs' and his or her own 'role to play'."*

The second trait of participatory democracy observed is its encouragement for citizens to engage in community activities. "New Public Commons" states that *"Each person in local communities"* are to get involved in *"activities as education or child-rearing, community-building, crime and disaster prevention, medical care and welfare."* Individuals are not only expected to take on a role, but also to collaborate with others. With a recognition that *"existence of all other people as invaluable,"* *"the nation, local authorities and people"* are *"to come together as one."*

In addition to participatory democracy, traits of associative democracy are also observed in the two policy initiatives. Associative democracy places importance on the wills of the active community members, and that their wills are expressed through various associations and institutions (Jones and Marsden 2010). The concept "emphasizes self-governing voluntary associations as the building blocks of participatory democracy (Ogawa 2009: 142)."

Traits of associative democracy is particularly strong in the initiative "Promoting the Society of Mutual Assistance." First is the emphasis on participation of people who had been inactive in communities. These include *"youth who could not find their place in the community,"* *"elderly who tend to be isolated,"* and *"women who could hardly raise their voice."* In a society of mutual assistance, these population participate actively with the will of *"the unheard voices of vulnerable people."*

The second observed trait is the role of community organizations, voluntary groups, or NPOs in reflecting citizens' voices for better ways to solve social issues. "Promoting the Society of Mutual Assistance" states, *"…diverse agents, such as the NPOs and general/public interest corporations, etc. (NPOs, etc.), private companies, social enterprises operators, financial institutions, educational institutions and the government, have started to take part in activities aimed to solve local challenges and involved in the promotion of the society of mutual assistance."*

9.4.4 Emphasis on Delivering Services with Participation

Close examination of the two policies reveals that the logics of neoliberalism and participatory/associative democracy are in play to legitimize the policy direction.

The logic of participatory/associative democracy has been received mostly favorably for enhancing the opportunity for citizen participation into the public sphere. Indeed, the two policies demonstrate strong beliefs on skills, knowledge, resource, and experience that each citizen can bring about in enhancing the quality of life in the community (Ogawa 2009: 117).

In contrast, the logic of neoliberalism has faced much scrutiny. Critics are concerned about the potential risk of community-level civil society organizations losing autonomy and turning into mere subcontractors to the public sector (Abe 2013). Indeed, in the policy initiatives, these organizations were assumed to play an instrumental role of delivering services to solve social issues with enhanced citizen participation. Doing so was considered to be a way to contribute to solving social issues while cutting involved costs and achieving more results. Such efficient and effective service delivery were believed to lead to development and growth of the communities, regions, and ultimately the entire country. Ogawa (2009) makes a strong argument against the use of neoliberalism in these policies, arguing that the institutionalizing NPOs through the 1998 Law was "an inevitable expansion of neo-liberal policy that has reorganized the Japanese public sphere. It is part of a calculated, strategic reorganization geared toward establishing small government in the post-Keynesian welfare state" (Ogawa 2009: 21).

The two policies that bring community-level civil society organizations to the center stage of local governance may have brought in every citizen to engage in making the communities a better place. However, the general understanding of these organizations is that they are actors that contribute to solving social issues in communities. In the following sections, the chapter argues that such view overlooks the other rich and vibrant functions of these organizations. Community-level civil society organizations are not just service deliverers. There's much broader roles these organizations play in the Japanese society.

9.5 Beyond Instrumental Function

9.5.1 The Four-Role Framework

What roles, in addition to delivering services, do community-level civil society organizations play in the Japanese society? That other functions of these organizations should the policy initiatives taken into consideration? To elaborate on these questions, the chapter introduces a four-role framework proposed by Peter Frumkin (2002) on nonprofit organizations. In discussing diversity of roles that nonprofits play in the society, Frumkin proposes develops a quadrant framework: service delivery, social entrepreneurship, civic and political engagement, values and faith.

This section examines these four roles closely with examples observed in Japan. Doing so will highlight the narrow view the current policies take in understanding the roles and functions of community-level civil society organizations. Below, the four roles are explained first. This is followed by a description of the two axes used to sort out the four roles as presented in Table 9.3.

Table 9.3 Four roles of nonprofit organizations

	Demand-side orientation	Supply-side orientation
Instrumental rationale	Providing services	Promoting innovation and Social entrepreneurship
Expressive rationale	Encouraging civic participation and political engagement	Presenting values and faith

Source: Adapted from Frumkin (2002), p. 25

9.5.2 Providing Services

The first role that community-level civil society organizations play is delivering services to fulfill the unmet needs in the society. This was exactly the view the policy initiatives of "New Public Commons" and "Promoting the Society of Mutual Assistance" had taken. This comes as no surprise as this role is "one of the most visible and recognizable functions (Frumkin 2002: 64)."

Nonprofits as service delivers is a role conventionally highlighted with the theories of government failure and market failure (Weisbrod 1977). The theory of government failure argues that NPOs fill-in for the government's inability to fulfill every social need that exist in the society (Salamon 1987). The public sector, operating on tax money, makes decision on the principles of quality and impartiality. Their decisions and operations aim to cover as much population as possible, but not necessary every single citizen. NPOs, operating based on their unique missions, are not confined to such principles. They are able to target a specific population or issues that are not covered by the government.

Market failure theory argues that the market, fundamentally a for-profit sector, are unable to provide all goods and services demanded in a society (Salamon 1987). Companies and firms operating on a market principle are unlikely to engage in selling goods or services that they cannot expect to generate revenues. This is where NPOs come in—they are more likely to engage even if with little or not anticipation for revenues.

An NPO "Mobility Support Rera (*ido shien rera*)" in Ishinomaki City, Miyagi Prefecture, is a symbolic example of NPOs providing services in response to government and market failure. Rera provides transportation services to those who are able to provide such on their own (Ido Shien Rera 2024). During the initial years after its founding in 2011, Rera served people affected by the largescale earthquake and tsunami. The affected people had lost their cars and even houses, and had no choice but to live in evacuation centers and temporal housing. Rera provided transport service for these population. Today, Rera has expanded the scope of users. They serve elderly people, those with disabilities, or those who cannot afford to own a car in remote areas, unable to secure transportation to go to hospitals, schools, or supermarkets to purchase essential goods for everyday life. Rera provides a transport service, picking up the users and taking them to wherever in need. The local government is reluctant to take action for these people who do not necessarily make up a considerable percentage of the entire population. Private transportation industry is also reluctant to move because these population are not necessarily prospective customers. Rera, an NPO, plays huge role in meeting the needs of those without mobility in the community.

9.5.3 Civic and Political Engagement

The second role that NPOs play is to encourage civic participation and political engagement. Nonprofits offer and create opportunities and space for people to speak up and to have their voices heard in the political arena.

Frumkin lays out six different ways in which nonprofits are linked in the political process (Frumkin 2002: 29–30). First, nonprofits build trust, cohesion and social capital in communities. Individual citizens connect with others and develop trusting relationships where they feel comfortable to talk about their concerns. Such may lead to solidarity and a sense of community. Second, nonprofits offer a door that opens onto the public sphere and a tool for demonstrating commitment to something greater than narrow self-interest. Third, nonprofits translate trust and civic engagement into direct political action. They organize people at the grassroots around interests and causes, register voters and spur them to get out the vote, or sometimes organize town hall meetings and a host of other participation and empowerment activities aimed at bringing the individual into the public sphere. Fourth, nonprofits engage in advocacy work. They inform and educate the public and policy makers on issues in question. Fifth, some nonprofits engage in direct lobbying around specific legislative issues. Sixth, nonprofit may figure prominently in the electoral system as campaign fundraising organizations, political action committees, or as party institutions.

A nonprofit "POSSE" is a symbolic example of this role in Japan. POSSE is an organization that engage in employment issues among young generations under the mission of "creating a society in which anyone can live and work without anxiety" (POSSE 2024). Their activities have three pillars: consultation, surveys, and policy recommendations. POSSE consults problems that young worker face and disseminating the details of those individual cases to the wider society. They do not confine themselves simply to solving individual cases. POSSE believes in the importance of bringing the voices of those who experienced work issues to the society and to challenge status quo and stimulate changes. They appear frequently in mass media, spreading the voice of those who are or went through labor troubles. A staff member says, "I believe that it is our role to raise the level of the environment for labor and poverty issues by asking these questions to society and creating public opinion (JAMMIN 2021)." Through their activities, POSSE offers young workers a chance to have their voices heard.

9.5.4   Innovation and Social Entrepreneurship

Another role that NPOs play in the society is to provide a space for innovative practices. Highlighted is a "role as a channel and vehicle for a new kind of social entrepreneurship (Frumkin 2002: 129)." NPOs offer space for people to challenge new
practices to solve social issues or to try new ways to fund their activities and initiatives. Those practices and trials are innovative and often new to the society. There's
indeed no guarantee that they will succeed—rather, there's a good chance the trial
will fail. However, NPOs offer a space for committed people to take a chance and
experiment. Through trial and error, these individuals and organizations might give
birth to brand-new ways and means to the society.

An NPO "Florence" is a well-known example for playing this role, particularly
for trying and establishing a sustainable system to provide care for sick child.
Conventionally, nurseries in Japan did not allow child with a fever over 37.5 degrees
Celsius to come, and had asked the parents to keep the child at home in such situations (Florence 2024). This had led to difficulties to working parents—it is certainly
not easy for most professions to make the change of schedule at 8 am in the morning. Given such challenge to balance work and childcare, it was not uncommon for
one of the parents—often mothers—to give up his or her professional career. To
transform this situation, Florence began a home-visit child care service in 2005.
Provision of such services come with many risks. However, Florence bravely gave
it a try, and a membership of 38 at the launch grew to over 100,000 cases of childcare in FY2022 (Florence 2024). Florence has won numbers of innovation and
social entrepreneurship awards as a pioneer, developing a sustainable system of care
of sick children.

9.5.5   Values and Faith

NPOs also serve as a space for those engaged to express values, commitments, and
faith that they believe in. Regardless of how people engage with the nonprofit—as
staff members, volunteers, donors, supporters, participants to the events—they all
do so because they share and believe what the community-level civil society organization do or aim to achieve. By offering activities in a wide range of fields, nonprofits provide a space for citizens to think, find out what they believe is important
or needed in the society, and put their beliefs into action in many different ways.

"Single Mothers' Sisterhood" is an NPO that provide peer support to mothers
raising a child by herself (Single Mothers' Sisterhood 2023). This group does not
regard single mothers as passive recipients of assistance, as seen in typical governmental interventions by the public sector in Japan. Rather, the organization sees
single mothers with a full potential of being empowered and they themselves taking
actions to contribute and make this society a better place. Under such vision, "Single
Mother's Sisterhood" implements programs to empower single mothers by

advocating for the importance of selfcare, learning, and building a network of peers as well as supporters. While the direct intervention of this organization is in providing peer support to single mothers, the organization also presents an alternative view to understand single mothers in the Japanese society. Those who sympathize with this view are not are given the opportunity to express their perspectives by supporting Single Mother's Sisterhood.

9.5.6 The Two Axes

As shown in Table 9.3, these four roles can be presented in a two-by-two quadrants with two axes (see Table 9.3).

The horizontal axis is labeled "demand-side" and "supply-side." This represents whether the roles respond to the needs that are already found in the society, or whether the nonprofit makes a proactive move to move the society ahead. In demand-side, the role of service delivery is to fulfil the unmet needs that already exist in the society. The role of civic and political engagement is to provide a channel for people's voices that already exist in the society to be heard and be reflected in the decision-making processes. In supply-side, NPOs in the role of innovation and social entrepreneurship offer the society brand-new ways and means to respond to a situation. In the role of values and faith, nonprofits offer citizens a new channel or ways to express their beliefs.

The vertical axis presents the rationales of nonprofits' roles. "Instrumental" refers to whether the proposed roles can be expected to lead to solving problems. Indeed, delivering services and trying out new ways have the chance of solving social issues. "Expressive" refers to the roles offering space for citizens to express their thoughts, beliefs, and values through action. Such may not necessarily lead to solving problems, but the significance is found in the fact that nonprofits offer a space to try innovative practices and for people to express their views.

9.5.7 Expanding the View of Roles

Frumkin (2002)'s four-role framework help to expand the view in understanding the role of community-level civil society organizations under study. These organizations are much more than service deliverers who contribute to solving social issues with enhanced citizen participation, just as the two policy initiatives had assumed. Understanding beyond service delivery—beyond the neoliberal view of cost-cutting, efficiency, and effectiveness—will help advance policy discussions on how community-level civil society organizations can contribute to better decision-makings, policy formulation, and policy implementation in local governance.

9.6   Conclusions

This chapter has argued that recent policies that put community-level civil society organizations as key actors in local governance have not paid sufficient attention to the wide range of roles that these organizations play in the Japanese society. As Frumkin (2002) argued, civil society organizations are more than providers of needed services with enhanced participation. These organizations go beyond such conventional role to offer space for innovative practices and social entrepreneurship, to encourage civic and political engagement, and to provide space for citizens to express their values and beliefs. Community-level civil society organizations are more than key actors to solve social issues; they not only respond to existing needs in the society but also make proactive moves to move the society forward. Their significance is beyond contributing to cutting costs in provision of public goods and services. Expanding the scope in understanding their roles, beyond service providers, not only contributes to nurturing vibrant civil society, but also to opening up broader channels through which community-level civil society organizations contribute to sustainable local governance.

References

Abe M (2013) "New public commons" and social policy ["Atarashi Kokyo" to Shakai Seisaku]. Soc Study Soc Policy [Shakai Seisaku] 5(1):5–14. (in Japanese)

Barber BR (2014) Participatory democracy. In: Gibbons MT, Coole D, Ellis E, Ferguson K (eds) The encyclopedia of political thought. Wiley-Blackwell, Malden. https://doi.org/10.1002/9781118474396.wbept0752

Cabinet Office (2009) Policy Speech by Prime Minister Yukio Hatoyama at the 173rd Session of the Diet. Accessed at: https://japan.kantei.go.jp/hatoyama/statement/200910/26syosin_e.html

Cabinet Office (2010) Declaration of "New Public Commons". Accessed at: https://www5.cao.go.jp/npc/pdf/declaration-english.pdf

Cabinet Office (2024) Cabinet Office NPO homepage [Naikakufu NPO Homupeiji]. (in Japanese). Accessed at: https://www.npo-homepage.go.jp/

Cabinet Office Gender Equality Bureau (2017) Promotion of gender equality for sustainable neighborhood association activities [Jizoku Kano na Jichikai Katsudo ni muketa Danjo Kyodo Sankaku no Suishin nitsuite]. (in Japanese). Accessed at: https://www.gender.go.jp/kaigi/kento/chiiki/pdf/report.pdf

Council for Promotion of the Society of Mutual Assistance (2015) Promoting the society of mutual assistance: aiming to build new "ties" (Summary). Accessed at: https://www.npo-homepage.go.jp/uploads/report33_8_youyaku_e.pdf

Evans B, Richmond T, Shields J (2005) Structuring neoliberal governance: the nonprofit sector, emerging new modes of control and the marketisation of service delivery. Policy and Society 24(1):73–97. https://doi.org/10.1016/S1449-4035(05)70050-3

Florence (2024) What is Florence? Florence in 1 minute [Florence toha? 1 pun de Wakaru Florence]. (In Japanese). Accessed at: https://florence.or.jp/about/

Frumkin P (2002) On being nonprofit: a conceptual and policy primer. Harvard University Press, Cambridge, MA

Fujiwara W (2006) Origins of private nonprofit organizations in Japan [Nihon no minkan hieiri soshiki no genryu]. In: Imata M (ed) NPO history in Japan: Reading the history of NPO, present, past, and future [Nihon no NPO shi: NPO no rekishi wo yomu, genzai, kako, mirai]. Gyosei, Tokyo, pp 1–16. (in Japanese)

Homma M, Deguchi M (1995) Volunteer revolution: experience of the disaster to citizen activities [Borantia Kakumei: Daishinsai no Keiken wo Shimin Katsudō e]. Toyo Keizai Inc, Tokyo. (in Japanese)

Ido Shien Rera (2024) Beginning of Rera [Rera no Hajimari]. (in Japanese). Accessed at: https://www.npo-rera.org/about.html

JAMMIN (2021) CHARITY FOR: Raising the Voices to Disseminate Labor Issues among Young People, Creating a Society where Everyone can Work "Normally"—NPO POSSE [Koe wo agete Wakamono no Roudou Mondai wo Hasshin, Daremoga "Futsu ni" Hatarakeru Shakai wo Tsukuru—NPO Hojin POSSE]. (in Japanese). Accessed at: https://jammin.co.jp/charity_list/210906-npoposse/

Jones N, Marsden H (2010) Associative democracy. In: Anheier HK, Toepler S (eds) International encyclopedia of civil society. Springer, New York. https://doi.org/10.1007/978-0-387-93996-4_493

Kotagiri Y (2014) Effectiveness of administration–citizen collaboration [Gyosei-shimin kan Kyodo no Kouyou]. Horitsu Bunka Sha, Kyoto. (in Japanese)

Makise M (2020) What are 'self-assistance, mutual assistance, and public assistance' that emerged since the 1990s? [90 Nendai kara Tojo shita 'Jijo, Koujo, Kyoujo' te Nandarou?]. (in Japanese). Project Design Online, Volume December 2020. Accessed at: https://www.projectdesign.jp/202012/assembly-ask/008643.php

MIC (2019) Results of a survey on the status of approval of organizations based on local ties [Chien ni yoru Dantai no Ninka Jimu no Jokyo ni kansuru Chosa Kekka]. Ministry of Internal Affairs and Communications, Tokyo. (in Japanese). Accessed at https://www.soumu.go.jp/main_content/000901474.pdf

MIC Group for Regional Vitalization (2024) Report on Survey and Research Project on the Formation and Sustainable Management of Region Management Organizations [Chiiki unei soshiki no Keisei oyobi Jizokuteki na Unnei ni kansuru Chosa Kenkyu Jigyo Houkokusho]. (in Japanese). Accessed at: https://www.soumu.go.jp/main_content/000874295.pdf

Ogawa A (2009) The failure of civil society? The third sector and the state in contemporary Japan. State University of New York Press, Albany

Okada A, Ishida Y, Nakajima T, Kotagiri Y (2017) The state of nonprofit sector research in Japan: a literature review. Voluntaristics Rev 2(3):1–68. https://doi.org/10.1163/9789004359468

Pekkanen R (2006) Japan's dual civil society: members without advocates. Stanford University Press, Stanford

POSSE (2024) About Activities of POSSE [POSSE no Katsudo ni Tsuite]. (in Japanese). Accessed at: https://www.npoposse.jp/katsudounaiyou

Prefectural Government of Mie (2005) Promotion Policy of the Public in the New Era ['Atarashi Jidai no Ohyake]. (in Japanese). Accessed at: https://www.pref.mie.lg.jp/common/content/000272863.pdf

Research Group on Regional Communities (2022) Report from research group on regional community [Chiiki Komyuniti ni kansuru Kenkyukai Houkokusho]. Ministry of Internal Affairs and Communications, Tokyo. (in Japanese). Accessed at https://www.soumu.go.jp/main_content/000816620.pdf

Salamon LM (1987) Of market failure, voluntary failure, and third-party government: towards a theory of government-nonprofit relations in the modern welfare state. J Voluntary Action Res 16(1–2):29–49

Single Mothers' Sisterhood (2023) White Paper on single parent's health: health survey on the mind and body of single mothers [Hitori Oya Kenko Hakusho—Shinguru Maza Kokoro to Karada no Kenko Hakusho]. (in Japanese)

Springer S, Birch K, MacLeavy J (2016) An introduction to neoliberalism. In: Springer S, Birch K, MacLeavy J (eds) Handbook of neoliberalism. Routledge, London. https://doi.org/10.4324/9781315730660

The Japan Foundation Center (2022) Status of foundations in Japan 2022—overview [Nihon no Josei Zaidan no Genjo 2022—Gaikyo]. (in Japanese). Accessed at: https://www.jfc.or.jp/bunseki-top/b1_2022/
Weisbrod BA (1977) The voluntary nonprofit sector: an economic analysis. Lexington Books, Lexington

Aya Okada is Professor of Civil Society Studies at Tohoku University Graduate School of Information Sciences in Sendai, Japan. Trained in sociology and policy studies, her research focuses on the design, implementation, and evaluation of communication process used by nonprofits as they seek to sustain their voluntary support in societies undergoing economic, social, and political change. Aya has a PhD in Public and International Affairs from the University of Pittsburgh. Her recent publications have appeared in journals including *Voluntas: International Journal of Voluntary and Nonprofit Organizations*, *Journal of Nonprofit Education and Leadership*, and *The Nonprofit Review*.

Chapter 10
Local Government and Social Marketing

Yoko Uryuhara ⓘ

Abstract Local governments need to promote voluntary behavioral changes among individuals for the overall well-being of society. The research question in this chapter examines whether mobilizing citizens to support policy implementation has a positive effect on policy promotion. Through case studies using educational leaflets and interviews with local government officials, this chapter aims to clarify the manner by which social marketing promotes behavioral change among citizens to mobilize them toward policy goals. Policymaking through social marketing differs from that of local governments as follows: (1) issues can be considered from the perspectives of residents; (2) a systematic and standardized policymaking process can be established; (3) segmentation and targeting can be used to set up detailed policies; and (4) the behavior of the citizens involved can be changed toward the social good. Based on these insights, this chapter examines the measurement of event outcomes, systematic process and framework, and marketing potential of citizens to determine a sense of efficacy in their relationships with local governments. The answer to the research question is to strengthen citizens' driving force for policy promotion and increase its effectiveness through social marketing, which can promote the planning and implementation of policies from citizens' perspectives.

Keywords Local government · Social marketing · Behavior change · Value creation · Benchmark criteria

Y. Uryuhara (✉)
Faculty of Commerce, Doshisha University, Kyoto, Japan
e-mail: yuryuhar@mail.doshisha.ac.jp

© The Author(s), under exclusive license to Springer Nature 　　　　　　189
Switzerland AG 2024
Y. Noda (ed.), *Local Governance in Japan*, Local and Urban Governance,
https://doi.org/10.1007/978-3-031-77322-8_10

10.1 Introduction

What image do you form from the term "social marketing?" You may think that "marketing" is something that is not related to local governments. However, social marketing is the key to policymaking by local governments from the perspective of citizens.

To achieve the Sustainable Development Goals (SDGs) and ensure the well-being of the entire society, it is important for all individuals to change their behavior toward a greater social good. Local governments need to promote voluntary behavioral changes among individuals. Lee and Kotler (2019) identify 50 social issues where social marketing can be useful, e.g., health-related (smoking cessation, excessive alcohol consumption, cancer screening, regular exercise, etc.), injury-related (drunk driving, seat belt/helmet, suicide, etc.), environmental protection (e.g., biodiversity protection, deforestation, waste reduction), and pro-social behavior/community participation (e.g., organ donation, blood donation, voting). All of these are related to policies implemented by local governments and other organizations.

In the U.K., a policy review was conducted by the government in 2004, and the usefulness of social marketing-based policymaking was confirmed. The National Social Marketing Center was established in 2006, and many healthcare policies have been developed and implemented based on social marketing (Uryuhara 2021). The key enabler to this is the training of policymakers. About 12,000 policy makers were trained in social marketing over ten years since 2006, and this has expanded to municipalities, creating a network of 7000 people who are learning and implementing social marketing in their tasks (Uryuhara 2023). Thus, it is clear from the examples of other countries that the understanding and utilization of social marketing in policymaking by local governments can help realize highly effective policies and contribute to citizens.

As local government policies are not automatically implemented once formulated, more attention is required in improving policy effectiveness. Although improving policy effectiveness is feasible when the policy is backed by ample budgetary and human resources and citizen support, it is difficult for local governments to deplete policy resources. However, policy implementers are not necessarily only local governments; in fact, they can be nonprofit organizations (NPOs), private companies, and citizens. The effect of citizen mobilization to promote policy-effectiveness improvement has not been adequately examined in the past. The research question in this chapter examines whether mobilizing citizens to promote policies has a positive effect. Therefore, this chapter aims to identify the manner by which social marketing facilitates behavioral changes in citizens for mobilization toward policy objectives.

The next section first discusses the history and theory of social marketing, the benchmarking criteria, and the procedure for formulating measures. Section 10.3 identifies the effective impact of citizen commitment through case studies using educational leaflets on the willingness to donate organs and follow-up research.

Section 10.4 discusses the benefits of learning and using social marketing through interviews with local government officials who attended educational programs in Japan. The results are used to identify the mobilizing effects of social marketing through behavioral changes among citizens.

10.2   What Is Social Marketing?

10.2.1   Definition of Social Marketing

Social marketing is a systematic, interdisciplinary framework for promoting change toward desired behaviors by creating social value for individuals, communities, and society, as a whole, for overall social welfare. The globally agreed upon definition of social marketing (International Social Marketing Association 2017) is as follows:

> Social Marketing seeks to develop and integrate marketing concepts with other approaches to influence behaviour that benefit individuals and communities for the greater social good. Social Marketing practice is guided by ethical principles. It seeks to integrate research, best practice, theory, audience and partnership insight, to inform the delivery of competition sensitive and segmented social change programmes that are effective, efficient, equitable, and sustainable.

10.2.2   History of Social Marketing and Its Introduction to Japan

Social marketing has about 60 years of history. In the 1950s, Wiebe, a psychologist at the City University of New York, asked, "Why can't you sell brotherhood and rational thinking like you sell soap ?," triggering discussions in the marketing field about expanding the marketing concept from being used only for commercial purposes to the social domain (Wiebe 1951: 679). Then, in 1971, Philip Kotler used the term "social marketing" and wondered if commercial marketing techniques "could be used for more social good" (Kotler and Zaltman 1971).

This practice began in the 1960s with family planning in developing countries (Manoff 1985; Ling et al. 1992), and in the 1980s, the World Health Organization (WHO) began to use the term "social marketing" and incorporated it into healthcare policy (White and French 2009). Furthermore, social marketing became a cornerstone of healthcare policy in the U.S. in the 1990s, and in the U.K. in the 2000s, mainly in the sphere of public health (Uryuhara 2023).

However, in the marketing field, concepts, and definitions continued to be examined, with Andreasen defining it in 1995 as the application of marketing techniques from the commercial field to programs designed to influence the voluntary behavior of the target population to improve the welfare of society (Andreasen 1995). He emphasized that the goal was to improve social welfare. Furthermore, in 2006, it was explicitly stated that the goal was to change not only attitudes but also behavior (Andreasen 2006). However, since then, social marketing practices have expanded, definitions have diversified in various regions, and a problem has arisen wherein social marketing is used without understanding its essence. Therefore, it was necessary to develop a globally agreed-upon definition, which was established in 2013.

Japan encountered the need to establish a research center for social marketing to spread internationally agreed-upon definitions and standards, and establish educational programs customized for Japan in the future. In 2018, the author received a mission from an international organization to introduce social marketing in Japan. At that time, it was recommended that first, an interdisciplinary research center must be established. It was advised to gather researchers from fields related to social marketing in its research center to study the points of contact and development and to expand the possibilities. It was also advised to develop a training program for professionals (social marketers) in accordance with international standards and establish a training system and network, especially for policymakers.

In April 2021, "The Social Marketing Research Centre" was established at Doshisha University. The center has 15 interdisciplinary members in 14 fields (as of December 2023), including Professor Jeff French, who established the National Social Marketing Centre in the U.K. and led social marketing research and education in the policy field. The mission of the Social Marketing Research Centre is to contribute to the advancement of academic research and the resolution of social issues by conducting interdisciplinary, multilayered, and creative research on approaches to inculcate socially good behaviors and implement the findings in society (https://www.jsocialmarketing.org). The Center has established a website (https://o-socialmarketing.jp) to provide accurate information on social marketing.

10.2.3 Difficulty in Behavior Change

Desirable social behaviors are often accompanied by physical and emotional burdens. For example, to exercise five times a week, new habits must be developed. Playing video games less frequently translates into less time for fun. Removing labels before recycling them requires more time and effort. While washing one's hands can prevent personal, family, and social infection, one is unlikely to realize that and do so regularly.

To promote new behaviors that entail physical and emotional burdens, the following four points should be considered: (1) create value that exceeds the physical and emotional burdens; (2) be based on behavioral science theories from diverse fields; (3) include benchmark criteria to enhance the effectiveness of behavior promotion; and (4) follow a systematic process that includes these criteria. Some key elements of the process are as follows.

10.2.4 Why Marketing Is Important in Policy Formulation: Creation of Social Value

The key concept in marketing is "exchange." For example, when we pay 100 yen for tea or water, we can enjoy the value of "quenching our thirst" or "drinking something delicious." When we wash our hands during outbreaks of infectious diseases, we enjoy the value of preventing infection. However, as mentioned above, socially desirable behaviors entail both physical and mental burdens. Therefore, the key is to create and provide "value to the individual and society that exceeds the burden." In other words, it is an exchange of new value for physical and emotional burdens.

To create this value, first, it is important to act from the perspective of citizens (the subjects of behavior change) rather than from that of the governing. Second, behavioral barriers and motivations for action should be thoroughly investigated to elicit insights. Third, pilot testing of measures should be conducted to incorporate citizens' voices and formulate them together with the citizens.

10.2.5 Use Behavioral Science Theories from Diverse Disciplines

Social marketing incorporates interdisciplinary behavioral science theories to determine intervention targets and formulate specific measures. For example, when determining intervention targets, the transtheoretical model (Prochaska and Velicer 1997) and the diffusion of innovation theory are used (Rogers 1995). Additionally, when considering the marketing mix, which is a combination of various measures, respondent conditioning (Pavlov 1927), operant conditioning (Skinner 1953), achievement motivational theory (McClelland 1961), expectancy theory (Vroom 1964), cognitive dissonance theory (Festinger 1957), theory of planned behavior (Fishbein 1967), the health belief model (Janz and Becker 1984), social cognitive theory (Bandura 1986), and choice architecture (nudge) are employed (Thaler and Sunstein 2008).

An important feature of social marketing is the selection of the most effective theory for the target audience from a variety of disciplines, including health behavioral science, social psychology, business administration, and economics, based on insights gained from formative research.

10.2.6   Factors and Formulation Process to Improve the Effectiveness of Behavior Change

Social marketing is often confused with social media marketing, education, and information- or knowledge-driven promotional campaigns. Andreasen (2002) defined six elements of social marketing, while The National Social Marketing Center in the U.K. added two more elements, proposing eight key elements as "benchmark criteria." The greater the inclusion of these eight benchmark criteria, the more effective the reported behavior change (Cairns and Rundle-Thiele 2014; Kubacki et al. 2015).

The first of the "Benchmark Criteria" is that the main objective is the transformation to "social good" behavior. It is not the end of empathy, but a commitment to action and persistence. Therefore, it is necessary to identify groups with similar beliefs, attitudes, and behavioral patterns and determine focus areas (Segmentation and Targeting). Once the intervention targets are determined, the reasons for their inability to act, concerns, and motivations for action are investigated, and their voices are thoroughly heard (Customer Orientation). Based on this formative research, it is important to extract unconscious behaviors and thoughts (Insights) and create value. At the same time, this is also key to considering the competition in action, providing "value" beyond the subject's concerns and determining reasons for not acting, and establishing an "exchange" that is attractive and convincing enough for them to act. Furthermore, it is important that behavioral science theories from various disciplines are combined and the marketing mix is tailor-made for each target group.

How should the plan be formulated? There are several planning methods, including the STELa model (French 2017), but the most basic and easiest to use in policy formulation is the Lee and Kotler model (2019) (Table 10.1).

10.3   Case Study of Implementation of Social Marketing-Based Measures Collaborating with Local Government

10.3.1   Background and Objectives of the Case Study

In Japan, there have been no reported cases of local governments implementing the social marketing processes described above. This chapter presents cases wherein university laboratories have taken the initiative to collaborate with local governments. The targeted social issue is the improvement in the willingness to donate organs. This case specifically concerns the process of creating an awareness leaflet together with the local government to increase public involvement.

Table 10.1 Procedure for formulating measures using the Lee & Kotler model

Step		Contents
1	Clarification of background, purpose, and focus	First, determine the social issues (health, environment, etc.) to be handled as the organization's activities. Clarify the background of the social issue, the nature of the problem, related issues, cooperative organizations, etc., through previous research and surveys. Next, establish the purpose of the activity. Objectives are at a higher level, and imply how society will be affected if the target individual is transformed into adopting the desired behavior. Furthermore, based on the previous research, we determine and specify what we will focus on from among the options that contribute to the objectives and proceed with the plan.
2	Situation analysis	Conduct a SWOT analysis of your organization that will influence strategy and decision-making.
3	Selection of intervention targets	First, divide the market into groups sharing common attributes (segmentation). Next, evaluate the segments using several variables, such as segment size, severity, and responsiveness to the marketing mix. Finally, select one or more target segments from among them.
4	Establishment of action objectives and goals	First, set one or two behavioral goals (specific behaviors to be encouraged in the intervention target). Next, establish a knowledge goal (information or facts that the intervention target should acquire to achieve the behavioral goal) and a belief goal (things that the intervention target should recognize or trust to achieve the behavioral goal).
5	Clarification of factors influencing behavior	Understand the behaviors (conflicts) that intervention subjects prefer over the "desired behavior," the perceived barriers to the "desired behavior," the benefits (values) they seek in exchange for that behavior, and their motivation to adopt that behavior. These factors are clarified through previous research surveys, both, qualitative, such as interviews, and quantitative, such as questionnaires. It is important to understand the four factors accurately, even if it means spending significant money and time on formative research.
6	Clarification of positioning	Clarify how you want the intervention target to consider the "desired behavior" you want to promote, compared to competing behaviors. Based on the four factors that influence behavior, it is important to create new values for the behavior.

(continued)

Table 10.1 (continued)

Step		Contents
7	Strategically develop a marketing mix	Develop a marketing mix (4P) to encourage the desired behavior in the intervention target population. (1) Product Strategy: Consider the Core Product (the most valuable benefit that the intervention target audience will gain from the desired behavior), the Actual Product (the plan provided at the intervention event), and the Augmented Product (additional items that support behavior change). The following products are considered. (2) Price strategy (Price): This refers to the cost paid by the intervention target for the target behavior, including both, monetary (the cost of goods and services necessary for the behavior) and non-monetary (time, effort, and psychological risk) aspects. We consider reducing these costs. (iii) Distribution strategy (Place): Think about when and where intervention subjects take action. Reduce psychological barriers regarding where to take action, working to ensure that the necessary factors to take action are available at the time of decision-making. (iv) Promotion: Activities that communicate what they want the intervention target audience to know and the benefits to be gained from the action. It consists of four components: message, messenger, creative logo or phrase, and channel.
8	Evaluation plan	Plan the evaluation and measurement of activities in advance. There are four main methods, but outcome measurement is essential. Input Measurement: Measures how many resources were used against the plan. Output measurement: Measures the response of intervention targets to the activities (e.g., number of visitors). Outcome measures: Measures changes in the behavior, knowledge, and beliefs of the intervention subjects. It is possible to assess how much has been achieved compared to the goals set in Step 4. Impact Measurement: Measures the social impact of a change in the behavior of the intervention target on a social issue.
9	Budget setting (of a computer or file, etc.)	Based on the draft plan, decide on a budget in light of the required funds. It may be necessary to modify the intervention targets, goals, and strategies in comparison to the funds available to the organization.
10	Preparation of implementation plan	Prepare a specific implementation plan that clearly identifies who is responsible, when it will be implemented, and how much it will cost. Ideally, this should be a 2–3-year mid-term action plan and a single year plan.

Source: The author created the table using these data, based on Lee and Kotler (2019)

Our organization primarily consists of university undergraduates. This study was implemented in Kyoto in 2017. We applied the Stages-of-Change Model (Prochaska and Velicer 1997) to promote general concern about social problems and encourage students to engage in positive societal actions. We focused on the specific issue of low rates of declaration of intent to donate organs in Japan.

We were asked by local governments to prepare educational leaflets on this topic. In the past, the use of educational leaflets was restricted to hospitals, public health centers, and ward offices. For example, traditional municipalities distributed leaflets only during events related to specific municipalities. Additionally, the content of educational leaflets was not designed in a way that is conscious of behavioral change, and individuals who are not interested in the issue do not take the leaflets seriously. Furthermore, it is difficult to assess whether educational leaflets influence behavior. Therefore, we aimed to achieve the following four tasks.

1. Create leaflets that encourage behavior transformation in people.
2. Develop methods to provide opportunities for people who are not interested in reading the leaflet.
3. Develop a method to assess behavior changes due to the intervention.
4. Promote actual behavior changes regarding declaration of intent for organ donation.

10.3.2 Methods

In our previous studies examining the five stages of the Action Change model, the "stage of interest" (transition from "not interested" to "interested"), and the "stage to decide attitude and move to action" (Transition from "attitude decision" to "intention display") was low, and it was clarified that there was a barrier in between stages. Because of the importance of intervention at this stage, the purpose of the leaflet interventions was to engage people in the different stages and help them form intentions in layer-deciding attitudes.

Commitment is an important factor for humans to take action (Skumanich and Kintsfather 1996). The degree of "involvement" in an issue, that is, the time and energy spent on considering a particular issue, influences the possibility of people taking action. We believed that it may be important to allow people to experience multiple leaflet proposals and create time to think about their intention to provide organs from various viewpoints. We believed that "voting" is an appropriate concrete event. Through the "voting" process, we created time to think about engaging people in the different stages by associating value with intention. By indicating this value from a new viewpoint, we thought that we could promote change at the stage at which the attitude was decided.

First, we created 20 leaflets, of which eight were selected for use. Next, we asked citizens to vote on their chosen leaflet over a certain period. Citizens voted (while discussing with their families during summer vacation) through a website associated with the local government.

At the time of voting, participants voted based on the four perspectives: "The leaflet that I would most like to choose," "The leaflet that I am most proud of declaration of intention to donate my organ or not," "The leaflet that I would most like to declare my intention to donate organs or not," and "The leaflet that I think overall is the best." We also asked questions about the views on the declaration of intent for organ donation leaflets, assessing the occurrence of conversations with the family, and the stage of behavior change regarding the declaration.

After the final leaflets were chosen, a follow-up survey was conducted and behavioral changes by voting (intervention) were measured.

10.3.3   Characteristics of Voters

In total, 1614 people voted during the 46-day voting period. Among them, the responses of 1154 subjects were analyzed, after excluding those with incomplete answers.

Among the participants analyzed, 51.7% were male and 48.3% were female. Regarding their age, 20.2% were in their teens and 68.8% were in their twenties. The participants were considered to belong to a generation accustomed to online voting. About one-third, that is, 33.4% of the subjects had discussed the intention for organ donation intention with their family, which was nearly equivalent to the public opinion poll.

10.3.4   Stage of Declaration Behaviors

Survey results showed that 17.2% (n = 197) of subjects declared and shared their intentions with their families (rate of intent declaration of whether to donate organs or not). Because 30.4% (n = 348) of the subjects were in Stage 1 (not interested), it was confirmed that the target layer was reached.

10.3.5   Perception for Organ Donation and Transplantation

Many participants (79.3%) considered organ transplantation "useful." Also, 64.4% had positive perceptions such as "thinking about each other," and 63.1% felt "connected." However, it became clear that 43.6% felt that organ donation was "scary" and 51.4% had negative perceptions, which can be described as "anxiety."

10.3.6   Results of Voting by Perception of Declaration of Intent to Donate Organs or Not

The voting results are shown in the table below. It became clear that the rankings of the selected leaflets differed depending on the viewpoint chosen (Table 10.2).

A chi-square test was conducted to examine the relationship between the perception of the declaration of intent to donate organs and the leaflet selected. It was

Table 10.2 The results of voting by viewpoints

Type of leaflet	The leaflet that I would like to pick up the most	The leaflet that I am proud of declaration of intention to donate my organ or not	The leaflet that I would like to declare my intention to donate organs or not	The leaflet that I think overall is the best
No.1 Declaration of intent for organ donation is a letter to family	24.8	29.7	28.4	29.5
No.2 Of course you do?	4.4	6.8	3.9	4.6
No.3 It is stylish to put it in black and white, is it not?	26.7	11.6	14.6	18.4
No.4 Kyoto people do it for granted	10.2	8.7	6.2	7.8
No.5 Not declaring intention for organ donation at the end of your life is not filial piety	7.0	16.9	18.0	11.3
No.6 Let us start with KYO	8.8	12.3	10.4	11.3
No.7 Did you choose??	6.2	5.0	8.8	7.9
No.8 Aim for the nation's No. 1 declaration of rate of intent for organ donation	11.9	9.0	9.7	9.4
Total	100.0%	100.0%	100.0%	100.0%

Source: Author's elaboration

revealed that those with perceptions of "scary," "uneasy," and "useless" toward intention display significantly chose "No.1" more, that is, "Declaration of intent for organ donation is a letter to family" (p < 0.001). It was suggested that it might be effective for a person with a negative perception to manifest a new viewpoint because that action of manifestation of intention becomes a "letter" to family members. Further, it was suggested to utilize a "loss frame" message was effective for behavioral changes.

10.3.7 Follow-Up Survey

Based on the above results, the leaflets identified as "No.1 Declaration of intent to donate organs is a letter to the family" and "No.5 Not declaring intention for organ donation at the end of your life is not filial piety" were chosen for distribution in the district.

Follow-up investigations were conducted with the voters after the final results were revealed. There were 102 respondents (6.3%). This investigation asked respondents about their behavior after voting. Results showed that "discussed with family about declaration of intent for organ donation (23.5%)," "studied about the declaration of intent for organ donation (17.7%)," and "discussed the campaign with close friends (14.7%)" were the most common behaviors, among others. These results suggest that new actions, such as dialogue and information retrieval, were caused by "voting."

Furthermore, we compared the behavior of 40 participants who responded to information regarding the stage of declaration behavior, both, during voting and the follow-up survey. We scored the responses as follows: not interested = 1 point, interested = 2 points, have made the decision but not taken action = 3 points, declare intention = 4 points, and share intention with family = 5 points based on Stages-of-Change Model. The average value was then calculated.

The average values at the time of voting and follow-up investigation were 2.73 and 3.02, respectively. Additionally, through conducting a t-test examining the difference between the mean values of the two groups, it was confirmed that the intention display behavior was statistically significant ($p < 0.001$ SE: $r = .47$). Also, as shown in the figure, 25% (10 out of 40 people) changed their behavior stage by one level, while 6.1% (2 out of 33 people) changed two or more levels.

10.3.8 Findings

The results of the voting behavior clarified the tendency to select leaflets in which the message theme, "gained one" or "lost one" is clearly indicated and associated with the behavioral change of declaring the intention to donate one's organs or not.

The trend differed according to behavior. Specifically, a leaflet showing a message that emphasized focus on "lost" by not indicating intention tend to be chosen as "the leaflet in which I would like to declare my intention to donate organs or not," and "the leaflet that makes me proud of my declaration of intention to donate my organs or not." On the other hand, a leaflet containing a message, emphasizing "what is obtained" by expressing intention was evaluated as "the leaflet that I would like to pick up the most."

Furthermore, differences were revealed in the leaflets chosen, depending on the respondents' perceptions. For people with negative perceptions, such as "scary," "anxious," or "useless" regarding the intention to donate, it was effective to provide a new viewpoint suggesting that the action of displaying intention could become a "letter to family."

10.4   Diffusion of Social Marketing in Local Governments

10.4.1   Educational Programs and Accreditation Requirements in Japan

In Japan, the need for professionals to utilize social marketing for policy formulation is being emphasized. Globally, guidelines for certification programs for individuals, who develop problem-solving strategies using social marketing, have been agreed upon, and educational programs, based on these guidelines, are already being offered (Lee and Kotler 2019), generating expertise on the subject.

Therefore, the author develops a standard educational program in Japan, based on the program offered by the International Social Marketing Association, as well as certification standards for professionals (social marketers). These standards are accredited by the International Social Marketing Association (Uryuhara 2023).

10.4.2   Contribution of Social Marketing in Municipalities

To increase the number of social marketing professionals in municipalities, the author conducted a training program for eight employees in a municipality in 2023. Although social implementation has not yet taken place, measures were developed in each policy area over a period of nine months according to the steps in Table 10.1.

At the end of the nine-month training, interviews were conducted with eight participants. They were asked about differences from previous methods of policy formulations. The results are summarized in Table 10.3.

The results can be roughly categorized into, "thinking from the residents' point of view," "establishment of a systematic and standardized process," "establishment of segmented measures," "creation of new added value," and "possibility of promoting behavioral change of the people involved." These are all characteristics of social marketing. In particular, social marketing contributes to local governments by enabling them to think from the residents' perspective and solve problems by enabling people in various positions to take socially beneficial actions.

Social marketing is a systematic process that helps citizens take new actions that are important to themselves and society, thereby improving their communities. Because it is not easy for people to take new actions, a "long-term perspective" is necessary. Additionally, it is important to first, thoroughly, "investigate and observe" the value of taking action, and the thoughts and needs of residents to clarify why they cannot take action. However, even if they were aware of this, it would have

Table 10.3 Contribution of social marketing compared to previous policy planning

Contribution point	Opinion
Thinking from the residents' point of view	To adopt a resident's point of view and think about how to permeate the policy in the community.
Establishment of a systematic and standardized process	The plan is a step-by-step policy plan. There is preliminary research and planning, and objectives based on that research and planning. 10 steps are covered in the planning process, so there is no need to overlook points that need to be considered. At the time of planning, outcome measurement and evaluation are also considered, eliminating regrets and haphazard actions.
Segmentation and targeting enable highly effective measures.	I felt that the perspective of targeting and setting up segmented measures was absolutely necessary.
Creation of new added value	By conducting in-depth and careful qualitative research, new and unexpected value can be found on the planning side.
Possibility of promoting behavioral change among the people involved	People from various walks of life will take socially beneficial actions, and this will generate solutions to problems.

Source: Author's elaboration

been difficult for them to formulate long-term citizen-oriented policies in their busy workplaces, where immediate action is required.

The responses of local government officials revealed that social marketing has a "systematic process and framework" that enables them to segment, deeply investigate citizens' thoughts, create value, and consider policies from multiple. The answers to these questions reveals the following. They feel that the above processes could be "utilized by local governments."

Finally, we discuss how social marketing can contribute to improving the sustainability of local government services with limited policy resources. The most important aspect of social marketing is to start from the viewpoint of citizens as beneficiaries. This means more than simply listening to the voices of citizens. It is a process of thinking, creating, and implementing policies together with citizens, based on behavioral science theory as well as sufficient research to elicit citizen insights. As summarized in Table 10.3, the social marketing process enables us to determine issues systematically, so we can take up the most needed measures, effectively discard unnecessary measures, and clarify the priorities of services. In addition, the effectiveness of policies can be improved through segmentation and targeting. The creation of new added value leads to the development of new policies, as opposed to policymaking that tends to follow precedent. In addition, a focus on behavior change will strengthen the promotion of policies. In this way, social marketing can enhance the prioritization and effectiveness of municipal policies and improve sustainability through the encouragement of citizen collaboration.

10.5   Conclusions

This chapter discusses social marketing, which is based on various behavioral science theories, and the factors and processes that facilitate behavioral change for the successful implementation of social marketing. The case study for examining the effects of behavioral change on citizens, is a series of campaigns, wherein citizens were asked to choose from various educational leaflets on "willingness to donate organs," conducted in collaboration with the local government and a university laboratory. Simultaneously, a follow-up study on citizens' behavioral changes was conducted.

These results confirms that voting on the website promoted the search for appropriate information, dialogue with family members, and willingness to donate, regarding organ donation. These results suggest that campaigns that leverage citizen commitment are effective. In addition, the case study in this chapter demonstrates the importance of local governments' collaboration with universities. Three key factors for success are identified. First, local government officials believes in the potential of young people and entrust them with creating leaflets and disseminating information through social networking. Second, students can work with the trust of the local government. This in turn helps them gain the trust of citizens, who also participates in the voting process in large numbers. Third, by partnering with a university research organization, students can design methods and conduct in-depth statistical analyses. In this manner, not only local governments but also citizens and universities become the driving force behind the positive promotion of policies.

Additionally, this chapter presents the results of interviews with policymakers in local governments to understand the recognition of social marketing by the officials who formulates policies. The findings of the interviews regarding the usefulness of social marketing are crucial for understanding and implementing policies with the support of citizens. The attitudes of public officials seeking to understand policies alongside citizens contribute significantly to policy formulation. Moreover, promoting policies by involving citizens enhances support for the policy through behavioral changes in the citizens and consequently improves the effectiveness of the policy. Additionally, increased awareness of segmentation and targeting can increase the effectiveness of policies and reconfirm priorities. A systematic process and framework are key in raising awareness regarding social marketing. This is because a systematic process clarifies the criteria for policy evaluation and increases the possibility of policy improvements based on practical evaluation.

Meanwhile, social marketing is still being developed owing to its short history and interdisciplinary nature. Ethical considerations on desirable behaviors to orient citizens are not examined in this chapter but more should be considered in the future than is currently done. Nevertheless, because social marketing focuses on mobilization effects, such as citizens' behavioral changes, various studies are expected to be conducted in the future through attempts to implement social marketing in society.

The conclusions of this chapter, based on case studies of citizens and interviews with officials, are that social marketing strengthens policy drivers and imposes a clear positive mobilizing effect through behavioral changes among citizens. We expect local government officials to develop and implement policies through social marketing, the benefits of which will spread to residents and others around them, thus improving their well-being.

References

Andreasen AR (1995) Marketing social change: changing behavior to promote health, social development, and the environment, 1st edn. Jossey-Bass, San Francisco

Andreasen AR (2002) Marketing social marketing in the social change marketplace. J Public Policy Mark 21(1):3–13. https://doi.org/10.1509/jppm.21.1.3.1760

Andreasen AR (2006) Social marketing in the 21st century. Sage Publications, Thousand Oaks. https://doi.org/10.4135/9781483329192

Bandura A (1986) Social foundations of thought and action: a social cognitive theory. Prentice Hall, Englewood Cliffs

Cairns J, Rundle-Thiele S (2014) Eating for the better: a social marketing review (2000–2012). Public Health Nutr 17(7):1628–1639. https://doi.org/10.1017/S1368980013001365

Festinger L (1957) A theory of cognitive dissonance. Stanford University Press, Stanford

Fishbein M (1967) Readings in attitude theory and measurement. Wiley, New York

French J (2017) Social marketing and public health: theory and practice, 2nd edn. Oxford University Press, Oxford. https://doi.org/10.1093/med/9780198717690.001.0001

International Social Marketing Association (2017) https://isocialmarketing.org/wp-content/uploads/2021/04/Global-Consensus-on-Social-Marketing-Principles-Concepts-and-Techniques-2017.pdf

Janz NK, Becker MH (1984) The health belief model: a decade later. Health Educ Q 11(1):1–47. https://doi.org/10.1177/109019818401100101

Kotler P, Zaltman G (1971) Social marketing: an approach to planned social change. J Mark 35(3):3–12. https://doi.org/10.1177/002224297103500302

Kubacki K, Rundle-Thiele SR, Pang B, Buyucek N (2015) Minimizing alcohol harm: a systematic social marketing review (2000–2014). J Bus Res 68(10):2214–2222. https://doi.org/10.1016/j.jbusres.2015.03.023

Lee NR, Kotler P (2019) Social marketing: behavior change for social good, 6th edn. Sage Publications, California

Ling JC, Franklin BAK, Lindsteadt JF, Gearon SAN (1992) Social marketing: its place in public health. Annu Rev Public Health 13:341–362. https://doi.org/10.1146/annurev.pu.13.050192.002013

Manoff RK (1985) Social marketing: the new imperative for public health. Praeger Publishers Inc, Michigan

McClelland DC (1961) The achieving society. D. Van Nostrand Co, Princeton

Pavlov IP (1927) Conditioned reflexes. Oxford University, London

Prochaska JO, Velicer WF (1997) The Transtheoretical model of health behavior change. Am J Health Promot 12(1):38–48. https://doi.org/10.4278/0890-1171-12.1.38

Rogers RW (1995) Diffusion of innovations, 4th edn. The Free Press, New York

Skinner B (1953) Science and human behaviour. Macmilla, New York

Skumanich SA, Kintsfather DP (1996) Promoting the organ donor card: a causal model of persuasion effects. Soc Sci Med 43:401–408. https://doi.org/10.1016/0277-9536(95)00404-1

Thaler RH, Sunstein CR (2008) Nudge: improving decisions about health, wealth, and happiness. Yale University Press, New Haven

Uryuhara Y (2021) Behavioral science for a better society: Solving social issues through social marketing [Kodo kagaku de yori yoi syakai o tsukuru: Sosyaru maketeingu ni yoru syakai kadai no kaiketsu]. Bunshindo Publishing Corporation, Tokyo. (in Japanese)

Uryuhara Y (2023) Contribution of social marketing to effective policy-making [Kokatekina seisaku no jitsugen ni taisuru *sosyaru maketeingu no koken*]. Doshisha Bus Rev [Doshisha Shogaku] 75(2):203–237. (in Japanese). https://doi.org/10.14988/0002000053

Vroom VH (1964) Work and motivation. Wiley, New York

White P, French J (2009) Capacity building competencies and standards. In: French J, Blair-Stevens C, McVey D, Merritt R (eds) Social marketing and public health: theory and practice. Oxford University Press, Oxford, pp 291–300. https://doi.org/10.1093/acprof:oso/9780199550692.001.0001

Wiebe GD (1951) Merchandising commodities and citizenship on television. Public Opin Q 15(4):679–691. https://doi.org/10.1086/266353

Yoko Uryuhara is a Professor at the Faculty of Commerce, Doshisha University, and the Director at the Social Marketing Research Centre, Doshisha University. She is an affiliated member of the Science Council of Japan. She was a former board member of the European Academy of Management and the first Japanese representative. Her research interests include social marketing, behavioral science, and organizational behavior. Recently, her book won the Japan NPO Society Award for Excellence.

Chapter 11
Hometown Tax Donation System and Local Governance

Tetsuharu Oba (iD) **and Tatsuki Kishimoto** (iD)

Abstract As attention to the hometown tax donation system has increased in recent years, it is important for practitioners to gain knowledge on what kinds of local government initiatives attract donations and what effects the system can have on local economies to provide appropriate information for making logical decisions. In this chapter, we examine both qualitatively and quantitatively how the hometown tax donation system, a unique Japanese donation system and one that has been in place for about 15 years, affect local governments. As a quantitative analysis method, we use two estimation models to analyze the relationship between local governments' efforts and the hometown tax donation system in relation to donation revenues. The results show that donors' self-interested factors such as financial incentives are statistically positively significant, while most of the altruistic factors are not statistically significant. The quantile regression model results also indicate that the trends are clearly different depending on the amount of donation. Specifically, for municipalities with smaller donation amounts, the positive associations with credit card payments and number of portals are larger. For municipalities with larger donation amounts, the positive associations with higher expense ratios, the number of returned gifts, and the presence of high-value returns of 10 million yen or more are larger. Additionally, a case study of the project 'Tokusan Doshiyo (What About Our Specialties?) Seminar,' in which the authors are involved as an academia-industry collaboration, suggests that the hometown tax donation system could contribute to construction of local ecosystems and enhancement of local governance.

T. Oba (✉)
Graduate School of Management & Graduate School of Engineering, Kyoto University, Kyoto, Japan
e-mail: oba.tetsuharu.5n@kyoto-u.ac.jp

T. Kishimoto
Graduate School of Management, Kyoto University, Kyoto, Japan
e-mail: kishimoto.tatsuki.64c@st.kyoto-u.ac.jp

Keywords Hometown tax donation system · Local governance · Sustainability · Local ecosystem · Heterogeneity in the relationship · Academia-industry partnership

11.1 Introduction

Japan has entered a society with a declining population since 2005, and raising concerns that citizen welfare, especially in rural areas, may decline due to reduced regional vitality and financial shortfalls caused by the population decrease. There are a wide range of issues related to citizen welfare, including maintenance of infrastructure such as transportation, water and sewage systems, and local medical care. However, local governments have limited means of securing discretionary financial resources, making it difficult to control them at will. Under these circumstances, the hometown tax donation system has gained attention in recent years as a financial resource for local governments. This system allows tax deductions from income and inhabitant taxes for donations made to any local government. In addition to the tax deduction, donors can also receive a return gift from the municipality. By effectively utilizing the system, municipalities that collect a large amount of donations have increased their expenditures on education, industrial development, and resident services, confirming that the hometown tax donation system plays a certain role as a source of revenue for local governments.

In addition, previous studies suggest that the hometown tax donation system can not only compensate for financial resource shortages but also revitalize local regions. For example, Nishimura and Seta (2017) show the possibility that the provision of hometown taxes could lead to the provision of new external resources, Hoda (2017) suggests the promotion of competition among regions and the occurrence of increased business motivation of local businesses through the provision of returned gifts, and Ito (2020) finds that emergent innovation is generated in public ecosystems such as the hometown tax donation system.

These findings indicate that the hometown tax donation system has the potential to be an effective tool for addressing the various challenges faced by local governments today, but it requires evidence-based policy making (EBPM) to determine whether limited resources should be allocated to it. Recent studies on the hometown tax donation system have primarily focused on the system's pros and cons or on lawsuits, with few scientifically and quantitatively verified cases examining the relationship between local government initiatives and donations or regional revitalization. There is also a lack of basic information for each local government to develop its own strategies. Therefore, the purpose of this chapter is to clarify the relationship between local governments' efforts and the hometown tax donation system. In particular, we focus on the relationship with donations and the relationship with the local revitalization effect caused by various activities to solicit donations. For the former, we use an econometric approach to quantitatively examine the question of which local government initiatives are related to hometown tax donations and whether the relationship differs depending on the amount of donations. For the latter, we provide specific examples of academia-industry partnership through the hometown tax donation system and examine the potential for regional revitalization based on the results obtained.

This chapter is organized as follows. First, in Sect. 11.2, the current status and issues of the hometown tax donation system are summarized based on statistical data and literature. The involvement of stakeholders such as local governments and private companies in the system is then reviewed. In Sect. 11.3, by constructing our own analytical dataset, we estimate the relationship between local governments' efforts and hometown tax donation revenues using least squares regression model and quantile regression model to identify the heterogeneity of the relationship at the median and specific quantile values. Section 11.4 discusses the need for local revitalization and regional development through the hometown tax donation system from the perspective of local ecosystem construction. Furthermore, we discuss the efforts of academia-industry partnership between an advertising agency and a university to enhance local governance, promote sustainable regional development, strengthen the formation and cohesion of local communities, and effectively utilize regional resources to revitalize the local economy. Finally, in the conclusion, we summarize the results obtained so far and discuss future challenges.

11.2 Current Status and Issues of the Hometown Tax Donation System

11.2.1 Origin of the Hometown Tax Donation System

Hometown tax donation is a unique donation system in Japan. It was launched in 2008 as a mechanism to contribute to hometowns through donation. This system is positioned as a means to promote a person's attachment and connection to their hometown against the background of the universal fact that hometowns are people's emotional support, as reflected in proverbs and quotes expressing values related to hometowns in both domestic and international cultures. Approximately 15 years have passed since the start of the system, and it has been used to raise tax awareness among citizens, to allow citizens to give back to the hometown or municipality to which they have a connection, and to promote competition among local governments.

Taxpayers who donate to local governments through the system gain a certain tax benefit from their income tax and individual inhabitant tax, excluding a 2000 yen copayment. The system is similar to the charitable donation system popular in Europe and the U.S. in that the donation amount can be deducted from income. However, the hometown tax donation system differs in that donations are made to local governments, donors can deduct donations to up to five local governments from their income without filing a final tax return through the one-stop exception

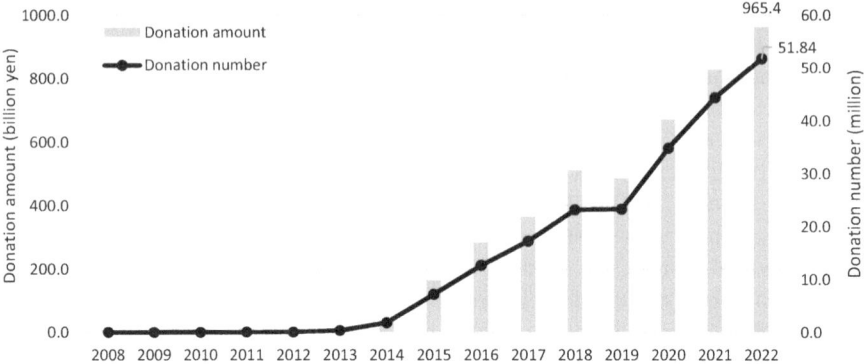

Fig. 11.1 Trends in the amount and number of hometown tax donation. (Source: Author's own design based on data taken from the MIC (2023))

system, and donors can receive local specialty gifts in return for their donations. Because donors can receive a variety of gifts for only 2000 yen, which is their own contribution, the economic benefits of this system have attracted increasing attention and the amount of donations has been steadily increasing (Fig. 11.1). According to the "Survey on Current Status of Hometown Tax Donations" released by the Ministry of Internal Affairs and Communications (MIC) in August 2023, donations in FY2022 amount to 965.4 billion yen in terms of value (approximately 1.2 times higher than the previous year) and 51.84 million in terms of number (approximately 1.2 times higher than the previous year). Incidentally, the total amount of donations is equivalent to approximately 1.2 times the amount of local tax revenues of Osaka City, one of Japan's major cities, and approximately 3.1 times that of Kyoto City.

11.2.2 Discussion on Hometown Tax Donation System

Given the aforementioned characteristics, the hometown tax donation system is not merely a donation system but also a unique ecosystem in Japan. Although the main purpose is to obtain donations, the secondary effects generated by the eco-cycle are also attracting attention.

For instance, Hoda and Kubo (2019) and Hoda and Richard (2021) conduct surveys focused on the effect of fostering local businesses through returned gifts and the survey results show that some local businesses are able to carry out more developed business strategies and expand their sales channels outside the returned gifts market. Yasuda and Koyama (2016) find a certain significance of hometown tax donation as a policy tool for regional development, citing examples in Miyakonojo City, Miyazaki Prefecture and Yaizu City, Shizuoka Prefecture, where the use of donations by the system contributes to regional economic revitalization through childcare support, environmental measures, and town development.

Elsewhere, Nishimura and Seta (2017) explain the possibility that donations can lead to the provision of new external resources in relation to the connection between local governments and donors and Ito (2020) reveals that emergent innovation can be generated in a public ecosystem such as the hometown tax donation system.

The literature also includes discussions on problems related to this system and its revision. For example, Mizuta (2017) points out that the hometown tax donation system conflicts with certain principles of taxation, such as the principle of return and the principle of sharing the burden in relation to the theory of taxation. In addition, he notes that it intensifies the competition for returned gifts in search of donations and that, although the value amount of returned gifts exceeds 2000 yen, which is a real benefit, donations without such a burden are antithetical to the principle of donation and cause inequality between donations to local governments and donations to other organizations. Hashimoto and Suzuki (2016) cite tax deductions as a problem with the system and note that phasing out such special deductions lead to increase the out-of-pocket percentage for high-value donations, which reduces the advantage of high-income donors. Other problems that have been pointed out are that fiscal democracy is being shaken, the revenue outlook becomes uncertain, and substantial tax collection costs are being incurred (Koike 2007).

11.2.3 Returned Gift Competition and System Revision

The majority of returned gifts are local specialties and services. However, some municipalities have offered gift certificates with high cash value, such as Amazon gift certificates, or excessive points, which are contrary to the principle of hometown tax donation and have attracted attention, resulting in the so-called "returned gift competition." Tsuchiya (2020) attributes the competition for returned gifts to an effect of the 2015 tax revision (i.e., an expansion of the hometown tax donation quota and the establishment of the one-stop exception system), which made it possible for municipalities to offer the aforementioned highly cashable returned gifts, the appearance of intermediaries on Internet sites. Hashimoto and Suzuki (2016) argue for the need to revise the system while expressing concern about the competition for returned gifts.

In response to the aforementioned circumstances, the government introduced the "Hometown Tax Designation System" for hometown tax through the 2019 tax revision. Local governments that meet the criteria set by the MIC are designated as eligible for the hometown tax credit, and donations to local governments that are not designated are excluded from the system. The criteria for designation by the MIC include the following: the local government must properly solicit donations, the amount of returned gifts must be less than 30% of the total amount of donations, and the returned gifts must be local products.

Nevertheless, even after the 2019 tax reform, the issue of incidental costs other than procurement of returned goods, so-called "hidden costs," and the practice of local governments procuring raw materials from other regions and processing them in their own municipalities, treating them as if they were locally produced goods, gradually became problematic, leading to further changes to the system in October 2023. Under the current system, the amount of total costs must be less than 50% of the donation amount, including incidental costs such as the one-stop exception and issuance of a donation receipt. In addition, only processed products such as aged meat and polished rice whose ingredients are produced in the same prefecture as the concerned local government are allowed as returned gifts. Furthermore, when local products are combined with products from other regions, the value of the incidental and local products must be at least 70% of the total value of the relevant offerings.

11.2.4 Relationships Between Hometown Tax Donation and Private Companies

A correlation diagram describing the relationship between local governments and private companies in the hometown tax donation system is shown in Fig. 11.2. First, hometown tax donation websites operated by private companies play an important role in connecting donors and local governments. Although each local government is responsible for soliciting hometown tax donations, the number of donors that can be gathered simply by providing information on the local government's website is limited. Especially for smaller municipalities, hiring sufficient staff to operate a dedicated website might not be possible. Therefore, most of the local governments in Japan have attempted to spread their information and accept donations by posting on websites operated by private companies.

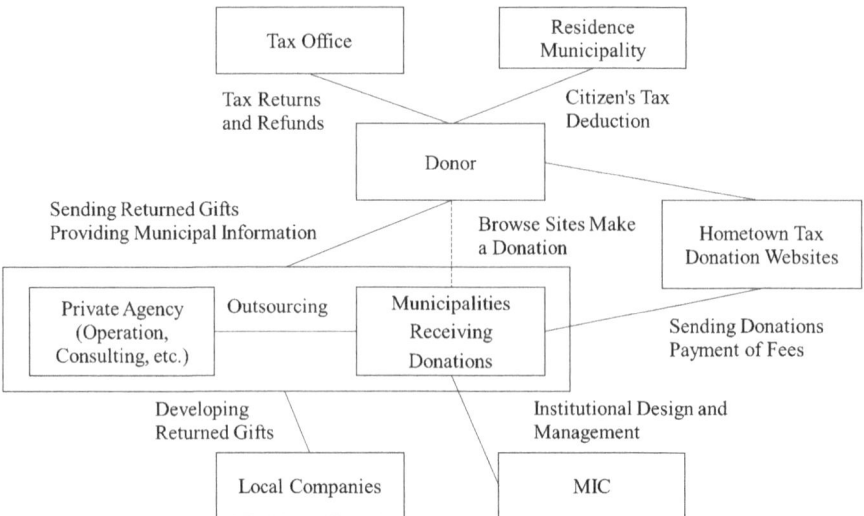

Fig. 11.2 Relationships surrounding hometown tax donation. (Source: Author's elaboration)

Furusato Choice (https://www.furusato-tax.jp/), Furunavi (https://furunavi.jp/), and Satofuru (https://www.satofull.jp/) are representative hometown tax donation websites.[1] These sites enable local governments to effectively collect donations, although they charge a fee. Hometown tax donation websites also make it easier for users to search for the returned gifts they want and to donate without visiting the local government office, thereby facilitating the use of the system. Some websites offer points based on the donation amount and are becoming increasingly popular because of the ease of donation.

For small municipalities and local governments with particularly large donation amounts, if all operations related to hometown tax payments were handled by municipal employees, the workload on each individual would be extremely heavy. To alleviate this problem, private companies act as agents for operational tasks related to hometown tax donations, ranging from daily administrative tasks (e.g., customer management, inventory control, production operations, and delivery arrangements) to marketing, promotion, and call-center operations. Because those agents have information about other local governments and general e-commerce site-operation know-how, they can utilize such knowledge and experience to attract customers more effectively. Some of these operations can also be performed by the aforementioned companies that operate hometown tax donation websites. In addition, some private companies not only perform operations on behalf of their clients but also provide consulting services on what returned gifts should be developed. Local government officials plan and operate the hometown tax donation system, utilizing the power of these private companies as needed.

Naturally, the relationship with local businesses that provides returned gifts is important for municipalities that solicit donations. Local governments (or agents) need to cooperate with local businesses to create attractive returned gifts. Such efforts, as mentioned in Sect. 11.2.2, encourage local industries to strengthen their management capabilities, which can result in the creation of new jobs and an increase in corporate tax revenues and should be an item to focus on for the sake of sustainable municipal growth.

11.3 Local Government Initiatives and Hometown Tax Donation

11.3.1 Review of Previous Studies

Section 11.2.2 clarifies that, although there are some problems with the hometown tax donation system, if well utilized, it can be a tool to compensate for the lack of financial resources of local governments and contribute to regional revitalization.

---

[1] Major corporations in various industries such as Rakuten (https://event.rakuten.co.jp/furusato/), ANA (https://furusato.ana.co.jp/), and au (https://furusato.wowma.jp/) also operate hometown tax donation websites. More than 30 hometown tax donation websites have been identified as of August 2022.

Therefore, this section reviews previous studies before presenting the results of an empirical study on the relationship between institutional utilization and donation performance.

First, in a research report, Musha (2019) analyzes the relationship between donation income and the efforts of local governments, including panel data on the relationship between the attributes of returned gifts and the amount of donations because attractive returned gifts affect the amount of donations. The results reveal that a 1% increase in the ratio of returned gifts increases the amount of donations by 26.2 million yen and that, in Hokkaido municipalities, the amount of donations increases when fresh food is offered as a returned gift. However, these findings are only the results of analyses in specific regions. In a similar study, Nishimura et al. (2017) point out that the amount of donations collected by local governments depends on the return ratio set by them. Yamamura et al. (2017) use panel data from 2008 to 2015 to analyze donation amounts and show that a 1% increase in return spending by a municipality led to a 0.61% increase in donations to the municipality in question. However, although these studies cover a wide range of municipalities, they do not examine factors other than economic incentives related to pure donations, particularly individual normative attitudes such as trust and reciprocity, which should be considered.

In a study focused on individuals' normative awareness, Takahashi et al. (2019) examin the influence of normative awareness factors and economic factors on hometown tax donations using an ordinal probit model based on questionnaire survey data and compared the results with those for general donations. Their results show that, although the awareness of reciprocity affects hometown tax donations as well as general donations, economic factors such as household income also affect hometown tax donations.

On the basis of the aforementioned studies, in Sect. 11.3.2 and thereafter, we conduct further in-depth empirical analyses to provide practitioners involved in hometown tax donation with useful basic information for considering effective initiatives in accordance with regional characteristics, complementing the topics addressed in the previous studies. Specifically, we conduct a quantitative analysis of the relationship between local governments' efforts and hometown tax donations, incorporating independent variables such as the expense ratio and the relationship with donors, which have been treated in previous studies, as well as unique indicators such as the number of returned goods and set prices that represent the status of local governments' efforts. In addition, focusing on the amount of donations, we examine not only the effect of the conventional average donation amount but also the possibility that the effect differs depending on the size of the donation amount.

11.3.2 Data Collection and Analysis Model

The data collected for the analysis are the latest status survey results published by the MIC as well as information posted on hometown tax donation websites. This chapter is not limited to a few regions but covers 1677 municipalities,[2] and we have constructed a highly unique dataset by combining the vast amount of statistical data published by the government with data collected on the basis of our own observations.

Regarding the analytical model, to quantitatively identify which municipalities attract donations, we use a regression model based on the ordinary least squares (OLS) with municipal initiatives affecting the amount or number of donations as independent variables, along with a quantile regression model (QRM) (Koenker and Bassett 1978; Koenker and Hallock 2001). For the OLS regression model, if the donation amount of municipality i is AD_i, it can be expressed as a one-logarithmic donation function as follows based on information about the municipality's initiatives, returned gifts, and characteristics.

$$\ln AD_i = \beta_0 + \beta_1 Selfish_i + \beta_2 Altruistic_i + \beta_3 Usage_i + \beta_4 Site_i \\ + \beta_5 Gift_i + \beta_6 Price_i + \beta_7 Area_i + \beta_8 PrevRank_i + \varepsilon_i \qquad (11.1)$$

In the equation, $Selfish_i$ is the donor's self-interest factor, while $Altruistic_i$ and $Usage_i$ are variables related to altruistic factors, $Site_i$, $Gift_i$ and $Price_i$ are dummy variables for returned gifts, and $Area_i$ and $PrevRank_i$ are variables for municipal characteristics. Note that ε_i is the error term and β_0 to β_8 are unknown parameters.

OLS regression models the effect of independent variables on the average value of the outcome by minimizing the sum of the squared residuals (for each observation, the residual is the difference between the actual value of the outcome and the value that is predicted using the regression equation). By contrast, the QRM, introduced by Koenker and Bassett (1978), is a method to evaluate the effect of independent variables on the distribution of the independent variable at various locations in the distribution by estimating the conditional quantiles or locations in the distribution, such as the median and the number of quantiles and deciles. That is, in addition to the effect of the average dependent variable, the possibility that the effect might differ for municipalities with particularly high or low donations can be quantitatively examined. In addition, because the analysis examines quantiles rather than averages, it can be robust to outliers. Given the donation amount for municipality i as AD_i, the dependent variable can be expressed as a one-logarithmic donation function at any τ quantile between 0 and 1, as follows.

---

[2] Of the 1741 municipalities that responded to the MIC survey, 1677 municipalities used Furusato Choice. As of September 2023, Furusato Choice is the most used website with 97.4% of the 1721 municipalities which have returned gifts adopting it.

$$\ln AD_i = \beta_{0\tau} + \beta_{1\tau} Selfish_i + \beta_{2\tau} Altruistic_i + \beta_{3\tau} Usage_i + \beta_{4\tau} Site_i + \beta_{5\tau} Gift_i$$
$$+ \beta_{6\tau} Price_i + \beta_{7\tau} Area_i + \beta_{8\tau} PrevRank_i + \varepsilon_{\tau i}$$

$$\tau \in (0,1) \tag{11.2}$$

Independent variables are the same as in Eq. (11.1). The estimated parameter $\hat{\beta}(\tau)$ from $\beta_{0\tau}$ to $\beta_{8\tau}$ can then be expressed as the solution to the minimization problem in the Eq. (11.3).

$$\hat{\beta}(\tau) = \underset{\beta_\tau}{argmin} \sum_{i=1}^{n} \rho_\tau \left(Y_i - X_i'\beta_\tau\right) \tag{11.3}$$

Note that $\varepsilon_{\tau i} = Y_i - X_i'\beta_\tau$, where Y is the independent variable and i is the explanatory variable vector, β_τ is the parameter vector at the τ quantile, $\varepsilon_{\tau i}$ is the error term at the τ quantile, prime $'$ is the transpose. $\rho_\tau(u)$ is called the check function and is represented by the Eq. (11.4). In this chapter, we set five quantiles: $\tau = 0.1$, 0.25, 0.5, 0.75, and 0.9.

$$\rho_\tau(u) = \begin{cases} \tau u & if \ u \geq 0 \\ (\tau - 1)u & if \ u < 0 \end{cases} \tag{11.4}$$

Table 11.1 lists the variables used in the estimation model, their definitions, sources of information, and basic statistics. As independent variables, we employ variables related to donor self-interest factors, such as the cost ratio for procurement of returned gifts, regular delivery, delivery date specification, one-stop special exception, credit card payment, and the existence of a point system. The expense ratio for the procurement of returned gifts can be paraphrased as the quality of the returned gifts, which is related to the economic incentive as well as the point system. Scheduled delivery, delivery date specification, one-stop special exception, and credit card payment are variables related to convenience. Variables related to the altruistic factors of donors are employed, such as the connection with donors, producer-supported products, the publicity of donation amount results, the publicity of utilization status, and whether progress and results are publicized. For the number of portal sites, we include dummy variables for the number of sites from 1 to 6 to account for the possibility of different relationships to the dependent variable depending on the number of websites subscribed to. Similarly, for the number of returned gifts and prices, we include dummy variables to account for heterogeneity in the relationship with the dependent variable in each band. In addition, the region to which the municipality belongs and its rank in the amount of donations received in the previous year are used as dummy variables.

Table 11.1 List of variables and basic statistics

Variables	Definition	Ave.	Std.
Dependent Variable			
lnAD	Logarithmically converted value of donations in FY2022	18.821	1.785
Independent Variables			
Selfish Factor			
S_Expense	Expense rate for procurement of returns (%)	0.261	0.074
S_Periodical	Takes 1 if there is a periodical delivery, otherwise 0	0.700	0.459
S_Delivery	Takes 1 if there is an item with a designated delivery date, otherwise 0	0.277	0.448
S_Onestop	Takes 1 if one-stop special exception is in place, otherwise 0	0.546	0.498
S_Card	Takes 1 if credit card payment is available, otherwise 0	0.963	0.189
S_Point	Takes 1 if a point system is in place, otherwise 0	0.106	0.308
Altruistic Factor			
A_Connection	Takes 1 if there is a donor connection, otherwise 0	0.430	0.495
A_Support	Takes 1 if there are producer-supported product, otherwise 0	0.165	0.371
A_D-Amount	Takes 1 if the company publishes actual donation amounts, otherwise 0	0.156	0.363
A_D-Use	Takes 1 if the status of utilization is publicly disclosed, otherwise 0	0.352	0.478
A_D-Progress	Takes 1 if progress and results are publicly disclosed, otherwise 0	0.465	0.499
Usage Dummy			
Choice_0	Takes the reference category if donor cannot choose a usage	0.023	0.151
Choice_1	Takes 1 if donor choose a usage, otherwise 0	0.747	0.435
Choice_2	Takes 1 if donor specifically choose a usage, otherwise 0	0.048	0.214
Choice_3	Takes 1 if donor can crowdfund a specific project, otherwise 0	0.182	0.386
Site Dummy			
Site_1	Takes the reference category if municipality uses 1 hometown tax donation websites	0.020	0.139
Site_2	Takes 1 if municipality uses 2 hometown tax donation websites, otherwise 0	0.046	0.211
Site_3	Takes 1 if municipality uses 3 hometown tax donation websites, otherwise 0	0.096	0.295
Site_4	Takes 1 if municipality uses 4 hometown tax donation websites, otherwise 0	0.185	0.388
Site_5	Takes 1 if municipality uses 5 hometown tax donation websites, otherwise 0	0.289	0.454
Site_6	Takes 1 if municipality uses 6 hometown tax donation websites, otherwise 0	0.359	0.480

(continued)

Table 11.1 (continued)

Variables	Definition	Ave.	Std.
Gift Dummy			
Gift_0.1T	Takes the reference category if the number of returned gifts is 1–99	0.223	0.416
Gift_0.2T	Takes 1 if the number of returned gifts is 100–199, otherwise 0	0.210	0.407
Gift_0.5T	Takes 1 if the number of returned gifts is 200–499, otherwise 0	0.337	0.473
Gift_1T	Takes 1 if the number of returned gifts is 500–999, otherwise 0	0.175	0.380
Gift_1T+	Takes 1 if the number of returned gifts is 1,000 or more, otherwise 0	0.055	0.228
Price Dummy			
Price_0.2M	Takes the reference category if the amount of returned gifts is less than 200,000 yen	0.089	0.285
Price_0.5M	Takes 1 if the amount of returned gifts is between 200,000 yen and 500,000 yen, otherwise 0	0.290	0.454
Price_1M	Takes 1 if the amount of returned gifts is between 500,000 yen and 1,000,000 yen, otherwise 0	0.153	0.360
Price_2M	Takes 1 if the amount of returned gifts is between 1,000,000 yen and 2,000,000 yen, otherwise 0	0.229	0.420
Price_5M	Takes 1 if the amount of returned gifts is between 2,000,000 yen and 5,000,000 yen, otherwise 0	0.139	0.347
Price_10M	Takes 1 if the amount of returned gifts is between 5,000,000 yen and 10,000,000 yen, otherwise 0	0.052	0.222
Price_10M+	Takes 1 if the amount of returned gifts is 10,000,000 yen or more, otherwise 0	0.048	0.214
Area Dummy			
Hokkaido	Takes the reference category if the municipality is in the Hokkaido region	0.104	0.305
Tohoku	Takes 1 if the municipality is in the Tohoku region, otherwise 0	0.131	0.338
Kanto	Takes 1 if the municipality is in the Kanto region, otherwise 0	0.177	0.381
Chubu	Takes 1 if the municipality is in the Chubu region, otherwise 0	0.182	0.386
Kinki	Takes 1 if the municipality is in the Kinki region, otherwise 0	0.131	0.337
Chugoku	Takes 1 if the municipality is in the Chugoku region, otherwise 0	0.062	0.242
Shikoku	Takes 1 if the municipality is in the Shikoku region, otherwise 0	0.055	0.227
Kyushu	Takes 1 if the municipality is in the Kyushu region, otherwise 0	0.135	0.342
Okinawa	Takes 1 if the municipality is in the Okinawa region, otherwise 0	0.024	0.153
Previous Rank			
Prev_Rank	Ranking of Donations Received in FY2021	886.26	515.40

11.3.3 Findings

The model estimation results are shown in Table 11.2.[3] The upper portion shows the estimated parameters and the lower portion shows the standard error. q10–q90 in the QRM are the estimated results at the 0.10–0.90 quantile points, where the 0.10 quantile point represents the municipalities in the bottom 10% of the donation amount and the 0.90 quantile point represents the municipalities in the top 10% of the donation amount.

One commonality between the OLS and QRM estimation results is that the variables related to the expense ratio of returns (Expense), the one-stop exception (Onestop), and credit card payment (Card) have statistically significant positive relationships. These variables pertain to the quality and convenience of returned gifts; however, they are related to the amount of donations. The variables related to periodical delivery (Periodical) and producer-supported products (Support) are not statistically significant, confirming that they are not related to the amount of donations. Many of the items related to building relationships with donors (A_X) are not statistically significant under all conditions. Thus, the results suggest that, under the current system, donors can prioritize selfish factors over altruistic factors and that, if the purpose is simply to collect donations, it is necessary to pursue economic incentives that benefit donors and build an environment that makes it easier for them to donate. If this is the case, as noted in the mass media, local governments become even more concerned about "competition for returned gifts" rather than "how they are used," suggesting that regions that do not offer marine products and meat, which tend to be popular returned gifts, might not be able to remedy the situation through local government efforts alone, placing them in an unfair situation.

The results of the quantile regression show that, for the expense ratio, the 0.50, 0.75, and 0.90 quantiles show statistical significance at the 1% level of significance, similar to the results estimated by OLS. However, there is no statistical significance at the 0.10 and 0.25 quantile points. In addition, focusing on the estimated parameters, we find that higher donation amounts lead to larger parameter values. That is, the positive relationship between the expense ratio and the donation amount increases as the donation amount increases. By contrast, when we examine the results for credit card payments, we observe the opposite trend from the estimation results for the expense ratio. That is, the parameter estimates become smaller as the donation amount increases and statistical significance is not secured at the 0.90 quantile point. The positive association with donation amount decreases as the donation amount increases. These results confirm the heterogeneity of the expense ratio and the presence or absence of credit card payment by donation amount.

---

[3] We used "statsmodels" (https://www.statsmodels.org/) for estimation. "statsmodels" is a Python package that provides statistical computations, including descriptive statistics and statistical model estimation and inference.

Table 11.2 Estimation results

Variables	OLS	QRM				
		q10	q25	q50	q75	q90
Intercept	19.1758***	18.5133***	18.7102***	19.1825***	20.3719***	20.7205***
	(0.183)	(0.233)	(0.165)	(0.159)	(0.205)	(0.295)
S_Expense	0.5737***	0.1045	0.2561	0.4967***	0.7637***	1.4135***
	(0.176)	(0.382)	(0.216)	(0.153)	(0.165)	(0.213)
S_Periodical	0.0177	0.0231	0.0313	0.0383	0.0139	−0.0243
	(0.033)	(0.031)	(0.028)	(0.029)	(0.037)	(0.050)
S_Delivery	−0.0689**	0.0250	0.0131	−0.0424	−0.0620*	−0.0723
	(0.031)	(0.031)	(0.027)	(0.027)	(0.035)	(0.048)
S_Onestop	0.0743***	0.0619**	0.0292	0.0662***	0.0607**	0.0896**
	(0.026)	(0.026)	(0.023)	(0.022)	(0.028)	(0.037)
S_Point	0.0342	−0.0520	−0.0085	−0.0228	0.0252	0.0962
	(0.043)	(0.045)	(0.038)	(0.038)	(0.048)	(0.063)
S_Card	0.2562***	0.4491***	0.4437***	0.2571***	0.1623*	0.0046
	(0.084)	(0.085)	(0.074)	(0.073)	(0.097)	(0.127)
A_Connection	0.0082	0.0474*	0.0293	0.0175	−0.0605**	−0.0029
	(0.027)	(0.029)	(0.024)	(0.023)	(0.028)	(0.039)
A_Support	−0.0028	0.0128	0.0085	0.0099	−0.0240	−0.0036
	(0.037)	(0.037)	(0.033)	(0.032)	(0.041)	(0.055)
A_D-Amount	0.1282*	0.2666***	0.0180	0.0689	0.1044	0.2168**
	(0.069)	(0.072)	(0.062)	(0.059)	(0.076)	(0.104)
A_D-Use	0.0306	0.0243	−0.0189	−0.0424	−0.0364	−0.0497
	(0.038)	(0.037)	(0.033)	(0.033)	(0.041)	(0.056)
A_D-Progress	0.0056	0.0534*	0.0398	−0.0184	0.0090	−0.0459
	(0.028)	(0.030)	(0.025)	(0.025)	(0.030)	(0.040)
Choice_0 (Reference)	—	—	—	—	—	—
Choice_1	0.0830	0.0776	0.1775**	0.1788**	0.0545	−0.2005
	(0.087)	(0.095)	(0.079)	(0.076)	(0.096)	(0.138)
Choice_2	0.2487**	0.1631	0.2551***	0.2495***	0.1643	0.1125
	(0.104)	(0.114)	(0.093)	(0.090)	(0.114)	(0.161)
Choice_3	0.1487	0.0876	0.2317***	0.2290***	0.1369	−0.0846
	(0.092)	(0.099)	(0.083)	(0.080)	(0.101)	(0.145)
Site_1 (Reference)	—	—	—	—	—	—
Site_2	0.8267***	0.4161**	0.8057***	0.9670***	0.1871	0.3278
	(0.148)	(0.191)	(0.135)	(0.128)	(0.174)	(0.239)
Site_3	0.9778***	0.6323***	1.1049***	1.1587***	0.2645	0.2840
	(0.143)	(0.187)	(0.129)	(0.124)	(0.172)	(0.234)
Site_4	1.1351***	0.9896***	1.3077***	1.2850***	0.4078**	0.2848
	(0.143)	(0.185)	(0.129)	(0.124)	(0.173)	(0.234)
Site_5	1.2034***	1.0315***	1.3500***	1.3344***	0.4483**	0.4212*
	(0.143)	(0.184)	(0.128)	(0.124)	(0.174)	(0.237)
Site_6	1.2099***	1.0420***	1.3761***	1.3474***	0.4470**	0.4266*
	(0.144)	(0.184)	(0.129)	(0.125)	(0.175)	(0.238)
Gift_0.1T(Reference)	—	—	—	—	—	—
Gift_0.2T	0.2860***	0.4088***	0.3248***	0.2270***	0.1921***	0.2143***
	(0.044)	(0.042)	(0.037)	(0.038)	(0.049)	(0.071)

(continued)

Table 11.2 (continued)

Variables	OLS	QRM				
		q10	q25	q50	q75	q90
Gift_0.5T	0.3429***	0.4432***	0.3449***	0.2537***	0.2803***	0.3581***
	(0.049)	(0.042)	(0.039)	(0.042)	(0.058)	(0.085)
Gift_1T	0.4118***	0.5102***	0.4024***	0.3108***	0.4309***	0.5259***
	(0.060)	(0.054)	(0.050)	(0.052)	(0.069)	(0.099)
Gift_1T+	0.6620***	0.5887***	0.5024***	0.5036***	0.7597***	0.9561***
	(0.079)	(0.078)	(0.067)	(0.069)	(0.089)	(0.125)
Price_0.2M (Reference)	—	—	—	—	—	—
Price_0.5M	0.0660	0.0688	0.0353	0.0111	0.0237	−0.0490
	(0.057)	(0.058)	(0.049)	(0.049)	(0.063)	(0.084)
Price_1M	0.0491	0.0968	0.0313	0.0038	−0.0011	0.0004
	(0.064)	(0.065)	(0.055)	(0.055)	(0.070)	(0.095)
Price_2M	0.0833	0.0933	0.0239	0.0106	0.0627	0.0207
	(0.063)	(0.065)	(0.054)	(0.054)	(0.070)	(0.095)
Price_5M	0.1017	0.1105	0.0371	0.0234	0.0587	0.0128
	(0.068)	(0.070)	(0.059)	(0.058)	(0.075)	(0.100)
Price_10M	0.0614	0.1956**	0.0705	0.0312	−0.0127	−0.1456
	(0.081)	(0.084)	(0.071)	(0.070)	(0.089)	(0.119)
Price_10M+	0.1837**	0.1218	0.1184	0.0931	0.1659*	0.2564**
	(0.082)	(0.083)	(0.072)	(0.071)	(0.089)	(0.121)
Hokkaido (Reference)	—	—	—	—	—	—
Tohoku	−0.0393	−0.0071	−0.0466	−0.0590	−0.0228	−0.0049
	(0.052)	(0.053)	(0.046)	(0.045)	(0.056)	(0.074)
Kanto	0.0642	0.0497	0.0551	0.0612	0.0849	0.1057
	(0.051)	(0.052)	(0.045)	(0.045)	(0.054)	(0.072)
Chubu	−0.0544	−0.0082	−0.0344	−0.0673	−0.0154	−0.0217
	(0.050)	(0.050)	(0.043)	(0.043)	(0.054)	(0.073)
Kinki	−0.0075	0.0012	−0.0028	−0.0143	0.0163	−0.0113
	(0.054)	(0.053)	(0.047)	(0.047)	(0.060)	(0.079)
Chugoku	−0.0659	0.0542	−0.0557	−0.0823	−0.1089	0.0072
	(0.063)	(0.064)	(0.056)	(0.055)	(0.069)	(0.095)
Shikoku	−0.0742	0.0193	−0.0572	−0.1109*	−0.0850	−0.0488
	(0.067)	(0.067)	(0.059)	(0.058)	(0.072)	(0.097)
Kyushu	−0.0588	−0.0608	−0.0696	−0.0854*	−0.0430	0.1054
	(0.054)	(0.053)	(0.047)	(0.046)	(0.058)	(0.077)
Okinawa	−0.1545*	0.0279	0.0037	−0.1681**	−0.1553	−0.0884
	(0.093)	(0.097)	(0.083)	(0.080)	(0.101)	(0.132)
PrevRank	−0.0028***	−0.0028***	−0.0028***	−0.0028***	−0.0028***	−0.0027***
	(0.000)	(0.000)	(0.000)	(0.000)	(0.000)	(0.000)
Observations	1677	1677	1677	1677	1677	1677
Adj. R-squared	0.914					
Pseudo R-squared		0.763	0.765	0.747	0.714	0.680

Note: *$p < 0.1$; **$p < 0.05$; ***$p < 0.01$

Regarding the number of portal sites (Site_X), compared to the municipalities that use only Furusato Choice, we confirm that the estimated parameter increases as the number of contracted sites increases in all estimation results. Naturally, as the number of sites increases, exposure to users increases and donations are generated from those websites; thus, the total amount of donations is expected to increase. However, focusing on the amount of change in the estimated parameter with the number of sites, we confirm that the amount of change differs between the 0.10, 0.25, and 0.50 quantile points and the 0.75 and 0.90 quantile points. Specifically, the former have a relatively large amount of change, whereas the latter have a relatively small amount of change. Also, some variables in the latter are no longer statistically significant. That is, the effect of increasing the number of portal sites is considered to be larger for municipalities with smaller donation amounts than for those with larger donation amounts. Municipalities with larger donation amounts might be affected by factors other than portal sites, such as the presence of repeat donors and donations made via each municipality's webpage. Notably, when the number of sites is restricted to areas with 4–6 sites, the amount of change is small in all of the estimation results. Thus, increasing the number of websites to 4 or more has a small positive effect on the amount of donations but the increase in the administrative burden can be inferred to negatively affect the amount of donations per website.

Regarding the number of returned gifts (Gift_X), compared to the municipalities that have less than 100 returned gifts, the estimated parameter also increases as the number of gifts increases in all of the estimation results. However, when we examine the amount of change, we can confirm that the trend differs for the 0.10, 0.25, and 0.50 quantile points and for the 0.75 and 0.90 quantile points. Municipalities with larger amounts of donations have larger changes in the estimated parameters than those with smaller or moderate amounts of donations. Municipalities with large donation amounts might be able to generate more attractive returned gifts that lead to donations, contributing to the amount of donations.

With regard to the price of returned gifts, no clear trend can be confirmed for the OLS and the 0.10–0.75 quantile points of the QRM; however, focusing on the 0.90 quantile point, statistically significant and clearly higher parameter value are found for municipalities with returned gifts of more than 10 million yen compared to the price of less than 200,000 yen. This result suggests that the municipalities in the top 10% have abundant know-how in the development of returned gifts and are able to develop attractive returned products, especially in the higher price range, and thus enjoy the support of high-income earners. Regarding the estimation results for the regional dummies, there is little statistical significance, although the parameters tend to be lower in the other regions except Kanto compared to Hokkaido.

The heterogeneity of the donation amount bands presented in this section is a new finding that differs from those of previous studies, which have assumed homogeneity in all donation amount bands, and requires local government officials and other practitioners to develop strategies based on current donation amounts to efficiently collect donations.

11.4   Local Governance and Sustainability

11.4.1   Building a Local Ecosystem Utilizing the Hometown Tax Donation System

As explained in Sect. 11.2, Japan's hometown tax donation system is a national initiative aims to revitalize and strengthen local communities by encouraging people to voluntarily donate to the prefectural and municipal governments of their choice. There are various opinions regarding the utilization of the hometown tax donation system, such as Fukasawa et al. (2020), who point out the distortion of uncooperative competition between local governments over donations, and Fu and Fujii (2023), who mention the efficiency of reviewing the lineup of gifts in return for hometown tax donation systems. In such a situation, to overcome the challenges of this system and achieve its goal, we need to establish local business ecosystems in which various public and private stakeholders cooperate in a mutually beneficial manner. Specifically, such local ecosystems should be designed to address the challenges that individual local communities face. As discussed in Sect. 11.3, municipalities use private-run websites and cooperate with local businesses in their jurisdiction to attract donors. However, the efforts of a small number of sections or departments of a local government are not sufficient to make drastic changes to the local communities. Solutions for sustainable change can only be achieved when various stakeholders engage. Interactions among residents, nonprofits, experts, academic institutions, and other parties that transform the traditional regulatory and business frameworks help maximize the strength of the local communities.

Creating effective business ecosystems that maximize the use of their resources and assets provides an avenue for sustainable growth. For example, businesses and innovations that take advantage of local specialties, cultural heritage, and tourist attractions stimulate the local economy and job creation. These ecosystems facilitate sharing of skills and know-how and thereby empower local economic growth. From this perspective, creating new platforms that assist commercial producers and manufacturers to improve and innovate their products is a first step toward these ecosystems because attractive products draw people who want them in return for their donation. In addition, creating new systems that nurture emotional connections with the donors or solve local challenges might also contribute to these ecosystems. Moreover, the participation of public relations agencies that are skilled in advertising local businesses, colleges, and other educational institutions that train and foster local entrepreneurs, and other parties with practical or academic expertise can contribute to local development. In the next section, we discuss possible activities that lead to sustainable business ecosystems by showcasing a project sponsored by the Kyoto University and Hakuhodo, Inc.: *Tokusan Doshiyo (What About Our Specialties?) Seminar*. This seminar was conducted in Amakusa, Kumamoto, to equip next-generation specialists with the skills to drive the local economy.

11.4.2 Academia–Industry Collaboration Seminar

For more than a decade, the Kyoto University Graduate School of Management has conducted research on regional revitalization design in local municipalities, including Amakusa. Meanwhile, the Mirai Business Division of Hakuhodo has been involved in supporting and activating the hometown tax donation system, leveraging their expertise in communication design and marketing. These two sponsors identified Amakusa as an experimental field to test their methods to develop new local specialties with a competitive advantage.

Hakuhodo is skilled in assisting local municipalities to build new brand image and value. They also help local communities monetize their resources. This joint project enables Hakuhodo to review and elaborate on their activities from the viewpoint of revitalization design while allowing the Graduate School of Management to scientifically evaluate the system's impact and provide feedback for improvement. Conducting the seminar over an extended period is expected to boost local activities.

This joint seminar is outlined below.

1. **Purpose and Nature of the Seminar**

The purpose of this seminar was to equip participants with enthusiasm for local revitalization and competency to productize and monetize available resources. This seminar consisted of 13 two-hour sessions held between November 2022 and February 2023. Because this period coincided with the COVID-19 pandemic, the lectures were held online. The lectures systematically addressed a wide range of topics from specialty development to sales promotion. Specifically, the seminar covered identification of local resources, flavor improvement, product design, quality control, measures to attract hometown tax subscribers, and hands-on training in collaboration with farm and agricultural producers. The first three introductory sessions of the seminar were open and freely accessible to local communities across Japan.

2. **Fostering Experts in Local Revitalization**

An open call for participants was announced online. A total of 20 students and employees from various parts of the country participated. Participants were divided into four groups and completed the course, which included hands-on practice to develop local specialties and a presentation to the mayor of Amakusa.

3. **Producer Cooperation and Support System for Specialty Development**

This seminar facilitated the interaction and cooperation between different sectors of producers, including those of red sea bream, oysters, Amakusa Daio chicken native to Kumamoto, and various seasoning products. It also provided comprehensive support and advice from a group of consumers, third-party business partners, and food-industry professionals.

The seminar's program was designed to accommodate topics other than specialty development. For example, it could be readily modified to address tourism promotion, community management, and other themes that reflect local needs. Conducting the seminar in many parts of Japan could help build a network that would provide comprehensive business advice and support services, train specialists, and revitalize local communities by overcoming their challenges.

Notably, Hakuhodo's activities to productize and monetize local resources and its joint seminar with Kyoto University primarily focused on gaining subscribers to the hometown tax donation system. Future efforts should address measures to take optimal advantage of the system's opportunities, such as opportunities to develop the return gifts that maximize net gains, determine the optimal use of the donations, and evaluate the system's effects on local economies.

11.4.3 Future Outlook

The hometown tax donation system possibly contributes to future sustainable development of local communities in Japan, including the strengthening of local governance, the promotion of sustainable regional development, the strengthening of community cohesion, the effective utilization of regional resources, and the revitalization of regional economies. Therefore, it is desirable to refine initiatives tailored to the characteristics of each municipality, taking into account the insights gained from the analysis results in Sect. 11.3, which highlighted the heterogeneity between municipalities with small and large donation amounts.

Particularly, heterogeneities in expense ratios, credit card payments, the number of contracted portal sites, and the number of return gifts, which have been overlooked in previous studies that assumed homogeneity, should be seen as clues for further refinement. Additionally, the practical initiatives introduced in Amakusa City in Sect. 11.4.2, although still in their early stages, are already showing tangible outcomes such as the expansion of human networks among producers and the development of new return gifts. Visible results are expected to gradually emerge in the future. Also, we cannot overlook the expansion to municipalities in other regions.

Recently, with the overheating of the hometown tax donation system, there have been instances where small and medium-sized municipalities outsource their duties to intermediary agents, and some funds are being siphoned off by unscrupulous intermediaries. Municipalities need to ensure that the benefits are returned to the local community, fostering local enterprises and linking them to regional revitalization. To achieve this, municipalities should create a mechanism that provides new platforms, as introduced in Sect. 11.4.2, to engage local enterprises and other stakeholders, thereby working on human resource development and public-private partnerships. Through these efforts, municipalities are required to strive even harder to build a rich and sustainable regional society and local governance.

11.5   Conclusions

In this chapter, we focus on the hometown tax donation system, a unique donation system in Japan, and develop our own database by collecting information on six private-sector intermediary websites in addition to the current survey results from the MIC in order to quantitatively clarify the relationship between local governments' efforts and hometown tax donations. Then, we estimate the donation function using two types of econometric models: a regression model based on the ordinary least squares (OLS) and a quantile regression model (QRM).

The results of the OLS estimation indicate that many of the variables related to donors' self-interested factors, such as expense ratio and card payments, are positively significant, while many of the variables relates to altruistic ones, such as building relationships with donors, are not significant. In other words, the results suggest that under the system in place at the time of the survey, donors may prioritize selfish factors over altruistic ones. Furthermore, for municipalities with smaller donation amounts, the regression coefficients vary more with the number of intermediary sites, while for municipalities with larger donation amounts, the regression coefficients vary more with the number of returned gifts.

These results suggest the importance of improving the environment for receiving donations, such as the enhancement of payment methods and the use of intermediary websites, for municipalities with small donation amounts, and the importance of developing returned gifts, including high-value items, for municipalities with large donation amounts. The heterogeneity of donation amounts shown in this chapter is a new finding that differs from previous studies by Musha (2019) and Nishimura et al. (2017), which have assumed homogeneity across all donation amount bands, and this finding requires local government officials and other practitioners to develop strategies based on current donation amounts to efficiently collect donations.

This estimation is based only on the donation amounts in 2022, and the MIC is planning further changes to the system in October 2025, in addition to the system change implemented in November 2023. An analysis using time-series data is required to explicitly capture the impact of these system changes, especially whether the heterogeneity occurring in the donation amount bands will change.

Finally, the project "*Tokusan Doshiyo (What About Our Specialties?) Seminar,*" an academia-industry collaboration, reveals its potential to contribute to the development of local ecosystems. It is essential for local governments to enhance the sustainability of local governance through mutually beneficial relationships and collaborations with private companies and universities using the hometown tax donation system.

Acknowledgments   The contents of Sect. 11.4 are part of the results of practical action research based on a joint research agreement with the Mirai Business Division of Hakuhodo Inc. We would like to thank Hakuhodo, and also Amakusa City, Kumamoto Prefecture for providing the research field.

References

Fu J, Fujii H (2023) Sustainable development of rural regions: Metafrontier data envelopment analysis of hometown tax in municipality K. Asia Pac J Reg Sci 7:775–806. https://doi.org/10.1007/s41685-023-00281-y

Fukasawa E, Fukasawa T, Ogawa H (2020) Intergovernmental competition for donations: the case of the Furusato Nozei program in Japan. J Asian Econ 67:101178. https://doi.org/10.1016/j.asieco.2020.101178

Hashimoto K, Suzuki Y (2016) Current status and issues of the hometown tax donation system [Furusato nozei seido no genjo to kadai]. Gov Auditing Rev [Kaikei kensa kenkyu] 54:13–38. (in Japanese). https://doi.org/10.51016/kaikeikensa.54.0_13

Hoda T (2017) Effects of supporting local business development through hometown tax donations [Furusato nozei ni yoru chihou no jigyosha ikusei shien kouka]. J Polit Econ [Kokumin Keizai zasshi] 216(6):59–70. (in Japanese). https://doi.org/10.24546/E0041344

Hoda T, Kubo Y (2019) Emergence of local entrepreneurship through hometown tax donation: unique local development system. Implications from development of new products and improvement of business capabilities by gift providers [Furusato nozei no chiiki antorepure-nashippu he no shisa –Yuniku na chiiki kaihatsu tsuru he: Henreihin teikyo jigyousha no shin shohin kaihatsu to keieiryoku shihyo koujo kara–]. Jpn J Reg Policy Stud [Nihon chiiki seisaku kenkyu] 23:90–99. (in Japanese). https://doi.org/10.32186/ncs.23.0_90

Hoda T, Richard BD (2021) Local tax benefits at a distance: Japan's hometown tax donation payment. Springer, Singapore. https://doi.org/10.1007/978-981-16-5138-0

Ito Y (2020) Innovation in an emergent business model for taxation: the case of the furusato nozei program [Zei seido ni okeru souhatsuteki bijinesumoderu no inobeshon –Furusato nozei no jirei–]. J Jp Soc Manag Infor [Keiei jouhou gakkai shi] 29(1):1–16. (in Japanese). https://doi.org/10.11497/jjasmin.29.1_1

Koenker R, Bassett G (1978) Regression quantiles. Econometrica 46(1):33–50. https://doi.org/10.2307/1913643

Koenker R, Hallock K (2001) Quantile regression. J Econ Perspect 15(4):143–156. https://doi.org/10.1257/jep.15.4.143

Koike T (2007) Local tax and fiscal reform and regional disparities in tax revenue-beyond the debate over hometown tax donations – [Chihou zeizaisei kaikaku to zeishu no tiikikan kakusa – Furusato nozei wo meguru giron wo koete]. Issue Brief Jpn Nat Diet Libr [Kokuritsu Kokkai toshokan ISSUE BRIEF] 593:1–10. (in Japanese)

MIC (2023) Results of the FY2023 survey on hometown tax donations [Furusato nouzei ni kansuru genkyo chousa kekka (reiwa 5 nendo jissi)]. (in Japanese). Accessed August 1 2023. https://www.soumu.go.jp/main_content/000897133.pdf

Mizuta K (2017) A consideration for "Furusato Nozei", a tax deduction system for donations to prefectural and municipal govermments out of donners' resident places [Furusato nozei seido to sono mondaiten –Kifukin zeisei no arubeki sugata–]. Nagoya Gakuin Univ Rev Soc Sci [Nagoya gakuin daigaku ronshu shakai Kagaku hen] 53(4):57–80. (in Japanese). https://doi.org/10.15012/00000897

Musha K (2019) Factor analysis of the amount of hometown tax payment received in municipalities in Hokkaido [Hokkaido nai sityoson ni okeru furusato nozei ukeire gaku no kettei yoin bunseki]. Sapporo Univ Res Inst J [Sapporo daigaku sogo keikyu] 11:49–57. (in Japanese)

Nishimura T, Seta F (2017) Study on the trend of donors making regional contributions through the "hometown tax" (donation system linked to one's hometown): focusing on the donor's empathy for the region [Furusato nozei no kifusha no chiiki koken ni taisuru iko ni kanrusu kenkyu –Kifusha no chiiki heno kyokan ni chakumoku site–]. Plan Public Manag [Keikaku gyosei] 40(2):90–97. (in Japanese). https://doi.org/10.14985/jappm.40.2_90

Nishimura Y, Ishimura T, Akai N (2017) Analysis of incentives for furusato tax (donation): empirical analysis based on donation acceptance data of individual municipalities [Furusato nozei (kifu) no incentive ni kansuru bunseki: kobetu jichitai no kihu ukeire data niyoru jisshou bunseki]. Jpn J Local Public Financ [Nihon chiho zaisei gakkai kenkyu sosho] 24:150–178. (in Japanese)

Takahashi Y, Yodo M, Kojima D (2019) Attribution and factor analysis of users of the hometown tax donation system: –validation through a comparison with conventional donations– [Furusato nozei seido no riyosha no zokusei to yoin bunseki –ippanteki na kifu tono hikaku kara no kensho–]. J Econ Policy Stud [Keizai seisaku janaru] 16(1):14–27. (in Japanese)

Tsuchiya H (2020) Problems of return gifts in the hometown tax donation system [Furusato nozei ni okeru henreihin kyosou no yoin to mondaiten]. J Kanazawa Seiryo Univ [Kanazawa seiryo daigaku ronshu] 53(2):29–39. (in Japanese)

Yamamura E, Tsutsui Y, Ohtake F (2017) Altruistic and selfish motivations of charitable giving: case of the hometown tax donation system (Furusato nozei) in Japan. ISER Discussion Paper, No. 1003. https://doi.org/10.2139/ssrn.2968260

Yasuda S, Koyama S (2016) Regional economy activation and the hometown tax payment system [Chiki Keizai kasseika to furusato nozei seido]. Josai Univ Bull Dep Econ [Josai daigaku keizai keiei kiyo] 34:49–78. (in Japanese). https://doi.org/10.20566/03866947_34_49

Tetsuharu Oba is a Professor in both the Graduate School of Management and the Graduate School of Engineering at Kyoto University. He is also a part-time instructor in the Graduate School of Urban Management at Osaka Metropolitan University. He was a visiting scholar at the School of Public Policy at the Georgia Institute of Technology from 2012 to 2013. His research interests include urban policy and planning, transportation and land use, urban management and society, and spatial analysis for public policy.

Tatsuki Kishimoto is a Ph.D. candidate of Management Science at Kyoto University. He received an MBA with a concentration in project-operations management from Kyoto University in 2024. He has worked in both the private and public sectors as an engineer. His work focuses specifically on urban management and public–private partnerships related to the hometown tax donation system.

Chapter 12
Bidding Behavior, Contract Prices, and Participant Numbers in Japanese Prefectural Procurement

Masashi Nishikawa (iD)

Abstract This chapter analyzes Japan's public procurement, focusing on bidding behavior patterns and contract price determination. The primary research questions are: How do different bidding formulas impact bidding behaviors and contract prices? What is the effect of the number of bidders on contract price ratios? To address these questions, this chapter employs multinomial logit models, OLS, Tobit, and truncated regression methodologies using data from over 22,000 cases in Ehime Prefecture (June 2014–March 2022). Evidence of collusive behavior, such as bid withdrawals and seemingly strategic phantom bids, influences procurement outcomes. A key finding is the necessity of discerning between the bidding behaviors in designated competitive bidding, characterized by frequent withdrawals and bids made at reservation prices, and those in general competitive bidding. Moreover, more bidders generally result in lower contract price ratios, suggesting increased participation enhances efficiency. Optimal participation is about 7–8 bidders, with each additional bidder reducing the ratio by nearly 0.01 points. Considering Japan's 25 trillion yen annual public construction investment in fiscal 2020, a 0.01 reduction in the price ratio could mean savings of around 250 billion yen (1.6 billion USD).

Keywords Local government · Public procurement · Contract price ratio · Collusion · Procurement policy · Designated competitive bidding · General competitive bidding

12.1 Introduction

In Japan, the Ministry of Land, Infrastructure, Transport, and Tourism (MLIT), serving as the regulatory body for the construction industry, plays a key role in establishing public procurement policies. Given this dual responsibility—promoting the healthy development of the construction industry as its regulator and acting

M. Nishikawa (✉)
College of Economics, Aoyama Gakuin University, Tokyo, Japan

© The Author(s), under exclusive license to Springer Nature
Switzerland AG 2024
Y. Noda (ed.), *Local Governance in Japan*, Local and Urban Governance,
https://doi.org/10.1007/978-3-031-77322-8_12

as a client for construction projects—MLIT tends to create a public procurement mechanism that, while advantageous to the construction industry, does not align with broader interests. This stance toward the construction industry also affects procedures within local governments, often exceeding what is typically expected due to a cultural inclination toward showing deference or anticipatory consideration to central authorities. This approach, along with other policies supporting private construction companies, has often aroused suspicions of corruption in public procurement among third parties. However, not all instances necessarily indicate insincerity; these decisions are partially caused by the necessity to accommodate various social needs, going beyond low cost and high quality for public procurement. This encompasses the concept of "passive waste" (Bandiera et al. 2009), which refers to inefficiencies in decisions governed by regulation and convention, although separating from private interests.

In Japanese local governments, strong centralized vertical fiscal transfers have led to an increase in passive waste. This situation is connected to classical economic problems, such as the common pool problem and fiscal illusion, as discussed in seminal works like those of Buchanan (1960), Goetz (1977), Wagner (1976), and Weingast et al. (1981). Decentralization reforms from the mid-1990s to 2000s aimed to address these problems. However, active waste, tied to public authorities' private interests and intertwined with passive waste, continues to be an unresolved issue in various areas. Furthermore, the divergence between benefits and costs, arising from vertical fiscal transfers (Nishikawa 2019), diminishes the incentive for voters to monitor waste, thereby leading to its persistent neglect despite the necessity. Mainly, this chapter investigates effective methods for distinguishing and preventing unnecessary waste, or at worst, active waste linked to the private gains of ordering entities, while acknowledging the inevitability of some passive waste in local government public procurement.

In seeking solutions to these issues, we delve into the detailed mechanisms of public procurement bidding. Japanese public entities primarily use two bidding formulas.[1] The first is designated competitive bidding (abbreviated as "designated bidding"), where only companies chosen by the procuring entity can participate. The other is general competitive bidding, where any interested applicant can participate. Waste reduction could be achieved through increased use of bidding formulas, which typically result in lower costs. Furthermore, if bid prices tend to decrease with more bidders, increasing participant numbers in projects could effectively lower bid prices.

In this chapter, we address the primary research questions of how different bidding formulas impact bidding behaviors and contract prices, and the effect of the number of bidders on contract price ratios. To explore these questions, this chapter uses data from over 22,000 cases in Ehime Prefecture (June 2014–March 2022).

---

[1] In Japan, there are three types of ordering procedures for public work procurement: two bidding formulas and a negotiation contract. Local governments seldom use the negotiation contract.

Our empirical analysis initially focuses on the difference in motivation between participants in the two bidding formulas. To measure participants' desire to win, a continuous variable known as the bid price ratio is commonly used. This ratio is the bid price divided by the reservation price and other elements, including estimated costs (De Silva et al. 2003; Onur et al. 2012). However, our approach encompasses more than just the bidders; it also includes those who, despite either declaring their intention to participate or being invited to do so, ultimately choose not to submit bids. Porter and Zona (1993) noted that withdrawing can also be a form of collaborative behavior. However, the tactic we observed represents a special type of withdrawal, attributable to the unique circumstances of the Japanese procurement system. We employ a multinomial logit analysis, where the dependent variable is a categorical variable that distinguishes among three behaviors: withdrawing, bidding at the reservation price, and bidding below the reservation price. The reservation price (the maximum price at which a contract can be awarded), is predetermined for all contracts in Japan's public procurement. For Ehime Prefecture, which was used for our empirical analysis, the reservation price is usually disclosed in advance, making it rare for a bidder to exceed it. Typically, bidders aim to secure contracts by submitting bids below this price. However, in the case of Japan, a non-negligible number of bidders bid at the reservation price. The reason for this, along with an explanation of the unique withdrawal process, will be discussed later. We estimate the likelihood of participants' behaviors regarding withdrawing and bidding at the reservation price, using the probability of bidding below the reservation price as a baseline.

Next in our analysis, we examine how the number of bidding participants impacts the contract price ratio (contract price divided by reservation price), accounting for the differences between the two bidding formulas. An increase in the number of bidders, assuming all other conditions (such as bidding formulas) remain constant, is likely to escalate competition and ultimately reduce the contract price ratio. This appears to indicate a negative correlation between the price and the number of bidders. However, expecting a reduction in the contract price ratio might diminish participants' interest, potentially decreasing the number of participants, suggesting a positive correlation between price and participant numbers. For instance, if the correlation between the number of participants (plotted on the vertical axis) and contract price ratio (horizontal axis) is negative when there are fewer participants, and the positive correlation gradually intensifies as the participant number increases, eventually becoming dominant, the relationship between these variables would form a U-shaped curve.[2] Iimi (2006) and Onur et al. (2012) suggest that the contract price ratio decreases as the participant number increases, whereas Gupta (2002) and Onur and Tas (2019) identify the number of participants as 6–8 and 7, where the contract price ratio is the lowest. This study analyzes the relationship between price

---

[2] An increase in the number of bid participants invariably leads to a lower probability of successful bids. From the bidders' viewpoint, this increases the latent burden of sunk costs for drafting technical proposals. Consequently, these costs are eventually reflected in the prices, and a visible increase in prices becomes evident when the number of participants exceeds a certain threshold.

and the number of bidders, employing three different estimation models in the process: OLS, Truncated regression, and Tobit.

12.2   Previous Research Using Japanese Data

Since its enactment in 2000, the Act for Promoting Proper Tendering and Contracting for Public Works requires entities involved in procurement to disclose public procurement information, thereby enhancing transparency and accountability. Currently, details such as construction period, bidding formula, reservation price, bid prices, contract price, and more are publicly accessible. This availability of data has spurred researchers to explore three key areas: the relationship between price and quality, detection of collusion and corruption, and the interplay between collusion, price, and bidding formulas.

Iwamatsu et al. (2001, 2003) initially use Japan's publicized bidding detailed data as analytical materials. These studies investigate the distribution of the number of bidding participants and the contract price ratio. Subsequent studies (Aizawa 2006; Sakon et al. 2007; Sato et al. 2008; Morimoto et al. 2007) demonstrate a positive correlation between prices and product performance. However, preliminary research by public authorities in the prefectures of Yamagata (n.d.) and Fukushima (2010), as well as the City of Takarazuka (2011), using their own bidding data, find no significant relationship between contract price ratios and project performance, challenging the notion that higher prices ensure better quality. Of late, studies of this type have focused on bidding data from municipalities, and the accuracy of the analytical methodology has improved. Hatsumi and Ishii (2022) use data from Ise City in Mie Prefecture and Nishikawa (2024b) uses data from Sagamihara City in Kanagawa Prefecture to perform quantitative analyses of the correlation between price and quality in public procurement, clarifying that lower prices do not lead to lower quality.

Ohashi (2009), Ishii (2013), and Kawai and Nakabayashi (2022) use data from the mid-2000s, when collusion became a public issue, to quantitatively show that collusion and other non-competitive elements exist in Japanese public procurement. Ohashi (2009) points out that adopting a transparent formula could reduce costs by 8%. Kawai and Nakabayashi (2022) suggest the likelihood of widespread collusion; notably, they, alongside Chassang et al. (2022), use the bid price difference ratio to detect collusion. We apply their methodology using our data, affirming its plausibility and effectiveness, albeit in certain specific conditions.[3]

Morimoto and Arai (2013, 2014) and Arai and Morimoto (2017) use long-term data from the early 2000s to the early 2010s. The former examines the impact of key systemic changes in the price floor system and the winner selection rule, whereas the latter indicates that bidding that includes new participants lowers contract price ratios by approximately 2%. Arai (2013) find that contract price ratios tend to be

---

[3] Nishikawa (2024a) provides the replicated figure.

lower in municipalities leveraging general competitive bidding. Chassang and Ortner (2019) use data across 2007–2016 from 14 cities in Ibaraki Prefecture to test and support whether introducing price floors can lower the winning-bid distribution.[4]

These in-depth analyses provide critical insights and enhance oversight capabilities. However, there are still gaps in fully understanding public procurement in Japan. This chapter aims to refine some of the remaining gaps.

Finally, the structure of this chapter is as follows: It begins with an introduction to the research questions, hypotheses, and methodology, as already described. Section 12.3 explains public procurement in Ehime Prefecture and discusses the data characteristics. Sections 12.4 and 12.5 present empirical analyses—Sect. 12.4 on bidding behaviors, and Sect. 12.5 on the ratios of contract prices. Finally, Sect. 12.6 summarizes the findings and concludes the study.

12.3   Public Procurement in Ehime Prefecture

12.3.1   Bidding Forms

The following analysis covers Ehime Prefecture, which is composed of 20 municipalities, has a total population of 1.3 million, and an area of 5600 km². Its local governments administer both depopulated and urban areas. The number of licensed construction businesses in Ehime Prefecture, which mirrored fluctuations in public works project volumes, declined until 2010 and subsequently stabilized.[5] The Prefecture's Accounting Division provided us with data regarding public procurement for more than 22,000 cases (involving about 113,000 accumulated participations conducted by nearly 1300 entities) from June 2014 to March 2022.

Table 12.1 summarizes these elements, showing that four types of bidding formulas (ordering procedures) as well as two types of winner selection criteria are used. Typically, designated bidding in Japanese local governments is paired with the Lowest Price Criteria (LPC), a winner selection criterion that considers cost. Meanwhile, competitive bidding, including its subtypes, is paired with the Most Economically Advantageous Tender (MEAT) method, which evaluates the price, factors in quality and other societal needs to select the winner. Due to its inherent characteristics, MEAT potentially results in higher contract prices than LPC. This implies that the contract price ratio associated with designated bidding, typically paired with LPC, is expected to be lower than that of general competitive bidding, commonly using MEAT. However, as illustrated in Table 12.1, the actual contract

---

[4] Nishikawa (2024a) provides a more detailed literature review.
[5] Nishikawa (2024a) presents a figure illustrating this condition.

Table 12.1 Bidding formulas and winner selection criteria for deals (Ehime Prefecture)

Bidding formula	Number of cases by the winner selection criteria		Contract price ratio by the winner selection criteria		Number of cases in Total	Number of cases without a floor price
	LPC	MEAT	LPC	MEAT		
Regular general competitive bidding	.	5	.	0.897	5	.
Designated bidding	15,430	.	0.953	.	15,430	3
Negotiated contracts	98	.	0.954	.	98	96
Post-review general competitive bidding	.	6,827	.	0.933	6,827	.
Total	15,528	6,832	0.953	0.933	22,360	

Source: Author's elaboration

Note: Excludes unexecuted biddings

price ratio for designated bidding is higher.[6] The upward pressure on the contract price via designated bidding exceeds the downward pressure from the use of LPC.

For simplification, this study excludes regular general competitive bidding and negotiated contracts listed in Table 12.1 from discussion, given their infrequent occurrence. This leaves two major styles of ordering procedure: designated bidding with LPC and post-review general competitive bidding with MEAT. In these biddings, the lowest price bidder occasionally does not become the winner. In designated bidding with LPC, approximately 1.9% of the cases resulted in the lowest price bidder not winning. This was due to disqualification for submitting a bid below the floor price, which is the minimum acceptable price.[7] In post-review general competitive bidding with MEAT, approximately 14.1% of the lowest price bidders did not secure the contract. Since MEAT evaluates both price and other factors, the lowest price bid does not automatically guarantee a win. In cases where there were more than two bidders tied at the lowest acceptable price (or tied for the highest score in MEAT), a lottery determined the winner by law.

Moving forward, we will refer to "post-review general competitive bidding" simply as "general competitive bidding" and adopt a straightforward framework to facilitate a clear comparison between general competitive bidding and designated bidding.

---

[6] In a comparison of mean values for contract price ratios "in total" between LPC and MEAT, the former is higher, and this difference is statistically significant in a t-test. Considering the number of observations, the high contract price ratio for LPC can be understood as a strong reflection of the high contract price ratio in designated bidding.

[7] There are two styles of "floor price" in Japanese public procurement. Although it is generally favorable to treat them separately, this study does not do so because of the data characteristics of Ehime Prefecture. See Nishikawa (2024a) for more detailed information.

12.3.2 Unique Incentives in Public Procurement

Local Japanese governments need to disclose their investment plans for public works in a timely manner to accommodate construction firms. This information includes details such as the scope of work, project size, work location, construction period, and bidding conditions, enabling potential bidders to make informed estimations. On the contrary, in the Guideline for Implementing Designated Bidding for Ehime Prefectural Construction Projects (the designated bidding guideline), the procuring entity is required to designate bidding participants based on project characteristics, as well as considering the locality and capabilities of each company.[8] Importantly, Article 5 of the guideline requests that each company's total volume of contracted work in the current fiscal year, alongside the number of ongoing projects, be considered. This policy aims to avoid the concentration of orders among highly efficient operators, thereby ensuring support for all businesses. Private firms, knowledgeable about the planned ordering amounts and guiding principles, can expect to receive invitations for bid on projects that align with their specialization and expertise.

Table 12.1 illustrates that designated bidding accounts for approximately 70% of the public works projects commissioned by Ehime Prefecture. The considerable share of funds allocated on a discretionary basis enables construction firms to anticipate consistent order volumes. Such predictability, in turn, facilitates steady business management and fosters a sense of security among participating firms. Conversely, the control exerted by designated bidding also limits the total volume of orders received. This restriction likewise affects the contract values from general competitive bidding, where the total annual amount is typically constrained, albeit not rigidly, to levels similar to previous years.

In construction works, the profit margin (desire to win a bid) for each company varies per project, even if the contract prices of the projects are identical. This variation is due to factors such as ownership of materials and machinery, proximity to the work site, and other physical constraints; profits can be increased by accepting jobs that align with the company's capabilities and conditions. Therefore, with a certain forecast about ordering projects, a strategy of abstaining from bidding on projects that do not match their specialties and waiting for high profit margin deals is rational. While waiting, if business entities are designated to participate in a bidding for which they have absolutely no interest, they are likely to withdraw from it. Withdrawing can occasionally be a form of collaborative behavior with other bidders, as Porter and Zona (1993) noted. However, even in such situations, withdrawal is not always the course of action.

Procuring entities attempt to maintain a certain number of bidders to ensure, or at least appear to ensure, competitive conditions in public procurement, thus avoiding numerous withdrawals. In Japan, under a highly centralized governance system, the bidding conditions of each prefecture and municipality are made publicly

---

[8] Most local governments have similar implementation guidelines.

available in a comparable manner by the Ministry of Internal Affairs and Communications. This transparency forces procurement officers to fulfill their accountability regarding the competitive environment in public procurement. Ensuring a sufficient number of participants is one of the primary monitoring points. Given these circumstances, procurement officers, eager to increase the number of participants, encourage local businesses not to withdraw. However, by pushing to boost numbers, they inadvertently increase the presence of participants with no real intention to win—such as "phantom bids" as described by Porter and Zona (1993) or "shill bidders" as noted by Conley and Decarolis (2016)—a consequence they seem willing to overlook. Since these bids are prompted by the government, they should not be considered bid rigging in the classical sense.

In practice, Article 4-4 of the designated bidding guidelines in Ehime Prefecture permits the exclusion of businesses if they repeatedly withdraw or show disinterest. This creates intense pressure on companies contemplating withdrawal, particularly if they are interested in securing future public works contracts. Given this situation, an alternative emerges for participants who have less incentive to win: they submit a bid equal to the reservation price, which is the price least likely to win. In Ehime Prefecture, the reservation price is disclosed in advance, allowing participants to select appropriate bid prices without the need for time-consuming, detailed calculations.[9] Even if the participant unexpectedly wins a bid at the maximum available price (via a lottery), they can minimize their opportunity losses.

12.3.3 Participants with Less Willingness to Win

Since general competitive bidding involves no involuntary participants, one might assume an absence of withdrawals. However, applicants may choose to withdraw after a closer examination of the bidding details. Bidders constitute a subset of participants in both designated and general competitive bidding processes.

Then, what is the distribution of the effective number of participants in each bidding auction, excluding withdrawals and reservation-price bidders from the number of participants? The left graph on Fig. 12.1, using the data shown in Table 12.1, illustrates the benchmark distribution of the number of participants in each bidding, including withdrawals and reservation-price bidders. For general competitive bidding, the percentage of biddings with few participants, including one bidder, is high. For designated bidding, since at least three participants must be designated under

---

[9]Bids that exceed the reservation price are automatically deemed invalid; this happens very rarely. Ordering entities regard such bidding as conducted by an operator having less incentive to win according to Article 4–4 or acting in bad faith according to Article 5, which would decrease their opportunity for future participation. As such, we treated these bids as unexpected mistakes made by "normal" participants who attempted to bid less than the reservation price.

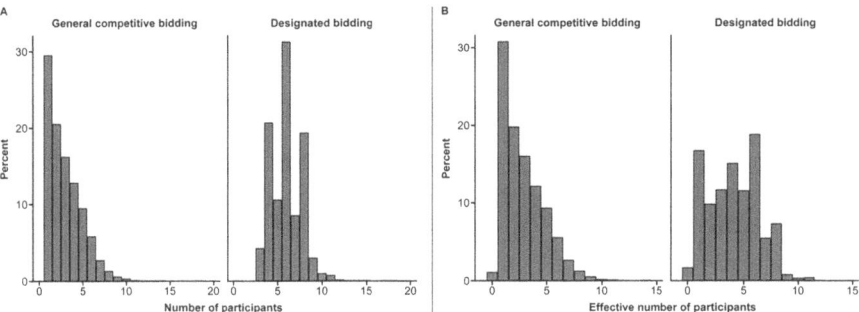

Fig. 12.1 Distribution of the number of participants in each bidding. (**a**) Number of participants in horizontal axis. (**b**) Effective number of participants in horizontal axis. (Source: Author's elaboration)

Article 3 of the guideline, there are no cases with two or fewer participants. Moreover, the number of designated participants is determined by the bidding conditions, showing a tendency toward certain numbers, such as four, six, and eight. On its right, Fig. 12.1 also displays the distribution of the effective number of participants, which excludes withdrawals and reservation-price bidders. In both the bidding distributions, there are biddings for which the number of participants is zero, suggesting that in these cases, two or more bidders bid at the reservation price and the winner was determined through a lottery. In designated bidding, a particular change is the thicker distribution in the range of a small number of participants and the reduced tendency for the number of bidders to concentrate on four, six, or eight. In both panels A and B, there are significant differences in the distribution of participants between the two bidding formulas. Distinguishing between the bidding formulas in the analysis can be beneficial for researchers.

12.4 Empirical Analysis

12.4.1 Participants Who Are Uninterested in Winning Bids

The first quantitative analysis focuses on the behavior of withdrawing and bidding at the reservation price. The number of observations is approximately 113,000 participants, and Eq. (12.1) is the estimation model. Descriptive statistics regarding the data used are presented in Table 12.2. The dependent variable is the decision Y_{ib} made by the company i in bidding b. Y_{ib} is a variable coded 0 when the bid price was less than the reservation price, 1 when the bid was identical to the reservation price, and 2 when the participant withdrew from bidding. We use a multinomial logit

Table 12.2 Descriptive statistics

Variable	For action					For bidder				
	Obs	Mean	Std. dev.	Min	Max	Obs	Mean	Std. dev.	Min	Max
Active	22,362	0.01592	0.12517	0	1	113,196	0.41795	0.75017	0	2
Bid below reservation price	22,362	0.98408	0.12517	0	1	113,196	0.74179	0.43765	0	1
Bid equal to reservation price	22,362	0.01592	0.12517	0	1	113,196	0.09847	0.29795	0	1
Withdraw						113,196	0.15974	0.36637	0	1
NBW: number of bids won						113,196	4.30157	7.22976	0	85
Contract price ratio	22,362	0.94690	0.04059	0.43590	1	113,196	0.94555	0.04041	0.43590	1
DD: Dummy designation (=1)	22,257	0.69327	0.46115	0	1	113,052	0.82108	0.38329	0	1
NP: Number of participants (centered)	22,362	0.00000	2.29292	−4.06198	12.93802	113,196	1.03857	2.05104	−4.06198	12.93802
NEP: Number of effective participants (centered)	22,362	0.00000	2.28788	−3.75217	10.24783	113,196	0.63100	2.41538	−3.75217	10.24783
Floor price rate	22,362	0.86868	0.06038	0	0.97423	113,196	0.87054	0.03327	0	0.97423
Reservation price										
Under 10,000,000 yen	22,362	0.55505	0.49697	0	1	113,196	0.59393	0.49110	0	1
10,000,000–15,000,000 yen	22,362	0.09776	0.29699	0	1	113,196	0.11053	0.31354	0	1
15,000,000–30,000,000 yen	22,362	0.17919	0.38352	0	1	113,196	0.19839	0.39879	0	1
30,000,000–45,000,000 yen	22,362	0.07625	0.26540	0	1	113,196	0.04303	0.20293	0	1
45,000,000–50,000,000 yen	22,362	0.01825	0.13384	0	1	113,196	0.01014	0.10019	0	1
50,000,000–60,000,000 yen	22,362	0.01731	0.13041	0	1	113,196	0.01032	0.10105	0	1
60,000,000–100,000,000 yen	22,362	0.04526	0.20787	0	1	113,196	0.02777	0.16430	0	1
100,000,000 yen or more	22,362	0.01096	0.10410	0	1	113,196	0.00589	0.07654	0	1
Month when winner is decided (baseline: January)										
Jan.	22,362	0.05487	0.22773	0	1	113,196	0.06015	0.23777	0	1
Feb.	22,362	0.05362	0.22527	0	1	113,196	0.05836	0.23442	0	1
Mar.	22,362	0.12517	0.33092	0	1	113,196	0.11939	0.32424	0	1
Apr.	22,362	0.10867	0.31123	0	1	113,196	0.09954	0.29939	0	1
May	22,362	0.03475	0.18314	0	1	113,196	0.03758	0.19018	0	1
Jun.	22,362	0.08711	0.28201	0	1	113,196	0.09416	0.29206	0	1
Jul.	22,362	0.08152	0.27364	0	1	113,196	0.08509	0.27902	0	1

Aug.	22,362	0.10214	0.30284	0	1	113,196	0.10237	0.30314	0	1
Sep.	22,362	0.15008	0.35715	0	1	113,196	0.13852	0.34545	0	1
Oct.	22,362	0.03908	0.19380	0	1	113,196	0.03693	0.18858	0	1
Nov.	22,362	0.08814	0.28351	0	1	113,196	0.08627	0.28076	0	1
Dec.	22,362	0.07486	0.26317	0	1	113,196	0.08164	0.27381	0	1
Work type										
Others	22,362	0.06073	0.23884	0	1	113,196	0.05418	0.22637	0	1
Civil engineering	22,362	0.64337	0.47902	0	1	113,196	0.63743	0.48074	0	1
Construction	22,362	0.01909	0.13686	0	1	113,196	0.01595	0.12527	0	1
Scaffolding and earthwork	22,362	0.07768	0.26767	0	1	113,196	0.08663	0.28129	0	1
Electrical engineering	22,362	0.04552	0.20845	0	1	113,196	0.04753	0.21277	0	1
Plumbing	22,362	0.01825	0.13384	0	1	113,196	0.01224	0.10997	0	1
Paving	22,362	0.11341	0.31710	0	1	113,196	0.12055	0.32561	0	1
Painting construction	22,362	0.02196	0.14655	0	1	113,196	0.02549	0.15760	0	1
Municipal type (location)										
Town	22,362	0.25463	0.43566	0	1	113,196	0.24614	0.43076	0	1
City	22,362	0.73679	0.44039	0	1	113,196	0.74606	0.43527	0	1
Multiple area or wider area	22,362	0.00859	0.09226	0	1	113,196	0.00780	0.08798	0	1
Fiscal year										
2014	22,362	0.08371	0.27696	0	1	113,196	0.07164	0.25789	0	1
2015	22,362	0.12861	0.33478	0	1	113,196	0.13674	0.34357	0	1
2016	22,362	0.13617	0.34298	0	1	113,196	0.14393	0.35102	0	1
2017	22,362	0.13577	0.34255	0	1	113,196	0.14947	0.35655	0	1
2018	22,362	0.14203	0.34909	0	1	113,196	0.15064	0.35770	0	1
2019	22,362	0.13044	0.33680	0	1	113,196	0.13086	0.33725	0	1
2020	22,362	0.13411	0.34078	0	1	113,196	0.12977	0.33605	0	1
2021	22,362	0.10911	0.31179	0	1	113,196	0.08693	0.28173	0	1
2022	22,362	0.00004	0.00669	0	1	113,196	0.00004	0.00594	0	1

Note: As in Table 12.1, this includes designated bidding, post-review general competitive bidding, 7 cases of regular competitive bidding, and 98 cases of negotiable contracts model by adding a random individual effect v_i on each business operator to the explanatory variables[10,.11]

$$Y_{ib} = \beta_0 + \rho X_b + \phi A_{ib} + \theta A_{ib}^2 + \gamma \left(A_{ib} \times X_b \right) + \beta_1 FP_b + \beta_2 FY_b + v_i + u_{ib} \quad (12.1)$$

The explanatory variables that are factors determining the behavior of company i in bidding b consist of the following. The designated bidding dummy, denoted as X_b (a binary variable that is 0 for general competitive bidding and 1 for designated bidding), is employed. It highlights disparities between designated and general competitive biddings.

Moreover, we use the number of bids won within a fiscal year as a representative variable for track record. Under their established bidding guidelines, local governments consider the track record of each business. As mentioned, this governmental approach significantly influences bidders' overall choices. Considering Japan's ranking system,[12] companies within the same rank tend to participate in bids of comparable size. Consequently, the difference in the amount of received orders among similarly ranked companies can be compared by the differences in the number of bids won; furthermore, this number allows for comparisons among different companies, even across various ranks. The number of bids won within the fiscal year for company i until immediately before bidding b is A_{ib} and the square of the number of bids won is A_{ib}^2. Intuitively, the fewer bids they win, the more eager they become to secure a job, leading them to bid below their reservation price.

Control variables are also incorporated. The floor price ratio (the standardized value obtained by dividing the floor price by the reservation price) is added to the explanatory variables. The floor price ratio when conducting bidding b, denoted as FP_b, indicates that a lower value allows for a larger room for price reduction. We also control for the fiscal year as a categorical dummy variable denoted as FY_b (representing 2014–2021).[13] Other available variables, such as the type of works, project size (reservation price), and project location, are not employed because these variables almost retain the same values for each operator, and their influence is absorbed into the individual effect. In Eq. (12.1), ρ, ϕ, θ, γ, β_1, and β_2 are all estimated coefficients or groups of coefficients; β_0 is a constant, and u_{ib} is a normal error.

---

[10] We cannot use a fixed-effects model. Due to the scope of this study, we should employ a dummy variable to distinguish the bidding formulas. However, a significant portion of the participants exclusively engaged in the same bidding formula, resulting in no variation across bidding formulas within individuals. This condition hinders the use of the fixed-effects model.

[11] The online supplementary material for this paper presents the results of a multinomial logit model. This model excludes individual effects and includes some potentially confounding variables, following the same procedure as in this study.

[12] See Nakabayashi (2013) for the Japanese ranking system.

[13] For fiscal year 2022, which began in April 2022, there was only one bidding event with four participants; therefore, we excluded it from our empirical analysis.

12.4.2 Probability of Withdrawing and Bidding at the Reservation Price

The estimation results are in Table 12.3. Among the participants' behavioral choices, the baseline behavior was bidding below the reservation price, with its probability serving as the reference outcome. The estimation results regarding the probabilities of bidding at the reservation price are in the left column, while the probabilities of withdrawing are in the right column. The coefficient of each variable estimated in the multinomial logit analysis helps confirm statistical significance, but interpreting these coefficients in practical terms remains challenging. To address this, we convey our analytical findings by visualizing the simulation results, which are based on these estimated coefficients. In Fig. 12.2, the horizontal axis represents the number

Table 12.3 Analysis of bidding behavior

	Bid price was less than the reservation price (baseline outcome)					
	Bidding at the reservation price			Withdrawing from bidding		
	Coefficient	Robust std.err.	P > z	Coefficient	Robust std. err.	P > z
DD: Dummy designation (=1)	2.6603	0.1394	***	3.4483	0.1560	***
NBW: Number of bids won within current fiscal year	0.0762	0.0168	***	−0.0042	0.0345	
DD X NBW	−0.0116	0.0129		0.0994	0.0369	***
Square value of NBW	−0.0012	0.0004	***	−0.0020	0.0006	***
Floor price rate	−5.4736	1.4629	***	5.8897	1.9124	***
Fiscal year of order (Baseline 2014)						
2015	−0.5917	0.0925	***	−0.4267	0.0882	***
2016	−0.4245	0.1015	***	−0.2956	0.0924	***
2017	0.0793	0.1160		−0.1894	0.1032	*
2018	0.4551	0.1153	***	0.2777	0.0957	***
2019	0.8040	0.1282	***	0.9516	0.1054	***
2020	0.7282	0.1296	***	0.9650	0.1192	***
2021	0.9710	0.1420	***	0.2899	0.1183	**
Constant	−1.7978	1.2922		−10.0542	1.6851	***
Var(u1)	7.3486	0.48238				
Var(u2)	6.0819	0.33479				
Number of obs	113,048					
Number of groups	1299					
Wald chi2(24)	1664		Obs per group:	Min = 1		
Log pseudolikelihood	−52,029			Avg = 87.0		
Prob > chi2	0			Max = 1781		

Note: Excludes four observation values that participated in fiscal 2022. ***: 1%, **: 5%, *: 10%

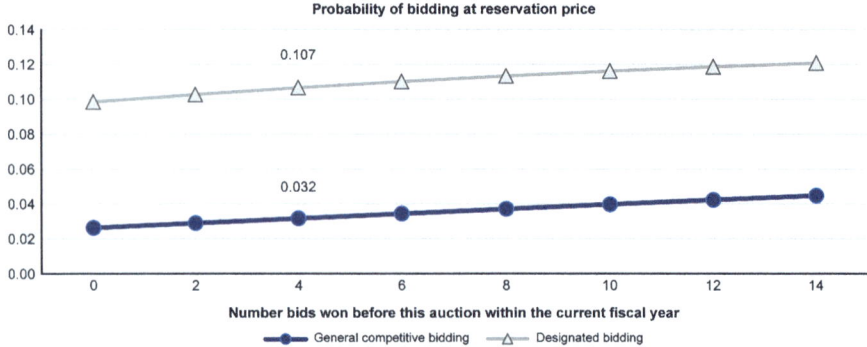

Fig. 12.2 Number of bids won and probability of bidding at the reservation price. (Source: Author's elaboration)

of bids won before the auction within the current fiscal year,[14] and the vertical axis represents the probability (predictive margin) of bidding at the reservation price. For calculating the probability of "bidding at the reservation price" for each specific "number of bids won", we first separated the bidding formulas. Subsequently, in the simulation process, we varied only the number of bids won while keeping all other variables constant. Figure 12.3 is similar to Fig. 12.2, but the vertical axis indicates the probability of withdrawing. The coefficients of (not all) variables related to the number of bids won are statistically significant (Table 12.3).

For this study, the data suggest a consistently higher probability of both bidding at the reservation price and withdrawing in designated bidding, compared with general competitive bidding. For example, when an entity has won four bids (with a mean value of 4.3) in designated bidding, the probability of bidding at the reservation price is 0.107, compared to 0.032 in general competitive bidding. Likewise, the probability of withdrawing is 0.350 for designated bidding and 0.059 for general competitive bidding.

Even in general competitive bidding, participants can withdraw for various reasons or bid at the reservation price with the expectation of winning. These behaviors occur with a certain probability in both bidding formulas. If this pattern of rational bidding behavior is consistent across different bidding formulas, then some of the observed disparity in behavioral probabilities between bidding formulas could be attributed to a lack of winning incentive for participants in designated bidding. Under average conditions, when comparing values in general competitive bidding with those in designated bidding, we observe gaps of approximately 0.075 (i.e., 0.107–0.032) and 0.291 (i.e., 0.350–0.059) for bidding at the reservation price and withdrawal, respectively. We interpret this 0.366 (i.e., 0.075–0.291) as partly indicative of a phenomenon in designated bidding, where the pool of participants with

---

[14]Less than 5% of the total bidders have won more than 14 bids before the auction within the current fiscal year.

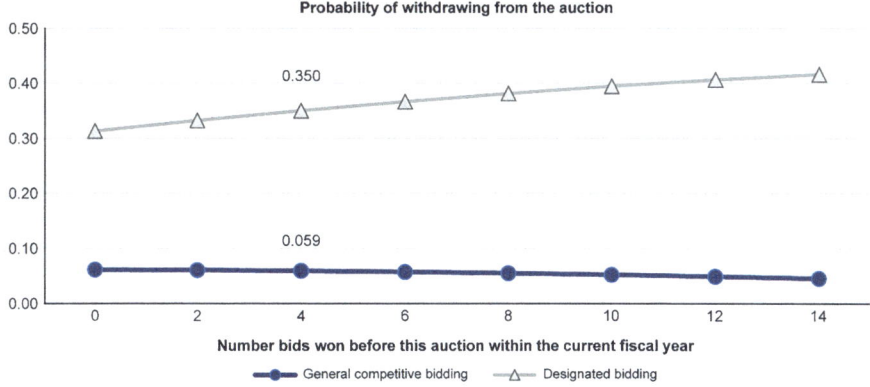

Fig. 12.3 Number of bids won and probability of withdrawing. (Source: Author's elaboration)

little interest in winning is expanded.[15] When studying Japan's public procurement, separately considering designated bidding and general competitive bidding is worthwhile because of differences in participants' interest in winning.

12.5 Participants and the Contract Price Ratio

12.5.1 Number of Participants and the Contract Price

We next examine the relationship between the number of participants and contract price ratio in approximately 22,000 executed auctions. The contract price ratio in public procurement is used as a metric representing the intensity of bidding competition from an economic perspective, depicting the degree of expense burden from a fiscal perspective and serving as a collusion detector from a political perspective. Assuming a consistent level of quality, a lower contract price ratio is considered more favorable. Since low-quality work is not permitted in public procurement, we can assume a certain level of quality.[16] To conduct an analysis of the contract price ratio for each auction, the primary concern variables and other control variables representing auction characteristics are included in Eq. (12.2).

$$CPR_a = \alpha + \rho X_a + \delta P_a + \psi P_a^2 + \xi \left(P_a \times X_a \right) + \beta_1 FP_a + \beta_2 FY_a + \sum_m \beta_m Z_{am} + e_a \qquad (12.2)$$

---

[15] In this scenario, when viewed from another perspective, procuring entities intentionally involve these participants to simulate a competitive market appearance. In reality, this approach allows public entities to easily direct orders to a targeted firm.

[16] Empirical studies using Japanese data did not find consistent evidence regarding the relationship between price and quality.

In Eq. (12.2), the dependent variable is the contract price ratio for the auction a denoted as CPR_a. The equation shows explanatory variables comprising the following: a designated bidding dummy denoted as X_a, the number of participants denoted as P_a, the fourth term as its square value of P_a, and the fifth term as the cross term of the designated bidding dummy and participant number. Using these primary variables, we attempt to compare the impact of the number of participants on the contract price ratio for both bidding formulas. However, if we incorporate the cross term into the model, the Variance Inflation Factor (VIF), which measures the degree of multicollinearity in a set of variables in regression analysis, exceeds 10 for some variables related to the cross term. To address this problem, P_a does not represent the actual number of participants; instead, the analysis uses the centering number derived by subtracting the mean number of participants (5.06) from each actual number.[17]

We add six explanatory variables. Initially, we control for the floor price ratio denoted as FP_a, and the tendering fiscal year denoted as FY_a. Additionally, four categorical dummy variables, Z_m (where $m = 3, \cdots, 6$), which influence each auction result, are included as follows: the work type dummy Z_{a3} comprised eight categories. The classification of work types was originally defined with 29 categories. For our empirical analysis, among these, the civil engineering group, construction group, scaffolding and earthworks, electrical engineering, plumbing, paving, and painting, which had 400 or more orders, are coded from 1 to 7, while the remaining ones are "others" coded as 8. The project location dummy, consisting of values 1–3, is Z_{a4}. This classification corresponds to towns, cities, and "others" (including multiple areas or broader regions). Intuitively, public works in towns are somewhat collusive, whereas those in others with diluted locality tend to be more competitive. We also introduce a categorical dummy for the reservation price for bidding a, with eight categories, denoted as Z_{a5}. Large-scale businesses participate in big-ticket deals, and small businesses participate in low-priced deals (see Table 12.4 for the breakdown). Finally, the winner decision month dummy, Z_{a6}, categorizes the month in which the winning bidder was determined. $\rho, \delta, \psi, \xi, \beta_1, \beta_2$ and β_m, attached to these explanatory variables are the estimated coefficients or groups of estimated coefficients; α is a constant; and e_a is a normal error.

As shown in Sect. 4.2, the probability of withdrawing or bidding at the reservation price indicates that, to accurately assess the number of genuine bidders, instead of relying solely on participant numbers, considering the effective number of participants is one of the preferable alternatives. When substituting the effective number of participants for the number of participants in the estimation equation, the 3rd–5th terms of Eq. (12.2) are replaced with those in Eq. (12.3).

$$CPR_a = \alpha + \rho X_a + \hat{\delta}\hat{P}_a + \hat{\psi}\hat{P}_a^2 + \hat{\xi}\left(\hat{P}_a \times X_a\right) + \beta_1 FP_a + \beta_2 FY_a + \sum_m \beta_m Z_{am} + e_a \quad (12.3)$$

---

[17] Using the centering value, the average value of the VIF is reduced to less than 2.4, and the maximum VIF value is less than 5.8.

Table 12.4 Impact of participant numbers on contract price ratio

	Participants			Effective participants			Participants		
	Model 1: OLS			Model 2: OLS			Model 3: Truncated regression		
	Coefficient	Robust std. err.	P > t	Coefficient	Robust std. err.	P > t	Coefficient	Robust std. err.	P > z
DD: Dummy designation (=1)	0.04044	0.00097	***	0.02497	0.00081	***	0.06050	0.00169	***
NP: Number of participants	−0.00767	0.00022	***				−0.00925	0.00040	***
NP squared	0.00083	0.00005	***				0.00182	0.00011	***
DD X NP	0.00308	0.00034	***				−0.00112	0.00072	
NEP: Number of effective participants				−0.01045	0.00022	***			
NEP squared				0.00119	0.00004	***			
DD X NEP				0.00554	0.00023	***			
Floor price rate	0.13441	0.04592	***	0.10772	0.03443	***	0.18735	0.07298	***
Fiscal year (baseline: 2014)									
2015	−0.00510	0.00129	***	−0.00495	0.00121	***	−0.00756	0.00212	***
2016	−0.00185	0.00109	*	−0.00139	0.00105		−0.00156	0.00183	
2017	−0.00123	0.00129		−0.00124	0.00117		0.00026	0.00219	
2018	0.00501	0.00119	***	0.00383	0.00109	***	0.01127	0.00210	***
2019	0.01022	0.00119	***	0.00742	0.00110	***	0.02207	0.00220	***
2020	0.00797	0.00115	***	0.00500	0.00108	***	0.01738	0.00210	***
2021	0.00380	0.00125	***	0.00345	0.00113	***	0.00924	0.00224	***
Reservation price (baseline: Less than 10,000,000 yen)									
10,000,000–15,000,000 yen	−0.00207	0.00098	**	−0.00508	0.00093	***	−0.00225	0.00174	
15,000,000–30,000,000 yen	−0.00217	0.00088	**	−0.00497	0.00081	***	−0.00245	0.00161	
30,000,000–45,000,000 yen	−0.00284	0.00129	**	−0.00423	0.00122	***	−0.00431	0.00230	*

(continued)

Table 12.4 (continued)

	Participants			Effective participants			Participants		
	Model 1: OLS			Model 2: OLS			Model 3: Truncated regression		
	Coefficient	Robust std. err.	P > t	Coefficient	Robust std. err.	P > t	Coefficient	Robust std. err.	P > z
45,000,000–50,000,000 yen	−0.00593	0.00204	***	−0.00673	0.00198	***	−0.01005	0.00351	***
50,000,000–60,000,000 yen	−0.00453	0.00204	**	−0.00504	0.00199	**	−0.00719	0.00358	**
60,000,000–100,000,000 yen	−0.00934	0.00159	***	−0.00956	0.00149	***	−0.01516	0.00264	***
100,000,000 yen or more	−0.01082	0.00260	***	−0.01108	0.00250	***	−0.01735	0.00417	***
Month when the winner was decided (baseline: January)									
Feb.	0.00056	0.00147		0.00119	0.00143		0.00081	0.00271	
Mar.	0.00003	0.00125		−0.00008	0.00121		−0.00020	0.00230	
Apr.	0.00177	0.00131		0.00514	0.00126	***	0.00333	0.00249	
May	0.00389	0.00146	***	0.00674	0.00144	***	0.00798	0.00285	***
Jun.	0.00183	0.00129		0.00331	0.00126	***	0.00323	0.00241	
Jul.	−0.00196	0.00135		−0.00020	0.00132		−0.00270	0.00239	
Aug.	−0.00032	0.00127		0.00055	0.00124		−0.00032	0.00228	
Sep.	−0.00018	0.00122		0.00030	0.00119		−0.00059	0.00219	
Oct.	0.00519	0.00153	***	0.00542	0.00148	***	0.00936	0.00299	***
Nov.	0.00465	0.00128	***	0.00602	0.00124	***	0.00904	0.00251	***
Dec.	0.00272	0.00135	**	0.00223	0.00131	*	0.00422	0.00251	*
Work type (Baseline: Others)									
Civil engineering	0.01679	0.00105	***	0.01336	0.00102	***	0.03219	0.00177	***
Construction	0.01672	0.00203	***	0.01213	0.00195	***	0.02887	0.00388	***

	Coef.			Coef.			Coef.		
Scaffolding and earthwork	−0.00635	0.00134	***	−0.00610	0.00131	***	−0.00565	0.00205	***
Electrical engineering	−0.00558	0.00160	***	−0.00856	0.00157	***	−0.00672	0.00250	***
Plumbing	0.01485	0.00201	***	0.01089	0.00193	***	0.02721	0.00405	***
Paving	−0.00811	0.00125	***	−0.00531	0.00119	***	−0.00795	0.00201	***
Painting construction	−0.00882	0.00200	***	−0.00994	0.00195	***	−0.00806	0.00295	***
Municipal type: Location (baseline: Town)									
City	0.00435	0.00052	***	0.00324	0.00050	***	0.00717	0.00098	***
Multiple area or wider area	−0.01197	0.00291	***	−0.01416	0.00279	***	−0.01544	0.00383	***
Constant	0.78070	0.04008	***	0.81713	0.03001	***	0.72416	0.06367	
/sigma							0.04635	0.00039	***
Var(e.cpr)									
Number of obs	22,256			22,256			21,921		
F	290			347					
Prob > F	0			0					
R-squared / pseudo R-squared	0.279			0.315					
Root MSE	0.034			0.033					
Wald chi2(32)							7986		
Prob > chi2							0		
Log pseudolikelihood							46,452		

Note: ***: 1%, **: 5%, *: 10%

Due to the consideration of the VIF for the effective number of participants, this analysis uses $\hat{P}_a$ as the centering value derived by subtracting the mean effective number of participants (3.75) from each effective number of participants for bidding a. $\hat{\delta}$, $\hat{\psi}$, and $\hat{\xi}$ attached to these variables represent the estimated coefficients. Regarding the estimation models in Eqs. (12.2) and (12.3), the distribution of the dependent variable, which is the contract price ratio, has a ceiling of 1. Considering this characteristic, we employed not only a standard linear regression model but also a truncated regression model and Tobit model. Each analysis used robust estimations that accounted for heterogeneity. The results are in Table 12.4.

12.5.2 Illustration of the Estimation Result

We conduct simulations to identify and compare the impacts of the two bidding formulas, focusing on the Dummy Designation (X_a), using the estimation results in Table 12.4. To calculate the predictive margin of the contract price ratio, we assumed that all auctions selected designated bidding. We then vary the number of participants, which ranged from −4 to 5 in integer steps (due to technical requirements for estimation, the participation numbers are centered), while keeping all other variables constant. This allow for calculating the predictive margin of the contract price ratio for each auction considering, a specified number of participants, when using designated bidding, based on Table 12.4. We apply the same procedure to general competitive bidding.

Table 12.5 summarizes the results. The numbers in the leftmost column represent the "after centering" number of participants (or effective number of participants). The values in each cell in Table 12.5 are the predictive margins derived from Models 1 and 2, Models 3 and 4, and Models 5 and 6 in Table 12.4.

Figure 12.4 displays the simulated values for Models 1 and 2, while Fig. 12.5 presents those for Models 3 and 4. Each graph on the left side is based on the estimation results from Eq. (12.2), whereas the right side is based on Eq. (12.3). In the

Table 12.5 Simulation of contract price ratios

	Fig.12.4				Fig.12.5				Omitted			
	Left		Right		Left		Right		Left		Right	
	Linear regression				Truncated regression				Tobit regression			
	Model 1: Participants		Model 2: Effective participants		Model 3: Participants		Model 4: Effective participants		Model 5: Participants		Model 6: Effective participants	
	General	Designation	General	Designation	General	Designation	General	Designation	General	Designation	General	Designation
−4	0.9567	0.9848	0.9828	0.9856	0.9852	1.0501	1.0283	1.0552	0.9571	0.9854	0.9856	0.9898
−3	0.9431	0.9744	0.9640	0.9724	0.9632	1.0270	0.9962	1.0261	0.9434	0.9748	0.9655	0.9750
−2	0.9313	0.9656	0.9476	0.9615	0.9448	1.0075	0.9690	1.0020	0.9315	0.9660	0.9481	0.9629
−1	0.9211	0.9585	0.9336	0.9530	0.9301	0.9917	0.9468	0.9829	0.9213	0.9588	0.9334	0.9535
0	0.9126	0.9531	0.9219	0.9469	0.9190	0.9795	0.9296	0.9687	0.9127	0.9533	0.9213	0.9467
1	0.9058	0.9493	0.9127	0.9432	0.9116	0.9710	0.9173	0.9594	0.9058	0.9495	0.9120	0.9426
2	0.9006	0.9472	0.9058	**0.9418**	0.9078	0.9661	0.9099	**0.9551**	0.9007	0.9474	0.9053	**0.9412**
3	0.8971	**0.9468**	0.9013	0.9429	**0.9077**	**0.9648**	**0.9075**	0.9558	0.8971	**0.9470**	0.9012	0.9424
4	0.8953	0.9480	**0.8992**	0.9463	0.9112	0.9672	0.9101	0.9614	0.8953	0.9482	**0.8999**	0.9464
5	**0.8951**	0.9509	0.8995	0.9522	0.9183	0.9732	0.9176	0.9719	**0.8952**	0.9512	0.9012	0.9529

Source: Author's elaboration

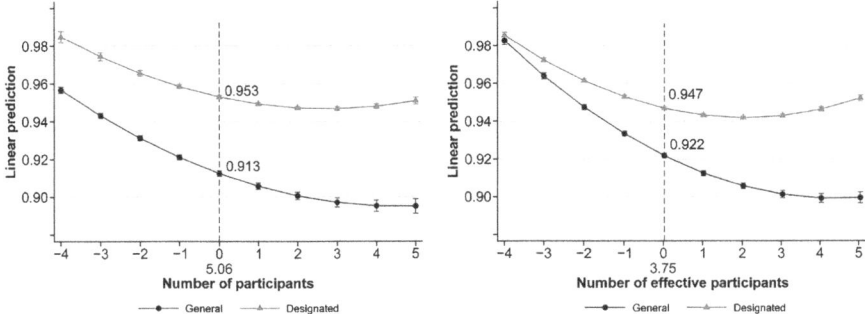

Fig. 12.4 Linear regressions. (Source: Author's elaboration)

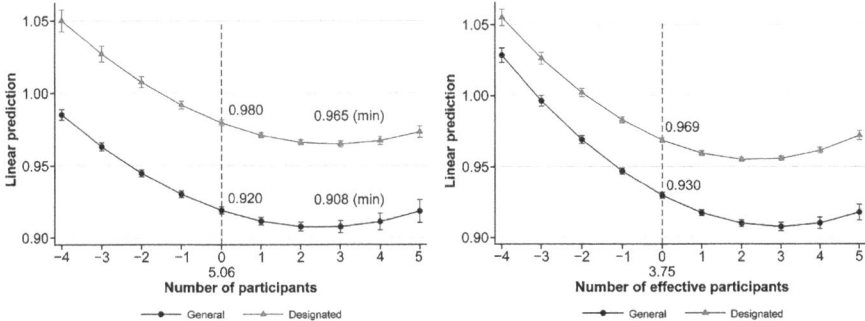

Fig. 12.5 Truncated regressions. (Source: Author's elaboration)

left graph, the value "0" on the horizontal axis represents 5.06, which is the observed value before it was subtracted and centered. Similarly, in the right graph, "0" corresponds to 3.75. The vertical axis represents the contract price ratio for both sides of the graphs. The curved lines represent the predictive margin of contract price ratios for the bidding formulas.

For example, in Model 1 of Table 12.5, if all bidders participated in the general competitive bidding with the "after centering" number of participants at 0 (while keeping the other variables constant), the average value of predicted contract price would be 0.9126. This value also denotes the predictive margins on the vertical axis for general competitive bidding when the number of participants is 0 on the horizontal axis in the left graph of Fig. 12.4. Alternatively, in Model 4 of Table 12.5, if all bidders participated in the designated bidding with the number of effective participants at 0, the average contract price would be 0.969. This value is reflected on the vertical axis for designated bidding when the number of participants is 0 in the right graph of Fig. 12.5. Note that we have omitted graphs for Models 5 and 6 because their shapes closely resemble those depicted in Fig. 12.4. Table 12.5 clearly indicates very minor differences between them.

12.5.3 Differences in the Definitions of Participants

In the left graph of Fig. 12.4, a comparison of contract price ratios between the two bidding formulas at a mean number of participants of 5.06 shows that the ratio for designated bidding is approximately 0.04 higher (i.e., 0.953–0.913). In the right graph, with a mean effective number of participants at 3.75, the contract price ratio for designated bidding is observed to be approximately 0.025 higher (i.e., 0.947–0.922). In Fig. 12.5, the estimation method is a truncated regression model, but the overall trend is similar to that of Fig. 12.4. In the left graph of Fig. 12.5, concerning the mean number of participants, there is a gap of 0.06 in the contract price; meanwhile, in the right graph, the gap is 0.039.

Examining these figures together, the gaps in contract price ratios are smaller for estimates using the effective number of participants (right-hand graphs) than the number of participants (left-hand graphs). In other words, when we conduct a comparison excluding withdrawals and reservation-price bidders, the contract price ratio for designated bidding approaches that of general competitive bidding. Nevertheless, merely changing the definition of participants (by excluding those who withdraw and those who bid at the reservation price) is not enough to fully explain why designated bidding results in higher contract price ratios.

12.5.4 Marginal Effect of Increasing Participants

These differences are interpreted as indicative of the gap in contract price ratios between bidding formulas under average conditions, which suggests a higher degree of "waste" in designated bidding, whether active or passive. However, employing designated bidding might be politically acceptable because it could fulfill social requirements, even if it entails some waste.[18] In fact, designated bidding is typically used for low-cost projects in which small and medium-sized firms participate. We can regard this approach as playing a crucial role in developing and preserving small businesses. Therefore, we propose a shift in perspective. Our goal is to reduce waste without altering the bidding formula.

The marginal impact of increasing the number of participants by one on the contract price ratio varies across conditions such as the absolute level of participants, bidding formula, and estimation model. For example, referring to Table 12.5 (the left graphs in Figs. 12.4 and 12.5), when the mean number of participants is around 0, the marginal change in the contract price ratio for general competitive bidding by adding 1 participant (moving from -1 to 0) is as follows: 0.009 ($=0.9211–0.9126$) for the linear regression model, 0.011 ($=0.9301–0.9190$) for the truncation regression model, and 0.009 ($=0.9213–0.9127$) for Tobit. Using the same procedure to

---

[18]Chever et al. (2017) quantitatively tested the economic reasonableness of restrictive tendering systems in small projects.

calculate the marginal change in the contract price ratio for designated bidding in the left graphs in the figures, we obtain 0.005 (=0.9585–0.9531), 0.012 (=0.9917–0.9795), and 0.006 (=0.9588–0.9533), respectively. From these calculations, when the number of participants is around the average, we can expect that if participants increase by one, the contract price ratio declines by approximately 1% for general competitive bidding and less than 1% for designated bidding. In reality, a reduction of just 0.01 in the contract price ratio could lead to a decrease of 250 billion yen in the annual government construction investment, which amounts to 25 trillion yen (as of 2020).

12.5.5 Minimizing the Contract Price

In the left-hand graph of Fig. 12.5, the minimum contract price ratio for designated bidding is 0.965, corresponding to approximately eight participants in actual number (i.e., 5.06 + 3). In the right graph of Fig. 12.5, the minimum contract price ratio is 0.955 (Table 12.5), equivalent to approximately six participants in actual number (i.e., 3.75 + 2). This procedure can determine the minimum contract price ratio, independent of the bidding formulas or estimation models.

Examining the actual number of participants, a metric commonly employed in other studies, reveals that the contract price ratio is lowest for both bidding formulas when the actual number of participants is between seven and eight in most cases. We can understand that an additional two or three participants are required to minimize the contract price ratio for Japan. Furthermore, this finding, with respect to the actual number of participants at the lowest contract price ratio, is largely consistent with Gupta (2002) at 6–8 participants and Onur and Tas (2019) at 7 participants.

12.6 Conclusions

The behavior patterns of procuring entities and suppliers in public procurement vary according to the bidding formula and other conditions. A lack of comprehensive understanding of these characteristics can lead to misinterpreting analytical results. However, empirical studies that take these factors into account are rare. In this chapter, we have clarified the strategic bidding behavior, including phantom bids and strategic withdrawals, and the relationship between winning bid prices and winning probabilities, while controlling for differences in bidding formulas that have not been adequately covered in previous research.

The analysis reveals that designated bidding has a higher probability of both withdrawals and bids at the reservation price compared with general competitive bidding. The probability of withdrawal is higher by approximately 29.1 percentage points, and bidding at the reservation price is higher by approximately 7.5 percentage points. According to our consideration in this study, this trend can be attributed to procuring entities frequently inviting participants who, whether intentionally or unavoidably, are less interested in winning. Furthermore, there is a difference in contract price ratios between bidding formats under average conditions, suggesting greater "waste" in designated bidding. Therefore, researchers should take care to note the differences among bidding formulas.

Designated bidding might be politically acceptable due to its ability to meet social requirements, even if it involves some waste. It would be reasonably valuable to shift our goal toward reducing this waste, without altering the existing bidding formula. The study estimations suggest that adding just one participant to the bidding process can, around the average scenario, decrease the contract price ratio by approximately 0.5–1% in both bidding formulas. The lowest contract price ratio may be achieved at 7–8 participants, which means adding 2–3 participants to the current situation.

This chapter highlights the issues of local public procurement, which unfortunately often fails to capture public interest. The substantial financial support that Japanese local governments receive from the central government means that local residents frequently lack a sense of direct fiscal responsibility or burden, which in turn reduces their incentive to monitor the efficiency of local government spending. Therefore, it is crucial for researchers to effectively communicate these findings to both voters and administrators, enhancing public procurement practices.

Acknowledgements This work received support from the Japan Society for the Promotion of Science Kakenhi Grants Nos. JP24530359 and JP17K03771 and from the Short-term Research Project 22210 and 23209 of the Institute of Economic Research in Aoyama Gakuin University College of Economics. I am grateful for the assistance provided by Atsushi Utsunomiya, Ryota Sudo, and Riu Hinokibara from the College of Economics at Aoyama Gakuin University in compiling this study. I also received valuable advice during the drafting stage from participants in the study group sponsored by the Japan Tax Association (chair: Taro Ozawa, Professor emeritus, Keio University) and participants in the Kurokawa Kazuyoshi research group. I would like to express my sincere gratitude to them.

References

Aizawa K (2006) Analysis of project performance assessments in civil engineering projects. [Doboku koji ni okeru koji seisekki hyotei no bunseki ni tsuite]. Public Works Manag J [Kensetsu manejimento gijyutsu] 2006(June):17–21. (in Japanese)

Arai K (2013) Effect of institutions: analysis of Japanese municipal public procurement. Int J Public Adm 36(9):638–648. https://doi.org/10.1080/01900692.2013.777928

Arai K, Morimoto E (2017) Construction industry and competition policy in Japan. Int J Econ Bus 24(3):345–363. https://doi.org/10.1080/13571516.2017.1332130

Bandiera O, Prat A, Valletti T (2009) Active and passive waste in government spending: evidence from a policy experiment. Am Econ Rev 99(4):1278–1308. https://doi.org/10.1257/aer.99.4.1278

Buchanan JM (1960) Fiscal theory and political economy. University of North Carolina Press, Chapel Hill

Chassang S, Ortner J (2019) Collusion in auctions with constrained bids: theory and evidence from public procurement. J Polit Econ 127(5):2269–2300. https://doi.org/10.1086/701812

Chassang S, Kawai K, Nakabayashi J, Ortner J (2022) Robust screens for noncompetitive bidding in procurement auctions. Econometrica 90(1):315–346. https://doi.org/10.3982/ECTA17155

Chever L, Saussier S, Yvrande-Billon A (2017) The law of small numbers: investigating the benefits of restricted auctions for public procurement. Appl Econ 49(42):4241–4260. https://doi.org/10.1080/00036846.2017.1279270

Conley TG, Decarolis F (2016) Detecting bidders groups in collusive auctions. Am Econ J Microecon 8(2):1–38. https://doi.org/10.1257/mic.20130254

De Silva DG, Dunne T, Kosmopoulou G (2003) An empirical analysis of entrant and incumbent bidding in road construction auctions. J Ind Econ 51(3):295–316. https://doi.org/10.1111/1467-6451.00202

Fukushima Prefecture contract oversight section (2010) Auction methods and construction work evaluation, Fukushima Prefecture Auction Oversight Committee Meeting. [Nyusatsu housiki to kouji seiseki ni tsuite] (in Japanese). http://www.pref.fukushima.lg.jp/uploaded/attachment/7344.pdf. Material 2 of 34th

Goetz CJ (1977) Fiscal illusion in state-local finance. In: Borcherding TE (ed) Budgets and bureaucrats. Duke University Press, Durham

Gupta S (2002) Competition and collusion in a government procurement auction market. Atl Econ J 30(1):13–25. https://doi.org/10.1007/BF02299143

Hatsumi K, Ishii R (2022) The effect of price on the quality of public construction in Japan. Jpn World Econ 62:101134. https://doi.org/10.1016/j.japwor.2022.101134

Iimi A (2006) Auction reforms for effective official development assistance. Rev Ind Organ 28(2):109–128. https://doi.org/10.1007/s11151-006-0012-x

Ishii R (2013) Bid roundness under collusion in Japanese procurement auctions. Rev Ind Organ 44(3):241–254. https://doi.org/10.1007/s11151-013-9408-6

Iwamatsu J, Akiyama T, Endo K (2001) Bidding strategies in Japanese construction projects: bidding behaviour that can be read from the disclosed tender data. [Kensetsu purojekuto niokeru nyusatsu senryaku ni kansuru kenkyu]. J Archit Plan Trans Archit Inst Jpn [Nihon kenchiku gakkai keikakukei ronbunsyu] 66(548):207–213. (in Japanese). https://doi.org/10.3130/aija.66.207_4

Iwamatsu J, Akiyama T, Endo K (2003) Bidding strategies in Japanese construction projects: 2 effect of enterprise scale on competitiveness. [Kensetsu purojekuto niokeru nyusatsu senryaku ni kansuru kenkyu sono2]. J Archit Plan Trans Archit Inst Jpn [Nihon kenchiku gakkai keikakukei ronbunsyu] 68(565):285–291. (in Japanese). https://doi.org/10.3130/aija.68.285

Kawai K, Nakabayashi J (2022) Detecting large-scale collusion in procurement auctions. J Polit Econ 130(5):1364–1411. https://doi.org/10.1086/718913

Morimoto E, Arai K (2013) Effects of spending mechanism of changes in examination trigger prices: analysis in terms of bidding behavior. [Shikokuchihoseibikyoku ippandobokukouji niokeru nyusatsukoudou kara mita teinyusatu-tyosa-kijyunkakaku kaitei no hakyu no bunseki]. J Jpn Soc Civil Eng F4 [Dobokugakkai ronbunsyuF4], 171–i(180) (in Japanese), 69(4), I. https://doi.org/10.2208/jscejcm.69.I_171

Morimoto E, Arai K (2014) Impact of the get out Dango declaration: analysis what happened since 2006. [Datsu-dangosengen no eikyo: 2006nen ni naniga okotta noka]. J Jpn Soc Civil Eng F4 [Dobokugakkai ronbunsyuF4] 70(2):38–54. (in Japanese). https://doi.org/10.2208/jscejcm.70.38

Morimoto E, Namerikawa S, Okamoto T, Yamanaka H (2007) Statistical analysis of the relationship between the number of times that the successful bidders were designated in past and quality of construction works focused on the "locality" of bidders. J Constr Manag JSCE [Kenstsu manejimento kenkyu ronbunsyu] 14:263–276. (in Japanese). https://doi.org/10.2208/procm.14.263

Nakabayashi J (2013) Small business set-asides in procurement auctions: an empirical analysis. J Public Econ 100:28–44. https://doi.org/10.1016/j.jpubeco.2013.01.003

Nishikawa M (2019) Harmful negativity bias under a decentralized system: retrospective voting in Japanese mayoral elections 1983–2015. In: Kunizaki M, Nakamura K, Sugahara K, Yanagihara M (eds) Advances in local public economics. Springer, Singapore, pp 279–314. https://doi.org/10.1007/978-981-13-3107-7_16

Nishikawa M (2024a) Supplementary Perspectives on Local Public Procurement in Japan. mimeo

Nishikawa M (2024b) Quality and price relationship in Japanese municipal public procurement (2011–2015) [Chihoujichitai no koukyou-tyotatsu niokeru hinshitsu to kakaku tono kankei]. Gov Auditing Rev [Kaikei kensa kenkyu] 69:13–33. (in Japanese). https://doi.org/10.51016/kaikeikensa.69.0_13

Ohashi H (2009) Effects of transparency in procurement practice on government expenditure: a case study of municipal public works. Rev Ind Organ 34(3):267–285. https://doi.org/10.1007/s11151-009-9208-1

Onur I, Tas BKO (2019) Optimal bidder participation in public procurement auctions. Int Tax Public Financ 26(3):595–617. https://doi.org/10.1007/s10797-018-9515-2

Onur I, Ozcan R, Tas BKO (2012) Public procurement auctions and competition in Turkey. Rev Ind Organ 40(3):207–223. https://doi.org/10.1007/s11151-011-9299-3

Porter R, Zona J (1993) Detection of bid rigging in procurement auctions. J Polit Econ 101(3):518–538. https://doi.org/10.1086/261885

Sakon H, Aizawa K, Yamamuro H (2007) Analysis of the construction results in public works. [Dobokukouji niokeru koujiseiseki-hyotei no bunseki nitsuite]. In Proceedings of the 25th Construction Management Research Conference. [Dai 25-kai kensetsu manejimento mondai ni kansuru kennkyu-happyo touronkai kouensyu], pp. 21–24. https://www.jsce.or.jp/library/open/proc/maglist2/02503/2007/mg01.htm (in Japanese)

Sato N, Matsumoto N, Kinoshita S, Tanno H, Ishinohachi S (2008) Study on the present state of excessively low-priced bidding for public works and its countermeasures. [Koukyokouji niokeru danpingu-jyutyu no jittai to taisaku ni kanusuru kousatsu]. J Constr Manag JSCE [Kenstsu manejimento kenkyu ronbunsyu] 15:261–272. (in Japanese). https://doi.org/10.2208/procm.15.261

Takarazuka city (2011) Report by expert panel members investigating the system for auctions and contracts. nNyusatsu oyobi keiyaku ni kakaru seido ni kansuru tyousa senmon iin houkokusyo [Nyusatsu oyobi keiyakuni kakaru seido ni kansuru tyousa semon iinkai] (In Japanese). https://www.city.takarazuka.hyogo.jp/shisei/keiyaku/1008681/1002699.html

Wagner RE (1976) Revenue structure, fiscal illusion, and budgetary choice. Public Chocie 25(1):45–61. https://doi.org/10.1007/BF01726330

Weingast B, Shepsle KA, Johnsen C (1981) The political economy of benefits and costs: a neoclassical approach to distributive politics. J Polit Econ 89(4):642–664. https://doi.org/10.1086/260997

Yamagata Prefectural Government (n.d.) Yamagata Prefecture land development department, construction planning section, each fiscal year. [Koukyou tyotatsu ni kakaru nyusatu keiyaku seido ni kansuru houkokusyo] (in Japanese). https://www.pref.yamagata.jp/180030/kensei/nyuusatsujouhou/nyuusatsujouhou/2nd_chotatsu/nyuusatsujouhou/kn/nks/index.html

Masashi Nishikawa is a Professor at the College of Economics, Aoyama Gakuin University. His specializations include public finance and public policy, within Japanese local governments particularly. His areas of expertise encompass vertical fiscal transfers, municipal amalgamation, mayoral elections, corruption in public procurement, and the nuclear power plants as Not in My Back Yard facilities.

Chapter 13
Key Directions for Improving the Sustainability of Local Governments

Yu Noda ⓘ

Abstract This book aims to derive key directions for enhancing the sustainability of Japanese local government services with extremely limited policy resources. From the perspectives of intergovernmental relations, political and administrative systems, local government-third sector relations, and local government-business relations, this book presents three key directions for improving the sustainability of local governments: (1) sufficient horizontal and vertical collaborations, (2) systemic changes based on the actual conditions of local government organizations, and (3) a stronger driving force to mobilize citizens. Collaboration addresses the challenge of resource depletion by allowing local governments to draw on the policy resources of other policy actors. To enhance horizontal cooperation with municipalities, non-profit organizations (NPOs), and businesses as well as vertical cooperation with prefectural governments, partnerships must be established regularly instead of only when the need for them arises. Systemic changes are necessary because traditional institutions and policy tools no longer adequately meet the needs of local governments or citizens' preferences. Systemic changes become inefficient when not adapted to the actual conditions of the local government organization. In addition, a stronger driving force on the behavioral changes required by citizens to increase the effectiveness of local government policies. Mobilization strategies focus on changing citizens' behavior are the driving force behind increasing the effectiveness of local government policies. The issues of local governance require policymakers and researchers to reconsider these measures.

Keywords Collaboration · Systemic change · Driving forces · Resource depletion · Local governance

Y. Noda (✉)
Faculty of Policy Studies, Doshisha University, Kyoto, Japan
e-mail: ynoda@mail.doshisha.ac.jp

13.1   Sustainability Clues in Intergovernmental Relations

What are the key directions for the sustainability of local governments with severely limited policy resources? To address the objectives of this book, this chapter summarizes the clues for improving the sustainability of local government discussed in the 12 chapters, considering intergovernmental relations, including central–local relations and interlocal relations, political and administrative systems, government-third sector relations, and government-business relations.

First, we focus on clues to the sustainability of local government in terms of central–local and interlocal government relations. Japan's central–local relations, examined in Chap. 2, are characterized by centralization and fusion, in which authority is centralized in the central government, but the implementation of individual policies is carried out collaboratively by local governments and national ministries. In central–local relations to the current date, local governance has been preserved through financial support provided by the central government to meet increasing citizen demands. However, each ministry secures budgetary resources through national financial support to expand its own organization and policy areas. Only when subsidies have been utilized by local governments have ministries succeeded in achieving their own objectives. Local governments also have a high incentive to use subsidies because they face financial difficulties, and the intentions of central ministries and dependence of local governments on subsidies have led to increases in their expenditures.

In addition, personnel exchanges have contributed to maintaining the amount of local government spending, with career bureaucrats from the central government being sent to key positions such as deputy mayor, general manager, or head of the finance section in local governments, returning to the central government after a few years, and being sent back for another assignment. Technically, it can continue to be possible for the national government to issue bonds to secure financial resources and make fiscal transfers to maintain local government expenditures. However, to maintain local governments in the future, when the population is declining significantly and fiscal difficulties become even more severe, the only options are a significant reduction in transfer funds, a reduction in the number of local governments, or collaboration among local governments. Japan has chosen collaboration, and Chap. 7 examined the strategies for reforming interlocal government relations.

Different forms of integration are available to promote intermunicipal cooperation. The central government promotes policy coordination, which has lower political costs. However, whether horizontal collaboration facilitated by the central government contributes to sustainability through increased population and tax revenues for municipalities must be clarified. Chapter 7 statistically demonstrates that municipalities with the Collaborative Central City-Region (CCCR) plans approved by the central government does not experience higher population and tax revenue growth than CCCR candidate municipalities that does not receive such approval. In countries with declining populations like Japan, municipalities with vulnerable policy resources of their own do not necessarily increase their available resources when collaborating with other municipalities. Moreover, according to the empirical study in Chap. 7, horizontal cooperation among local governments does not necessarily increase the sustainability of local governments. In this context, local government cooperation is now focused not only on horizontal relationships among municipalities but also on vertical cooperation between municipalities and prefectures. Prefectures, which are expected to be oriented toward regional governance as a more extensive government, have been recognized as governments with different roles and functions from those of municipalities, which are the basic government closer to citizens. However, in the future, prefectures increasingly require to assume the position of major services performed by municipalities. In this case, because prefectures are responsible for a wide range of areas, they are less transparent than municipalities from the perspective of individual citizens, and the procedures for participation are less proactive and more psychologically distant. In other words, the prefectures are less democratic for citizens than the municipalities. Hence, prefectures need to actively encourage the participation of municipal residents and strive for transparency when replacing the main services of municipalities.

13.2   Sustainability Clues in Political and Administrative Systems

13.2.1   Institutional Improvements in Dual Representation System

In the context of a declining population and financial difficulties, decisions on whether to downsize local government organizations or collaborate with other governments are determined by a system of dual representation in which the head (mayor or governor) and the council make decisions. Dysfunctional political systems are a fundamental problem for the sustainability of municipalities. Failure to resolve this problem leads to the ineffective promotion of policies and inefficient collaborations with other policy entities. In Japan, the head of the local government has a great deal of power in terms of the distribution of authority, including the right to submit budgets and to supervise and control all administrative organizations. However, the leadership of the head of government does not always function well, depending on the political system. The council plays a role in controlling the arbitrary policy management of the head of government, but Chap. 3 reveals that Japan's unique election system, the Single Non-Transferable Vote system, arguably results in distorted policy decisions based on preferences that emphasize council members' special interests.

Unlike candidates for the head of government, who seek to motivate a wide range of voters throughout the local government, councilor candidates target specific voter segments because the electoral threshold for winning a seat is low; therefore, when there are multiple constituencies, candidates prioritize the interests of specific voters over the interests of the local government as a whole. As a result of the council members' focus on the specific interests of limited constituencies, policies that change the status quo would be difficult to implement. Spending cuts are hardly agreed upon among stakeholders, thereby preventing local governments from achieving efficient administrative management.

Since the 2010s, the author has observed that Japanese local politics have been characterized by both the rise of the Osaka Restoration Association (ORA) and the splitting of the Liberal Democratic Party (LDP) in gubernatorial elections. The emerging regional parties including ORA are expected to constitute a new driving force in local governance through the strong political leadership of reformist local leaders. However, such movements are currently centered on specific regions and do not appear to be sufficiently influential to spread throughout the country. The LDP's split in the gubernatorial elections shows that in the absence of any change in the prevailing local political landscape, intra-party rather than inter-party competition has become the primary concern.

In this context, the author focuses on the reform of the electoral system as an institutional environment that promotes competition among political parties by clarifying the policy differences between them at the local level. In particular, a proportional representation system can realize competition based on policies with party labels for prefectural and ordinance-designated city electoral districts. Alternatively, to maintain plurality voting, another option is to divide prefectures and municipalities into multiple electoral districts with single-seat constituencies while considering the issue of the disproportionate number of voters.

The challenge for the future is to investigate how systemic changes related to local elections can realize policy debates in local politics in Japan and how this interacts with the executive branch of the head of government in a two-party representative system. Chapter 3 thus addresses the pressing need for institutional and systemic reforms adapted to the current realities of policymaking and local politics.

13.2.2 *Organizational Management Improvements*

Chapters 4 and 5 discuss the dysfunctions of the administrative system, deriving aspects of systems failure to meet the actual conditions. As discussed in Chap. 1, local governments in Japan are organized in a very large pyramidal structure, with the mayor or governor at the top and a clear chain of command. However, in the context of a depletion of policy resources, such as the declining population and financial difficulties, strategies such as the application of digital technology, administrative reform, and resource sharing need to be prioritized. Based on these key issues, Chap. 4 quantitatively examines the effects of the introduction of digital technology into administrative operations, and Chap. 5 on administrative reforms examines the implications for sustainability based on the characteristics and challenges of Japan's evaluation activities.

Municipal service efficiency is affected by a number of factors, not just cloud adoption, but the most fundamental of these factors are population and finances, which are directly related to policy resources. Chapter 4 presents a quantitative examination that also considered factors, such as population concentration in local governments and vertical cooperation with higher-level governments, that contribute to financial support. Consequently, no efficiency improvement is confirmed through the introduction of the administrative cloud. Instead, the productivity of municipalities that introduced cloud computing at an early stage is relatively low. The author's view of this result is that uniform digitization of all operations, including those that do not require digital transformation (DX), in fact, requires more effort and is inefficient. Certainly, DX is significant and has a higher potential to contribute to municipal efficiency. However, efficient administrative operations are best achieved by implementing DX in a manner best suited to the size of each local government and the desired workflow within the organization. To perform DX in the first place, a detailed analysis of the workflow is necessary to understand the commonality of work within the administrative organization in depth and the possibility of computerization. However, in Japanese local governments, such workflow analysis is not always sufficiently conducted. An accurate understanding of system operations is a fundamental prerequisite for achieving systemic changes. On the other side, Chap. 4 reveals that vertical cooperation with the national government and prefectures is effective in improving the efficiency of local government administrative operations. This point is similar to the discussion in Chap. 7 presented earlier.

Next, an autonomous and effective evaluation system is essential to reduce wasteful spending and clarify policy prioritization with respect to large local government organizations. Improving the sustainability of local government services requires reducing the workforce, streamlining the organization, and improving the payroll system to keep administrative costs and the size of the government under control. All these approaches have already been addressed to some extent by Japanese local governments in the process of creating and implementing administrative and fiscal reforms. Such administrative and fiscal reforms are needed in the future, but as a prerequisite, it is imperative that local governments conduct evaluation activities to eliminate waste and prioritize measures on their own. However, as confirmed in Chap. 5, the evaluation system of local governments in Japan is strongly influenced by the central government, making it difficult for autonomous evaluation to function.

In contrast to performance measurement efforts in other countries, Japan's evaluation system has been developed independently by local governments, without central government involvement. The extent of central government involvement has increased since the 2000s, as ministries and agencies have demanded that local governments formulate and evaluate plans to implement national policies. Consequently, the volume of evaluation activities conducted by local governments has expanded, suppressing the degree of autonomous organizational management by local governments. In this situation, the author points out that an evaluation system is needed to enable local governments to ensure their own organizational management, but this necessitates the redesign of an integrated intergovernmental indicator system between local governments and higher-level governments to prevent local governments' evaluation work from becoming bloated. Such a redesign facilitates systemic change toward an accurate evaluation of improving the policies of local governments.

Chapters 4 and 5 discuss how the dysfunctions of the administrative system can be resolved as follows. DX should be introduced according to the desired workflow and the efficiency of municipal evaluation activities should be improved by linking central and local government evaluation systems. In other words, these are administrative system changes that are based on the actual conditions of the local government organization.

Local government organizational management cannot be improved simply by restructuring organizational structures and workflows through digital technology and administrative reforms. Chapter 6 discusses resource sharing in crisis management administration with other local governments, businesses and third sectors, and policy actors. Crisis management is mainly handled by local governments in Japan. Thus, resource sharing with other local governments and the private sector is vital as policy resources become depleted. Therefore, for the sustainability of local government, in addition to disaster management activities in cooperation with voluntary disaster management organizations, it is necessary for local governments to deliver supplies to evacuation sites, procure supplies themselves, and strengthen volunteer activities through collaboration and transportation agreements with the private sector, as well as with volunteer organizations.

As information sharing among actors is difficult to achieve after a crisis occurs, the mutual promotion of communication on a routine basis is required to maintain crisis management response capabilities at all times. Among the municipalities unable to improve their response capabilities through horizontal collaboration are those with limited financial resources. In such areas, prefectures must take the initiative in crisis management response. Moreover, in the event of a larger disaster, vertical collaboration, such as disaster recovery assistance from the central government or increased flexibility in the dispatch of Self-Defense Forces, can provide powerful support to overcome the limitations of collaboration among local governments. Vertical cooperation facilitates financial support, particularly in terms of scale. Therefore, in the crisis management response of local government organizations, in addition to sharing policy resources, such as information, human resources, and material resources through horizontal cooperation among local governments, the effective mobilization of financial resources through enhanced vertical cooperation with the national government is a requirement for the sustainability of local governments.

13.3   Sustainability Clues in Local Government–Third Sector Relations

Local governments are expected to operate democratically and efficiently, with all citizens in the jurisdictional area placing their taxes and rights in trust with the government while the local government considers the citizens' preferences. In such cases, citizen participation must also be reconsidered. In addition, citizen organizations such as neighborhood associations (NHAs) and nonprofit organizations (NPOs) are essential for carrying out self-governing activities. Similar to Chap. 6, which deals with crisis management, Chaps. 8 and 9, which deal with the relationships between the third sectors, such as NHAs, NPOs, and local governments, discuss the need for sufficient collaborations despite contextual differences. Meanwhile, Chap. 10 highlights the importance of policy drivers through citizen mobilization.

NHAs have achieved meticulous services such as garbage separation, evacuation guidance, community beautification, welfare activities, circulation of administrative and event information, mobilization for events, weddings, funerals, festivals, and identification of community issues. NHAs in Japan have been regarded as co-producers of public services, and municipal policy resources, such as human and financial resources, have been depleted. The NPM briefly diverted the interest in collaboration, but the governance debate has reignited interest in collaboration. Chapter 8 discusses how municipalities faced with limited human and financial resources have mobilized community-based organizations, particularly NHAs, to promote public policy. Co-production in Japan has the potential to enhance the efficiency of public service delivery and strengthen democracy through citizen participation and trust in government, both of which enhance the sustainability of local governments. Surprisingly, few empirical studies confirm whether these effects have emerged. The main research question examines the extent to which NHA activities contribute to the financial efficiency of local governments and the quality of public services. In addition, a systematic review of the accumulated Japanese NHA research is considered an eagerly awaited step in developing international knowledge of coproduction.

Chapter 9 focuses on how the ideas of the New Public Commons and the Society of Mutual Assistance spread in Japan and what makes them unique in terms of participatory/associative democracy. In Japan, the Great Hanshin-Awaji Earthquake of 1995 triggered the formation of many volunteer organizations and an increase in NPOs based on the Law for the Promotion of Specified Nonprofit Activities in 1998. Since then, NPOs have become a common sight for citizens, and local governments have provided subsidies to NPOs, making them leaders in community development. This study examined the role of community-level civil society organizations, such as NPOs and organizations based on local ties, which are important actors in local governance with respect to the sustainability of local governments.

They are not just providers of services, but they also function as a vehicle for citizens' political participation, promote innovation and social entrepreneurship, and serve as a place for citizens to express their values and beliefs. Considering these roles, they afford local governments, with increasingly depleted policy resources, more channels and tools for effective governance. Fully understanding the advantages of this as a venue for citizen participation and the expression of values through these actors, public officials are expected to collaborate with these organizations on a more regular basis. This regular collaboration, as mentioned above, is the source of increased flexibility in crisis management responses.

In addition, ensuring that citizens understand their government and fully appreciate the intent of its policies and services is a topic that has not been sufficiently researched but is, in fact, extremely significant. This is because the effectiveness of policies can be legitimately assessed when citizens are fully aware of them. Moreover, for policies that need citizen behavior, local governments can leverage social marketing as an essential tool to improve policy effectiveness. Chapter 10 includes a discussion of the effectiveness of educational leaflets on the "willingness to donate organs" and the change in citizens' behavior through follow-up surveys. Other policies that require citizen behavior include garbage collection and sorting, basic health checkups, immunization against infectious diseases, and elections of chiefs and councilors. Furthermore, when local governments formulate comprehensive plans or develop large-scale facilities, they hold citizen participation meetings, but often, the problem is that citizens' spontaneous participation is not easily realized. In particular, young and hard-working citizens do not participate in such meetings. Social marketing strengthens the driving force to solve these problems. Thus, it should be used to promote local government policies in the future.

Local governments trusted by citizens need to be policymakers who first trust their citizens. One of the benefits of social marketing identified in Chap. 10 is that local government officials develop attitudes that consider citizens' perspectives, which is highly instructive. In Japan, the need for specialists to utilize social marketing in policymaking has been emphasized, and its systematic use is expected to improve the sustainability of local governments by strengthening their driving forces.

13.4 Sustainability Clues in Local Government–Business Relations

Private businesses, for local governments, are subjects of the production and supply of public services as well as subjects of tax revenue supply when they are located within the local government's area. The role of private businesses as service production and supply entities includes garbage collection, welfare and childcare, food services, medical care, education, water supply, public transportation, road maintenance, facility construction, and certain other services, as well as the transportation of goods, as discussed in Chap. 6, Crisis Management. In addition, they generally outsource support for the formulation of administrative plans to private think tanks and the printing of public information papers and plans to private companies. Thus, there is a wide range of services for which the private sector is responsible for the specific production and supply. However, in a society with a declining population, these businesses are likely to withdraw from the municipality. Accordingly, municipalities are required to proactively develop environments and systems that make it as easy as possible for the private business sector to manage these services, as they are essential partners in maintaining public services. If private businesses withdraw, municipalities must maintain services directly, which decreases tax revenue.

Chapters 11 and 12 deal with the relationship between corporations and local governments. The former considers companies as policy actors responsible for the future of the region—similar to local governments—and discusses the need for mutually beneficial collaborations. The latter is based on a study that discusses the role of systemic change in increasing the number of firms involved in the bidding system.

Chapter 11 examines the factors that enable local governments to collect more tax revenue through the hometown tax donation system, which allows citizens to pay taxes to a municipality different from the one in which they reside. The empirical study reveals that municipalities offering more returned gifts were able to collect more tax revenues from hometown tax donations. Additionally, the higher the expense ratio, the greater the amount of tax revenue received. Moreover, municipalities with the highest tax receipts benefited from the tax increase effect of the development of higher-priced returned gifts. This difference in tax receipts is a result of local governments' product development expertise, efforts, and marketing. In municipalities with weak finances, there is an urgent need for product development through mutually beneficial collaboration between municipalities and the business sector.

In addition, local governments supply not only services but also facilities, the information system infrastructure within administrative organizations, and government buildings. Public procurement of such facilities and infrastructure is carried out through a bidding system in which the private sector participates, which has the potential to reduce cost waste. In Chap. 12, we find that general competitive bidding, in which bidding information is publicly announced, applications for participation are solicited, and contractors are selected through competition among applicants, has a lower probability of declines and bids at reserved prices than competitive bidding in which the government determines the participating companies in advance.

The study also discovers that the contract price ratio could be lowered because of the greater number of participants in the public bidding process. Although public procurement uses a large amount of taxpayer money, issues such as the bidding system are technically and institutionally difficult to understand; therefore, local residents frequently lack a sense of direct fiscal responsibility or burden at the local level. The study concludes that the role of the researcher is to reveal specialized knowledge to citizens and society by systematically improving complex methods that are difficult for citizens to control. Local government systems are highly specialized and confusing, causing waste in some cases in such systems themselves. It is necessary to promote research on local government by researchers who have clues to promote systemic change in local government.

13.5 Conclusions

The relationships between local governments and various actors have provided clues for improving the sustainability of local governments. To further summarize them, we can categorize them into three key directions: sufficient horizontal and vertical collaborations, systemic changes based on the actual conditions of local government organizations, and a stronger driving force to mobilize citizens.

The first is sufficient horizontal and vertical collaborations. When local governments themselves have limited resources, sharing resources with other governments, the private sector, and other actors can be effective, resulting in increased sustainability of regional governance, crisis management, NPOs, and community relations. Collaboration addresses the challenge of resource depletion by allowing local governments to draw on the policy resources of other policy actors. However, collaboration requires inter-entity relationships in which the sharing of resources is also deemed desirable for other policy actors. For instance, between local governments, there are cases in which mutually funded joint-use facilities are established, and between local governments and NPOs, in which the NPOs recognize that collaboration can lead not only to their involvement in service implementation but also to the creation of new value for themselves. Regarding collaboration with NHAs, NHAs have few members due to the declining population. Therefore, local governments need to spread awareness among citizens about their membership to enrich their neighborhoods. Additionally, measures for revitalizing the region while building mutually beneficial cooperative relationships with private businesses for product development in the hometown tax donation system were discussed. Moreover, building relationships through collaborations takes time and effort; thus, regular collaborations are essential.

However, for many municipalities with weak finances, building relationships with these other policy actors is not always easy. In such cases, vertical cooperation is expected not only to replace municipal services with those provided by higher levels of government, such as prefectural and central governments, but also to provide financial resources to municipalities. For these reasons, improving the sustainability of local governments depends on regularly engaging in horizontal and vertical cooperation. In addition, vertical cooperation differs from horizontal cooperation, which preserves the democracy of a municipality and cooperates with other municipalities but emphasizes the efficiency of service provision and organizational management rather than democracy. Therefore, even when vertical cooperation is established, democracy must be ensured by promoting citizen participation in the prefectures and advancing administrative transparency. Nevertheless, the future demand for vertical cooperation by prefecture is quite high in Japan, as most regions, with the exception of Kanto and Tokai, are municipalities with tightened finances and sharply declining populations.

Second is systemic changes based on the actual conditions of local government organizations. These are necessary because traditional institutions and policy tools no longer provide services that sufficiently satisfy the efficiency of local governments and citizens' preferences. Systemic changes to improve the sustainability of local governments were part of the electoral system. Citizens are the main actors in determining policy prioritization for sound local government administrative and fiscal management. Local representatives elected by the citizens do not have an environment in which to present the policy differences between political parties. However, reform of the electoral system must create an environment for interparty competition in the future. Many different systems can be reformed, such as the relaxation of service retention mandated to local governments and decentralization, which transfers both authority and financial resources to local governments. Regarding minor systemic reforms, we discuss the inefficiency of the central government's involvement in the evaluation system, the adoption of an information system unsuitable for the workflow, and a bidding system that generates waste in public procurement. Such apparently trivial but beneficial institutional reforms have yet to be fully uncovered and explored. Researchers have a role to play in revealing such beneficial systemic changes to the public. The findings of this publication suggest the need for systemic changes that are adapted to the actual conditions of the local government.

Third is a stronger driving force to mobilize citizens. Strengthening the driving forces focuses on the behavioral changes required on the part of citizens to increase the effectiveness of local government policies. Public policy is most effective when accompanied by a change in citizens' perceptions and behavior as a result of information dissemination from the local government. In this context, the behavioral change of citizens through social marketing is vital to the sustainable operation of local governments. Cumulative research in behavioral economics and behavioral public administration, which conduct similar discussions, further accumulates knowledge of social marketing, which focuses on behavior change based on more extensive discussions and social implementations. More specifically, in policies such as garbage collection separation and basic health checkups, the de facto effectiveness of policies can be ensured based on behavioral changes in citizens. Changes in citizen behavior through social marketing strengthen the drivers of local governance in a variety of policy areas. Local government policies that have increased in effectiveness due to the mobilization of citizens contribute to the sustainability of the municipality.

In countries with dwindling policy resources, policymakers and researchers can obtain clear clues about the sustainability of local governments by rethinking local governance in terms of collaboration, systemic change, and strengthening driving forces.

Yu Noda is Professor at the Faculty of Policy Studies, Doshisha University. He was a Fulbright Visiting Scholar of Public Administration and Policy at Georgetown University in 2014. Since 2024, he has served as Principal of Doshisha Elementary School. In addition, he provided research guidance to graduate students at the Graduate School of Policy and Management at Doshisha University. His educational activities span all age groups from children to older adults. His research focuses on inter-municipal cooperation, performance information and learning effects of citizens, citizen satisfaction with government services, trust in local governments, and governance reforms. His recent articles have appeared in prominent journals, including *Public Administration Review*, *Public Management Review*, *Local Government Studies*, *International Review of Administrative Sciences*, *Asia-Pacific Journal of Public Administration*, and *International Journal of Public Administration*.

Index

The manufacturer's authorised representative in the EU is Springer
Nature Customer Service Centre GmbH, Europaplatz 3, 69115 Heidelberg,
Germany. If you have any concerns regarding our products, please
contact ProductSafety@springernature.com

Printed and bound by CPI Group (UK) Ltd, Croydon, CR0 4YY

28/08/2025

01945963-0001